A Lifetime of Church

A Journey From Law to Grace

by

Tom Speicher

Xulon Press

Copyright © 2004 by Tom Speicher

A Lifetime of Church
by Tom Speicher

Printed in the United States of America

ISBN 1-594673-35-7

All rights reserved by the author. The contents and views expressed in this book are solely those of the author and are not necessarily those of Xulon Press, Inc. The author guarantees this book is original and does not infringe upon any laws or rights, and that this book is not libelous, plagiarized or in any other way illegal. If any portion of this book is fictitious, the author guarantees it does not represent any real event or person in a way that could be deemed libelous. No part of this book may be reproduced in any form without the permission of the author.

Unless otherwise indicated, Bible quotations are taken from the Holy Bible, New International Version. Copyright © 1973, 1978, 1984 by the International Bible Society.

Introduction

Ordinary? Or extraordinary? How does one define these terms? To whom, or to what do they apply? Who decides? Indiana could be described as an ordinary State within the United States of America. Milford is a very ordinary little town in the rural northern area of the ordinary State of Indiana. Into this ordinary rural community was born an ordinary baby boy on Wednesday, October 14, 1952. Thus began an ordinary life. Or was it extraordinary? This baby boy was taken to an ordinary home on an ordinary family farm to his two older brothers by his ordinary nineteen year-old mother. Or was she extraordinary? When the second Sunday arrived the family did the ordinary thing and took the baby to church. Thus began an ordinary lifetime of church. Or was it extraordinary?

A Lifetime of Church is my autobiography. We become who we are as the result of many factors. We begin with our genetic makeup and our characteristics, personalities, and values are molded by the interaction of our influences and experiences. I am no exception to this phenomenon. My early years were framed by the predominate influence of the customs and traditions of the church denomination of my maternal Grandparents. These customs and traditions contributed strongly to creating a heritage that formed my sense of identity and my sense of worth and belongingness. From my adolescence through my early adulthood I knew no distinction between my cultural and religious heritage. In my mind, choosing a religious path that was different than that of my forefathers was equivalent to impugning their character and the testimonies of their lives. Even in my adolescent years I knew that there was no acceptable path for me other than that of my forefathers. To explain how I became who I am it was necessary to go back three generations and reconstruct five marriages that came to be within the church denomination of my heritage. The first three of these marriages were the fruit of the church practices and the last two of them, including my own, came about despite the church practices. *A Lifetime of Church* is my narrative of three distinct periods of time in my life. The first era begins with my heritage and an examination of the religious beliefs and practices of my forefathers. It continues with the lives of my parents, how my mother struggled emotionally and spiritually, and how my parents became married despite all the forces in play against their union. The account then turns to my own birth and early years and what it was like to grow up in this religious context, how I viewed life and why I viewed it as I did. My home life is described, including both the blessings I enjoyed growing up in the shadow of my maternal Grandparents and the frustrations my parents dealt with because of their position in the church and in my mother's extended family. This first period of my life ends with me becoming a member of the denomination of my forefathers and my marriage. I doubt anyone outside of my early-life religious context would describe the process of attaining this membership and becoming married and the associated events as being ordinary.

The second distinct period of my life began when I was drafted into the United States Army. Having served my time in West Germany, I moved away from home and completed my college education. These two physical separations from my earlier influences sowed in my mind the first seeds of independent thinking, although it would require years for these seeds to grow and begin to produce fruit. A twist of fate brought me back to my home town after college. With this move came my immersion back into the lifestyle of my heritage. Six years and three children later I found myself holding the office of lay minister in the denomination of my forefathers. One would search in vain to find anyone who would describe my ascent to this position and circumstances surrounding it as ordinary. In addition, I cannot think of anything that would have made my place of honor more secure in my Grandparents' eyes than me serving as a minister in the denomination of my heritage. Running parallel to my ascent to the office of minister, however, was the beginning of a spiritual renaissance within me. I had no sooner become a minister in the denomination of my heritage than I began to realize my independent study of the Bible was leading me to faith in doctrines that my own denomination strongly opposed. Further fueling this introspection was my tense relationship with a local church leader who was both insecure and lacking in leadership skills. Within two years I had come to realize that I could no longer continue to be a part of the denomination of my heritage. This war between my intellect and will was both intense and painful. My daily journals from this time period and correspondence with others help reconstruct this metamorphosis in my Biblical faith. The departure from the denomination of my heritage was framed by circumstances that could not be accurately described as ordinary.

The third distinct period of my life began with the founding of a new local assembly of believers, the Wawasee Community Bible Church. It is not unusual for a new church to be planted. It happens often. Wawasee Community Bible Church, however, was not an ordinary new church. It began meeting in the cafeteria of a local school. It began with no facilities, assets, or programs and grew into a large congregation for a small town and surrounding rural area. For thirteen years I was the Senior Pastor. Throughout this period of time my children grew from toddlers to teenagers and my wife and I owned and operated a community pharmacy. In this third section I describe the many challenges, blessings, hurts, successes, and failures along this journey.

Ordinary? Or extraordinary? There would no doubt be differing opinions among those who know me as to which of these terms apply to my life and my lifetime of church. It is my opinion that am a very ordinary man who has enjoyed some extraordinary experiences and who has been extraordinarily blessed by God.

Chapter One

T he day began like many before it. "Tom, time to get up! We are running late. The boys need in the shower. You have four minutes." And then, as my dear wife Tammy got up from the bed and left the room she repeated over her shoulder, "Four minutes!"

As I tried to gather some coherent thoughts, I chuckled to myself, "Four minutes! We are being ***really*** precise this morning. Usually it's at least five or ten."

I began to pray. "Lord, thanks for another day. Please be with the kids today. Please protect them on the road and help them to make wise decisions. Help them to live for You. Lord, help me to be honest and to be a light to others today. Thanks for Tammy and the kids and the abundance of good things that you have given me. Father, I really do want to do Your will for my life — You know I do. Please make me aware of it. Thank you most for Jesus Christ. In His name I pray. Amen."

As I moved to get out of bed, my feet didn't hit the floor when I thought they should. "Oh, yeah," I thought, "we just got a new bed." As I stood up I thought, "Man, my joints are stiff in the mornings these days." The second and third toes on my left foot were tingling like they were just waking up from being asleep, a reminder of a herniated disc from some years ago. I did not fret, though, because I knew that, with a little movement, I'd soon be OK.

I stumbled to the kitchen to take my daily dose of Prilosec for my chronic stomach acid and then to the bathroom to brush my teeth and shower. Tama was scurrying about, as usual. She greeted me with a "Good morning" before reminding me to "Hurry" because my son Travis' friend would be getting up in a few minutes to use the shower.

As the water from the shower brought my mind to functional alertness I again chuckled at the "four minutes" admonition. "Man," I thought, "where would this household be without her?"

I went through my usual routine: Apply Head and Shoulders shampoo to my hair, leave it on while I systematically soap up, then lather up the whiskers and shave blind. It's always a relief to rinse the razor and begin the final rinse from hair to toe. As I stepped out and dried off I began a carefully choreographed (if not compulsive) routine of drying off the fixtures and folding and hanging the towels. I especially hate it if a drop from the showerhead lands on the bathtub faucet. Usually it takes several dryings to prevent this!

By the time I made it back to the bedroom I was alert and happy. I started with Bobby (the friend who had stayed over with Travis), "Good morning, Robert! How great is life?" I then moved on to Tama, "What a woman! Are we on schedule? I think I made it up within my four minute window!" She ignored these comments, as she generally does with my mindless banter. As I dressed I was thrown off my routine by not having somewhere to sit, our new mattress being too high, so I finished in the living room.

I had half an hour before I needed to go, so I took the luxury of eating some breakfast. As I was munching on some cereal Travis came stumbling down the stairs. I was delighted to have the opportunity to torment him with excessive energy and happiness. "Travie! Good morning! Isn't it great to get up in the morning?! I always say 'the earlier, the better!' Are you excited for another opportunity to learn today!?" By this time he was already heading out the door with a scowl and a sweet utterance suggesting that I cease speaking (actually, "Shut up!"). I truly love irritating people with happiness in the mornings, a trait I inherited from my father.

This morning was not routine, in the sense that usually I am not up before Travis. It is one of the perks of being a pharmacist, not having to be at work until 8:30am, so usually I miss the thrill of irritating others who do not like to get up. Life would be a lot more productive if I needed less sleep, but I do not function well without it, so I will persevere.

A Lifetime of Church

After watching the news for a while I noticed it was 7:40am and time to go. I asked Tammy, "What's the plan for the day?" I ask this each day partly because it amazes (and somewhat amuses) me to hear her rattle it off and because I really want to know. Without a millisecond of hesitation she recited the day's activities in detail, not only for herself, but for Travis and me also. What a woman! I grabbed a few papers and some continuing education articles as I headed to the garage. I rarely, if ever, get to them, but I take them just in case I cannot find some other diversion.

The Suburban is generally mine to drive, so I hopped in. I put in a tape of the Bible (end of Genesis, beginning of Exodus today), reset the trip meter (even though it is always the same distance), and left. Somewhere during the twenty-six point four mile drive and hearing a genealogy on the tape, my mind began to wander. Over and over I was hearing "So and so had so many children and so many possessions, and then he died." I never think about my own death, but this morning I found myself reflecting about the fact that I am forty-eight years old and not a young whipper-snapper anymore. For some reason I was trying to think back as far as I could.

The earliest memory that I have is that of being at Grandpa (Charlie) and Grandma (Pauline) Speicher's house in Milford. I had walked from the living room to a room that faced the railroad that ran behind their house. In this room they had a large stuffed white owl. I was trying to reach up and touch it when Grandpa came out of a small adjacent room and said "No. Don't touch that." My second memory also concerned Grandpa Speicher. I was sitting on my aunt Marguerite Hoerr's lap in a car. We were in the Apostolic Christian Church parking lot. I remember it as a bright and sunshiny day. Marguerite said to me "Your Daddy is very sad today." I looked up and saw my Dad walking in front of the car towards the church. I remember him as being thin and in a suit. His head was down and he was hunched over. Several years ago I related this memory to my parents and they confirmed that Marguerite watched me on the day of Grandpa Speicher's funeral. I would have been two and a half years old.

I was thinking, what an irony that my first two memories were of a man I never knew — and that one of them involved the Apostolic Christian Church. I suppose that my memories begin with Grandpa

Speicher because his death was such a profound tragedy for the family. To this day my father finds it difficult to talk about his death.

It seems that Grandpa (Charlie) Speicher was a life long melancholy man. After completing an outstanding sports career in High School, he married, fathered four sons (Lewie, Bill "Bugsy," Jim "Lip," and Pat), and spent his adult life working for a low, but steady wage for the railroad. It seems that he was always a sad, quiet man, whose insecurities and inadequacies were exacerbated by my Grandma, who had few money management skills and who tended to be a somewhat dissatisfied and demanding woman.

Throughout the older boys' early lives Grandpa Speicher was emotionally stable, as the boys excelled in athletics and were the pride of the town. But after Uncle Jim went to the Navy he became deeply depressed and despondent. The family thought that they had dodged a bullet when he unsuccessfully attempted suicide by ingesting a large number of aspirin. It was not too long after this, however, that Uncle Pat went to the garage to get the lawn mower and found Grandpa hanging from a rope, dead. Pat was fourteen years old. I was two and a half years old, but neither of us has forgotten it. No one in the family ever will.

It was a shock to my mother's family when the Speichers asked my Grandpa Theo Beer to have the funeral in the Apostolic Christian Church. They did not attend church there. But ask they did and there it was held. I often worried about Grandpa Speicher's soul in my early years. It wasn't until about ten years ago that my Uncle Pat told me that once he and Grandpa went to an evangelistic meeting in the area. Grandpa was obviously searching because he was not known to have an interest in spiritual matters. But Uncle Pat clearly remembers that when the Gospel was presented and the invitation was given that night that Grandpa went forward and prayed to receive Jesus Christ as his Savior. I do not know if there was ever any follow up counseling or teaching. No one knows of any. With no intervention techniques or effective medicines for depression, Grandpa got more and more despondent until, in despair, he took his own life to still the pain. How sad, because he had so much life ahead of him and so many reasons to live. He might still be alive today, having retired with a nice Conrail pension that would have come in his working days. I am certain he would have loved to know us grandchildren. Medications to help with his depression would have come along during his normal life span, too. How sad.

As I neared Mentone it occurred to me that for my story to be told I have to go back at least two more generations. Besides, it was time to go to work! As I turned off the tape I was nearing the end the Book of Genesis and Joseph had just met his brothers in Egypt.

Chapter Two

Some years ago I had a brainstorm that I am very thankful I followed through on. My Grandpa Theo Beer was in his mid-nineties and his mind was still sharp. I had been a part of several family conversations in which we spoke of the need to get his memories on videotape, so one morning I took our new video camera to his house. I was prepared! I had made a list of everything I wanted to ask him about so we could both keep on track. After setting up the camera on a tripod and touching "record," we began.

Grandpa's story began with one of his uncles who had emigrated from near Bern, Switzerland before the United States' Civil War. Grandpa recalled stories this uncle would tell him as a boy of being present at slave auctions in Missouri. He spoke about how the slaves would wail when separated from family members, of how strong young males would bring about prolonged bidding, and how older men and women would stir little interest at all.

When the Civil War broke out, this uncle was conscripted into the Confederate Army. He was able to pay the three hundred dollars to get out of the obligation. When he was conscripted the third time, he decided to move north. This he did and he ended up in Upper Sandusky, Ohio. The war claimed more than six hundred thousand lives, mostly of young men. This created a wealth of economic opportunity for those who survived and opened a door very wide for immigration. Grandpa Beer's uncle wrote to his family and explained about the ample opportunity in America. Upon hearing this, my Grandpa Beer's father, Simon Beer, and two more of his uncles made the decision to emigrate. They came to America on a clipper ship with a total of eight dollars. The year was 1866.

From time to time I try and imagine what it must have been like for them to emigrate and what it must have been like for their parents to allow them to! The odds were strongly against ever seeing one's parents and siblings again. Indeed, Grandpa Beer explained that only one of the four brothers ever went back for a visit. In addition, they came to America with little more than the clothes on their backs, with no skills, and speaking only the German language. When I think of how hard it is for me to go more than a day or two without communication from my immediate family, I scarcely can imagine the courage and sacrifice of the early immigrants — and the conditions in the "homelands" that made immigration seem attractive. One of Grandpa Beer's stories illustrates this: One year there was a crop failure in Switzerland and his grandparents' family, including his father, lived an entire winter on turnips! Yum.

When Simon Beer and his brothers arrived in America they headed for Sandusky, Ohio, only to find that their brother was not there to meet them. It turned out that their inability to speak English had landed them three hours, by train, away from their objective of **Upper Sandusky**, Ohio. Once they finally arrived their brother agreed to give them room and board while they learned his trade of barrel making. They began to receive pay when they were able to make one watertight barrel per day. Grandpa was quick to point out that it was not too long until his father, Simon, was out on his own, making a living as a cooper (barrel maker).

There was another factor that strongly contributed to the assimilation of these brothers: the Apostolic Christian Church. This denomination had sprung from the Anabaptist movement in Europe. There will be much to follow on this subject later, but suffice it to say that this church served as a mechanism for cultural and ethnic preservation in addition to being a place of worship for the Swiss-German immigrants of the day.

It was not long before Simon met his first wife, Ursula Meyer, through the church. They were married in 1871 and settled in Mansfield, Ohio, where they farmed, made barrels, and raised four of their six children. Two of their children died in infancy.

Grandpa Theo once described the process of making a barrel to me. His brother Otto was a barn builder and always said that making a barrel was far more difficult than building a barn. I cannot imagine how difficult it must have been to make one watertight barrel a day in order to begin to draw a wage. The process began with a walk through the woods in search of a white oak tree with the approximate diameter of the barrel that was to be built. Once a suitable tree was found, Simon would pay the farmer "a dollar or two" for it and cut it down. A chunk of the log the height of the prospective barrel was then cut off. If it would split cleanly, the tree was usable. If not, it was discarded and another tree selected. I cannot imagine having white oak trees in such abundance today! If the chunk split cleanly, it was split in half, then in fourths, etc, until one had enough staves to build the barrel. Other acceptable chunks of the tree were cut off the trunk until the first branches were reached. With the first branch came a knot in the trunk and the wood could no longer be cleanly split. The staves were then shaped by tapering them on all edges so that they would fit together to form a round barrel that was bigger at the center than at the top and bottom. They also had to be grooved at the top and bottom so that more staves could be fit into them to form a watertight top and bottom of the barrel. All of this shaping was done with hand tools. The precision required to produce watertight joints in all directions challenges my imagination. I can remember playing with some of these tools as a little boy. They were in various buildings around the farm. Sadly, I am sure that I contributed to losing them. Once all the pieces were shaped, Simon would build a fire. He then began assembling the barrel at one end, fitting all the staves together with one set of end staves. He would then slip one of the small metal bands over the end to hold it in place. Next he would slide the large center band over the top. The fire was then used to heat the lower parts of the staves. Once heated, they could be slowly pulled together with a rope. Soon the center band was in place and once the lower parts were heated enough, the other end staves were put in place and the final small band would secure them. As liquid was put in the barrel the joints would swell and produce the final seals. Simon stated late in life that in his "prime" he was able to make five barrels in one day! I cannot imagine the skill and precision that was necessary to accomplish this task. Amazing.

Simon's first wife died in 1891 in her mid-forties. Grandpa Theo always said that she died of "her change." My best guess from the description is that it was cervical cancer or some related fatal disease. Becoming a widower with four children is always a life-altering event and Simon Beer was no exception. He became a melancholy and hopeless man. Grandpa Theo explained that after some time had passed that Simon was encouraged by a friend to remarry. He is said to have asked "But who would have me? I'm a poor man and I have four children." The friend encouraged him to make it a matter of prayer and he agreed to do so.

Simon Beer was a member of the Apostolic Christian Church. This denomination largely defined by its time-honored customs and traditions. Some of the practices of the Apostolic Christian Church that makes them distinct from other Protestant denominations are their courtship and marriage customs. Among the single members of the church there is no dating, and marriage to one outside of the denomination is not allowed. Social activities of single members are limited to groups of young members in church-sanctioned events like "singings." The basic program of a "singing" includes group singing of hymns, a scripture reading, a prayer, food, and fellowship. Groups of young members within the denomination are also active in visiting other Apostolic Christian Churches on Wednesday nights and on weekends. In these activities friendships are formed and single members can become acquainted with prospective spouses.

The marriage process in the Apostolic Christian Church begins with a brother in the faith deciding that it is time for him to be married. The brother makes it a matter of prayer that God will show him who is to be his wife. Once a sister in the faith is selected the brother speaks to his father about it. With the father's blessing the brother then takes his proposal to the Elder, or leader, of his local church. If the local Elder feels the request is reasonable and that the brother's spiritual life is in order, he will forward the request to the Elder of the prospective bride's church. If this Elder feels that the request is reasonable and that their spiritual lives are in order, then the proposal is forwarded to the father of the prospective bride. If the father is in agreement then the proposal is forwarded to the sister in the faith. She is to then make it a matter of prayer to determine if it is

God's will that she marry this brother in the faith. If she agrees, then the proposal is announced to their respective home churches. Marriages generally follow short engagement periods, as strict church discipline, including excommunication, is applied to those who have premarital relations.

This solemn process continues to this day. In theory, the process produces marriages that are literally "made in heaven." Quite often the process and the results have been a great blessing to all involved. Unfortunately, though, the process also often results in some striking mismatches, particularly for the women involved. There are four reasons for this. First, the man is always the initiator and when traits such as interests, personality, and intellect cannot be known without some significant social interaction, one is left to choose primarily on the basis of physical attributes. People in general and men in particular are first attracted to beauty. It has been my experience that very average and less than average looking brothers are more often than not "led by God" to ask for the hands of beautiful sisters than sisters who would be physically equally yoked with them. Secondly, the sisters in the faith know that there are many more young sisters than young brothers in the faith. Simple math tells them that many of them will never receive a proposal of marriage at all, let alone receive multiple proposals. This creates pressure to accept the first proposal they get, in case that is their only chance. Furthermore, despite the solemn and prayerful nature of the process, refused proposals are soon widely known about and the refusing sister is stigmatized. Thirdly, the process amounts to a dramatically "stacked deck" against the sister. Why? Consider the proposal she receives: The brother has prayed about it and believes it is God's will that they be married. His father, his Elder, her Elder, and her father all feel that the proposal is legitimate, at least to the extent that it has been passed along to them. As the sister in faith begins to pray about the proposal she has to be under enormous social and religious pressure to confirm that God led the others in the process correctly. The first and second reasons listed above further contribute to this social and religious pressure.

Fourth, and finally, the doctrinal base of the Apostolic Christian Church pressures the sister to accept the proposal of marriage. In the Apostolic Christian Church salvation is believed to be a process. One is exhorted continually to live a life of self-denial and separation from the world. One's "hope" is to have more holiness than shortcomings in order to preserve the work of Christ in obtaining salvation. Submission is considered the path for women to be "made worthy." This is submission to religious leaders as well as to one's husband. Submission, as practiced in the denomination, is often more closely related to the concept of obedience than to the voluntary placing of one's will under the will of another. This makes it very, very difficult for a sister to refuse a proposal of marriage. Consider a sister's options when presented with a proposal of marriage:

> (1) Say "Yes." Be married to a man you trust is God's will for your life. Have faith you will learn to love him and share his interests. Many have done this and lived very happy lives. Others have said yes and have lived lives of misery, knowing that they were in marriages that would have never come about under any other circumstances, all the while hoping that God will reward them eternally for their submission and long-suffering.

> (2) Say "No." Be known as a sister who said "No." Take a big chance of never being asked again, knowing that marriage outside the denomination brings loss of church membership, which some in the denomination equate with loss of salvation.

My existence had come about as a result, at least partially, of several generations of these church-produced marriages. As far as I know, in my ancestry the marriages worked out well. In three instances, great acts of faith and commitment brought about marriages and families that produced my mother. The account of the most amazing of these marriages requires me to return to the story of my Great Grandfather, Simon Beer. Grandpa Theo told the story many times over the years. One time he was "on the record" as a part of one of the grandchildren's school projects. In a transcript of an audiotape, he told the story as follows. The year was 1892. Simon was a forty three year old widower with four children.

"..he (Simon) *was in debt heavy and lost his* (first) *wife and was discouraged. So he went to a neighbor and the neighbor said 'Sima, vie gehts?' -asked him how it goes. Father replied, 'I'm discouraged.' The neighbor replied, 'well, you just mustn't be discouraged.' The neighbor continued, 'I'm going to tell you something. Honor lost, much is lost. Money lost, much is lost. But courage lost, all is lost. I advise you to get married again.' Simon replied, 'Who would want to step in to four children, and I'm heavily in debt?' The neighbor insisted, 'There is a woman someplace for you.'*

"So he went home and he remembered that when his wife died a maiden lady of the church rode in his wagon, a spring wagon. She rode on the front seat where he was driving. Father remembered that she was a nice person. He remembered her name and where she lived, but that was about all. So he said after he was a widower a year he told the Elder in his church that he wanted her. He asked the Elder to write her a letter and tell her that he would have faith and hopefully he can love her; that she should be his wife and mother to his four children. (The reason the Elder wrote to her directly is because she was no longer living in the home of her father.)

"She (Catherine) *came from Switzerland when she was nine. At age fourteen her family had hired her out (to a wealthy family), and at age twenty-nine she was still at the same place. She had always said that her prayer was that if there would ever be someone worthy...who would be good for me...even if he's poor...(she made some reservation)...that she would consider it.*

"After receiving the letter she deliberated quite a while and went to her own minister in the Toledo church. She told him the situation and that she would have faith and maybe she should accept the proposal. The minister replied, 'if you want to be a servant all your life, why just go that route.' Mother said that just discouraged her to no end. So she wrote back to Mansfield, to my father's minister, and told him what the head of the church in Toledo said. My father's minister wrote back and said, 'He should not have said that. He (Simon) *is a good man. He is poor and he is a widower and he needs help. As far as being a servant, you won't be. You will be his wife.'*

"So she (Mother) *said she would accept him* (Father). *Father then wrote to her, 'would you be willing to come to Mansfield, that's about*

sixty miles? I got the children. I got my chores. If you could come to Mansfield to my church, we'd be married the first Sunday you come.' We often laughed at that. We thought that girls wouldn't do that nowadays. But she did. And she never met the children (beforehand). (While Simon expected to be married on this first Sunday, Catherine was not sure if it was going to be then. It was a remarkable understatement when Grandpa Theo stated "girls wouldn't do that nowadays!") *"The Sunday came and after the church service, then Elder announced that there was going to be a wedding. 'Simon Beer is marrying Catherine Meister.' So they were married and then father went out and hitched up his team to his spring wagon. And mother came out and got on the spring wagon with him. The children weren't at church. They were at home with the oldest boy who was already old enough to take care of them.* (Children normally did not attend church services in those days until they were old enough to sit still. Generally an older sibling stayed home and watched them while the parents attended church.) *"They drove five miles on the spring wagon and drove into the yard and drove up to the hitching rack. And right in front of the hitching rack was a picket fence. He* (Simon) *said to Catherine 'there's your family.' The four children were leaning over the fence. Mother looked at them. She said it didn't scare her. That's something now, isn't it?"*

Grandpa Theo related that it was a difficult transition for his mother to make. She "turned the corner" when she gave birth to her first child, a son named Otto. Six more children would follow: Hulda, Ezra, Theophilus, Henry, Saloma, and Peter. Through the first decade of the new century, Simon and Catherine kept busy with farming, making barrels, and rearing children. The Apostolic Christian Church was the center of their non-working lives. Grandpa Theo, at age eighty nine, wrote of these years as follows:

I was the fourth child of Simon and Katherine Beer. (I was) *born January 23, 1898.* (Note: Grandpa always said that he got his name "Theophilus" because his father said the night he was born was "the awfulest" of his life. The weather on the night of his birth was "awful" and his father had to ride a horse to get the doctor in the middle of the night.) *Father was married before. I had three half* brothers and a half sister. Charley and Matilda were home as I can remember. Charley was often unwilling to help Mother. She (Mother) *needed his father's help* (to make Charley obey), (as) *he was supposed to turn the washing machine. Matilda was a good help to mother. She was a nice looking girl about twelve. I remember she took care of us much of the time. Father and Mother would leave us in her care on Sundays. She would take the baby to church with her. As a young boy I did not go to church. As I grew older I would go and sit with my father. But I never liked the way he sang. I had a squeaky voice, he sang bass. I thought he was off tune. Later I learned there are four parts people could sing. The sermons were in German. All I can remember* (is) *the quote "von ewigkeit zu ewigkeit"* (equivalent to the English phrase "for ever and ever"). *Bro. Engwiller, Bro. Sabo, and later Bro. Stavenick, who also spoke in English* (were the preachers). *Father loved to hear Bro. Stavenick. He said "when he preached, it was preached!" I started school when I was five and a half years old. I spoke some English. I soon spoke well. I learned it fast. School was easy for me. I enjoyed playing games with the other kids. As I remember I wore felt boots. When inside we would take the rubber boots off and walk in our felt boots. I played hard with any one who would play with me. Brother Ezra did pretty well. Brother Henry would play awhile and quit. He had likes that I didn't have. Otto was grown. He was my hero. He could hunt squirrels and was a good trapper. He made one hundred dollars one year trapping and hunting raccoon, skunk,* (and) *muskrats. I shot my first rabbit when I was eleven years old. I had a single shot rifle. I knew I would have to find one sitting if I would ever be able to get one. It was a great thrill when I saw one in a clump of weeds. I took aim and fired. He jumped up about two feet, but he could not run. I grabbed him and wrung off his head. I felt I really did something. I brought it home to mother. She said she would fry it, but would not skin it. I skinned it. This was the best rabbit I ever ate. One time Brother Otto tracked a skunk to a hole along a fence row. He asked me if I would help dig her out. We dug from two holes, hoping we would come to the skunk. Otto finally said "I see his tail." He took hold of the tail and threw him out. I was supposed to kill him with my shovel. He threw him out, and I hit him hard with my shovel. I got a real dose of skunk on me,* (and) *I could hardly breathe. Otto said "I see another tail." He did as he did before. I got another dose as bad as the first. We got seven skunks from that hole. It was a stinky mess, but we sold the pelts for thirty five dollars. We felt it was worth it. When I was eleven years old I worked for my brother Joel for five dollars a month. I worked three months and he paid me fifteen dollars. My folk's agreed I could buy a bicycle. I ordered one from* (the) *Sears catalogue. It cost fifteen dollars and seventy five cents. Dad paid the seventy-five cents. I had that bicycle for at least eight years. It was red and white. I sure was proud of it. I always liked baseball, but we never had a good place to play. I finally went out in the calf pasture and measured out the bases. I filled a sack with straw for the bases. But I never could get enough kids in to play at one time, so I never did use the ball diamond. In my last year of school in Ohio we had a school picnic in a woods, all seven of the township schools. Our school played another school. I was the catcher. I think our school lost. We had a picnic of plenty of food. Lemonade was made in a fifty gallon barrel. It was really good. I still feel I can taste it. There were about one dozen tin cups tied to strings so no one walked off with them. A farmer hauled us to the picnic with a flat bottom rack. Horses and wagon was decorated with streamers.* (It was) *always a red letter day to go to the last day picnic. We were poor but didn't know it. We were happy anyway.*

As Simon and Catherine's family began to mature some circumstances presented themselves that would bring about a major change in their lives and the lives of their children. The first factor was a split in the Apostolic Christian Church denomination.

The Apostolic Christian Church had its roots in the Anabaptist movement in Europe. A man named Samuel Froelich founded the denomination in 1836. Originally there was an evangelical mindset. Samuel Froelich is said to have spent Sunday mornings knocking on doors, inviting people to church while others were conducting and attending the services. From the beginning the church advocated holiness doctrines, steadfastly teaching that a Christian's life was one of simplicity, separation, submission, and self-denial. As the denomination spread into different European countries, what constituted obedience to these disciplines began to become adapted to the various cultures.

The Mansfield, Ohio Apostolic Christian Church congregation had been founded by immigrants from similar cultural backgrounds, as had most of the American congregations. What constituted acceptable attire and appearance within the American churches began to be seriously disputed when Hungarian immigrants began settling in the communities. The "flashpoint" issue of Simon Beer's day was mustaches. The Hungarian men of the day wore long "handlebar" mustaches, while the other men wore only beards. Soon there was trouble as many of the Swiss-German members began to demand that the Hungarians trim their mustaches and conform for the sake of unity. It was reasoned by many since the Hungarians had been assisted by the church members in coming to America that they should be willing to conform to the American church's custom.

The particular complaint was that it was unpleasant for the other men to greet the Hungarian members with a holy kiss, which was a custom in the Apostolic Christian Church. Apparently the mustaches were thought to be unclean by the American members. Grandpa Theo said the American brethren felt there was "just too much hair on the lips to greet them." Before long the American Apostolic Christian churches divided over this issue. To this day there are two major types of Apostolic Christian Churches in America, who refer to each other as "sister churches."

A generation after the split of Simon Beer's day there was a serious effort for reconciliation. By this time the one branch allowed no beards or mustaches, while the other branch allowed mustaches. Reconciliation work had progressed a long way when it broke down over the definition of a "neatly trimmed" mustache. An influential Elder from the Simon Beer side of the split defined "neatly trimmed" as being "as close as a scissors can cut." This severe definition effectively ended the reconciliation attempt.

This sad division probably had very little to do with mustaches. Much more likely it had to do with underlying issues like ethnic and cultural identity, and power — who had the right to dictate how things will be. These issues are seen in the New Testament churches. For example, in Acts 6:1 we read, *In those days when the number of disciples was increasing, the Grecian Jews among them complained against the Hebraic Jews because their widows were being overlooked in the daily distribution of food.* We see other examples in Acts 15, Galatians 2, and Galatians 3:28. Similar divisions continue until today. Today we see them manifested in styles of worship, as well as among races, ethnic groups, and differing cultures. This is very sad and it must be an affront to God who so clearly laid out His plans for "Oneness" in Jesus Christ. (Matthew 28:18-20; John 13:34,35; Acts 1:8; Galatians 3:28.) This division deeply hurt Simon Beer, who had friends on both sides of the issue. He saw no need for a separation and Grandpa Theo remembers that for a period of time he did not even want to go to church because of it.

A second circumstance that contributed to Simon and Catherine's life change also had a Hungarian connection. Grandpa Theo's older brother Otto began to spend too much time with the Hungarian girls. Catherine, in particular, was concerned about this. Otto was even sent to Milford, Indiana, one summer for work in an effort to break off this contact. One time Grandpa Theo and I talked about this. At the time he was well into his nineties. He remembers, "They (the Hungarian girls) were after me, too. Mother really worried about this." Thinking this to be an issue of Swiss versus Hungarian, I asked him if it was simply because they were not Swiss. "No," he quickly replied, "It was because they put out!" In 1987, Grandpa Theo had written about this issue:

"We had a large family of Hungarian children we played with. We played hide and go seek. We played serious. I remember one time I crawled into a crawl space to hide. And in there were two girls, older than I. I didn't think too much of it then, but since I got older I became wiser. I think this will be all on this topic of my life as I grew to manhood." (Beers have historically had a keen understanding of and appreciation for issues of human sexuality!)

The third circumstance that led to Simon and Catherine's life change was religious in nature. It seems that some time before 1910 Simon took an interest in the Jehovah's Witnesses and their prophecies. This was something that Grandpa Theo did not talk about much, but on several occasions we did discuss it. How Simon became interested in Jehovah's Witness' prophecies is not known, but it became a source of conflict between Catherine and him. Grandpa Theo recalled Simon telling Catherine that if a certain prophecy did not come true that he would throw away all the Jehovah's Witnesses' literature and be done with it. It cannot be known for certain, but comparing accounts and history, the prophecy in question is probably what follows. In 1904 *The Watchtower*, the official publication of the Jehovah's Witnesses, stated:

"The stress of the great time of trouble will be on us soon, somewhere between 1910 and 1912, culminating with the end of the 'times of the Gentiles,' October 1914."

When the time came and went without any hint of fulfillment, Simon was done with the Jehovah's Witnesses. Beers are historically people who are very decisive, not dwelling on the past.

The connection with the State of Indiana began with Grandpa Theo's brother Otto moving there to work. In addition, Simon's brother Ulrich had moved to Indiana from Illinois. Adding to this the church split, the Hungarian girls, and the Jehovah's Witnesses produced an atmosphere that made a change of location seem attractive. When a land agent came to Simon with some farms for sale in Indiana, he was ready to look. When he and his son Otto left for Milford, Indiana, Catherine implored him not to buy anything. Guess what? He bought a farm. Grandpa Theo wrote about this in 1987:

"...Then something happened that changed my whole life. A land agent from Milford came and tried to interest Dad to come and look at several farms he had for sale in the Milford area. Dad's brother Ulrich had settled there from Illinois. The church was built already. We had eighty acres paid for. It turned about that we traded our eighty acres for one hundred sixty acres where I live now. Mother was unhappy about it at first, but she got over it. The first night she cried all night. March first 1912 we moved to Milford. Otto and Ezra rode in the boxcar with the horses, cows, and chickens. There were three cars all together. We moved all our furniture and farm implements. Mother and father and we five children came by train. It seemed a kind of a new venture for me. I was willing to leave our

home and friends. I hoped I would like our new home. We stayed at Ulrich's home till the cars came. Then the church people came with wagons and so our home was now Milford."

Simon and Catherine were to live out the remainder of their lives in Milford, Indiana. Grandpa Theo added some interesting personal notes about them in his writings of 1987:

"My father was a strong man. (He was) *five feet ten inches and weighed around one hundred eighty pounds. He always seemed to be pretty old, he always wore a beard...Dad was diligent to teach us to work, and he always said to us boys 'be honest in your dealings, and work, and God will bless you'... One thing I want to mention is that Dad was <u>very, very</u> cautious how much money he would give us. A quarter a week was the limit. Ezra and I told him once that this was not enough; he said 'how will you spend it?' We were foolish enough to tell him* (that) *to take a girl to a show and ice cream would take fifty cents. To my knowledge he never raised our twenty-five cents allowance, but we worked out once in a while and earned a little money, which he left us keep. We were no different than our friends, — they* (also) *had to make their allowances go as far as possible. As I got older I often thought this was good for us — we learned money did not come easy. So Dad was good to us after all. Dad missed his ninetieth birthday by twenty days. Mother died at eighty-three. Both died suddenly, for which we were all thankful."*

Grandpa Theo also added some interesting personal notes about his mother Catherine. A consistent family testimony is that Catherine was more of a refined woman whose influence served to moderate some of the crudeness and stubbornness of Simon. She apparently was a very spiritual woman as well. One of Grandpa Theo's nephews recently said of Catherine that many who knew her said "If she had been a man she would have been a preacher."

"Mother was more a delicate woman. I always felt she might die before I could be grown. But she always rallied to duties of bearing and caring for her children. She was a smart person. We kids could fool our Dad, but not our Mom, she could read our

thoughts... Mother was our spiritual advisor. She told us of her conversion and baptism. She and one other soul were baptized when they had to cut a hole in the ice. I often said that it was awful to go into such cold water... Our mother told us she loved her Lord, and felt that the cold water would not hurt her.

Chapter Three

A second church-produced marriage that illustrates the character and devotion of my ancestors is that of Benjamin and Eliza Speheger, my mother's maternal grandparents. Benjamin Speheger was born in Ohio to Swiss immigrants. He later moved to Bluffton, Indiana where he lived on his father, John Sr's, one hundred sixty acre farm. Eventually Ben and his brother, John Jr, each bought half of the home farm from their father. The farm was heavily wooded and Ben worked his entire adult life clearing it for farming. Walter Speheger, Ben's youngest son and a brother to my Grandma Naoma Beer, wrote an interesting article many years ago that encapsulates this family's experience with their eighty acre farm:

"My grandfather (John Speheger) *bought one hundred sixty acres of ground here* (Lancaster Township). *John Speheger Jr.* (son) *got eighty acres to the south and Ben* (son) *my dad the eighty acres to the north. The ground all had to be cleared in order to farm and build. The barn was built in 1902 and the house two years later.*
With the huge equipment of today it is amazing that I would farm and plow this ground with two horses and a one row walking plow.
At times my dad, when a boy, would see an Indian come from the woods and drink water from the hog trough. The water there was pumped fresh and he probably knew that the water from a puddle would be contaminated with malaria germs. On the hill on the south end of the farm was a log cabin at one time. A man and woman lived

there. The man could play an accordion and for entertainment my dad would go there and listen to him play. He later bought the man a new accordion from the Sears Roebuck Catalog. Many stones and Indian relics were found on this hill as well as broken dishes. The man died but there is no account of what became of them.

Due to the large family and the aging of my parents the farm fell into debt. Mom and Dad could not pay off the loan. A man from Prudential Insurance Company came one day and said, I know you are trying but unless the money is paid in two years we will have to take the farm.

In the meantime I was able to save $1500.00 and as the time drew near I applied for a loan for ten years at the Federal Land Bank. They asked if I had any money and I told him of the $1500.00, but I wanted to keep that in case of illness. The loan was granted and the first loan was paid off, much to the surprise of the Prudential Company. The loan office was on the top floor of the tall Lincoln Tower building in Fort Wayne.

By raising hogs and milking several cows night and morning and a job which was offered me in the AAA office by Jim Gordon, I was able to pay the loan off in three years and save the farm. From then on things went better."

Ben met his wife-to-be, Eliza Dubach, when the Speheger and Dubach families made the move from Ohio to Bluffton, Indiana. The story goes that Ben and his brother John were so shy that they walked the entire way rather than ride on the wagon with the Dubach girls. Eliza had been born in Berne, Switzerland in 1871 and had immigrated to America with her family. She was a young woman and a member of the Apostolic Christian Church when she became pregnant by a hired hand where she worked. She gave birth to a daughter, whom she named Olga. Ben loved Eliza and was undeterred by her out of wedlock child. He apparently overcame his earlier shyness, as the two of them married and had twelve children together. Their daughter Naoma was my Grandma Beer.

Ben and Eliza lived their entire married lives under the discipline of the Apostolic Christian Church. Eliza was under discipline because of her out-of-wedlock child. Ben was under discipline because he married Eliza. It is also speculated by some in the family that Eliza may have been pregnant with Ben's child when they were married, but there seems to be no agreement on this. Whatever the reason, the two of them were under discipline of the church, and understanding their status in the church requires a description of the doctrine of church discipline, as practiced by the Apostolic Christian Church.

Chapter Four

Church discipline is a clear doctrine in scripture (Matthew 18:15-17; Romans 16:17; I Corinthians 5:1-13, compare with II Corinthians 2:5-11; Galatians 6:1,2). Church discipline preserves the testimony of the church to unbelievers. Another purpose is to turn an unrepentant believer from an on-going sin. The objective of church discipline is always the restoration of a believer to fellowship within the body. It is an extremely difficult doctrine to obey, as it requires a clear understanding of the issue in question, reliable witnesses, unity among church leaders, and a congregation that is both trusting of and submissive to the leadership. In our day it is even more difficult because there is so little commitment among believers that only the most spiritual will be a part of the process. Most simply conclude that the congregation is unloving and move on to find another congregation. I know of no clear doctrine in scripture which, when applied, causes more problems in the local church.

In my own experience we always tried to faithfully follow the process which Jesus laid out in Matthew 18:15-17. In my thirteen years of pastoring we never had to bring an issue of sin before the congregation because either there was repentance and restoration of the individual in question or the individual simply left the church. Whenever we knew that an individual who was subject to discipline had become a part of another church we would make their leaders aware of it. Usually this information was graciously received, but sometimes the response was "So?" Because of the difficulty in properly applying the doctrine of church discipline, most churches simply ignore it. This is tragic for three reasons: First, to ignore a clear doctrine is sin and God never blesses sin. Secondly, to ignore one doctrine in scripture is a first step to ignoring others. The ultimate result of this is to rob the Bible of its authority and then there are no absolutes by which to live. It is no accident that the world is now full of churches that hold the Bible to be only "a source" of truth rather than "the source" of truth. Thirdly, when church discipline is applied correctly and consistently it is a beautiful and holy process.

To the credit of the Apostolic Christian Church, they openly and consistently apply church discipline, as they understand it. Having spent my first thirty-three years in the Apostolic Christian Church and my last fifteen years out of it I have concluded that the only thing worse than not practicing church discipline at all is to practice it in an unbiblical manner, which I believe is the case in the Apostolic Christian Church.

To understand the Apostolic Christian Church's practice of church discipline, one must first understand their view of salvation. In the Apostolic Christian Church it is believed that salvation comes about as the result of a process that is called "repentance and conversion." While evangelicals believe that salvation comes about when one by faith accepts Jesus Christ as their Savior from sin, Apostolics believe that salvation comes about when God accepts them as a result of repentance, conversion, and water baptism.

The repentance process of the Apostolic Christian Church begins when an individual decides that it is time to get right with God. The terminology is generally that one "is repenting' or "joining the church." This is encouraged in the denomination when one "reaches an age of accountability." This age of accountability is believed to be entered into at some point during the teenage years. Most often the repentance process begins shortly after high school. The main reasons for this are because once one "repents" they can no longer participate in organized sports or actively continue to be a part of relationships with people outside of the church. I am one of many who can remember praying throughout high school that God would let me live long enough to "receive the call" and "repent," or "join the church."

When an individual makes this decision to repent, they visit the Elder, or leader, of their congregation and confess their sins. This confession is officially "to God in the presence of men." All sins are to be confessed. During this confession, the Elder is also free to inquire into areas of the convert's life where he knows others have had trouble in the past. Once the confession has been made the convert is spoken of as having "made a beginning." Next follows a period of contrition, restitution, and reconciliation in which past wrongs are made right as much as possible. The individual becomes faithful in church attendance, begins to conform to church customs and traditions, and limits social activities to church functions and church people.

After a period of two to three months the convert has done as much as he or she knows to do. It is believed that at this point one receives "peace." "Peace" comes to converts in a variety of ways, ranging from mystical "signs" to intellectual assent. What it means practically is that the convert no longer feels guilt over past sin and knows that nothing more can be done to make past wrongs right. If the church Elder agrees, then the convert is announced to the church as having "found peace." This ushers in a period of time during which the convert is to be willing to receive admonition from other members of the church who may have concerns about his or her repentance, appearance, or lifestyle.

If nothing serious arises, the convert is then announced for baptism. On the Saturday evening before Baptism Sunday the church membership assembles for a "proving" service. During this service the convert is brought to the front bench of the church. From the pulpit the Elder begins the service by asking the convert why they have come. The convert then gives a brief recounting of how the "call" came and how repentance began. The remainder of the service is then conducted in a question and answer format. The Elder questions the convert about their repentance process, their beliefs, their appearance, their feelings about the customs and traditions of the church, and their willingness to submit to the leadership. Assuming the convert answers to the satisfaction of the Elder, the Elder then asks various people in the audience for their impression. Usually parents, spouses, and grandparents are asked. The reply is rarely more than "Well satisfied" or "I've seen a big change." The service culminates with the Elder asking the convert if they mind if the church is asked for their support for his or her baptism. The church is then asked "If you can support the baptism of (the convert) tomorrow, please indicate so by standing." If everyone stands in support, the convert will be baptized the next day. They have been "proved."

Only in very rare instances is one hundred per cent approval not given. The first reason for this is that the congregation has been given ample opportunity to register concerns beforehand. To harbor concerns and not come forward before the proving would be sinful in and of itself. Secondly, to not support the baptism would be tantamount to challenging the Elder's judgment, in that he has presented the convert for approval.

One of these rare instances occurred after the "proving" of my Grandma Naoma Beer, who was the most humble and godly woman I have ever known. There were some in the congregation who refused to stand in support of her because she wore a collar on her dress, which was considered to be too fancy. Her baptism was delayed for a while as a result. I can never know for sure, but I feel the fact that her parents were under discipline also played a role in the matter. Grandma Naoma was none-the-worse for the incident, but it was an embarrassment that she took to her grave.

On the Sunday following the proving the convert is baptized (by immersion, in the name of the Father, Son, and holy Spirit, one time face up). Following the baptism there is a "prayer of consecration." As the Elder prays with his hands on the convert's head, "The Holy Spirit is poured out upon such a cleansed and purified heart, to lead it upon the pathway of truth and righteousness." (Quoted from *The First Hundred Years*. This is a book about the history of The Apostolic Christian Church.) This prayer is also commonly referred to as "the sealing of the Holy Spirit," an apparent reference to Ephesians 1:13,14. Following this prayer the convert is welcomed as a new member of the church and is greeted with a holy kiss for the first time by all members of the same gender. In the New Testament, believers are instructed to greet each other with a "holy kiss" in five different passages. (Romans 16:16; I Corinthians 16:20; II Corinthians 13:12; I Thessalonians 5:26; I Peter 5:14) In these passages the holy kiss is meant to be a pure expression of Christian love between men with men and women with women, with no sexual overtones. Most Christians believe that the principle of expressing warm, loving, and sincere greetings among Christians is a universal imperative, but that the practice of a literal kiss to express these greetings was rooted in the culture of the first century church. The Apostolic Christian Church denomination believes that the physical act of the kiss is imperative and practices it accordingly.

After water baptism the new member of the Apostolic Christian Church is considered converted and born again. Many church members relate that this day is the only day in their life that they were sure of their salvation. Officially, the church strongly maintains that salvation is only "our hope" as long as we live, that only those who "stay true and faithful unto the end" will enter heaven. According to Apostolic Christian Church doctrine, one can never know for sure that they are going to heaven. They can only hope they will make it. Many Apostolics maintain that salvation is never attained until death. Others, however, believe that one can possess salvation in this life, but that it can be lost. Within this group, opinions vary widely about what is necessary for one to lose salvation. If there is one Bible doctrine that is universally most opposed by the Apostolic Christian Church, it is the doctrine of eternal security.

A critical question in this religious context is "How does one remain true and faithful until the end?" The simple answer, in the Apostolic Christian Church, is to remain a member in good standing. For many members this includes prayer, scripture reading, faithful attendance, a loving spirit, and sincerely denying oneself worldly pleasures. For many others it simply means remaining a member in good standing. In its simplest form this means not "rocking the boat" and not taking part in activities that the church deems to be worldly, especially when other members are watching. In either case this amounts to a salvation that is maintained by "doing good works." Combining this with a carefully choreographed "repentance and conversion" process makes it dangerously easy for Apostolics to erroneously equate attaining church membership with attaining salvation. There is much more to follow on this subject later.

Chapter Five

With this background information on the Apostolic Christian Church's view of the process of salvation, we return to the doctrine of church discipline, as practiced by the Apostolic Christian Church. The following excerpt from *The First Hundred Years* summarizes the church's view of church discipline.

"Church discipline requires that all members adhere to and faithfully obey the teachings of Jesus Christ and the Apostles, exercising all Christian virtues as exemplified by these, abstaining from the lusts and pleasures of the world, from vanity and pride."

One more explanation is necessary to understand the denomination's practice of discipline, and that is to understand what is "sin" in the life of the church member. It is understood that church members are not perfect. The leaders of the Apostolic Christian Church speak of two general classes of imperfections. First, there is the broad category of imperfections called "mistakes and shortcomings." Included in this category would be such things as envy, vanity, pride, anger, gossip, slander, greed, discord, selfish ambition, dissensions, factions, and the like. These are viewed as human frailties which must be warred against, but which are rarely, if ever, disciplined. The second category of imperfections is called "sins" and includes fornication, adultery, and other sexual sins. On rare occasions, financial failures, like a bankruptcy judged to be the result of a member being prideful or seeking after vainglory will be viewed as a "sin." On other rare occasions, anything blatant and ongoing from the first category of imperfections is deemed to be "sin."

"Sin" requires church discipline. Such discipline is viewed as "punishment" for the sinning member and it is administered whether the sinning member is repentant or not. For a serious sin like adultery or fornication a standard procedure is followed. Within the Apostolic Christian Church denomination, each congregation is led by an Elder, who is supported by a varying number of local ministers. The first step in the discipline is confession to the local Elder by the one who has committed the sin. Most often the penitent sinner comes to the local Elder because of his or her own guilt, but other times the Elder seeks out the sinner after learning about the sin from another source. Once the sin has been confessed, the local Elder will then consult Elders from other congregations. If they are in agreement, a special members-only church meeting will be called. At this meeting it is announced that the individual has fallen into sin and will be punished. The individual is identified and the sin is made known. Once the punishment is announced the entire membership is asked to stand in support of the Elders and the action being taken.

The punishment begins with the church placing a "ban" on the individual. The scripture cited as the authority for this "ban" is I Corinthians 5: 1-13. During this "ban" period the individual is required to attend all services but is to be shunned by the membership. The membership is to have no conversation or fellowship with the individual. The practice of the denomination on Sundays is to have a morning preaching service, then a simple meal, followed by an afternoon preaching service. The individual under the "ban" is not allowed to come to the dining area for the noon meal. Generally the individual's immediate family will sit silently with them in the auditorium, sharing their shame during this mealtime. After a period of time, ranging from several weeks to several months, the ban is lifted. The individual can then be spoken to and may attend the noon lunch again, but they are no longer members of the church. As such they cannot take communion or greet with a holy kiss, and they are not referred to as "brother" or "sister" anymore.

When the sin is adultery, the individual's membership will

never be restored. I clearly remember being present at a national conference and hearing one prominent Elder in the denomination defend this life-long punishment as being equivalent to a diabetic needing life-long doses of insulin to save his life. Repentant fornicators can be restored in our modern age, but only after years of faithfully submitting to the discipline.

Lesser punishment is reserved for "sin" other than adultery and fornication. It generally consists of the individual not being allowed to partake in communion and to greet with the holy kiss for a period of time. When to apply church discipline for lesser sins, the form the discipline takes, and the duration of the discipline varies greatly, largely depending on who the Elder is and whom the individuals in question are.

The object of discipline in the Apostolic Christian Church is to punish the sinner in order to pay for the sin. This understanding meshes well with their "repentance- procured" and "faithfulness-maintained" view of salvation.

Chapter Six

My mother's maternal Grandparents, Benjamin and Eliza Speheger, were highly respected people in their community. They were known to be hard-working, honest people who lived quietly on their farm raising their large family. Both Ben and Eliza were members in good standing at one time in the Apostolic Christian Church. As mentioned earlier, Eliza lost her membership when she bore a child out of wedlock. Benjamin lost his membership when he married Eliza. In their day fornicators were never restored. This seems especially harsh, even for that day and time. They faithfully attended church services throughout their lives, despite not being considered to be a brother and sister in faith by the other members, despite not being allowed to greet with a holy kiss, and despite never being allowed to partake in the Lord's Supper. Every Sunday brought these overt reminders of their standing in the church. The story is told that one time some Elders visited their home. One of the Elders, who was not from Bluffton, moved to greet Benjamin with the customary holy kiss, but was pulled back by a local Elder. Despite such constant reminders of their past sin they never complained or wavered in their support of the church.

It is difficult for one who has never been in this denomination to understand the ramifications of this long-term discipline on individuals and their families. As an illustration I offer the discipline of one of my aunt's sisters. This woman became involved in an extramarital affair. She repented of her sin and confessed it to her local

Elder. The church excommunicated her. During the period of her "ban" her husband backed over one of their children in the driveway and killed him. In the midst of this unspeakable personal tragedy the church members would not speak to her throughout the visitation and funeral for her child. While this woman remains in the denomination to this day, her brothers all rejected the Apostolic Christian Church as a result of what they perceived to be profound cruelty to their sister. One might think, "So? They can just go to another church." It is not this simple. It must be understood that while children are not members of the church, they are taught early on that their church is the only one which follows "the whole Bible," that other churches are taking the "easy way," that other churches' members are not sufficiently devoted to a separated life. While only a very small percentage of Apostolic children eventually become members in the denomination, many of them do not want to be a part of any other church either.

In the denomination everyone knows who is under discipline. People under discipline are identified and defined by it, even by members of other congregations. This is particularly difficult for children of disciplined parents. The children of Ben and Eliza Speheger were no exception to this. My Grandma Beer often spoke of how she "thought of them no different than regular members," that they "never spoke of it" in their home, and that her parents "never complained about it." The fact that Grandma Beer explained this to me on many occasions, however, leads me to believe it was a source of shame to her throughout her life. How sad.

When Ben was an old man the Elders of the church offered to restore his membership. He refused, thinking it would be better that he remain in his standing. This decision was very likely out of love for Eliza as well. This sort of humility, steadfastness, and devotion is part of a heritage that I am proud to call as my own.

Chapter Seven

The third church-produced marriage illustrative of the character of my ancestors is that of Simon and Catherine Beer's son Theophilus (Theo) and Benjamin and Eliza Speheger's daughter Naoma. This union produced my mother. This union also produced the physical and spiritual framework in which I grew up. I had the privilege of growing up next door to my grandparents, Theo and Naoma Beer. This essentially amounted to having two sets of parents, a double blessing to me.

Grandpa Theo's two older brothers, Otto and Ezra, grew up and left the farm when they were of age. He remained on the farm. He wrote of this period of his life as follows:

"I worked at home and helped farm til I was twenty-one years old. Dad said he would give me $30.00 a month during the summer months. So I helped farm til the corn was in. We cut the corn and shocked it. Then we would pull down the shocks and husk them by hand. We had a wagon there (and) *we would throw the ears into the wagon. We would tie the fodder in bundles and again set them up in shocks. The corn we would shovel off by hand, always before meals, which was the part I thought was the hardest. When I was nineteen years old I painted our old buggy with yellow paint for the wheels, and the body was black. We never had a real buggy horse, so I drove the nicest work horse we had. I had several girlfriends which I would take a ride in my buggy. Once I drove to Wawasee Lake*

with a girl, there was something going on all day. I had a nice time but my girl friends and I never got serious."

Grandpa Theo must have been a dashing gent in his younger days. He often would speak of his girlfriends and the other girls who wanted to be his girlfriends. By all accounts, he was a handsome young man. He was also a life-long master conversationalist. With these two attributes it is no wonder that he was popular with the ladies. But it was always his intention to marry a church girl, so he never allowed himself to get serious. It must also be noted that Grandpa Theo's recollection of himself as handsome and desirable to the ladies was not pride — it was just true (of course!).

When Grandpa Theo was twenty-three he wanted to return to Mansfield, Ohio. He never really spoke of any specific reasons for wanting to go back. Probably he was just bored in Milford. This decision to return to Mansfield was life changing for Theo, as it brought about his repentance and salvation. Grandpa Theo wrote of this episode of his life in 1987.

"November 25, 1921, I asked if I could go back to Mansfield for the winter. I said I would try to get work there. Mother was very reluctant for me to go. She feared I would get in bad company and get into trouble. I assured her I would be careful and I told her I would go to church on Sunday mornings. So I packed my clothes and took the street car to Warsaw, and from there by train to Mansfield. I did not feel bad by going, but Mother did, she warned me again don't go to bad places, and go to church. This advice I remembered, and it helped me when I was tempted to stray. I worked at the Westinghouse Electric Company for several months. I enjoyed my work and city life. And I felt I might stay there and work, the farm life did not seen to attract me as much as the factory work. I dated a few church girls but we were never too serious. I did enjoy my life in the city."

Grandpa Theo often told me the story about being a part of a group of young men who decided to visit a "bad house." He went along with them but said that when he came to the door he turned back. He told me, "I remembered my promise to mother and I just couldn't do it." Later one of the men who went in told him that he was really sick with a bad "dose" he had gotten from that night. Grandpa also told the story that he had bought some dance lessons in Mansfield. He only took one lesson before he became ill. When he told me this story, he laughed and said I could go and take the rest of the lessons if I wanted to. Theo's story continues:

All went well till in the middle of February I took down with a bad flu and bronchitis. I was rooming with a cousin's mother. She was good to me, but she worked through the day. I was all alone in the house for about one week through the day. One day I felt better so I dressed and walked up town to see a doctor. I got most of the way, then I began to chill and feel worse, so I started back to my room. That night I had fever and really sweat. I began to worry, maybe I won't get over this, then what? For the first time I began to think of home and I knew Mother could see me through this illness. And here I am all alone, and nobody cares. I always prayed in a fashion before, but this time I prayed "Lord, see me through this, I cannot handle it alone." I started to cry and I could not stop. Finally the cousin's mother looked in on me, and saw me crying, and said I should not cry. "You will soon be well and will go out with the boys and have a nice time." I wanted her to leave. I was so distressed with myself. It is then I made a promise to God, who I did not know in fullness, (that) if he would let me get well and let me go home again I would surrender my life to Him.

I (soon) got some better and I made plans to go back home. The church young people had a farewell party for me, but I just did not enjoy it as I did before. So I bought a ticket to go back home. On the way home the enemy of my soul tempted me to not keep my promise that I made to Him (God) while I was sick. I fought it all the way home. When I got home Mother was glad to see me. I had wrote to her that I was sick, and (she) was worried. She and the family seemed so good to me. I wondered why I ever left to go to the city. I said to my brothers (that) I would not help with the chores my first night home. So Mother and I were alone in the house. I went to the organ and with one finger I played. I finally came to the song "Jesus Lover of my Soul." I began to think about this song. Does Jesus really love my soul? I was so deep in my thoughts about this that I did not see my mother looking over my shoulder. She said to me do you believe that Jesus loves your soul? It is then I broke down and cried. She said "Theophilus, what is wrong with you?" I said "You tell me. I (have) *felt this way during my sickness." She said "I know what's wrong with you. Jesus is calling you. I could feel it when you wrote that you were coming home."*

Now I knew that Mother (knew) *of my feelings. We had a long talk of my feelings. She convinced me the Lord was calling to me to give my life to Him. She went* (back) *to preparing the evening meal. I was alone with my thoughts. I finally made up my mind to turn my life around and follow Jesus wherever He would lead me. I went to church on Sunday. My friends came and found me sitting up farther than usual, and they wondered what was wrong. At noon I told them I was going to change my life. They told me they had plans for me to take girls out on Sunday eve. I said I could not go with them. They were shocked but on Wednesday George Graff* (a friend) *said he was going* (joining the church) *with me. My brother Ezra and sister Saloma made up their minds also, so I was not alone. I started to read the Bible and prayed the best I could. I didn't know just what to do next. My Mother said I should go the talk to our German minister Ed Haab. I went to his home and he was gone. I came home discouraged, but Mother stood by me* (saying) *I should go again. I finally took courage and went. He was in his shop working. He was nice to me and asked if he could help me. I said my life was in a turmoil,* (that) *I don't know what to do. He said he made the same experience when he was young. And God helped him through until this present day. With his help and encouragement I opened my heart to him of my burdens. To my surprise he said he did the same thing to his minister. He told me he also was a sinner and needed help, and God kept His promise. I felt I now am on the way to salvation. I told both Father and Mother* (that) *I'm not going to give up. They encouraged me. It was several months till we four were announced for baptism. I was living in peace and now had a hope for the future.*

(On) *October 25, 1920 Brother Henry Sauder of the Leo church came and heard our testimonies, we were all four baptized at the well west of the old church. The water was pumped out of the well. It was cold but it did not hurt any of us. Now I was a member of the* church. *The old people accepted me well and I felt at home with them. (My) Brother Henry was taken in* (became a member of the church) *while I was at Mansfield. He and Joe Rassi were the* (only other) *single members.*

My Grandma Naoma's history is not as well documented as Grandpa Theo's. As I began to write about Grandma Naoma's pre-marriage years, I realized that I knew almost nothing. This seemed strange to me in that I had known of Grandpa Theo's life for many years. I asked my mother to provide some details. She readily agreed to do so. As we talked I realized that my not knowing about the early years of Grandma's life was understandable. She would never have spoken about herself unless asked, and then only in the most humble and self-minimizing of words. Grandma Beer was one of the very few truly humble people that I ever have known.

My mother offered the following memories:

"Naoma Marguerite Speheger was born on February 16, 1901, to Benjamin and Eliza Dubach Speheger. She was the fourth child of the couple and she grew up on the family farm east of Bluffton, Indiana. Her parents had a total of twelve children, six boys and six girls, all of whom were raised on the farm.

Her playground was the woods next to her house, the barn, and the windmill, which she loved to climb. Her friends were her siblings and the Myer children, who lived across the road. They were the undisciplined children of John and Laura Myer. John was an alcoholic and a cruel man. His children seemed to follow in his footsteps and often terrorized the shy little girl Naoma. She said her brothers were protective of her, but she seemed to be very affected from the fights that went on involving the Myer family. Aunt Irene, a younger sister of hers, eventually married one of the Myer boys, Orlando. She said her parents were very troubled over this.

Naoma and her siblings attended "The Little School" which was less than a mile from their home. It was a typical one-room school that was common at that time. She went through the eighth grade twice because she was too young to be out of school. Naoma was a straight-A student. Her friends often became jealous of her and this made her sad.

Naoma often talked about being a sickly child. She contacted the flu during the epidemic around the First World War, which left her very fragile. She became a victim of tuberculosis after this and spent a long time resting and sleeping on the open porch in the fresh air. Naoma never told us this, but Uncle Walter's wife said the family often talked about how they nearly lost her.

Naoma told about the time she and her siblings were playing in the barn and she fell out of the haymow on her head. They all thought she was dead, but it only knocked her unconscious. She had a concussion that left her with a severe headache for a long time.

Naoma also talked about the fun they had in the woods. They climbed trees and pretended they were in a fairyland. I believe the young years were happy and full of imagination for her.

After she was out of school she spent a few years helping her mother and her sister, Olga, raise the younger children. Olga was soon married with children and Naoma often helped her out. Naoma learned to sew and made most of her own clothes and also clothes for her younger sisters. Lorene and Irene, her twin sisters, went to high school, and Naoma helped them with their clothes so that they always looked nice.

When Naoma was seventeen she felt the need of a Savior in her life. She repented and wanted to join the church. The Apostolic Christian Church of Bluffton is where her family always attended. Grandma and Grandpa Speheger had been members of this church but were under lifetime punishment because Grandma had a child out of wedlock. Since Grandpa married her after this, his membership was taken away.

When Naoma was proved the first time, (went before the church to be accepted for membership) she was rejected by the membership because they felt her clothing was not humble enough. Naoma accepted this as God's will and willingly waited until they were satisfied.

Naoma had reached a time in her life when she felt the need to get a job that could help the family out. She enrolled in a business course at International Business College in Fort Wayne, Indiana. This was a very brave thing for her to do, because she had no high school training and she had to find a place to live away from home for the first time. Her parents were concerned for her but they also knew it was a wise thing to do. She found a room in the home of a Catholic family in Fort Wayne. She said they were very good to her and respected her faith and religion. She felt these people really knew the Lord.

After her business course she accepted a job at the bank in Bluffton. Since she had no transportation, she moved in with her brother Charlie and his wife Mary, who lived in town. She loved her job and enjoyed working with the public. With her paycheck she was able to pay Charlie a small rent and help her younger sisters and brothers with their money for clothes and school. When her younger brother Ben was in medical school, she was consistent in putting money in his shirt pocket after she ironed it. Service to others was a major part of Naoma's nature and her entire life was spent serving others.

Naoma was a very pretty, dark-haired girl with black eyes that sparkled. When she began to work in the public she was admired by many men. She said she had to stay on her guard because they made passes at her and wanted to date her. Being a member of the church, Naoma did not date. She became concerned that she would be tempted and compromise her faith. I wonder if this is part of the reason she changed jobs. She next went to work at the Hartman-Dotterer Feed Mill as a bookkeeper. One of the owners was a member of her church, which would make it a safer haven for her.

In His sovereignty, God had brought Grandpa Theo and Grandma Naoma to the point in their lives when they were willing to marry each other in faith. The year was 1925. Grandpa Theo's side of the story, recorded on several occasions, goes as follows:

"I was twenty-two years old when I was converted. I did not do much traveling at first. Once I was invited to a wedding in Bluffton of one of my friends, Joe Klopfenstein. Minnie Ladig, my sister Saloma, and I went to the wedding. The brother who met me at the street car told me that he had a girl he wanted me to meet. So we went to the place she worked and he introduced me to Naoma. I will admit that she struck me, that she was nicely made and very friendly."

Grandpa often said over the years that Naoma was the most beautiful woman he had ever seen.

"And I made a pretty good point to make her feel like I had more than a passing interest in her. But I didn't say anything about it. A man who worked in the office said to the boss 'You see that young fellow leaning against the counter? He is going to take that girl out of this office.' I learned of this later.

After the wedding we worshiped in the church on Sunday. I didn't see Naoma much, but it stuck. I told myself I'll have to see more of this girl. So on various visits to the Bluffton church I always made it a point to meet her and to visit with her and tried to get involved in her group of friends.

I was farming for Dad. I got one fourth of the income. He paid the expenses. I had saved $1500.00 and I had faith and love that I was going to ask for her heart and hand in marriage. Soon after this our bank failed and my money was tied up. I could not draw out any at all. This postponed my proposal."

This bank failure was a preview of what would soon follow during the Great Depression. This Milford bank invested too heavily in the construction of the Tippecanoe Golf Club. When the project failed, Grandpa's money was lost. There was no FDIC to protect investors. Many years later Grandpa got back three hundred of his fifteen hundred dollars.

"I kept working and praying and saving my money. I felt I needed to have some money to set up a home. I prayed that when I was ready to get married that she (Naoma) would still be single.

Fifteen months later I had saved $1500.00 again. So I had the faith to ask for her hand in marriage through my minister. I prayed during that time that she would be of the same mind.

Later she told me that she always felt a proposal from me might be in the foreground. She feared it because she had a good job and had become kind of independent at age twenty-four. But when the proposal came she knew she had to make a decision. She said that she always respected me, she liked me, but she had to have faith that love would come. I had love for her when I asked for her.

Eventually the answer came back yes and we were announced to the church. Two months later we were married in the Bluffton church. Brother Rauch was the Elder who performed the ceremony in the

German language. Our honeymoon was spent around Bluffton. We started home on Saturday after the wedding. On the way we stopped at Hartman and Dotterer's Feed Store where Naoma had worked when I first met her. Brother Henry was nice to us but he said something I did not like to hear. He said 'Naoma, I will give you six months and you will be back in Bluffton.' It has lasted sixty-one years and she never asked me to move her back to Bluffton."

Thanks to my mother, we also have the story from Grandma Naoma's perspective:

"It was at the feed mill that she first met Theo Beer, the man who would win her heart. He had stopped in to visit Henry Dotterer, her boss, and was delighted to meet his new bookkeeper. Naoma said he was nice looking and very friendly. Too friendly for her liking. Naoma was currently being noticed by several young church member brothers and she didn't seem very interested in Theo at that time."

Grandma Naoma once told me that one time in church she was standing with some other young people when one of them said "Look, there is Theo Beer!" Grandma said he was surrounded by a bunch of single people and she said "I'm not interested in him at all." She felt he was too friendly.

"Theo was persistent with his attention and if he didn't impress Naoma he surely impressed her mother and father. They became very found of him and told Naoma she should not let him get away. She must have decided to check him out a little more. She and her friends went to visit the Milford church to visit the young people there. While there she went to Grandma and Grandpa Simon Beer's home for a visit. This gave Theo a chance to talk to her and show her where he would live when he got married. It happened to be a run-down shamble of a house on the farm where they were raising chickens. Naoma was not impressed."

Grandpa Theo told me when he showed her this house that Grandma Naoma laughed. It really disappointed him. He also mentioned that his brother Otto was raising raccoons in the house at the time, in addition to the chickens.

"Theo assured her he would fix it up to be a nice home. Theo was a good salesman and with God's help he won her heart. They were married on October 25, 1925, when Naoma was twenty-four years old and Theo was twenty-seven. They moved into the house that once housed chickens."

Chapter Eight

The house that had served as the home of chickens and raccoons was quickly transformed into the home of my Grandpa Theo and Grandma Naoma Beer. Nearly thirty years later it was the home that I was brought home from the hospital to. A lot of "elbow grease' and remodeling went into it over the years. Grandma told me that in the early years of their marriage that she would always clap her hands before descending the basement steps so that the rats would run out. This was the home of either my parents or Theo and Naoma all the way into the twilight years of the twentieth century, when Theo and Naoma went to be with the Lord and the farm was sold.

In 1924 Grandpa Theo had bought a retail milk route from his cousin Frank Beer. This supplemented his farm income in the early years of their married life. He wrote of their livelihood in the early years as follows:

"We were milking twenty cows so we produced the milk that I sold. We delivered it in quart and pint bottles. Naoma made cottage cheese which sold well also. I got up to two hundred fifty quarts a day.

During the depression we always had some money. We sold and collected almost all our sales, so the depression did not affect us too much. We also sold fat hogs for six cents a pound. Grain prices were way down but we kept faith that God would provide for us, and He did.

In 1936 I was faced with pasteurization. I did not want to go into that so I sold out to a large dairy who delivered to Milford. Today milk is sold in stores."

(Anyone who knew Grandpa Theo can appreciate this last statement. He was a master at stating the obvious!)

Grandma Naoma had some difficult times in the early years of the marriage. She had a fear of intimacy to the point that their marriage was not consummated for months. Grandma Naoma's fears were likely rooted in her childhood observations of the evil Myer boys, who lived on a neighboring farm. Grandpa Theo was understanding about her fear of intimacy, which testifies to his character and love for Grandma. In his years as an Elder in the church Grandpa told me that he always counseled the young brothers to be patient with their new brides, for "the whole prize," as he put it.

My Aunt Marguerite was born sixteen months after their marriage. Grandma Naoma often spoke of her birth, which was long and extremely difficult. The doctor needed to use forceps and a great deal of leverage to deliver the baby. This, in turn, tore Grandma from vagina to rectum. It is a miracle that this did not result in a lethal infection. Grandpa Theo recalls that Marguerite's head was badly misshapen from the birth. While the doctor worked on Grandma Naoma, Noama's mother took the baby, applied lard to the head and reshaped the skull. Grandpa said he was sure at this point that Marguerite would never be normal. Apart from a scar on her forehead, however, Aunt Marguerite was none-the-worse for this traumatic beginning.

After the birth of Marguerite, Grandma went into a deep depression. Grandpa said she often would only sit and stare. Before too long, though, she began to get better. Grandma was a woman especially devoted to her God, her husband, and her family. She likely reasoned that if God wanted her to suffer pain in childbirth and to be depressed that she would accept it and make the best of it. She eventually fought her way out of the depression and continued on in life.

When Marguerite was eighteen months old an event took place which would come to direct the family's activities and priorities permanently: Grandpa was made a preacher in the Apostolic Christian Church.

In the Apostolic Christian Church there are no professional or seminary-trained pastors. Ministers are chosen by a vote of the congregation. In our present day, the congregation is polled when a need occurs on the pulpit. The local Elder and one or more visiting Elders then interview those receiving sufficient support. If the candidate is deemed to be solid in support of the teachings and traditions of the denomination and is deemed to be willing to submit to the Elder(s), then his name may be one presented to the congregation to be voted on.

This sort of formal "screening" of candidates did not take place in Grandpa Theo's day. There was a need for a minister in the Milford church and the church was asked to pray about whom God would have to fill the need. Grandpa Theo, his mother, and those who spoke about the upcoming election were certain that the next minister would be Theo's younger brother Henry.

Grandpa had good reason to believe this. Henry had become a member several years before Theo. He was also educated through high school, something that was exceptional at that time. Henry was a deeply spiritual man who was gifted in the arts and letters. He was a florist, a poet, a songwriter — all things that were thought to be strange in his conservative agrarian social context. Henry had also contributed heavily to the translation of the church hymnal from the German into the English. Furthermore, Ed Haab, the Milford Elder, had taken Henry "under his wing" and was grooming him for the ministry.

The day came when the church was asked to vote. When the Elders came back from counting the votes, the visiting Elder announced that a "dark horse" candidate had been chosen. He then announced that Theo Beer had received the church's support. Grandpa said he was absolutely stunned and began to cry. In the Apostolic Christian Church the tradition is that men sit on one side of the church and the women on the other. Soon Grandma Naoma came over to his pew and sat beside him. She told him "Theo, stop crying. These people are counting on you." Thus began Theo's ministry in the Milford Apostolic Christian Church. It lasted fifty-two years. The first time Marguerite saw him on the pulpit she said loudly "I don't want my daddy up there." It was a sentiment that all the children felt at one time or another over the years.

Chapter Nine

To understand the life of Theo Beer, one must begin with the fact that "the church" came first in everything and that "the church" meant the Apostolic Christian Church. Grandpa was a good preacher and an even better "people person." In the Apostolic Christian Church the better preachers are often invited to visit other congregations. Grandpa often received such invitations and traveled a lot through the years. He gained the reputation as an especially good funeral preacher. He and Grandma were also known for their hospitality. A Sunday seldom went by that Grandpa did not invite guests home after church for dinner. It was not uncommon for the number of guests to be such that multiple seatings at the table were necessary to feed them all. Grandma knew that this was her gift and that it was a way to team with Grandpa in his ministry. She never complained — at least so that the guests could hear! My mother recalls one occasion being in the kitchen with her listening to Grandpa tell the guests that the large meal was "no trouble" and that Naoma "does it so easily," to which Grandma Naoma quietly responded "Right, it is easy — for him." I can recall several times hearing Grandma say that she wished Grandpa would let her know ahead of time when he was bringing guests home. But the guests always came and she always cooked and it always looked easy. She was totally devoted to her husband.

Throughout Theo's ministry, two things were "constants" on Sundays: Preaching in Milford or another Apostolic Christian (AC)

Church, and entertaining after church at home or being entertained in a home of someone in the church being visited. The Beer children understood this. For them there was no other way to spend a Sunday. Whether they liked it or not, it was to be no other way.

Such large meals required a lot of kitchen help and the daughters were Grandma's helpers. Guests were to be waited on. Grandpa also frequently had the girls sing for the guests as well. He was very proud of his family and introductions with a pertinent fact or two were mandatory. I can remember many times in my own childhood years sneaking around outside so that I would not be called in for introductions and small talk. Usually it did not work.

The children were expected to attend church functions. Grandpa knew that his children were exceptional and assumed that they would live accordingly. Grandma made it clear to them that while they were not expected to be any better behaved than other church kids, they were not to be any worse, either. While they were allowed to participate in school activities and have non-Apostolic friends, it was understood that they were "church kids" and that ultimately their lifelong associations would be with other Apostolics. This was especially true about who they would marry. Apostolic Christian Church spouses were a foundational expectation of Theo for his children.

Grandpa was a stern and authoritarian father. This was especially true with the older children, as is generally the case in families. His standard answer to any request was "No." Grandma used to have to admonish him to "At least listen to what they have to say before you say no." Slapping and spankings were summarily dealt out for backtalk, bad attitudes, disobedience, and general insubordination. This sort of "one size fits all" discipline generally brings mixed results and Grandpa's children were no exception. The compliant ones got along reasonably well, while those determined to find ways to express their wills did not. His love was to be understood. Hugging, touching, and verbal expressions of it were not necessary. Grandpa mellowed over the years to the point that those of us who only knew him as "Grandpa" found the "young Theo" hard to imagine.

Another constant in the Theo Beer family was work. Laziness was absolutely not tolerated. Everyone had their jobs to do and was expected to do them. "Fun" was in the eye of the beholder. Anything that Theo did not enjoy doing tended to be viewed as leisure and was to be enjoyed only when all work was done. The problem was that what he enjoyed doing, others saw as work — things like preaching, visiting, selling, entertaining guests, and, most of all, seeing to it that others were working. "Bossing" was his special gift. Before he left to do what he enjoyed doing, he would always be sure that others were started in their work.

This bossiness was so predictable that in the end it resulted in a lot of humor within the family. Two other "gifts" of Grandpa have also contributed to our family laughter over the years. They were his bluntness and tendency to state the obvious. To illustrate this, I list the following postings to our family web site this past year. The first is from my cousin Doug Hoerr. "I took Tracy (my wife) to the nursing home to meet Gramps (Theo) for the first time. He looked her over a fair bit...if I recall. He took her hands and said to me, 'Well, Doug, she looks like a good woman, try not to mess it up this time.' And THEN asked if we planned on having kids, after he expressed concern I might be getting too old. He told Tracy 'Don't be afraid of childbirth...it's the only way children can get into this world.'" My father (Lewie) loves to recall the time there was a large dinner at the small farmhouse. Two tables were set up and full with guests. There was a knock at the door and Grandpa Theo went to answer it. Having greeted the man, Grandpa turned and called to Lewie in the next room, "Lewie, there is some fat guy here to see you!" One day my wife Tammy and I met Grandpa on the street in Milford. After exchanging pleasantries he said to Tammy, "Tammy, you are looking more like your Mom every day — you know, that middle age spread!" It was meant as a compliment, of course. He always thought women looked better with a little extra weight. My sisters still laugh as they recall the horror they felt as Grandpa Theo looked at them, knowing that a "compliment" about their weight was likely coming! Another time Grandpa was describing a woman to a houseful of guests (which included my Aunt Marguerite): "She's a big woman, kinda like Marguerite." Our Ritzman cousins still laugh at a memory about Grandpa. One time he had all of us out walking through newly mowed mint, picking out the weeds, and throwing them on a wagon. It was demanded of Grandpa, "Why are we doing this?" He replied that we have to be "weed conscious." Grandpa also liked to point out to boys in early puberty, "Your nose is getting big. That's a sure sign you are manning up." It is an understatement that Grandpa Theo tended to be bossy. One day a car needed to be towed to a neighboring town to be worked on. My good friend was there that day and was going to sit in the car and steer it as it was being towed. Grandpa was going to tow it with his truck. Once everything was hooked up Grandpa walked back to my friend's car and instructed him, "You follow me." For years my mother Mim would bring Grandpa coffee at a certain point during his breakfast. She got to the point that she would try to sneak to the coffee pot before being told "Get me some coffee." After years of filling Grandpa's same prescription, he still would tell me where it was on the shelf as I walked to get it. Having Grandpa ride in a vehicle with you was a predictable event. At every corner, every time, without fail he would tell the driver when to go and which way to turn. If there were conversation going on, he would just motion with his left hand. Either way, the driver was instructed. My Uncle Bernie had the misfortune of following my Uncle Alan, who was an honor student, in school. He recalls that the ultimate bad day was when report cards came. One time he came home and showed Grandpa Theo his report card. Grandpa looked at it, looked up, and inquired, "What are you, a moron?" Grandpa Theo loved to ask the employers of us grandchildren, "How is Tom (or whomever) working out?" Grandpa Theo also always wanted to know if we "could see our way clear" whenever we bought anything. I find myself thinking and repeating one particular saying of Grandpa Theo more and more as the years go by: "A woman is never more beautiful than when she is pregnant."

 The person who coined the phrase "he never met a stranger" must have had Grandpa in mind. He could strike up a conversation with anyone. Over many years I observed him doing this and concluded that there were three key elements in this ability. The first was that he could remember people's names, amazingly so. The second was his ability to "connect" people with other people that they both knew. The third was in getting people to talk about themselves. Many, many times I stood idly by or sat in the pickup listening to this skill play out. It made him a master salesman, particularly to the Amish and other conservative farmers.

I found it interesting that while Grandpa was such an effective communicator, he was not easy to tease with. He seldom "caught" jokes or ironic comments. My uncle Bernie put it best once when he said "How would you like to be a comedian and have all Dads (Theos) in the audience?"

Naoma Beer was also a remarkable individual. She was a woman absolutely devoted to her God, her family, and her husband. She seldom used the word "I" in any other context than "I am thankful, I am unworthy, I will help, I am willing, or I affirm you." Grandma always tried to say something nice about someone. Even when there seemed to be nothing positive to say about someone or something she would come through. There were times when her attempts were so far-fetched that it was humorous. She was ever the encourager, always nurturing others, praising their efforts, and building them up. She was especially resourceful. There were few occasions that she could not prepare a banquet at a moment's notice. "I will make a little something," she would say. There seemed to be nothing that she could not make or repair with a sewing machine. There were very few people whom she could not make feel better about themselves. She conveyed her disapproval with a hard, deliberate blink of her close-set brown eyes. Her amusement was expressed in a sweet abdominal chuckle. She would often offer excellent, common sense advice, like "Always take the in-law's side in disagreements. Your kids will forgive you, but the in-laws won't." The Spehegers, in contrast to the Beers, were witty people and Grandma was no exception. She gave and received teasing well.

There was nothing in the lives of Theo and Naoma Beer that was not in a "God context." Their mindset was like that of David, King of Israel, when he said in Psalm 16:8 *"I have set the Lord always before me."* Conversations were sprinkled with expressions of "God's blessing," or "God's will," or "God's grace," or "God's Word." God was truly the center of their home. One story illustrates this. When my Uncle Bernie was a young boy he was driving the tractor in the circle drive. Being too young and inexperienced, he turned too sharply. The front wheels stuck sideways and the tractor began to pivot in a circle. Grandpa and others were frantic, trying to get on the tractor to stop it, all the while knowing that if Bernie fell off he would surely be run over. Someone finally was able to jump on and stop the tractor. Bernie was spared. What he remembers most about the ordeal is that Theo did not say a word until he had knelt down and said a prayer of thanksgiving.

Grandpa and Grandma always taught us that salvation was a gracious gift of God that came through the Person and work of the Lord Jesus Christ. This was good. This teaching, however, was coupled with the insistence that the only sure and acceptable institution for salvation was the Apostolic Christian Church. This was not good. "Are there other genuine believers in the world who are not Apostolics?" If asked this question, Grandpa and Grandma Beer would have replied "Yes, of course there are." Nearly all Apostolics would agree with this. If asked to name one, however, they (Apostolics in general) would be hard-pressed to do so. One of Grandpa Beer's favorite expressions, when referring to professing believers who were not Apostolics or to other seemingly sound churches was "I 'spose they have a little something."

If one is bound to a denomination where salvation is a future prospect instead of a present possession, to a denomination where adherence to customs, traditions, and membership requirements are integral parts of the definition of a "true believer," there are no other answers that can be given to such questions. When it is believed that salvation is a future prospect that depends on our satisfactory degree of "faithfulness," the question is not "Who is saved?" but "Who has the best chance of making it?" or "Who has the best chance of holding on to it?" And if it is believed that the questions are "Who has the best chance of making it?" or "Who has the best chance of holding on to it?" then one's denomination becomes critical.

I hasten to add that the Apostolic Christian Church is not unique in this. Any group that does not believe salvation is a secure present possession that one receives by Grace alone, through Faith alone, through the Person and finished work of Jesus Christ alone, must of necessity set parameters and benchmarks for measuring the sanctification of their adherents. There is no end to the possible forms this can take, as we see throughout the world.

The child-rearing years of Theo and Naoma Beer were likely not atypical of the times in which they lived. Neither were the work ethic, the order, and the discipline. What *was* different was the lay ministry in the church — and it was a big difference. The Beer children were all very intelligent and capable kids. They all received a mixed bag of blessings and burdens from being the children of a church leader. I did also.

Chapter Ten

The Apostolic Christian Church did not produce the fourth marriage that illustrates the character and devotion of my ancestors. It came about in spite of the Apostolic Christian Church — the marriage of my parents, Charles Lewis Speicher and Miriam Frances Beer.

Exactly when facts begin to form in the mind of a child is not understood. Why they form is the result of what he sees and hears. I was always a happy and secure child. I never remember feeling any other way. But the following facts framed my early childhood: My Dad was a great basketball player. We did not have enough money. My Grandpa was a preacher. My Dad and Mom had to get married. My Mom never seemed to be happy. I wanted my Mom to be happy.

Some weeks ago I asked my Mom to write about her life growing up. After some initial hesitation, she did. The first part of what she wrote follows.

I was born on a sunny Sunday morning the first day of May in 1932 to Theo and Naoma Beer. I was born on my brother Philip's second birthday. I had one older sister, Marguerite, who was five at the time. I was told it was an inconvenient time to be born because my father was the only preacher at the Milford Apostolic Christian Church at that time and as I was coming in to the world he needed to be there to preach.

I think my brother was proud to have a new little sister for his birthday present at first. As he grew older whenever I irritated him in any way, he threatened to cut my birthday off of his. This would always throw me into a frantic crying fit where Mom had to assure me he could never do that. To celebrate our birthdays Mom always made two cakes. A white angel food for me and a chocolate angel food for Philip. Once our day came, we shared it equally and it was a happy time. Philip was my best friend as I grew up. Except for the birthday thing, he was nice to me and shared his toys. My sister, Marguerite, was my idol. She knew how to do everything and could do it so well. I wanted to be just like her because she made Mom and Dad so happy. At that early age I knew I had no special talents on my own. I always tried to be like someone else. This was not a recipe for happiness.

When I was two and a half years old, my sister Mary was born. Thirteen months after her my sister Rebecca made her appearance. Thirteen months after Becky, my brother Alan was born. To say Mom was busy was certainly an understatement. Dad was increasingly busy with his farming, bus driving, and most of all, the church.

Dad loved company and always invited people to visit and eat with us. Weekends seldom went by without someone visiting or at least eating with us. When we weren't entertaining Dad was expected to visit other churches and he always wanted Mom to go with him.

When we were all small my parents hired a girl to help out around the house. Kathryn and Lena Ruch were two who lived with us over the young years so that Mom could fulfill all her obligations. I have fond memories of them. They were very kind to us.

I was a healthy child and was strong and could work pretty well for my age. When I was six I started to help with the milking. I didn't enjoy this and I felt like Marguerite got the best deal because she got to stay in the house and help Mom. I started morning and evening with one cow but I soon worked up to three cows. If I went too fast I had to help milk some more. It didn't pay to hurry. After milking in the morning I carried corn to the pigs and fed and watered the chickens. In the evening I gathered the eggs. I really hated this job because the chickens pecked me when I had to reach under them. We always had at least one rooster in the flock and they were mean. They would fly at me and peck really hard. When I cried to Dad he just said, "Don't be a baby. They won't hurt you." That settled that. I used to carry a stick and poke the chickens off the nest and pound on the roosters. I guess I wasn't so nice to them either.

When I was nine years old my brother Bernie was born. It was Christmas Day and he was born in the Warsaw hospital. He was the only one of us to be born there. He was a very special Christmas present for all of us. Dad took all six of us to the hospital to see him. We all thought he was wonderful.

By this time the three oldest ones in the family were able to do a lot of work. Marguerite was expected to stand in for our parents at a young age (13 or 14) when they were traveling. Philip was responsible outside and I was able to help. Mom and Dad always bragged on Marguerite and Philip because they were so responsible. I was given credit for being strong and a good worker, but, they always added, I grumbled a lot. I guess I did.

Mary and Becky were sick a lot with sore throat or some ailment. Mom always made us feel so special and loved when we were sick. As I said before I never got sick, so one day I said I wished I'd get sick once so I could be babied like they were. That was not a good thing to say. Dad spanked me and said I was a bad girl and I should be ashamed of myself.

Mary and Becky were a special joy to Dad. They were the same size, both had curly hair and they were best friends. They always walked around holding hands and playing together. Beside all that they sang beautifully together. When we had company Dad would always make them sing for people. If I was around, I had to sing with them. Why would I want to do that when they were so adorable? As I look back, I never felt that I contributed anything worthwhile or admirable to the family. I was only praised for my working ability; even then, my bad attitude was always mentioned. I know I was unhappy. I was ashamed that I didn't appreciate all the talents of my siblings. I wanted some of my own.

It is ingrained in my mind how Dad used to introduce his children to people. Marguerite was the oldest, a wonderful student and able to handle any job they gave her. Philip was the first son and so responsible. He caught on so fast to the farm work. He was another great student. Miriam was their "blondie" (whatever that meant). Mary and Becky, the little girls, were such close friends and they sang together so beautifully and so on. I used to think, "I wonder what I will be good at someday?" I had no self-esteem at all. I used to look at myself in the mirror and think "I wonder why I was born?" I believed I was the stupid one in the family. I wanted so badly to be smart and make my parents proud. Depression is a terrible thing. When I was grown and married I found my old report cards. I was amazed at my good grades. If I had thought they belonged to someone else, I would have been so envious and had wished they were mine. My bad attitude caused Mom and Dad a lot of concern. It was the cause of many spankings from Dad. My feelings of worthlessness and unhappiness were inexcusable to Dad. He believed my feelings were a sign of weakness and he had no patience with me.

    The five oldest of us went to Miller School, a one room school about a mile from home. There was a wood-burning stove for heat, an outside pump for water and outside toilets. All eight grades were in one room so we learned from each other. We became very close to our fellow students and we had some good times and some bad, but mostly I have pleasant memories of that experience. There were only two of us in the second grade class so we could progress at our own speed. We finished all our books by the end of the first semester so they moved us up to third grade. This was not good for my self-esteem because the third graders resented us and wouldn't share their books. They wanted us to fail and when we didn't they finally accepted us. By the time we were fourth graders we were friends and got along okay. It was hard to keep good teachers in a school that small and we became victims of a very bad one in my sixth grade year. At this time Mom decided she would send us to the Milford school so that the conditions would be better. When our family pulled out of the school there weren't enough students to continue and they closed the school. When they needed a bus to haul us there, Dad took the job. My cousins who went to Milford told us how hard it would be for us in the new school. I was scared to death. I thought I would really be in trouble. To my surprise, it was far easier than we had before. We went so much slower because of more students. I felt good about the move. I made friends with a lot of girls and I soon saw some boys were trying to get my attention. I suddenly was excited about life.

Work went on at the farm. Milking became an even worse experience for me because I couldn't wash the cow smell off my hands for school. I became more reluctant to work in the barn and there was always friction between Dad and me. Dad was so busy with all his jobs, preaching, bus driving, selling feed and planting mint, that he hired Amish boys, along with the Ritzmans (our cousins from Ohio), every summer. I hated it when the Amish were there. They stayed over night and destroyed what family privacy we had. Planting and distilling mint was a killing job. I didn't help much with the distilling, but planting was a backbreaking job. The best part was the wonderful meals we had at noon, thanks to Mom. It was a somewhat wild time in the field with Dad trying to make a dozen kids pull whole plants and plant them properly. There was more monkey business than work.

About the time I was in high school Dad decided to buy a milking machine. I was elated! I was sure I finally could quit helping with the milking. To my dismay, Dad planned on teaching me to use the milkers. I fought that idea with everything I had. I threw myself on Mom's mercy. To my surprise, she agreed that I had helped in the barn long enough. She told Dad that he had enough help in the barn without me. I think that she was also a bit irritated that he could find money to buy what he wanted outside, but they never could afford what was needed for the house. What a glorious feeling to be rid of that awful job! I was now a little more like the town kids whom I admired so much. I began to feel feminine.

I was very young for my class and my friends were much more mature than I. In my eighth grade year I began hearing that Lewie Speicher liked me. I didn't even know who he was at that time. My friends kept telling me how cute he was and what a great basketball player he was. I decided I should check him out. He seemed to be all they said and we soon began writing notes and spending our free time together in school. It was so great to go to the games and watch him play. We had a winning team and he was the star. I was very happy.

At home things were not so good. Mom and Dad became concerned about my choice of boyfriends and began to pressure me to date church boys. During this time, whenever Dad traveled to another church I went along. He hoped I would meet more suitable boys. I did meet a lot of them from Bluffton, Bremen, Chicago, Peoria, and Francesville. I even dated some of them for a while, but this caused a lot of friction between Lewie and I. Dad and Mom were happy, but Lewie was miserable and I was so confused about where my loyalties belonged. Again I began to wonder why I was born. Every time I did something that made me happy I made others miserable. I either had to lie to Lewie to make Mom and Dad happy or lie to Mom and Dad to make Lewie happy. Neither way made me happy. I think I cried myself to sleep every night during this time.

(My sister) Marguerite got married to Bob during this time and moved away. I missed her so much. The bright spot in my life at that time was when she had a daughter, Becky Ann. I fell in love with her and she was a real special addition to the family. I never knew one could love a baby so much as I loved her. When I held her I could forget my unhappiness.

During the end of my junior year in school things went from bad to worse. I realized that I was pregnant and I had reached the end of my rope. I knew this would destroy Mom and Dad and the only choice I had was to kill myself. I almost felt a peace about coming to the end of my misery. First I wanted to go see Marguerite and Becky Ann one more time before I ended it all. In my mind it would be such a relief to my family.

While I was in Peoria with Marguerite and Bob, God intervened. Lewie's folks came to tell my parents the truth of the situation and totally changed the picture. Mom called me at Marguerite's and said I had to come home and make decisions. I didn't want to, but there was no choice. Mom was in bed with a migraine when I got home and Dad looked like he had been kicked in the stomach. It was the worst day of my life. I couldn't believe it when Dad hugged me and told me he loved me. That was the first time I ever remember that happening. I must have cried a bucket of tears that day. The decision of what to do was a hard one for Mom and Dad. They felt, because of my age, it would be better to have the child and let them help raise it. This was heartbreaking for Lewie and he pleaded with them to let us get married. After he assured them that he loved me and would be good husband they agreed to a wedding.

We were married at my home on June 22, 1948. Lewie's brother Bill and his wife Joan were our attendants. Our neighbor, Rev. Leroy

Fisher, married us. (Dad was a preacher but he was not allowed to marry anyone who was not a member of his church.) A trio of my cousins sang as I descended the staircase. My cousin Marion made my bouquet of blue delphiniums and white lilies. It was so beautiful. Mom made a cake and decorated it with flowers. Both families were there, along with a few special friends. It was a happy day.

After I was married, I decided this was what God had in mind for me so I was determined to make it work and be a good mother. We lived with the folks until the baby, our son Ned was born. The birth was hard and I had no training to understand what was happening to me. They used forceps to get the baby out after many hours of labor that was going nowhere. When I first saw my baby with his bruised, misshapen head, I thought he was the most beautiful child in the world. What a joy it was to hold him and realize he was a part of Lewis and me and he was all ours. I had no idea what euphoria one would feel after the birth of a child. I felt fulfilled and needed.

We lived with Mom and Dad until Ned was three months old. Then we moved to town into a new little house on Fourth Street. I always wanted to live in town and I loved it. It was like a little dollhouse and I loved making it pretty. Lewie worked on the railroad with his Dad and I took care of the house and Ned. We were happy.

We lived in town for only two years. Our second son, Ted, was born. Our two little boys were the pride of our lives, but we were still kids ourselves. Lewie had sports in his blood. Two nights a week he played ball on independent teams in the county. That left me at home with two children alone or I could take the boys along to watch. Either way was hard.

When my brother Philip was drafted into the Army during the Korean conflict, we moved into the little house on the farm to help Dad in place of Philip. Lewie had never farmed and had a lot to learn. Dad was never a patient teacher but I kept trying to keep Lewie from discouragement. He worked hard and learned fast, but his personality was so different from Dad's. He often felt he hadn't measured up to the task. I tried very hard to encourage him but it was not easy. Never in my lifetime, to that point, did I believe Dad could be wrong. He was in charge and we were at his mercy. It seemed that everything he did for us, we were to be eternally grateful for, because we obviously didn't deserve it. It seems I spent most of my time defending Dad's position on things to keep peace. In my heart I felt things were not as they should be, but who were we to complain? We had really messed up our lives. It was our fault. The one thing we all agreed on was our now, three, boys. Tom had been born by then. Dad and Mom and all my siblings adored my sons. Dad would often take them with him to town and show them off like they were his own. He truly loved them. I felt like I wasn't even given credit for being the mother of my own sons. The boys thrived like healthy little animals on the farm. They made the whole farm a happy place with their antics. Grandma and Grandpa adored them and I began to feel as if I indeed had a purpose for living.

The church continued to be the center of our lives. Lewie had promised the folks he would come to church with me. For the most part, he did. He didn't enjoy it because the ways of the church were so foreign to him. It was hard trying to justify all the traditions because they seemed strange to me, too. I was always told, "the Elders know best." The time came, when I was seventeen, I knew I needed forgiveness for my sins. The church was the only way I knew to receive this forgiveness so I proceeded to join the church. Lewie was willing that I do this, but he didn't have the understanding, at that time, to join me.

Intersecting the life of this beautiful, gifted, but insecure girl was the life of my father, Charles Lewis Speicher. He offers the following brief account of his own early life.

I was born on May 28, 1929 to Charles Austin Speicher and Pauline Angie O'Haver in Milford Junction, Indiana. I was their first child. My mother grew up in Syracuse and my dad in Milford Junction (Milford Junction is north of Milford at the railroad junction.) When I was very young we moved to Milford and lived in three different houses. At age six we moved back to Milford Junction into the old Speicher home place, where we stayed until I was fifteen. My dad bought this house for $800 dollars but worried all the time we were there that he could not afford it. He sold it when I was 15 for $1,000 and then wished he had it back. This sort of worry was the story of his life. From here we moved to a house east of Milford Junction for one year and then to Milford, where I stayed until I got married after High School.

My brother Bill was one and one-half years younger than me. I gave him the nickname "Bugsy." Bill and I both loved to hunt, fish, and play ball. Each spring we loved to hunt mushrooms. Later on we had two more brothers, Jim and Pat, who also loved to do the same things we did. For years Bill and I would walk to town and back for everything we wanted to do. There came a time when I finally got enough money for a bicycle. It made a big difference. I could stay in town until dark and then ride home. I was always scared to death when I rode by the old sinkhole south of town. I rode with all my might to get past it.

Times were hard and there wasn't much money. The only thing to do was to play sports. We did this all the time to entertain ourselves and became very good at it. My dad worked on the railroad and sometimes there wasn't enough work. We had big gardens and canned a lot of vegetables. My parents were good people who worked hard and taught us a lot of good things.

As soon as I was old enough I had a job. Bill and I worked in the muck fields when we were young, weeding onions, carrots, and potatoes. Later in the season we would top the onions and carrots and pick up the potatoes. We also planted mint. I even had a job in a bowling alley setting pins. We worked for 10 cents to 25 cents an hour and were glad to get it.

When I was thirteen Bill and I would hitchhike to the Tippecanoe Golf Course and caddy for men who had enough money to play golf. I got to be really good at watching where the shots went and this was appreciated. Later I got to where I could carry two sets of clubs and double my income. I remember the first time I made three dollars for a day's work. I thought I was the Rich Kid. All these things were good for me.

When I got to High School I met this beautiful young girl named Mim and very soon knew she was the one I wanted to spend my life with. We went together all through High School. At times it was tough because her folks didn't want her dating anyone who wasn't a church boy (someone from the Apostolic Christian Church). I didn't understand this. I knew the church boys and thought I behaved as good as they did, but it didn't matter. I loved her and never gave up.

As I went through school I was lucky to play ball with so many *good players. In basketball we won two county tournaments and two sectional championships. In my senior year we went unbeaten, to be the only Milford team ever to do it. That year (1948) we were state ranked. I was lucky enough to lead the team in scoring all three years and was also the county leading scorer my senior year. I made many county and sectional first teams and was all-state third team. In track I set the school record in the 100 yard dash. This record stood until the school closed in 1968. I also was the county 100 yard dash champion that year. In my four years of High School we won the county championship in fast-pitch softball every year. I played shortstop and second base. I often bunted because I was fast and could beat the throw. I don't mean to be bragging about all of this, but I want my grandchildren to know.*

I did not go to church very often when I was young. There was not any pressure about church either way from Mom and Dad. But deep down inside I knew what I should do — go to church.

Mim and I got married right after I finished High School. Once I was in the family her folks accepted me well. I had told her folks that I would go to church with her when we got married and I did this almost all of the time. I did not understand the Apostolic ways but everyone treated me great. Soon Mim joined the church. This was fine with me but I did not want it for myself. After a few years there was a lot of polio in our area. There was no cure and there was no sure way of knowing you would not get it. This got me thinking seriously about my soul. I had a young family and did not want to die or be crippled without being right with the Lord. I decided to give my life to the Lord. Since all I knew was the Apostolic Christian Church that was the way I went. I still did not agree with a lot of their ways but I wanted to be saved. It was tough being married with children at a young age but we both worked at it. Even in the hardest of times we never even considered not staying together. We had five children and it all worked out. I am really thankful for my wife and my children Ned, Ted, Tom, Sue, and Amy and also for their spouses Deb, Sandy, Tammy, Jerry, and Tom. I am also very thankful for my grandchildren and great-grandchildren.

I don't know if it is possible for one outside the social and religious context to understand the predicament my mother found herself in at fifteen years old and pregnant. She was a "church girl." My father was a "world boy." Church girls, in general, and Theo's daughters, in particular, were to marry only church boys. She had spent her first fifteen years feeling unloved and disapproved of by her father — and feeling unworthy of his love even if she had felt it. He was a minister in the church. In her mind she had made him miserable for fifteen years. Now she would humiliate him as well. There was no question in her mind now that everything that she believed her father felt about her was true. When the "solution" of suicide was undone by the intervention of Grandpa and Grandma Speicher, the only solution left to her was unconditional surrender to her father. Translation? "I *am* bad. I deserve what has happened to me. I deserve all the misery that surely will come in my life. I *am* unworthy of happiness. I will try my best, but I know I will never be able to atone for my wrongs and be able to measure up to others. And I am mad at Lewie for being so happy about our marriage and baby."

For my father, the situation was simple. He loved my mother and wanted to marry her. Her father had tried to break them up and had not succeeded. Now they were married. The ways of the Apostolics were as foreign to him as chopsticks — they may have had a use for some people, but not for him. If Mim did not feel her father's love, his love would take the place of it.

The complexities of Mom's feelings about herself were bewildering to him. Fifty-three years later they still are.

Chapter Eleven

I was born on October 14, 1952, the third son of Lewie and Mim. I weighed eight pounds five ounces and joined two older brothers. Ned was four and Ted was two. Dad remembers that it was a cold, rainy fall night. It was a Wednesday and the farmers were having a hard time getting the corn harvested. My first identifiable characteristics have remained constant throughout my life — I was chubby, very white, and happy. "Chubby" came from both sides. "Very white" came from Mom. "Happy" came from Dad.

As a toddler I had a favorite blanket. I carried it around with me, working one corner of it between the fingers of one hand. With this corner ("torner") I rubbed my nose while sucking my other thumb. This "torner" eventually got to be about eight inches long. The blanket became so ragged from dragging that Mom cut off the corner with the "torner" for me to carry with me. Mom tells me that I used to come to her in the afternoon and ask to be laid down for my nap.

When I was very young Dad and Mom took us to see Niagra Falls. I was not three yet, but I distinctly remember three things about the trip. The first thing I remember is sitting on the front seat of the car looking straight up at a red traffic light. I remember looking at the front door of a building and Mom telling us that Dad had to go inside to pay a fine for going through the red light and that everything would be alright. The second memory is standing beside a railing really close to some wild and fast water. I remember being scared by it. The third memory is standing by a rail looking down at the river way below. A tiny man got in a tiny car and drove it away. I thought it was funny that tiny people drove play cars down there.

We lived in the small farmhouse, the one Grandma Naoma had laughed at when Grandpa Theo first showed it to her. My earliest memories in this home include the stairway leading to one bedroom upstairs, the heat stove in the living room, the screened-in porch along the front, and the huge garden behind. I remember my fifth birthday. Mom made a triple-decker cake. She sat me on a counter in the kitchen beside it and took a picture. The picture was lost over the years, but I remember from the picture that the cake said "Happy Birthday, Cowboy." I looked pretty cherubic, even in a cowboy suit. One very odd early memory is that of my brothers and I walking through the east part of the barn, ankle deep in the manure. I was bare-footed. I can't imagine why I did this — the memory gives me chills. One could not pay me enough to do such a thing now! Antics like this certainly contributed to the premature "graying" of my mother.

Another early memory is of the birth of my sister, Sue. I was five at the time. I remember making a fishing pole in the barn. I did it by the strawmow. The pole was a stick. I used baler twine for the line. At the tip of the twine I stuck a safety pin. I was walking down the cow lane to the ditch to go fishing when I remember Ned running up to me. "Where have you been?" he exclaimed, "Mom's going to have the baby and she wants to see you!" Ned was offering rebuke and correction even at the tender age of nine.

What strikes me about this memory is the fact that I was walking to the ditch alone. The ditch was a good half a mile from the house. It had steep banks and enough water to give a five year-old trouble. Apparently, no one worried about it. I know that I did not. Many, many hours of my childhood were spent there.

My first educational experience was at church. My teachers were Helen (Kaiser) and Martha (Ruch). Our room was a little converted closet off of the "landing" in the church. I have no idea why this area was called the "landing." It was an area between the sanctuary doors and the steps that led to the basement. I also remember us gathering to sing in the basement. My brother Ted and Bruce Beer were always goofing off during this. I found their antics very funny. One time Ted had his back to the song leader, not paying attention. Bruce was beside him. The leader snapped at Ted "Turn around!" Both of them turned around — Ted to the front and Bruce to the back. I can see this in my mind as if it happened yesterday. I was greatly amused. The teacher was not. I can never remember not liking Sunday school.

My public education began in the Milford Public Library basement, where we had kindergarten. My teacher was Mrs. Templin. She was a homely, impatient woman who obviously did not like children. Our families car-pooled for our transportation. One day I remember getting a haircut at Harry Good's Barber Shop while the car-pool car load waited outside — bet they appreciated this! It was in this car-pool that I first met Dave Baumgartner, who would later become one of my two best friends. Mrs. Templin was so mean and Dave was so nervous that he soon dropped out. We sat at tables on little wooden chairs. One day I fell over backwards and everyone, including Mrs. Templin, laughed. I told my Dad about it when I got home. When he asked about what the teacher said I told him she laughed. My cousin Bob Ritzman was there and replied "I bet she won't laugh next time." He was right. I did it again, this time on purpose, and she really scolded me. It was clear to me that the laughter of my classmates was not worth the embarrassment. One day Mrs. Templin told us to write out our ABC's. I could sing them with no problem, but writing them was tougher. I did not get them right. Maybe it was because in the song I sang "LMNOP" as "elemento P." I am told that singing was my "gift" from the time I could walk. Mom would often put me on display at the request of family and friends and I would sing for them. I only remember one instance of this. We were in Sorg Jewelers in Goshen. My great aunt Lorene picked me up and stood me on a glass jewelry case. Mom insists that I was no older than two when this happened. I do not remember what I sang.

One time my Dad picked me up from kindergarten. It was a beautiful day outside. We drove to the railroad tracks and looked for mushrooms. I remember finding some yellow ones in the grass near the car. As I look back, Dad must have planned this carefully. It was spring and the weather was nice — there had to be plenty of work to be done on the farm. But picking me up was a perfect opportunity to sneak off and do a little mushroom hunting. Between

Grandpa Beer and Mom, there was little time for such things. I do not think he ever fooled Mom once, though. I am sure glad he slipped this one in, though, because it gave me a life memory. The work that went undone has long since been forgotten.

Another special memory took place one day after kindergarten. Dad was plowing in the "back forty" of the muck. Mom let me walk down there so I could ride back on the tractor. Dad was just finishing when I arrived. I got on the tractor, an International "M" that was pulling a three-bottom plow. We drove on the ditch bank along the "little ditch." I asked Dad to look for turtles. He drove slowly and stood up to get the best look possible. Soon he stopped and told me to be quiet. As he got off and started down the bank I saw the turtle, too. It was a box turtle in the middle of the water — a big one. My heart pounded out of my chest as Dad got closer and closer. When he was in "grabbing distance" he took off his glove and grabbed the turtle. When he lifted it out of the water, along came another one. It was a double decker — two box turtles who were mating. I was astonished and can still feel the thrill. To get two box turtles, my favorite kind, in one grab was more than any turtle hunter might dare hope for! It might have been this exceptional moment that started my obsession with turtles. What a memory.

After kindergarten one day I went out to find Dad. It was chilly outside. I found him in the old corncrib where he was shoveling popcorn ears on an upper part that was over the drive-through. I climbed up and watched him. At one point he began stomping and jumping frantically. When he stopped he told me that a mouse had run up his pant leg! He then took his pants and underwear off, gave them to me, and told me to take them to Mom. The memory ends here. For over forty years this strange request remained a mystery to me until one day it occurred to me that he must have messed his pants in his horror! Dad remembers the mouse, but even under intense interrogation will not admit to remembering the incontinence. But he won't deny it, either. He just looks down with a slight grin, shakes his head, and mumbles. Anyone who knows Lewie knows this is "code" for "Yes, but I'm not admitting anything."

My kindergarten graduation was held in the little gym of the elementary school. I remember being there. I remember that I sat beside a boy named Ricky and thinking that his pants were really tight. Apparently the proceedings did not keep my attention! We wore white graduation hats with tassels. A picture of this exists somewhere. What I **really** remember about kindergarten graduation, though, is that Dad and Mom gave me a present. As if it was yesterday, I remember opening it and finding not one, but **two** BB Guns! One was a pistol and the other a rifle. I never remember playing with the pistol and I do not know what happened to it. It is equally possible that Dad worried I would hurt myself (or others) with it and hid it or that my brother Ted took it and lost it.

Chapter Twelve

My elementary school years were also very happy years. My first grade teacher was Bessie Suntimer. She was a sweet lady and a good teacher. I only remember a few things about learning that year. One day we were reading our "Dick and Jane" reading books and we came to a new word. I was the one who knew the word. I remember being both surprised and proud about this. When we had our achievement tests at the end of the year I was sitting at a round table in the back of the room with some other kids. I remember not understanding what I was supposed to do on the test, so I asked a boy named Jeffrey about it. Pointing to three pictures on the paper, he replied, "it's simple — frog, dog, log." I knew what the pictures were of, but I still did not know what I was supposed to do. I am sure I flunked that test.

Once on the playground I was on the teeter-totter with another kid. He jumped off when I was in the air. I hit the ground hard enough that it knocked the wind out of me. As I lay there writhing in pain I remember envisioning a skeleton suit and knowing my skeleton was broken. The memory ends here, so there must have been no long-term consequences.

During the winter we were always cautioned to not get our pants wet. If we did we ran the risk of having to wear a dress. One day this happened to me. During recess we were frolicking in the snow and I came back to class with wet pants. Dennis Hart and I had to go down to the boiler room. There we took off our pants. The teacher laid them on top of the boiler to dry. She gave me a long skirt to put on. I wrapped it around me and went back to class. The other kids stole glances and snickered. I didn't appreciate this, but overall the experience wasn't too traumatic. We would have a lawsuit over such a thing today.

I got my first spanking (outside the home) in first grade. It happened at the end of music class. The way it went in those days was that a piano was rolled into the classroom and a music teacher had us sing for an hour. The music teacher was a grouchy, obese woman by the name of Mrs. Robinson. As she was wheeling the piano out one day after class, I was chewing on some scissors — I have no clue why. She yelled across the room "Get those scissors out of your mouth, Tom!" I had a cousin named Tom Beer who, unfortunately, happened to be sitting next to me. He immediately yelled back "I don't have any scissors in my mouth!" Mrs. Robinson instantly stomped toward us, exclaiming "You may get away with talking like that at home, but you're not getting away with it here!" She yanked Tom Beer out of his desk and spanked him. When I saw what was happening I put my head on my desk and covered up with my arms. No sooner had she finished with Tom Beer than she grabbed me out of my seat and spanked me. I was stunned. The spanking wasn't too bad — probably half a dozen wacks on the butt — but as soon as Mrs. Robinson left the room the whole class erupted in laughter. I yelled back "Shut up! It isn't funny!" But it was to no avail. By the time the following recess was over, however, Tom Beer and I were "folk heroes." Tom said his spanking was like "taking a helicopter ride." Our peers were all amazed how well we endured this fractuosity.

I met my first girlfriend in first grade. She was a short, cute girl named Karen Graff. One day after school I went to her house to play. Her Mom had lunch waiting for us when we arrived. Hot dogs were the main course and I remember that Karen burped as she was eating and talking. I really wonder why I remember such odd details about things. It doesn't seem like this would be an inherited characteristic, but I also see it in both of my daughters, especially Traci. Karen was my girlfriend off and on until fifth grade, but this was the only time I ever went to her house. There was never any more to it then an occasional note and the understanding that we were boyfriend and girlfriend.

My second grade teacher was Mrs. Anglin. She was a good teacher who never seemed to have any discipline problems. I can remember working hard that year on correctly printing the letters. I also filled page after page with consecutive numbers. Karen Graff was better at this than I was. I was amazed when she showed me one day that she had reached 2222. Such a number seemed unattainable to me.

One day during recess we were playing on the monkey bars. My cousin, Tom Beer (the one who got me the spanking), got provoked about something and began shouting words I had never heard before. I learned that these were cuss words — words never to be said at home. It was not long, however, until we were all using foul language when no adults were around. Tom Beer would be an amusement to me and one of my instructors in the baser elements of life throughout my pre-high school years. He was very bright, funny, and athletic. He was very gifted musically. He was just a bad boy. To this day those of us from his youth know him as "Filthy Nip."

It was in second grade that I had my first literary work. It was a success, as it was published in my second grade yearbook. It was called "The Hibernation" and was about my favorite subject, turtles.

The Hibernation
by
Tom Speicher

Old Grandfather Turtle was tired of hibernation. He went to see his nephews, but they were not hatched out of their eggs. Grandfather hoped for five girls and five boy turtles. He thought that they would be hatched in two weeks, so he went back to sleep for two weeks. In two weeks he woke up and wondered if his nephews were hatched, so he went to the egg hatchery. He hoped his nephews had hatched. When Grandfather got there his nephews had hatched. Old Grandfather Turtle said to himself, "I'll bet when they grow up to be 63 years old it will be the same thing over and over and over again."

It was also in the second grade that my nicknaming "gift" began to manifest itself. My friend, Roger Korenstra, was the recipient. I had met Roger several years before, when he lived across the field from our home. I was riding on the tractor with Dad when we saw Roger playing in his yard. Dad said "Why don't you go play with that boy?" So I climbed the fence and crossed the road to his yard. When I asked how old he was he held up five fingers. Turns out he was one week older than I was. We were good friends from the get-go and it has continued until this day, although early on I tested the friendship by taking his cowboy guns and holster home with me. Our moms soon had the problem resolved.

Roger was a chubby boy, but combative and hard to say "no" to. One day at lunch he talked several kids out of their hot dogs. As we were leaving the cafeteria I asked him "Man, how many hot dogs did you have?" To this he pounded his chest and exclaimed "Just call me Mr. Wieners." It has been many years and I'm still honoring his request. His mother, Mary Lou, never liked this nickname (understandably). When we boys were in High School Mary Lou spoke to my mom about the name one time, wondering if Mim would talk to me about not calling Roger "Wieners" anymore. As is usually the case with Moms intervening, it only made the name more famous. Please do not misunderstand, however. Wieners was fully capable of stopping this if he wanted to. None of us would have been any match for him in a fight. He would not have needed his Mom's help.

My sister Amy was born when I was in third grade. I distinctly remember being told that Mom was going to have another baby. I was called into Dad and Mom's bedroom on a Sunday morning, while they were getting ready for church. My brother Ned was in the room and simply said "Mom is going to have a baby." I do not remember any particular feeling about this news, but I clearly remember Dad immediately adding the admonition "Now don't go telling a bunch of people!" I guess pregnancies were to be kept secret during the early months in those days. The news obviously got around, because my third grad teacher, Mrs. Watts, knitted a pair of baby booties for Amy. Nothing else stands out about this year, except that I remember Mom being very unhappy about having another baby.

My fourth grade teacher was a man I will call Mr. K. He and I got along well, but he had a bad temper. He would slap both boys

A Lifetime of Church

and girls right across the face for backtalk. When we played baseball at recess he always called me "Easy-out." This didn't bother me, though, because I was a good batter and knew he was kidding. Mr. K. had only one child. She married a man from an Apostolic family and the two of them later joined the Apostolic Christian Church. Mr. K. did not have much use for the AC Church and did not mind using me as a vehicle to express his disdain. One time in class he mentioned that "Tom's church" did not have a piano. The other students looked at me like I was from Mars. Another time he asked me in class if my parents had taken me to a certain basketball game. When I said "No" he told the class that my church did not believe in going to ball games. I distinctly remember one girl turning around and saying to me in astonishment, "That's weird! Why?" I can still clearly remember my face turning red with embarrassment. These remarks produced no lasting harm, but it is sad to think that an adult authority figure like a school teacher would embarrass a child simply because he did not like the church the child's parents were rearing him in. It has been my observation in life that things like this will produce one of two reactions in a child. Either the child will begin to resent that which is being made fun of, or he will begin to defend it. My brother Ted and I were an example of each reaction. At a young age he began to rebel against the AC Church and to want anything to do with it. I took the other path and began to defend it. My defense was indirect, however. I never stuck up for the customs and traditions of the Apostolics. Instead I took shots at other kid's churches as being filled with fakes. Even at a young age I **knew** that the Apostolic Christian Church was the only true, sincere church. It was inconceivable to me that my family could be wrong about anything, but especially about anything as important as church.

The Cuban Missile Crisis took place when I was in fourth grade. I remember watching President Kennedy announce the naval quarantine of Cuba and my Dad exclaiming, "Man, he really means business!" It was a scary time for our family because my Uncle Pat Speicher was in the U.S. Navy on a ship in the Carribean Sea. For a while it looked like war with the Soviet Union was inevitable. Thank God war was avoided in the end.

My fifth grade year was the only year that I had some discipline problems. We had a teacher named Mr. Babb. He kept no discipline in the class. That year a boy named James was in our class. His Dad was in the Army and he had been in many different schools already. I realize today that this boy was a textbook case of attention deficit hyperactivity disorder (ADHD) and would be on medication for the problem today. In those days, though, he was just a "problem child." He was very bold and mouthy and I found him to be incredibly funny. He was paddled in the hallway on several occasions. The entire class could hear what was happening and I remember grimacing at each "whack." These spankings made no difference in James' behavior. The teacher tried to put his desk in the far rear corner of the room to isolate him. This did no good, either. He would do things like fart and say "Excuuuuuuse meee!" really loud. I had never encountered anyone like him before. In my experience it was unthinkable that a child would defy authority like he did.

I soon learned that I could make the kids laugh also. I never remotely approached the boldness of James but I became disruptive enough that I got paddled in the hall once. I was scared to death, but Mr. Babb went easy on me. It did not even hurt. I crossed a line, however, when I got a "U" (unsatisfactory) in citizenship on my second report card that year. To say that my Mom was furious would be a gross understatement. She yelled and cried and prophesied doom on my future — that I would "Never turn out!" and that "God would judge me for behavior like this!" and "Where did she go wrong?" This crushed me. I knew that what I had done was bad, but I did not think it was **that** bad. Mom was sad so often in those days. The last thing I wanted to do was to make her even more miserable. This was exactly what I had done, though. It was also clear to me that she was not as upset with me as she was with herself for being such a bad Mom. I concluded right then and there that I would try really hard to not upset her like that again.

For the most part I lived up to this resolution from then on. I really tried to be polite and obedient and helpful. The problem was, however, that I did not do this for the right reason. I did not do it simply because it was right — I did it because I did not want to upset Mom. During my growing up years I was every bit as mischievous as my brothers, but I became an expert at keeping it from Mom. This was no small accomplishment, either, because I have never known anyone with a better "nose" for bad behavior than Mom. Her "hit and miss" ratio for successfully "sniffing out" bad behavior was artificially high, though, because she always assumed the worst. This way she was always right when it came. Poor Mom. In these early years she was either feeling responsible, guilty, and deserving of the crisis she was in or she was worrying about when and where the next one would strike. How did Dad weigh in on my "U" in citizenship? As he usually did: "Come on, now! Don't do that again." Dad knew that "boys will be boys." The only thing that would anger him is if we were mean to other kids.

My shame and resolve were dramatically reinforced the very next day when I made a mistake of gargantuan proportions on the school bus. As I got on the bus a boy stood up and yelled to me from the front "Hey Tom, what did your folks say about your U in citizenship?" I did not want to talk about it so I just replied in a mocking tone "Blah! Blah! Blah!" This amused my friends, but not my brother Ned. In those years he struggled with Pharisaic tendencies and something like this simply could not go unreported. That night it was even worse for me at home. After letting me know that she knew about how I had mocked her, she just cried. She had obviously failed with me. I was beyond hope. This response hurt me far more than anything else could have.

The next grading period I worked really hard to improve my behavior in school. I only recall making Mr. Babb ("Babbo") angry once. He had a swivel chair at his desk that he liked to lean back in while he taught. While he did this one day he fell over backwards, flat on his back. This was beyond funny to me and I simply could not stop laughing. He must have remembered this because I only raised my citizenship grade to a "S-" on the next report card. I thought this was unfair but Mr. Babb saved the day when he put a note next the "S-" stating "Tom is trying."

James moved away over Christmas that year. I remember a sad incident regarding him that has always helped me have sympathy for stigmatized kids like him. In the third grading period we had a section on astronomy. James loved it and took an active part in the class. When the grades came, however, Mr. Babb gave him a "C." He began to cry and lashed out at the teacher from the back of the room. I can vividly recall him yelling through his tears. "I loved astronomy and I behaved myself and I got all the answers right and you STILL gave me a C! It's not fair!" I really felt sorry for James and I also wondered why he got a C. I have never forgotten this. It has helped me understand why kids like him tend to simply give up and drop out.

One day some kids and I were playing on a frozen-over mud puddle. I was standing near the edge when a boy came sliding toward me. The next thing I remember I was on my back looking up. Some kids were standing over me, staring. They told me I had fallen on my head and was knocked out for a little bit. They also wondered what was in my mouth. I had been chewing on an old football mouthpiece that a cousin had given me. I'm sure that it did look strange to them. As they helped me up I realized that my shoulder hurt. They took me to the teacher who had me lie down in a little room just inside the east door of the school. As I was lying there another boy came through the door and exclaimed, "Someone shot President Kennedy! Right in the head!" A while later our principal, Mr. Young, came on the intercom and said "President Kennedy is dead. He has been shot and killed in Dallas, Texas. This is a very sad time for our country." Upon hearing this I distinctly remember thinking, "I hope it wasn't a black man. They will be really mean to the black people if it was." As I look back, I must have been moved by the scenes of the early days of the civil rights movement to think this.

After school that day Mom took me to see Dr. Rheinheimer. He took an X-ray and found that I had chipped my collarbone when I fell. The next days were very sad for everyone. I remember that the adults were scared about what would come next. During the President's funeral and funeral procession I remember Mom crying, especially when John Kennedy, Jr. saluted the casket.

Soon after this the Chicago Bears won the NFL championship. We were watching the game with some of our cousins, the Ritzman boys. Late in the game the Bears had the ball near the goal line. The defense was set, waiting for the Bears to come to the line. It was cold out and the NY Giants were panting. You could see their breath. I was very amused when the Ritzmans said, "Look! They are blowing on the ball, trying to move it back!" The Ritzmans were very witty. The fact that I remember something as strange as this indicates how amusing I found them to be. Mom says they always brought out the worst in me.

After the Christmas break we had a new fifth grade teacher. She was an old lady. With James Heckaman gone the whole class settled down. I only remember two things about this teacher. She would pray with us in the morning before we started class. I never had this happen any other time in school. I also remember her telling us how she had gotten an infected hangnail which landed her in the hospital and which later required her to wear a bag of antibiotic liquid over it for a long time. You are right. It is a strange thing to remember.

This teacher must have only been filling in because we soon had another teacher. She was a pretty woman who was very young. Somehow it became known that she was a Catholic. I vividly remember a fat, ornery boy in my class exclaiming one day "You mean to tell me that beautiful woman is a Catholic?!" It must have gotten out of hand because one day Mrs. Watts, who had been my third grade teacher, came in to the room to talk to us about it. Among other things she told us that our teacher was very hurt about how we acted when we learned she was a Catholic. I was really ashamed after this talk.

One day this new teacher took us for a walk. We went to the bridge that crossed over Turkey Creek. I had been there with Ted and some of his friends not too long before. They had pointed out to me where the sewage pipe emptied into the creek — yes, raw sewage was released directly into the creek in those days — that some condoms were stuck on some branches in the water. I apparently thought it would be a good time to be funny, so I called the teacher over to my side of the bridge and pointed to them and asked her what they were. She acted like she did not see what I was pointing at, so after several attempts I let it drop. The next day I got called to the principal's office. The teacher followed me there. I was very scared, wondering what I had done. Mr. Young told me he was very disappointed in me for embarrassing the teacher at the creek and for laughing at "double-meaning words like rubber." He said if it happened again he would talk to my parents. The thought of this struck fear into my heart and I was a model student for the rest of the year.

Another significant event occurred while I was in fifth grade. It came to my attention one day when the teacher asked us to go to the blackboard and write a sentence. We could choose what to write.

The same ornery fat boy who had made the comment about our teacher being Catholic went to the board and wrote, "There is a new singing group coming to America called the Beatles and they have a song called 'I Wanna Hold Your Hand.'" It was the first time I had ever heard of them. I remember watching their first appearance on the Ed Sullivan Show at Uncle Bob and Aunt Marguerite Hoerr's house. The adults all thought they and their long hair were the beginning of the end of western civilization as we knew it, but I loved their music. I still do.

Chapter Thirteen

My story cannot be told without remembering life on the farm. I feel very blessed to have grown up there. In many ways my childhood seems like a fairytale because of memories from the farm.

Memories of the farm must begin with a description of life in our home on the farm. Our farming arrangement was basically that of an owner and a tenant. Grandpa Beer owned everything — the houses, the land, the livestock. My dad was his farmer and tenant. Dad and Mom had moved to the farm when my uncle Philip was drafted into the Army and sent to Korea. Grandpa Beer needed help and jobs were hard to find in the sluggish economy, so the move seemed to be a mutually beneficial one. Grandpa and Dad split the expenses and the profits fifty-fifty. Our situation differed from a conventional owner-tenant operation in two important ways. First, the two houses were side by side on the same farm and, secondly, my father was a son-in-law instead of a son or another non-related person.

The blessing for us children was that we essentially had two sets of parents. In addition to Dad and Mom we were the beneficiaries of the daily influence of Grandma and Grandpa Beer. But what was a blessing for us was not always a blessing for my parents' marriage relationship. When Grandpa Theo was around there was only one boss — him. Things were done in Theo's timing and in Theo's way.

We lived on his farm and in his house. If we boys were not up in the morning when he thought we should be, he felt free to come in the house and get us up. If we stepped out of line, he would discipline us. If he had work for us to do, his wishes came first. If Dad and Mom made a decision he did not agree with he would wield his veto power. My mother was generally dealt with more as his daughter than as my father's wife. I remember one time my parents bought a car. It was not new, but it was new to us. Like my brothers, I was excited about it. Grandpa Beer felt that we did not need this car and insisted that they take it back. They did. I could see that my parents were very upset about this and they simply told us that Grandpa made them take it back. I was not sure why this was wrong, but I knew it was. My brother Ted was especially upset about this and will still speak of it today. My mother recalls that when she would protest things like this to Grandpa he reminded her that everything came from the farm — and he owned the farm. While I do not doubt that Grandpa sincerely had what he thought was their best interest in mind, it sent a clear and ongoing message to my parents: You are not capable of running your own lives.

At this point in time Dad and Mom were still very young. Being young and married with three children and from different backgrounds with different expectations produced enough tension on its own. The authority structure of the farm created a lot more. Intellectually, Mom knew that her first loyalty was to her husband and her children. She knew that this was also biblical. Warring against this truth was her need to gain her father's approval. She felt she had failed miserably when she had gone against his will in the past and was going to "get it right" in the future. Decision making was a dilemma; while she resented her father's continuing authority and knew it was not correctly being imposed upon her, she felt she had no choice but to obey. This resulted in her defending him to Dad, even when she felt he was wrong. Dad resented Theo's control over them and protested it — but to Mom, not Theo. Mom thus found herself constantly in the middle. If she pleased Dad (and often herself), she was in conflict with Theo. If she pleased Theo (which she felt she had no choice but to do), she was in conflict with Dad. Add to this her life paradigm of "I don't have anything — I will never have anything apart from Theo's provision — I don't deserve anything anyway" and you have the production of a lot of anger and frustration. Since she did not feel free to express this to her father it was often vented on my father. It seemed like there was always arguing going on when I was a little boy. This is the only thing about my childhood that I really hated. I never understood what it was about and it seemed to be so unnecessary. To this day I cannot stand it when people argue in my presence. I find that I immediately move to try and stop it or to remove myself from it.

My father was a man who was very different from Theo Beer. Dad was a man who was generally content with life. He knew life required work and so he worked. But it was never his passion. It was not important to him to "get ahead" if this meant buying farms and accumulating possessions. Other than in his sports career, it was never important to him to have authority or to be a leader of others. He trusted Christ as his Savior and loved the Lord. He was a morally upright man who went to church, but who had no desire to hold offices in the church that would require speaking in front of others. He didn't like to visit other Apostolic Christian churches or to interact much with Theo's guests. He was satisfied to milk twenty cows and to get up in the morning at 7:00 a.m. to do it instead of the customary 5:00 a.m. While he did not seek a lot of leisure time, he enjoyed it when he could and did not feel guilty about enjoying it. For the most part, he was an uncomplicated and happy man. In all these ways he did not fit the stereotype of the ever-working, authoritarian, no-nonsense, moneymaking Apostolic Christian Church male. Grandpa Beer illustrated the stereotype. I believe that Mom deeply resented them both in these early years, but for very different reasons. I do not believe, however, that poor Mom would have known what she wanted even if she could have custom-ordered it. She was just too conflicted about her own wants, desires, and self-worth to make sense of anything in her life.

Grandpa Beer clearly felt he was my father's benefactor in the early years. I believe that many of the church people felt this way as well. I can remember on more than one occasion Grandpa Beer asking me if I thought my Dad would have "turned out as good" if he had not married my Mom. Even as a little boy I sensed that this was an inappropriate question. I did not like it, but I did not feel I could tell him so. I agreed with him, knowing that somehow I had just insulted my Dad. I knew also that many of the "successful" farmers in the church felt superior to my Dad. I'm not sure how I knew this as a little boy, but I did — and I hated it. My Dad must also have sensed this. I remember one time we were doing something outside and he asked me "Do you wish Flip (my uncle) was your Dad instead of me?" I suppose I remember it because it surprised me so. I would never have even conceived of wanting another Dad. He teased me and was funny and played ball with me and caught turtles for me and took me places and made me feel special and I knew he was the best basketball player Milford ever had. What more could a little boy want in a Dad? He was sad when he asked me this question and it still hurts me that life had brought him to the point where he felt he needed to ask it. The very concepts of being a "good farmer" or the importance of buying a farm or "turning out better" for having married into Grandpa's family were unknowable to me as a little boy. It wasn't until many years later that I began to understand the pride of the Apostolic Christian Church "proper" male. I learned that one's "worth" tends to be directly proportional to one's financial portfolio and that financial success is viewed as proof-positive of God's stamp of approval on one's life. Such views, while widely held among Christians of many persuasions, are thoroughly contrary to the letter of Scripture (Matthew 20: 25-28) and to the life-model of our Lord Jesus Christ.

Very recently I asked my Dad about this. He said, "I knew they thought I could not manage or get ahead, that I wasn't much of a farmer." I asked him if it bothered him. Surprisingly, he replied, "No, it really didn't, because I went to school with most of them and knew they could not begin to compete with me athletically. And I always felt they would have wanted that more than what they had over me then." I found this to be a very interesting view, one consistent with Dad's simple view of life. And he is probably right.

One thing I am sure of is this. Despite the conflict in our home and the social and religious factors that brought it about, Dad and Mom were both absolutely devoted and loving parents. Mom was inexhaustible in working to provide us with the best food, the best care, and an immaculate home. We were given opportunities and clothing at a level far above what we might have expected from our family income. I always felt adored by both Dad and Mom. There have probably been very few children ever who have enjoyed more parental devotion than we did. The older I get the more I thank God for their devotion to the institution of marriage. They never gave up on it and we children are the beneficiaries of their devotion to what was right instead of what might have seemed expedient.

Chapter Fourteen

The obsession of my youth was collecting turtles. It may have begun in Kindergarten when Dad caught the two box turtles, but I am not sure. I cannot remember a time when I was not fascinated with them.

Many times I remember peering over the dashboard of the car as we went back and forth to town. With four drainage ditches and some swamp acreage in the three-mile distance to town it was a prime area for turtle crossings, particularly in the spring of the year when they laid their eggs. Any distant speck on the road made my heart pound. Was it a turtle crossing the road? It rarely was a turtle, but it was often enough that I jumped at any opportunity to ride to town. Even Mom would stop to pick up a turtle in those days — whether I was with her or not.

In the first few years of my "turtle era" I did not keep them very long. I would catch one or someone would give one to me and I would keep it in the "horse tank" (the cattle watering tank) down by the barn or in one of Grandpa Beer's tanks. He sold feeders and watering tanks in those days that were "seconds," or slightly damaged. He had a display area between the house and the barn, so there was never a shortage of places to keep a turtle or two. It was not long before the turtles would come up missing. Either I would get them out to play with them and forget to put them back or someone else would. Or maybe they just "got out." I still marvel at how resourceful turtles are at getting away. One time I had a big snapping turtle in a tank down by the barn. I had thrown some little fish in the tank the night before and found them floating headless the next morning. The water in the tank would only stay clear for a few days and I could not see the bottom. I wanted to get the snapper out that day, but I could not see where he was. With no sense of the danger in doing this I simply dunked my arm in and felt around for him. When I felt his tail I pulled him to the surface. I was shocked to see that I had grabbed the snapping turtle's head instead of his tail and his mouth was wide open, ready to snap. A turtle of his size could have easily bitten off a finger or two. I instantly let go, but I knew I had been lucky and I never groped around blindly for a snapping turtle again.

When I got a little older I began catching more turtles on my own. My oldest brother Ned taught me a great way to do it. My technique until this point was to walk along the top of the ditch bank until I saw a turtle on a patch of moss, sunning itself. I would then try to sneak down to them and grab them. Despite my best efforts, though, I rarely was able to sneak down to them before they swam away. After observing what I was doing, Ned suggested that I go and stand in the patch of moss and quietly wait. He said the turtle would eventually need to come up for air and when they did I could catch them. Sure enough, it worked. This was the "great leap forward" in turtle-catching technology. Soon I began catching more turtles than I could store.

I began to conceive the image of the ideal turtle pen when I saw an old bathtub in one of the buildings. Ned and Ted helped me build my dream turtle pen between the garage and the shop at home. First, we buried the bathtub so that the top of it was level with the ground. We then built a wooden frame around it. The frame consisted of four two-by-four corner posts, connected at the top by one-by-six boards. From old pictures I suppose the perimeter was about eight feet by ten feet. We then took chicken wire and nailed it to the wooden perimeter frame on top, on the outside of the top board so that the turtles would not be able to have any surface to get their claws onto and climb out. We buried the bottom of the chicken wire about six inches deep so the turtles could not dig out, either. When finished, this pen was the standard by which other turtle pens were judged. For a number of summers all guests on the family farm were given turtle pen tours as part of the hospitality package.

All spring and summer I would collect the turtles. I would carve my initials on the shells of my favorite ones. I was able to keep track of things this way and I caught the same black box turtle three years in a row. The third year I caught him he was four miles upstream from where I had released him the previous fall. Another odd turtle that I caught two years in a row was a large brown box turtle that only had two legs, one in the front and one in the back, on opposite sides. No doubt this handicap made him easier to catch than a normal turtle.

When I was in first grade the teacher told us we were going to have a turtle race the next day. I had just caught an especially fast one a few days before, plus I knew more about turtles than anyone in my class. There was no doubt in my mind that my turtle would win. The next day at recess we put them in the middle of a circle and let them go. To my shock and dismay my turtle just sat there and looked around. Another boy's turtle won easily. It was a very traumatic experience.

One day I decided to change the water in my turtle pen. Ned helped me. We put a board across half the pen and put all the turtles on the other side. Once all the water was dipped out and replaced with clean water, we decided to count them as we put them back. Ned filled a bucket with water and dipped them in it before putting them in the tub. This kept the water clean longer. When the last turtle was put back we had reached a count of forty-nine. I was incubating some turtle eggs in an aquarium at the time so we decided we would report the number at fifty. This happened in mid-summer, so I'm sure the number even surpassed fifty by the summer's end.

In those days we butchered livestock for our meat. My Dad hated liver, so liver became my turtles' main food. They loved it. Each fall I had to turn them loose at the ditch. I can remember filling five-gallon buckets with them for the trip there. Several years I know I cried. The other years I just left with a huge lump in my throat.

No one can remember for sure when I stopped collecting turtles. I suppose it was about the time I got to middle school. It has been a lot of years ago, but I still get excited when I see a turtle on the road. I still love to play with them and take them to children whom I know will have an interest in them. The "turtle years" were an exciting period of my life.

Chapter Fifteen

When I was a child we raised spearmint and distilled it for its oil. It was a labor-intensive endeavor that required a family effort. The muck ground was well suited for growing mint. This low lying flat ground guaranteed hot, dry working conditions.

In the spring of the year we would transplant mint plants into new acreage. This was the worst part of the whole process. The transplanting process began with the acquisition of mint plants. Usually we would buy them from another farmer. These plants were sold by the crate, which was about an eighteen inch wooden cube. We would go into an existing mint field and begin pulling up plants, which we put in the crates. It was important that we pull them gently in order to get the roots as well as the tops. We kids tended to just yank and stuff whatever we got into the crates. When we thought we had a crate filled, Grandpa Beer would invariably come over and compact it to half of its previous volume and tell us to continue. When the crates were filled to Grandpa's satisfaction we would put the crates in a tank of water to keep the roots (what roots there were) from drying out.

Very soon after collecting the plants we would transplant them in a prepared field. We had an implement for this job. This transplanter had four metal seats that corresponded to four transplant wheels. On these wheels were a number of receptacles into which a mint plant was placed. As the wheel turned, it planted it in the ground. The job required a minimum of six people: four to sit on the seats and place plants into the transplant wheels, one to walk along behind to distribute plants to the four people and to be boss, and one to drive the tractor. Of course, Theo was always the distributor of plants and the boss. One day Grandpa got his pant leg caught while walking behind and it pulled him to the ground. I thought this was very funny. My Mom fell off one of the seats once when she was little and was run over by the transplanter. When Grandpa dusted her off and saw that she was not hurt, he spanked her. This was not the best thing to do to an insecure girl who felt unloved. It is an understatement to say that this was long, hot, tedious, boring work.

My job was to drive the tractor. It was an entry-level job that required no skill at all. The tractor was in first gear and idled as low as it would go. All I had to do was keep the wheels straight and not fall asleep. I gained a reputation for daydreaming at this job. Grandpa used to say that my rows "were crookeder than a dog's hind leg." My brother Ted was found lacking as a transplanter also. Being older, he got to sit on one of the seats and feed the plants into the wheel. One summer he became obsessed with his hands getting dry. By the end of the rows he was hysterical and would run to dunk his hands in water, crying "Ohhhhh, dry hands!" as he ran.

At the end of each row Dad or Grandpa would relieve me to turn the transplanter around. I would always sprint to the ditch bank to see if there were any turtles. One time I saw a big snapper in the water. I slide down the bank and into the water and grabbed him. He was a big one and very grouchy. When we broke for lunch that day someone was at the house to buy some feed or something from Grandpa. When they saw the turtle they remarked how they liked to eat turtle. At this, Grandpa gave the turtle to them. This launched me into a tantrum. How dare he give my turtle away! I can vividly remember jumping up and down and crying as that pale green car drove out our back lane — with my turtle.

Once a field was transplanted it required special care the first summer. The transplanted plants were about six inches apart in rows that were forty inches apart. We would cultivate between the rows with a tractor, but once in the first year we would have to walk the rows and weed between the plants with hoes. By the end of the first summer we were able to cut the row mint and distill it one time. In the fall, we would plow the field over and the next spring it would come up spread throughout the field.

The distilling process began with cutting the mint with a tractor and hay mower. We would let it dry a day to lower the moisture content. It was important to not let it get too dry, though, or the leaves would fall off the stalk. The leaves held the oil. We would then load the mint on wagons and take them to the house where the mint distill was. Once there a chain hoist would lower big knives onto the wagon. We would shove these knives into the mint. The hoist would then lift the mint off the wagon and we would turn the boom so the mint came inside. Once inside over the tub we would pull a rope to release the mint. It fell into the tub. When the tub was full we would all get on top of it, join arms, and jump up and down together. This packed the mint into the tub. As we did this we all said "hoo-sha, hoo-sha, hoo-sha." We referred to this as "Doing the Jess Haab." I don't think it meant anything in particular.

When the tub was packed tight with mint we would lower the lid and attach the clamps all around. The steam valve was then opened and steam began to pressure-cook the mint. The vapors ascended in pipes to the top of the mint distill, where they entered a series of coils in water tanks. Eventually, the distillate came back to ground level into one small separator. At the end of the process it was a thrill to pull the lever that shut off the outflow of water. This caused the water in the separator to rise. The oil, which rose to the top, flowed out from a metal spout at the top. This was then put into a fifty-gallon drum to be sold later.

Once the distilling was complete the steam was turned off and the tub opened. What had entered green was now brown and shrunken in mass. These were called the "mint pummies." I am unable to find this word and the correct spelling. I loved taking out the pummies. To do this an empty wagon was pulled along the side of the building. On this wagon we placed two slings. They were long enough to hang over each side. On the one end was a wood piece about three feet long and four inches in diameter. Chains were attached to each side of this. These chains lay across the top of the wagon and were joined by a metal ring on the other side. The hoist lowered the knives into the tub. We got into the tub and stomped the knives into the pummies. The hoist then pulled the steaming mass out of the tub. We then swung the boom out over the wagon and pulled the release. The pummies plopped onto the wagon. A tractor would then pull the wagon into a field. We unhooked the wagon and drove the tractor to the wagon's side. A chain was then attached to the ring of the sling, thrown over the top of the pummies, and attached to the tractor. The tractor pulled away and the pummies were flipped over onto the ground. In the fall we spread them out with a tractor and loader and plowed them under the next spring. This whole process of loading, distilling, and unloading usually took about three hours. There were two tubs in the mint distill, so in a good day one could do six wagon loads of mint.

A furnace needed to be fired to heat the boiler and produce the steam. To fuel this fire we burned every scrap of wood we could accumulate throughout the year. When the wood ran out we used coal. Ted and I used to love to play with this fire. We threw things in it to watch them burn all the time. We even threw in some 22-caliber bullets from time to time to hear them explode. We noticed that Grandpa Beer would always grab some ashes from the ash pile to wash his hands with before dinner. One day we decided to play a trick on him. Right before dinner we threw some hot ashes on the pile by the water faucet and waited for him to come. He came right on cue and grabbed a handful of the hot ashes. He just threw them down, saying "whup - whup," grabbed another handful from a different spot, and washed his hands as usual. He was oblivious to our trick. Maybe Grandpa Theo did not notice our trick because his mind was on the meal he would soon enjoy. The mealtimes were unquestionably the highlight of working in the mint operation. Grandma Naoma created Thanksgiving Day-like meals every day during mint season. I do not ever remember food tasting better.

Spearmint oil was very strong. It would burn like fire if you had it on your finger and rubbed your mouth and eyes. We had a flat stick that we used to separate the last of the oil from the water when we took it off. One day between jobs Ted came up to me, looked inquisitively at me, and asked me to stick out my tongue. Without thinking I did it. He instantly took the flat stick with oil on it and rubbed it on my tongue. I rubbed my tongue, spit and gargled over and over to get the fire out of my mouth. Ted was greatly amused by my agony. It was not funny at all when it happened to me. But I knew I would do the trick to someone else the first chance I got.

Working the mint was akin to a three-ring circus most of the time. Usually a Ritzman cousin or two were around. They were good workers, but were very ornery and constantly got Ted and me into crazy situations. One time Bob Ritzman and my uncle Bernie had grabbed Ted and me and dangled us by our feet over the manure in the barn. I can vividly remember my face right next to the manure. The next day they were sleeping upstairs at Grandma Beer's house, probably recovering from the night before. I grabbed a twig off a thorn bush and followed Ted upstairs. We roamed around the room for a while trying to decide how to pay them back. As we were walking out, an idea came to me. I remember that Bob was lying on his stomach. I slowly pulled up on the elastic of his underwear and put the thorn twig inside. We continued on downstairs where Grandma had a roomful of company. Shortly thereafter we heard a shout from upstairs. Bob came bounding down the stairs. He was angry and came across the room. He grabbed me hard on the arm and exclaimed, "Don't you ever do that again!" All this took place in a roomful of guests with Bob in his underwear. Bob always teased us. This, in turn, brought retaliation from us. Bob knew that Ted was behind most of my actions, so one day he grabbed Ted and threw him in the horse tank. Of course Ted came up madder than a "wet hen" and ran to Mom. Mom then scolded Bob. He still laughs about it and says that in dunking Ted he had simply "gone to the source."

Bob Ritzman had three younger brothers named Paul, Jerry, and Eric. Paul was a year or so younger than Bob. Jerry was a year older than my brother Ned. Eric and my brother Ted were the same age. Paul was very handy on the farm, but the biggest teaser of them all. My Mom always said he reminded her of Eddie Haskell on the "Leave It To Beaver" television show. Mom hated it when the Ritzman cousins came in the summer because they turned Ted and me into wild monsters.

Paul Ritzman kept us in line with the threat of a "treatment" if we didn't listen to him. A "treatment" was a series of different physical torments that included, but was not limited to, ear pops, head thumps, Indian burns, knuckle twists to the ribs, skin twisters, and Dutch rubs. A treatment was always concluded with "the claw." This was a hand-claw to the abdomen. "Treatments" were a very effective tool for overcoming our wills and in modifying our behavior.

One day Paul and I were coming home from Uncle Flip's on the "Putt-Putt." This was a Korean War era Army surplus motor scooter. I was standing on the platform, holding on to the handlebars. Paul was on the seat behind me, reaching around me. We suddenly veered off into the ditch alongside the road and crashed. I never knew why, but maybe I pulled on the handlebar too hard. I have a scar on my left eyebrow to show for this incident.

Another time Paul left this Putt-Putt running in the front yard of Grandma Beer's house while he went inside. I climbed on the seat to pretend I was driving it. I did not know that the engine was accelerated with a twist of the one handgrip. I twisted it, the Putt-Putt took off, and we ran right up the side of the large maple tree. When we came back to ground level, the Putt-Putt came down on my leg. It hurt very badly but did not break any bones. Grandma Beer was driving up the lane and saw this happen. She ran the car into the bushes before she got stopped.

One day Bernie, Bob, and Paul came home with some fireworks. They had the really good M-80's and Cherry Bombs. Ted, Eric, and I wanted some of them badly and were begging. Paul said to Ted and Eric "If you two fight for awhile we will give you some." They immediately went at it right in the yard between the two houses. Before long Bernie stopped the fight. Paul then said, "I've changed my mind. I'm not giving you any." Ted and Eric were both young enough that they started crying. The three older guys really thought this was funny. I do not remember whether they eventually gave them some firecrackers or not. Probably not.

The mint wagons were always pulled through the barnyard to the side of the mint distill. Of course the barnyard was full of manure. One time Ted wanted to ride to the field with Bob. Bob said he could not go with him unless he cleaned out the treads on the tractor tires. Without hesitation Ted took his hand and began cleaning the manure out of the treads. Bob really laughed and let him ride along.

Hay often needed to be baled when we were doing the mint. Sometimes we would take a break from the mint to do it. Other times we would split into two crews. I usually got stuck with the hay baling crew because I could drive the tractor that pulled the

A Lifetime of Church

baler. Far worse than the hay baling crew, though, was the milking crew. I tolerated the afternoon milking but I absolutely hated the morning milking. For some unknown reason I was given the job of helping Dad milk on Sunday mornings. Many Saturday nights I sank into melancholy moods at the very thought of getting up to milk the next morning. What a cross to bear!

By late summer the upper floor of the barn was stacked high with hay bales. After supper one night I walked up to the barn to find Ned and Ted swinging on a rope. This rope was attached to the old track at the peak of the roof. They were swinging from some hay bales in the center of the barn to a tractor, which they pushed off of with their legs to send them back to the starting point. It looked like they were having a lot of fun so I asked if I could take a turn. I climbed up the bales, took the rope, and swung out. I forgot to put my feet out and slammed flat into the tractor. This opened a gash in my forehead that bled profusely. Dad and Mom took me to Doctor Rheinheimer, who patched me up. I bear a scar from this, but it could have been much worse.

The bad part of this incident is that the blood from the wound ruined my favorite T-shirt. Some time before I had received a patch which said "Training Command" in a Cracker Jack box. Mom had sewed it on a T-shirt for me. Since I was a chubby little boy Bob Ritzman promptly gave me the name "Lard Can Training Command." This name stuck quite awhile, even after my shirt was ruined. Another name I had was "Heavy" after Burger's Ice Cream "Heavy Pack." Ted gave me this one. The third name I had was "Doonce." Once I had tried to insult someone by calling them a "Dunce," but when I wrote it I mis-spelled it as "Doonce." I think it is pretty impressive that I even knew the word "dunce" as a tyke. My Aunt Becky Doll still occasionally calls me Doonce forty years later.

The mint operation continued until I was about to enter middle school. One spring we had a late frost and it killed all the mint. We never planted any more. This was probably because the distilling equipment was worn out and Grandpa was getting older. Mint oil prices had also dropped very low due to the introduction of synthetic oil. This closed one of the most interesting chapters in my life. Grandpa Beer had often said that he paid off the farm with a few good mint crops.

Chapter Sixteen

Ned, Ted, and I were classic illustrations of personalities one would expect from our birth order. I never remember a time when Ned was not a "little man." He could always see what needed to be done to accomplish a task. He was efficient and goal-oriented in his work. He loved to boss Ted and me whenever he could. He understood authority and tried to please the authority figure in his life — Grandpa Beer.

Ted was a typical second child. He was very independent. He was determined to make his own decisions about what he would do and what he would believe. Early on Ted was interested in clothes, cars, and other possessions. Early on he made it clear that he did not like the farm work and he did not like the Apostolic Christian Church. Ted wanted to be his own authority. He would argue for his independence and would fight for it whenever necessary. Ted did not take on many projects, but when he did he was very organized and saw them through. He and Ned got along reasonably well, as long as Ned did not try to impose his will on him.

I was a typical third child. I tended to be very compliant. I loved to work with other people and never wanted to be the boss. I did not question authority much. I assumed that if my grandparents and parents went to the Apostolic Christian Church, that it must be the best. I hated arguments and conflict. I worked hard to defuse tension. Unless something was important to me, I generally let others have their own way. It was not that I was noble in doing this,

I just generally did not care one way or the other. As long as I was fed and things were peaceful, I was usually happy.

Among the three of us the dynamic was pretty constant. If Ned got to me first, I would assist him in what he was trying to accomplish. He, in turn, would help me in what I wanted to do, but lacked the expertise to do. Catching turtles and building my turtle pen are two examples of activities that illustrate this.

If Ted got my attention first, it usually involved going somewhere, playing a game of some sort, or causing some sort of mischief. Most commonly it was Ted and me against anything which others were trying to do. I remember Dad once telling someone about the quality of help I was on the farm. He said, referring to me, "He can be the best or the worst, depending on the day." This was true, and the determining factor was generally whether I was allied with Ned or Ted for the day.

The summer after my kindergarten year Ted and I rode our bikes to a boy's house several miles away. The boy's name was Jonnie. He was a year older than Ted. Jonnie would have been referred to as a "hood" in those days. Ted had gotten to know him on the school bus, so we rode over for a visit. The three of us then rode our bikes down to the ditch south of Jonnie's house. There was a big steel suspension bridge over the ditch there. We sat on this bridge and talked. Before long Jonnie pulled out a pack of cigarettes. They were Lucky Strikes. I distinctly remember the big circle on the pack. He lit one up and was sharing it with Ted. Ted held it out to me and said "Here, try this." I took a puff and gave it back. Before long we rode back home. Ted forgot to tell me that I should not say anything about the cigarette, so the first thing I did when we got home was to tell Mom about it. Big mistake.

Smoking became one of the "bad" things we would do once in awhile. Every summer Uncle Pat and Aunt Laurel Speicher would take us to a Cubs baseball game in Chicago. This was something we all looked forward to for months in advance. And it was the only way we were going to see a game since, as Apostolics, Dad and Mom could not take us. One the way up and back we always stopped along the Toll Road. In these restaurants they had vending machines that sold cigars. Ted and I would usually get one purchased without being seen. I only remember several times actually smoking it, though, and then thinking it tasted horrible.

Ted had quite an imagination. We used to take our BB guns and play war around the farm. He was the leader, of course. He told me about the enemy troop movements and devised strategies for fighting them. This went on from the back yards of the houses to the barn and back. I really enjoyed doing this.

Another activity we enjoyed was playing tricks on our cousins and our friends from town who came to visit. One of our favorite tricks was to get people to touch the electric fence. This fence went down to the muck and around a number of fields. To get the cows into different pastures or to pen them in the barnyard for milking required grabbing a hold of the fence and changing it to another side. Of course we turned the fence off before we did this. The "shocking" of others had several variations. One way was to simply ask them to unhook the wire and bring it to you. This only worked one time per person. Another way we did it was to ask them to "test" the fence to see if it was on. When we seriously wanted to do this we would use a dry twig or a dry blade of grass. This would only result in a "tickle" of electricity. If you used a green blade of grass the shock was near normal. This also only worked one time per person. Our favorite way was to unplug the fence at its electrical source in the mint distill. We would then handle it ourselves in front of the intended victim. When they were confident it was off, they would help. The problem was that someone else was back inside the mint distill watching, who would plug it back in. We played this game with each other also. I can distinctly remember many times straining my eyes to see if anyone was in the mint distill before touching the fence. I need to add that this "shock" was not strong enough to hurt anyone, but it was strong enough to make one not desire to receive it. The two dumbest incidents in this "shocking" game were both with our cousins. One "tested" the fence with a piece of wire. But even dumber than this was the cousin who urinated on the fence to test it! Both of these cousins were very intelligent and are now successful professionals. These "testings" were not their finest hour intellectually.

My younger cousin Dan Doll remembers Ted devising strange games. One time he put us back to back. He took a chain and attached one end of it to my leg and the other end to Dan's leg. We then were ordered to run in opposite directions! We did this without hesitation. Other times he would tie us to posts in the barn and we would try to get loose. One day I remember he had me ride my bike down the barn bank. As I passed by him he would throw a stick at my front tire to see if I would crash. I do not remember crashing. Ted went through a stage where he was obsessed with making a perfect "handprint." He claims that he learned the art of "handprinting" from the Ritzman cousins. Smacking a bare back with his open hand did this. If done right it made a beautiful image of the hand. If I needed persuasion he would simply say "Handprint!" and I was persuaded. One day I ran for the house rather than be persuaded. I was running with all my might for the door of the screened-in-porch of the little house. Ted was rapidly "closing the gap" when Grandma Beer yelled at him to stop. I was spared a "handprint!"

There were only two times that I remember making Ted "pay" for his aggression. Both instances would probably be better classified as pre-emptive strikes to deter aggression. Ted and I were both very young when these pre-emptive strikes took place. The first incident was really stupid. I had a pack of Dentyne gum. Apparently Ted wanted some of it and I did not want to share. All I remember is that I put all the sticks in my mouth and he decided to go in after them.

The problem was that I clamped down on his finger when he did. The harder he pounded on my back with his free hand, the harder I bit the index finger of his other hand. I do not remember exactly how the standoff ended but I am pretty sure I kept the gum and he kept his finger.

The second incident was nearly as dumb. I was sitting on an old implement trailer pounding peanuts with a hammer. I have no idea why. Ted hopped on the trailer and said "Let me try that." I said "No!" and hit him on the head with the hammer. He ran screaming to the house. I must have been in a really foul mood that day because I remember following him in to the house a short time later. Dad and Mom had Ted leaning over the bathroom sink, apparently cleaning up the wound. I walked by and mocked "Waaahhhhh!" Mom turned and yelled to me "You were very bad to do this. You should be ashamed of yourself!" In retrospect, I cannot believe that I did not get spanked for this. Dad and Mom must have figured that Ted had done something to deserve the whack on the head — and he probably did. I have just forgotten what it was!

One time one of Ted's tricks backfired on him. He was mad at our cousins for something, so he prepared a trick to get even with them. In the north end of the upper floor of our barn was the straw mow. One half of this mow contained two wooden bins where grain or feed was stored. On the roof of the grain bin was a trap door through which the grain could be put in. The distance from the floor to the trap door was about seven feet. The grain bin was empty except for a little grain left on the floor. Ted had gone up the ladder to the top of the grain bin. There were straw bales up there. Ted stacked up the straw bales around the open trap door to a height of about five feet. As one climbed up the ladder it looked like it was continuous straw bales to where Ted was hiding. He called to me to come up to him. I was in a great mood so I scrambled up the ladder, ran a few steps, and jumped to where Ted was. As if it were yesterday I can see his face with wide-eyed horror as he yelled, "Wait!" It was too late. There was no straw bale where I jumped. There was nothing. I fell all the way down to the grain bin floor, landing on my back. I can still see Ted's face looking down on me from above in shock. The fall knocked the wind out of me, but that was the extent of my injuries. I remember that my Uncle Flip's hired man was standing outside the grain bin, looking at me and laughing. I desperately wanted to tell him to shut up, but I could not get enough breath to yell it. I had fallen from a great enough height to seriously injure myself, but the only long-term result was that I have a great story to tell. I think this incident really scared Ted and I never remember anything like it again.

Ted and I knew that Eric Ritzman was coming to visit one time so we thought we would play a trick on him when he arrived. I suggested that we put several pins between the mattress of his bed and the cover sheet, sticking up. As soon as Eric arrived we went up to our room and showed him where he would be sleeping. Right away he went and sat on the edge of his bed. The trick worked perfectly. He jumped back up and saw the pins that had stuck him. Ted and I were laughing hysterically. Eric got so angry that he began to cry. Through his tears he shouted "I come here to have good time with you guys and you do something like this to welcome me!" I felt terrible about what I had done. I think Ted did too.

There used to be an old orchard to the west of the little house. We liked to play out there, climbing trees and chopping limbs for forts. One day Jerry, Eric, Ted and I were out there. We had a 22-gauge rifle. One of them shot at a bird. We heard a sharp "crack" by the house and realized that we had shot in that direction without thinking. When we walked to the house we saw that the bullet had hit the front hood of Grandpa Beer's car. It left a "quarter-size" dent where it had ricocheted off. We were greatly amused by this. As far as I know, Grandpa Beer never noticed.

One more story again illustrates the lack of good judgement that children have. One afternoon Ted, Eric, and I were the only ones around so we decided to take Eric's parents' car for a drive. Ted and Eric could not have been more than middle schoolers at the time. Eric drove and I rode in the middle of the back seat. After driving around for a while, we headed home. A couple of miles west of our front lane, Eric "floored it." We were going close to one hundred miles per hour when we passed the last crossroad. The intersection was elevated and we went air born. When we hit the road Eric nearly lost control as he swerved from side to side. They thought it was hilarious. I was scared to death. This was one of many times when God was watching over us. At that speed with no seatbelts I doubt we would have survived a crash.

These stories make Ted seem mean, but he really wasn't. He could be ruthless if provoked. Most of the time, however, he was a great companion that I had a lot of fun with. There were two things Ted would never tolerate. One was for anyone to pick on me, other than him. The other was if someone bullied an underprivileged or helpless kid. Such a bully would pay a high price for his actions.

Summer baseball was another factor that made my childhood special. The whole community seemed to take part in the Little League program. My first direct experience with baseball was as manager of Ned and Ted's team. Uncle Bernie Beer was the coach. The team was having a good season. They lost a crucial game near the end of the season. A factor in that game was one of our batters being called out for not having a batter's helmet when he came to the plate. Guess whose responsibility it was to be sure that batters had their helmets? Turns out that I had wandered off to look for

A Lifetime of Church

turtles. I was crushed when Uncle Bernie scolded me for this.

I turned out to be a pretty good baseball player. I played shortstop or second base. I was a good fielder and made very few errors. When I did, they were usually throwing errors. Once they tried me at catcher but it did not work out. On the first batter I was distracted by the swing of the bat and the ball hit my right hand instead of the gloved one. Ouch! I also pitched to one batter one time. It was Denny Replogle and I hit him on the thigh with my first pitch. Despite these outings I still almost always played on the All Star Team.

My forte, though, was batting. I nearly always batted third or fourth in the lineup. The biggest thrill of my baseball days happened when I was still one of the younger players in the league. We trailed by a run or two in our last at-bats. Our team had loaded the bases with two outs when I came to the plate. The pitcher was an older kid who threw hard. I swung hard at a ball and hit it very high. I ran for first base with all my might. By the time I got to first base I realized everyone was cheering wildly. It was then I realized that I had hit a grand slam home run, over the center field fence. I was astonished. Of course I was mobbed by my teammates. More than this, though, I remember my coach driving by as we were walking uptown afterwards. He honked and yelled "Hey, Hey, Grand Slam!" What a memory. I hit other home runs, but never another one like this one.

For three years I also participated in Punt, Pass, and Kick, the last year being the fall before my sixth grade year. The first year I remember Dad taking me into the CS Myers Ford Dealership in town to register. There was a big picture of Mike Ditka in his Chicago Bears uniform. I practiced very hard for the big day. When I got there I realized that I would be competing against some boys from the grade ahead of me because the birthday cutoffs were from January to January instead of with the school year. This disappointed me but I decided to just do my best. I do not remember my punt or my kick, but on my pass the announcer said "That made the chalk fly!" This meant the pass was perfectly straight. When the winners were announced my name was not mentioned for third or second place. I was absolutely stunned when my name was called for first place. I received a Chicago Bears athletic jacket and was on top of the world.

The next year I ended in a tie for first place with Steve

Wolferman. We had to do it over again and I beat him. I was really proud about this because Steve was "The Man" in the grade ahead of me. I received a Chicago Bears helmet and a plaque for this.

The pressure was really on me for my third year. No way I could retire without defending my crown. My punt and pass went pretty well. As I approached for my kick, I really gave it all I had! To my shock and horror, my shoe came off and went straight up in the air. The ball rolled off to the side. My embarrassment came to full measure when the announcer exclaimed, "I think his shoe went farther than the ball!" Man, this was far more embarrassing than getting a spanking in first grade. Obviously, I was not one of the top three finishers.

When I got home I walked to the muck where Dad was working ground. He probably was too nervous to come and watch that day. I know Mom was there. It would have been permissible for him to come, because things like this and Little League were "gray areas" in the Apostolic Christian Church's "no sports attendance" policy. The "good" church members did not attend. The "nominal" church members did attend. Even the "good" members, though, would at times skirt this rule for Little League. The common "acceptable" way to do it was for a parent to come early to pick up their child and then stand apart from the other fans to watch the end of the game. This way one was not "really there." Dad thought I was kidding at first when I told him what had happened, but was very understanding. He really felt bad that I had to endure such public ignominy.

Chapter Seventeen

When I was about ten years old I began to sense that something was wrong at church. I noticed that the aunts and uncles would gather at Grandpa Beer's on Sundays and talk seriously, in tones that were not meant for us children to hear. In addition to this, I noticed that my cousin and best friend on Sundays, Tom Beer, did not come to church regularly anymore. In school he told me they went to the Bremen Apostolic Christian Church sometimes. This did not make any sense to me at all because Bremen was twenty miles away.

One Saturday afternoon Ned and I were working on something outside. I noticed that there were many cars at Grandpa Beer's house. When I asked Ned what was going on at Grandpa's he told me that they "were Elders." He added that "They are after Junie's a...!" I did not know why this would be and I did not think much more about it until the following Monday when I went home with Tom Beer after school. We were good friends and this is something I did on occasion. I remember that his mom looked surprised when she saw me and said "Oh Tom, what are you doing here?" I knew something was not right so I soon called Mom to come and get me. When I got in the car she was upset with me. She said "Why did you go there today! Don't you know those people hate us?" When I asked why they hated us she told me that many people had left the church the day before and that they had been very mean to Grandpa Beer.

It was not long before what had happened began to unfold in my mind. The Milford Apostolic Christian Church was mainly comprised of several large, extended families. One of these families was the Simon Beer family. The branches of Simon's children in Milford included Otto Senior, Ezra, Theo, Henry, and Hulda. Another family was the Graff family. Otto Beer, Senior and Hulda Beer were married to Graff's. A third family was the Haab family. Ezra Beer had married a Haab.

Otto Beer, Junior ("Junie") was quickly identified as the troublemaker. From his own testimony, Junie recalls that he grew up a staunch supporter of the church. Throughout his teens and early twenties he prayed that God would not take his life until he was able to "join the church." He eventually married a church girl from the Bluffton Apostolic Christian Church and soon, thereafter, they repented and joined the church. He was a committed AC church member until he heard the preaching of Billy Sunday and Billy Graham. Through these ministries he began to believe that he was not a Christian at all because he never placed his faith in Jesus Christ for salvation, but had simply "joined the church" thinking this was the way to salvation. With his new faith came a zeal for evangelism and missions. He set out to change the Apostolic Christian Church. What he sought was wholesale change, not only in the customs and traditions of the church, but in their foundational doctrines. Junie advocated that salvation was by grace through faith in Jesus Christ alone, that one is complete in Christ, that one is secure eternally in Christ.

This immediately began a division within the church. It brought Junie into direct conflict with his uncles Theo and Henry Beer, who were ministers in the church. It brought direct conflict with most of his cousins. The division, for the most part, went along family lines. The fiercest antagonists were the descendants of Otto Beer, Senior and Ezra Beer. Junie Beer will quickly point out two facts in retrospect. First, that he was a "Beer" and knew how to fight. Secondly, that he was full of zeal, but it was a zeal that was misguided.

The split in the church came when the Apostolic Elders annulled the memberships of Junie and his followers. The Otto Beer, Senior family all left the Milford AC Church after this. Some other members also left, but the biggest defections were in the

A Lifetime of Church

married "friends of the church," people who attended, but who were not members. A split also occurred in the Bremen Apostolic Christian Church shortly thereafter and the two groups came together to form a new church in Bremen, Indiana called Community Gospel Church. This new church experienced rapid growth from its inception.

This split was devastating to my parents and grandparents. It produced bitterness among some on both sides that still lingers 40 years later. What hurt my family also hurt me. This doctrine of "once saved always saved" was incomprehensible to me. ***Anyone*** knew this was ridiculous. What's more, I was around some of Junie's followers who claimed to be Christians. They sure did not look or act like what I thought Christians should look and act like. Besides, they were too young to be Christians. What was worse than the split itself was the fact that Junie kept "bothering" people who stayed with the church. My Uncle Pat and Aunt Laurel Speicher began to believe like Junie did. They became zealous in their faith, too. We all noticed that Uncle Pat stopped smoking and drinking right away. This was impressive. Lifestyle changes like this tended to catch the attention of Apostolic people and it might have been an effective part of a testimony to challenge my parents' thinking if Uncle Pat had approached them right. Sadly, this was not to be the case. Instead of exalting Christ and seeking common ground with Dad as a basis for discussion about his new faith, Uncle Pat needled my dad about being an Apostolic. On one occasion he told my dad that we kids did not respect him because he was an Apostolic. He also spoke negatively about the AC Church and about Grandpa Beer to my brothers and me. I never once remember him trying to share the Gospel with me. I only remember the negative comments. I was very hurt by this when I was a boy. This sort of behavior only made me angry. It did nothing to advance the cause of Christ.

The incident, however, which caused the most bitterness in the Theo Beer family took place when Otto Beer, Senior died. His children were willing to allow his funeral to be in the Apostolic Christian Church if one of their ministers could have the service. It is a time honored tradition that only Apostolic ministers speak in Apostolic Christian Churches, so the funeral was held at Bremen in the Community Gospel Church.

Three things are prominent in my mind about how I felt as a boy about all of this. First, they were wrong and we were right. Secondly, they were just looking for an easy way to heaven. Thirdly, they were against my family and my church, so I was against them. What I **do not** remember anyone in my parents' family debating at the time is what the **scripture** had to say about the doctrines in dispute.

In the Milford Apostolic Christian Church there was anger and uncertainty in the aftermath. It still was not known how "solid" a number of people still were. Some were sympathetic to Junie, yet decided to stay. For most, however, one thing was certain: Junie Beer was a troublemaker who had forsaken his family, his heritage, his church, and, in the minds of some, his salvation, in order to pursue heretical beliefs.

The Milford Apostolic Christian Church received a strong dose of encouragement several years later when a dozen or so young people repented and joined the church. Among them was my big brother Ned.

Chapter Eighteen

In the fall of 1964 I entered the sixth grade. It was a big deal for me because the sixth grade was in the same building as the middle school and high school. My brothers Ned and Ted were entering their sophomore and freshman years, respectively.

This year marked a distinctly new era in my life. This was about the time that my turtle collecting ended. The mint days were now over on the farm. Ned took full-time summer work and I do not remember Ted being around much. Without the Ritzman boys around in the summers things were not as exciting on the farm. I was now Dad's main helper and this was fine with me. I liked most of the work and I still had a lot of independence. I helped Dad on the farm until the summer following my graduation from high school.

With my former "cronies" not around much I began to spend most of my free time with my two best friends, Dave ("Toad") Baumgartner and Roger ("Wieners") Korenstra. We spent a lot of time at each other's houses, which were within a mile of each other. At first we got back and forth with bicycles. This soon graduated to tractors. By the time we were in eighth grade we were driving pick-up trucks around the neighborhood. When we had hay to bale, they were the ones we hired. We three often helped other farmers with their hay and straw baling, too. We generally just hung out together. There was never any serious mischief.

The only other person I spent much time with in those days was my cousin Fred Hoerr. We had great times together spearing frogs.

It sounds strange now, but we loved it. Several evenings a week in the summers we would ride our bikes to one of the local drain ditches. On our shoulders were our spears — six-foot long wooden poles with four-pronged metal spears on the end. We would sneak along the ditch banks and spear frogs. Once we had accumulated enough we had family frog leg dinners. I remember one hot summer day deciding to go to the ditch that ran through the muck ground on the family farm to spear frogs by myself. I rode my bicycle and carried my frog spear on my shoulder. All I was wearing was a pair of blue jean shorts. I turned off the road and followed a lane we had through the muck to the ditch. My mind was somewhere other than with my body when I suddenly felt a jolt and landed flat on my back on the ground. As my mind cleared I realized that I had run into a length of barbed wire that was stretched across the lane as part of a cow pasture. I also realized that I was covered with blood. Checking myself out I found six gashes, beginning on my stomach, under the armpit and along the arm, and finishing with my chin. Most of them were an inch or two long and they were deep. I knew I needed to get home so I picked up my bike and began running along side of it. I remember thinking after a while "Why am I doing this?" and began to ride it instead. I decided to stop at a neighbor lady's house that was about half way home. This woman was very kind. It was common for us to stop at her house for cookies when we went by. This day she took me in. She washed the wounds and I remember her putting Porter's Salve on them before sending me home. Mom was shocked and worried when I got home, but after consulting with Grandma Beer it was decided that I was patched up enough and a visit to the doctor was unnecessary. I was pretty sore for a day or two but was soon back at my regular activities. The wounds did not heal pretty, producing puffy scars. At least two of them should have been stitched, but if they had been I would not have been able to see my children's eyes fill with wonder the first time I showed them the scars and told them the story. It was a bizarre little incident, but well worth it. It made a great story.

    My only experience dealing with a bully happened in the spring following my sixth grade year. A boy in the grade ahead of me had been bullying some others and me throughout the year. It was not anything serious, just annoying. Had I breathed a word of it to Ted the problem would have been taken care of instantly. But the bully was a friend at times, too, so I never said anything. One evening this boy, Tom Beer, and I were at the Milford Cemetery together. It was probably around Memorial Day. The bully was punching and pushing us, as usual. For some reason this time I pushed back. We were instantly in a full-fledged fight. To my astonishment, I soon had him on the ground in a "head-lock" and he gave up. At this Tom Beer went ballistic, laughing and shouting "Kevin got beat up by a sixth grader!" I had never gotten into a fight before. It was totally out of character for me.

This fight instantly became "front page" news in the Milford middle school community. I was famous. Kevin was humiliated and demanding a rematch. He was telling everyone that I had only beaten him in wrestling, that there was no way I could beat him in boxing. I was content to rest on my laurels. This was until Ted got wind of what was going on. He immediately set about promoting a rematch. He was so effective that I am sure Don King must have studied under him. The rematch came before the end of the summer. Mom had taken us to the beach to swim at Waubee Lake one evening. Ted and some of his friends soon had Kevin and me lined up for a boxing match. We all went to the nearby abandoned Boy Scout Cabin. I wanted no part of this. I was scared to death. Ted, however, was not to be denied. He told us to start boxing, so we did. The rematch did not amount to much. Before long I had Kevin in a corner and he quit. Ted could not have been prouder. I was on top of the world — until we got back to the beach where Mom was. It turns out that Tom Beer's brother Kent had told her about the big fight.

After this I had the reputation of a "tough" guy. It would have been hard to find a kid less inclined to fight than I was, but this strange twist of events had others thinking of me this way. Helping reinforce this image was the fact that I ran around with Wieners Korenstra. He was big, strong, athletic, and aggressive. Toad Baumgartner was no wimp either. By the time I retired undefeated in eighth grade, I was involved in four more scrapes, only one of which bears mentioning. It took place when the Milford Apostolic Christian Church Sunday School went on a weekend bus trip to visit the Detroit Apostolic Christian Church Sunday School. By Sunday evening of that weekend Ted and a boy from Detroit were testing each other. During the farewell dinner the Detroit boy was telling Ted that his little brother was pretty tough. To this Ted replied — loud enough for me to hear it two tables away — "My little brother could beat that fat a.. brother of yours!" I tried to act like I did not hear it, but soon everyone was outside waiting for the fight to take place. The little brother was a lot bigger than I was, but he was fat and not too athletic. Ted and his big brother had bet a dollar over who would win.

It was not much of a fight. Ted had made me box with boxing gloves enough that I subdued the brother easily. I threw one punch too many, though, because I got hit hard from behind and fell into a ditch. As I gathered myself and looked up I saw that Ted and the big brother were in a serious fight. It turns out that my opponent's big brother had knocked me into the ditch to stop the fight. Ted, in turn, attacked him. Soon the big brother gave up, but not until he had a bloody nose, a loose tooth, and a torn suit. He was wearing a "Nehru" jacket that the Beatles had made popular at the time. The final insult to this boy was that Ted made him pay the dollar bet. Ted remembers that our uncle Phil Beer took him aside and told him that he was very ashamed of him for what had happened. He really felt terrible after he realized the embarrassment he had caused. I feel bad as I look back on this incident too. This had to be a humiliation for these brothers, especially the younger one. I hate to cause anyone to have a bad day. I always have and this is one time I definitely did. I wonder what became of them.

In seventh grade I was on the baseball team, my first participation on an official school team. Our first game was with Syracuse. I was really nervous because I was the only seventh grader to "start" on the eighth grade team. I played second base. The pressure was really on because I was the leadoff batter. To my delight, I got a hit. I know we lost the game, but I have no more memories of the rest of the season whatsoever. My baseball playing ended with this season. I chose to play football instead thereafter. When I was a sophomore in high school, baseball was changed to a spring sport, but I never took it up again. This was probably a mistake because I now feel baseball was the sport I had the most ability in.

A Lifetime of Church

In seventh grade I had my first official girlfriend. She was an eighth grader and we went together until the following summer. Our dads had played together on the same basketball team in high school. I was sure this had to have some significance, but we eventually broke up anyway. This was the first girlfriend that I kissed. It was quite an experience, but not too romantic, as it took place on a fan bus on the way home from a basketball game — with all of our friends watching.

Football became a sport in our school in the fall of my eighth grade year. We felt we had really made the "big time" when we received our first equipment. It was *so* exciting to actually play in it. Our season consisted of only two games, one with each of the corporation schools, Syracuse and North Webster. The first game was at North Webster. They played Syracuse. We Milford kids went to watch. Syracuse beat them very badly and we were sure the same thing would happen to us the next week. They were big and had a really fast running back.

The day of the big game we were very nervous. Once we got started, however, we saw that we had over-estimated them — or under-estimated ourselves. We won the game 21-7. I played halfback and cornerback. My friend Wieners Korenstra was our fullback and was the star of the game. The Syracuse kids tried to shoulder-tackle him and he just carried them along. The next week we beat North Webster easily to complete our undefeated season!

My middle school athletic experience also included basketball and track. We had better than average teams and I was a better than average athlete. I always enjoyed playing sports but I knew early on that I would never be famous for doing so, like my father.

Over the years I have not come across a religious denomination, other than the Apostolic Christian Church, that views all high school athletics as worldly and something that Christians are to have no part of. I spent my first thirty-three years in the denomination and never did clearly understand why they hold this view. We were told that participation in sports was competitive and unbecoming a Christian. We were told that attendance at sports activities was "emulation." We were told that regarding sports we should be like the Apostle Paul who said that when he became a man he "put away childish things." Indeed, one would not be allowed to be a member of the AC church, which is equated with being "a Christian" and participate in organized sports. It was a strong denominational conviction. "Good" church members stayed away from sports altogether. They did not participate in them or attend them. They did not coach in Little League or attend when their children played. "Nominal" members would attend sports activities of their younger children and an occasional special activity of their older children. "Bad" members would attend all their children's sports activities. They would attend some sports activities even when their children were not involved. Some would even go so far as to coach their children's Little League teams. The likelihood of such people of teaching Sunday school or holding an office in the church was very remote without agreeing to refrain from such activities in the future.

As I mentioned earlier, this view of sports probably was rooted in the desire of immigrant farmers to keep their boys home to help on the farm. Perpetuating the view in the present day is difficult to do. There are a number of reasons why. First, there is no reasonable basis in scripture for condemning all sports interests and activities as worldly. Secondly, the church condones other activities that are equally competitive. A flash point example of this among members of the Milford Apostolic Christian Church was 4-H and the County Fair. The competition to win here is as intense as in any sporting event, yet even "good" members wholeheartedly attend these activities. Other examples are high school drama, music, and choir. These activities often contain less-than-wholesome material, yet the church allows its members to attend them and support their children. I never understood why it was considered acceptable for Apostolic children to play in organized sports, but worldly for their parents to support them in doing so. Granted, the children have not yet joined the church and are not considered Christians, but one would think that activities considered to be too worldly for member-parents should be considered too worldly for non-member children also. The church leadership is left with empty explanations that only the faithful can accept, like "we have found this to be good" or "we must preserve our precious faith" or "this is a small thing for you to give up for the sake of unity," or "if we start changing, then there will be no end to it and we will be like all the other worldly churches."

A Lifetime of Church

My parents always attended our little league games. This was not a problem with most of the church members, although Grandpa Beer always felt it was necessary to point out to Mom that her time could probably be better spent doing something else. This was especially true when the games were on Wednesday night, the night of mid-week church. Sports attendance began to be a problem when my brothers entered high school. They were athletes and it was not acceptable for Dad and Mom attend their games. Dad and Mom had known this was coming for years. Early in their marriage Dad still played on independent basketball teams. Mom attended until she joined the church. If she attended after this it brought conflict with Grandpa Beer. After they moved to the farm she stopped going altogether because attending was not worth the trouble it caused. Dad's sports days ended when he joined the church and it ceased to be an issue, for the most part, until we boys began to participate in sports.

A turning point came when I was a sixth grader. Ned would have been a sophomore in high school and Ted a freshman. Dad wanted to watch them play basketball and Mom could not see any valid reason why he should not. They knew, however, that conflict with Grandpa Beer and the church would be sure to follow. They had faced an even thornier issue several years before when considering whether to buy a television set or not. The church was strongly opposed to members owning television sets. Dad and Mom had purchased one over Grandpa Beer's objections when they faced the facts that we kids were going to friends' houses to watch TV and that they were going to Dad's brothers' homes to watch TV also. This was the first time that I know of that Mom did not give in to Grandpa Beer's opposition. She struggled greatly with guilt, however, after Grandpa Beer came into their bedroom late one night and told them that we kids would never "repent" (join the Apostolic Christian Church) because of their decision.

Attending Ned and Ted's basketball game for the first time was the result of a long deliberation. When and where to attend was decided in accordance with a foundational legalistic principle: if no one knows what you are doing, then it is all right to do it. I remember the evening very well. The game was played at a neighboring town called Larwill. Dad and I were the ones who went. I remember driving east on US 30 as Dad explained why what we were doing was not wrong but that it was important we keep quiet about it. The evening passed without the "sky falling." By the time Ned and Ted were upperclassmen Dad and Mom openly attended many of their games. I am sure they were considered "nominal members" for doing so, but it would have been hard for them to attain "good member" status under any circumstances.

When Ned repented and joined the church after graduation from high school he attended some of Ted's games. This brought about an ugly confrontation in the church that I remember well. One Sunday evening at a church program I walked into the Sunday school wing of the church. There in the stairwell was one of the "good member" women angrily confronting Mom. I walked by as if I had not noticed, but I remember my stomach churning. Soon someone came to where I was and exclaimed, "Man, they are really fighting!"

When we got home I stood around the corner and listened while Mom explained to Dad what had happened. The "good member" woman was furious because Ned had allegedly asked her "good member" son to attend a basketball game with him. And while she was on the subject she let Mom know how awful Mom was for attending games herself. After all, she pointed out, she and her "good member" husband had not attended when **their** son had played. Dad was in a rage after the explanation. Several days later Grandpa Beer had the two couples together at his house and mediated a peace treaty, but not before Ned and a friend had to apologize to the "good member" family — all this for an alleged invitation to a high school basketball game. Mom later told me that Dad had really scolded the "good member" couple for their public rebuke of her. It made me happy to realize that she was proud of him for aggressively defending her.

One vivid memory and a strange little incident from my middle school years illustrate the degree of my Apostolic Christian Church indoctrination at that point in my life. The vivid memory goes back to a film we watched in class one day. It was a film about the hazards of smoking. In this film they were interviewing a man who was dying of throat cancer. He was smoking a cigarette through a hole in his throat. The man was expressing his sorrow over smoking and ruining his health. I remember him saying "All I have to look forward to is dying and going to be with Jesus." I distinctly remember thinking "This is so sad. You can't go to heaven if you smoke."

Another strange little incident that illustrates my indoctrination took place in my eighth grade year. A new teacher came to the school. He taught science, physical education, and was the eighth grade basketball coach, so I had a lot of exposure to him. We generally got along well, but he had a mean streak and enjoyed needling me about the Apostolic Church. One day he said something which bothered me so I shot back with "I go to church every Sunday and know the Bible better than any of these people, but I'm no hypocrite." He had me where he wanted me and asked "So you *are* a Christian, then?" I replied, "I said I'm no hypocrite. When I get older and join the church I'll do it right." He just laughed at this, but I was angry. Soon after this I overheard my friend Wieners telling someone in astonishment, "Spike was fighting to say he was not a Christian." I remember thinking that they did not understand at all what I was trying to say. As I look back on this, three things strike me about this encounter. First, I *did* know the Bible well. But I only knew the stories and Apostolic cliches. I was woefully ignorant about doctrine. Secondly, there was nothing about the behavior of either my Christ-professing peers or this teacher that made me think they were any different than I was. If they had lived Christ-like lives, perhaps I might have been challenged in my thinking. Thirdly, by this point in my life I clearly held two beliefs about salvation — that young people could not be saved and that joining the Apostolic Christian Church was the way one attained salvation. I'm sure by this point in my life I was pleading with God every day to let me live long enough to do this very thing.

Chapter Nineteen

A chapter in my life that I still feel ashamed about took place mostly in my sixth grade through freshman years. The focus of this sad chapter was a boy named Ronnie. Ronnie was a farm boy who lived several miles to the south of us. He was a classmate of mine throughout school. We went to church together until his family left in the split. Ronnie was active in 4-H and band. He was kind of a quiet boy and a loner. When spoken to he did not have much of a personality. He could be blunt and argumentative as well. He dressed very plainly. He had short hair when it was not in style. Physically, he was chubby and unathletic. I do not know how, when, or why the teasing started, but by middle school it was full-blown. I do know that two things helped perpetuate it. One was the fact that Ronnie fought back. He would fight back verbally with odd expressions that made matters worse. He would fight back physically with unusual techniques like kicking or stabbing with pencils or scratching. Again, all things that made matters worse. The second factor that made matters worse was that his parents fought for him, oftentimes directing their efforts at other kids rather than at the kids' parents.

There was an irony in this whole sad chapter of my life. On the one hand, Ronnie and I got along fairly well face-to-face. I cannot remember a single time that we had "words" with each other. At times I would make an effort to talk with him. I remember one time I felt sorry for him so I sat by him in the gym for a school convocation.

As I was trying to make small talk with him, he turned to me and simply said, "Your breath smells bad." This was typical of Ronnie. The poor guy did nothing to help himself.

So, on the one hand we got along well. On the other hand, though, I was a catalyst behind much of the teasing. The worst antagonist towards Ronnie was Tom Beer. By this time he had the nickname of "Nip" because he had stolen some beer and been caught. This name evolved to "Filthy Nip" when Ronnie called him a "filthy thing" one day. In conversation I began referring to Ronnie as "Big-R" and to Tom as "Filth." Before long our imaginations had developed a situation comedy with their two characters: "Big-R' was the equivalent of "Superman" and "Filthy Nip" was the evil-doer he had to combat. A genius friend of mine even produced a comic strip called *"The Adventures of Big-R."* This whole phenomenon became so well known that our class once burst into laughter when our freshman algebra teacher referred to the big "R" in an equation. The entire class obsessed about a puritanical religious community we studied about in Indiana History that had a name similar to Ronnie's last name.

In the fall of the year many of our homes were the targets of pranks like "TP-ing" or soaping windows. It was soon discovered that Ronnie's dad would get in the car and chase pranksters. This was the worst possible thing he could have done. Soon everyone wanted to try and successfully "prank" Ronnie's house. One evening Ronnie's dad chased some of us in his car. He was on us bumper to bumper with bright lights before we stopped. He was furious and demanded that we come back and clean up what we had thrown in his yard. As we were doing this he demanded to know our names. My friend Toad got bold and proclaimed, "My name is Baumgartner, Dave Baumgartner. My father's name is Hank Baumgartner." To this Ronnie's dad made a slur about Baumgartners. As the rest of us cleaned up Toad and Ronnie's dad stood toe-to-toe trading insults about their respective families. What a scene. From this point on Toad was as bad an antagonist as Filthy Nip.

This chasing game was a very dangerous one. One evening the kids put tape over their license plates and kept fleeing until Ronnie's dad gave up. I was not involved that night but learned later that the chase involved very high speeds.

One afternoon my brother Ted, Toad, and I were in a pick-up truck on our way home from Warsaw. Toad suggested that we drive by Ronnie's. We stopped in front of the house. Toad got out, checked under the hood, got back in, and we drove off. The third time we did this Ronnie's dad came running toward us with his big dog on a leash. I was sitting in the middle of the truck, between Ted and Toad. Toad was the one getting in and out so I was expecting another argument between the two of them. Instead, Ronnie's dad directed his anger at me. He called me the ringleader and began insulting my parents. At this Ted became furious and had to be restrained to keep from fighting him — all of this in the middle of the county road.

By the time I got home Ronnie's dad had already been there. He had unloaded on Dad and Mom and Grandpa Beer about how I had been persecuting him and threatened legal action if it did not stop. Understandably, Dad and Mom were very upset with me. My initial reaction was anger because I really had been an innocent bystander in what had just happened. Also, why did he attack my family and me instead of Toad and his family?

Once I calmed down I began to think rationally about the whole situation. Ronnie's dad had acted shrewdly. While I may have been innocent in this one instance, I often had been the ringleader in the past. Furthermore, he knew that my parents would reign me in. Toad's Dad would have told him to get lost. I felt very bad that I had caused my parents this trouble. I decided that the best thing for me to do would be to go to Ronnie's house and apologize. This is what I did. That same afternoon Ronnie, his folks, and I sat in their kitchen and talked. I listened to what they had to say for quite awhile but it was not as bad as I had expected. I said I was sorry for the trouble I had caused them and asked for their forgiveness. They forgave me and I promised I would not be involved in anything regarding them in the future. I was true to my word in this. As I was driving home I remembered thinking that when I got older and joined the church this would be one home I would not have to visit. The memory of this episode of my life has been a classic case of the forgiving and forgetting. I know God has forgiven me for this many years ago. I know that Ronnie and his parents forgave me. Despite this I still hurt from time to time about the pain Ronnie must have felt during these years. As my own children grew up I often had to fight off worry that God would "pay me back" by hurting them. Intellectually I knew this was not God's way but I still had to war against such thoughts. I can only imagine how hard it must be for those who have had lives of crime or lives of cruelty or lives of failed relationships or lives of abuse to feel truly forgiven and new in Christ. I thank God that the home I was reared in and the values which were instilled in me early on spared me many, many things in my youth which I might otherwise have had to contend with.

Chapter Twenty

In the 1960's the Indiana General Assembly passed the School Consolidation Act. The objective of this legislation was for the many small schools in our state to come together and form new, larger high schools. It was believed that this would streamline secondary education, making more and better opportunities for Indiana children. As we enter our fourth decade since this began, the results are mixed. One thing everyone agrees on is that small communities really suffered when they lost their high schools. Many have since lost their middle schools also.

I had known it was coming throughout middle school, but it was still intimidating when I entered Wawasee High School for the first time in the fall of 1968. The three small communities of Milford, Syracuse, and North Webster had come together to form the school. I was a sophomore. Ted had graduated with the last class at Milford High School. There were twenty-seven kids in his graduating class.

In the fall of 1968, our country was being torn apart from within from race riots in major cities after the assassination of Civil Rights leader Martin Luther King. Like most of white America, I thought King was a troublemaker. I was ignorant of the appalling conditions of blacks in the southern states and their lack of equal justice under the law at the time. I can even remember the first time I saw a black man. I was probably in mid-elementary school and was traveling with Grandpa and Grandma Beer to Akron, Ohio. In a restaurant along the Toll Road I saw two black men sitting at a lunch counter.

I must have stared at them because it is a vivid memory. Up until that moment I thought Mexicans were Negroes. The night Martin Luther King was shot Dad took me to my Sunday school teacher's house for choir practice. As he stepped out to the house to greet me, Dad asked him if he had heard that "They shot King?" He squealed "Yippee!" with glee at the news. I remember thinking this was not appropriate from a Sunday school teacher, but I did not say anything. How sad this all was as I look back. That spring Robert Kennedy was also assassinated after he won the California presidential primary. It was a time of real uncertainty in America.

The country was also in turmoil over the war in Viet Nam. Ned had told me several years before that the war in Viet Nam would get worse than the war in Korea had been before it was all over, and time had proven him right. The government was drafting eighteen and nineteen year-olds right out of high school to fight this jungle war and the casualties were starting to touch most communities in the nation. The nation was mostly in two camps. One was very vocal and felt that the war was illegal and immoral and that we should get out at any cost. The other camp saw the war as necessary to contain the spread of communism. They felt that US honor was at stake and that we should escalate the fighting until we won. Most of small town America was in the latter camp in the summer of 1968. Most were appalled at the lack of respect for authority shown by those in the Anti-War movement. I was solidly behind the government. I viewed the protesters as anti-American cowards. I could not imagine why these protesters did not see the threat that communism was to the world. I was unable to understand why they could not see the evil, brutal, anti-God governments that communism had produced. Surely they did not think this would be good for the world. I also did not agree with the "free sex" and drug use of those in the Anti-War movement. But this all still seemed pretty far away from Milford, Indiana in 1968. It was far more important to me that I fit in well at Wawasee High School.

When I was a little boy, one of my fears was needing to change schools. The very thought of it scared me. But going to Wawasee High School turned out to be no big deal at all. By the first day of school I had already been in football for several weeks and knew a lot of the other boys. Things actually went pretty smoothly the first

A Lifetime of Church

day. In the afternoon the sophomore class met to elect officers. Someone nominated me for student council. I had never given the first thought to student leadership before this. I remember thinking how humiliating it would be if I was not elected, but the worry was short-lived because I was.

Things went well for me in football. I was made a starter at defensive corner back and second-string halfback. Our first game was played on a Saturday afternoon at Wawasee. As we drove the ball down field on our first possession the coach sent me in with a play where I would run the ball. I took the ball from the quarterback and ran around the right end and scored. This is a record that will never be broken in that it was the first touchdown in WHS history. We won the game and ended up having a pretty good year.

In our last game of the season I received some bruised ribs. It was painful but I really did not mind the injury because I was not excited about playing basketball. After a week, however, I joined the basketball practices. It went surprisingly well. By the second game I had enough practices to play. The game was at Concord and I played most of the second half of the JV game. I did well enough that the varsity coach complimented me between games. The next week I played even more, but got my lower lip split open late in the game. One of the JV assistants took me to the doctor's office. He looked at it and decided it needed to be stitched. He said "By the time I numb the area I can be done" and he began. It hurt very badly. I decided if I ever needed stitches again that I would insist on a local anesthetic. The varsity game was over by the time I got back so I went to visit a girl that I was supposed to have a second date with that night. She babied me for a while but the lip was throbbing and I soon went home.

The next day I went rabbit hunting with two friends. As we were walking a rabbit ran across the top of a ridge that was between one of the boys and me. He shot at the rabbit without realizing that I was directly in his line of fire. The dirt sprayed me and I realized that I had been hit. As we checked my head out we realized that I had been very fortunate. Only one BB from the shotgun had hit me. It had gone through a sweatshirt hood and a stocking hat and had lodged in the cartilage of my right ear. We went to Dr. Rheinheimer, who cut the BB out and put several stitches in the cut. I did not think much of this incident until I got home and told Dad and Mom. They were very upset. I would have been too if I was in their shoes.

The next week the JV coach moved me into a starting guard spot. I was not expecting this and began to think I might come to like Wawasee basketball after all. On the Saturday of the game I went rabbit hunting again. We saw more rabbits that day than I ever had before or since. I was running late when Ned came to where we were cleaning the rabbits. He chewed me out and told me to get going or I would miss the game. As I got in the car to leave, he sarcastically shouted, "Lets see you crack it up now!" referring to the car we shared. It was snowing hard and getting dark as I headed home. I saw a car ahead of me that was stopped. I could not figure out why it had its bright lights on as I approached it. In an instant I saw a steel bridge in front of me as I hit it. I realized that I was in a wreck, but my thoughts were scattered. I darkly remember my friend asking me if I was all right. I remember being in the ambulance as Dad and Mom arrived. My mind began to clear in the hospital. It turned out that all I had was a concussion and a very sore neck from hitting the windshield. The car was totaled. The bridge that I had hit was replaced the next summer so it was as wide as the road. The driver of the car with the bright lights on knew it was a narrow bridge and had stopped so I could pass. Poor Ned really felt bad for what he had said as I was leaving. Obviously, I missed the basketball game.

My injuries from the wreck were not serious, but they were chronic. I had headaches, neck aches, and backaches for months afterwards. I quit basketball after the wreck. I did not mind this at all, but I worried Dad would be upset. When he was not upset, I was relieved to be done with it. Wieners and Toad were both on the wrestling team and I began hanging out with them. The coach asked me if I would be interested in learning to "tape up" the athletes. I was soon the tape and injury man. I really enjoyed doing this. I did this for the wrestling and track teams until I graduated.

My Wawasee girlfriend and I were still together as January of my sophomore year rolled around. I wanted to break up with her, but did not want to hurt her feelings. She was nice enough and cute but she was not a good conversationalist. In addition to this, I had not been able to get a girl out of my mind that I had seen the previous summer. I had seen her one night when Wieners and Toad and I were driving around (illegally) in Grandpa Beer's pickup. She was working at the Root Beer stand in Nappanee. I first saw her as she was carrying a tray to a car as we drove around the stand. I thought she was the most beautiful girl I had ever seen. It was like in the movies when the camera focuses on a face and everything else around it blurs. I was "struck" by this first sight to the point that I "felt it" in my stomach. I had immediately set about to find out if she was available, only to learn that she had a boyfriend. I found out that her name was Tammy Sheets.

My brother Ted's wife Sandy had a younger sister named Vicki. She was a year younger than I was and attended NorthWood High School. She and I had become friends. I had an idea that led to a plan. The Wawasee - NorthWood basketball game was coming in a few weeks. My girlfriend worked as a waitress on weekend nights. This seemed to present a good opportunity to have Vicki fix me up with a NorthWood girl. I called Vicki and suggested that I could fix her up if she would fix me up. I did not specifically ask her to ask Tammy but I asked a lot of questions about her, hoping she would take the hint. Why did I not just ask her to ask Tammy? I was very insecure about such matters. I never asked a girl to do anything unless I was sure she would say yes. Vicki must have taken the hint because one week before the game she called to say that Tammy Sheets would be my date for the night. I was so excited. Ted knew it was a big night for me. He made sure I was properly transported, letting me use his 1969 Chevy Nova 396 for the occasion.

That Friday night Vicki and Tammy were at Ted's house in Milford when I picked them up. I walked into their kitchen, where Vicki met me. She said Tammy would be right out. Soon she walked into the kitchen. At the very sight of her I got the chill in the stomach that I had felt the first time I saw her. She had a nervous smile on her face and simply said "Hi." Vicki said, "This is Tammy" (as if I didn't know). She was dressed in a skirt and a NorthWood cheer block top. I immediately took note of the fact that she was "nicely proportioned" (to use Grandpa Theo's terminology) in addition to being beautiful. I started chatting right away but my mind was racing. What was she thinking? Did she think I was staring? Was she disappointed? How can I impress her? Man, she is gorgeous! Don't mess this up, Tom!

She and Vicki rode to the game in Ted's car with me. I noticed she kind of turned toward me with her knees toward the gearshift. This brought the flutter to my stomach again as I mentally noted that the posturing was a good sign. I could not wait for the game to be over so we could leave. As everyone was exiting the gym after the game, a potentially disastrous development presented itself. I rounded the corner and there was my girlfriend! She had gotten off work early and had come to the school to surprise me. She accomplished her objective! I was acting excited to see her when Tammy and Vicki walked past us without so much as a sideward glance. I was grace under pressure as the lies began to issue forth. I explained that I wish I had known she was coming because I had already promised to spend the evening entertaining a freshman cousin from NorthWood. To my shock and delight she believed me. I said I would call her the next day and she left for home. Had I not been so giddy about getting back to Tammy I would have felt really bad about what I had just done.

Tammy and I and Vicki and her date spent several hours driving around before heading back to Ted and Sandy's. Vicki's date left from there. Tammy and I parked Ted's car in the garage and talked for a while. I thought she was staying with Vicki at Ted's. I was thrilled when she asked me to drive her home. As she directed me to where she lived I was stunned. She lived about five miles from where I lived. This was beyond good. When I got home I could not sleep. I kept trying to visualize her in my mind. As I drifted off to sleep my mindset was like the line from the old Herman's Hermits song, "Something Tells Me I'm Into Something Good." Time has proven my initial feelings to be correct. After meeting Tammy I never even considered dating another girl. It was a classic example of love at first sight. It has been over thirty years since this first date and the growth of my love for her still has no end in sight.

Those close to me saw how I was "taken" by Tammy. Soon after we began dating Toad told me that he and Wieners had talked about it and both felt that Tammy and I would "be together for a long time." My classmates were also impressed by their first "visuals." The essence of the initial comments was "Way to go, Spike!" Soon after we began dating Tammy went with Fred Hoerr, Teresa Beer,

Sally Beer, and me on a Sunday evening to sing in the Fort Wayne Apostolic Christian Church. Fred took me aside on the way home and told me "Man, that's by far the best you've done!" I was so proud to be seen with her. I still am.

Having had one date with Tammy I knew it was over with my previous girlfriend. I struggled with a graceful way to break up. I hated the thought of hurting her feelings. As I was trying to figure out what to do, the word spread like wildfire that I had a new girlfriend. Of course it got back to her. Earlier I had told her that I would go with her back to visit her former high school. She came to me after class one day and said "You told me you would go with me to my old school, but I suppose that's not a good idea now, is it?" I said, "No, it probably isn't." She just shook her head and walked away. I felt terrible about what I had done and how I had deceived her, but the happiness of dating Tammy overpowered my guilt. A year later I still felt bad about it so I talked to her and really apologized. She forgave me and said it meant a lot to her that I came to her. When a girl in my class who was familiar with the ways of the Apostolic Church heard about this she asked me "Are you repenting (joining the AC Church) or something?" I remember telling her "No, but if I do join the church some day this is one thing I won't have to take care of."

Chapter Twenty-One

In the spring of my sophomore year in high school I made a decision. It was a decision I made without much thought. Even today I cannot explain why I made it. It involved a leap into an area that I never had any interest in before. It involved a lot of risk of embarrassment if I was not successful, the type of risk I had never been willing to take before. The decision shocked my parents and my friends. It also shocked me, once I thought about what I had decided. It was also a decision that began to give direction to my life. The decision? I decided that I would run for Wawasee High School Student Body President.

I had enjoyed my year on the Student Council. I respected the student body president. He seemed to like the job and was good at it. I also was impressed with the number of activities the student council was in charge of. My cousin, Fred Hoerr, was the Junior class president that first year and had told me he was going to run for student body president instead of running for senior class president the next year. He saw it as the ultimate student office in the school. I had not given any thought to running for the office until that spring when the school announced the application period. That evening Toad and I were discussing the upcoming election as we rode home on the bus. We had just dropped off my cousin Teresa Beer when Toad said, "Spike, you oughta run for it. You could win." As I was discing ground later that day in the "Jess Haab field" I began to think about what he had said. I was enjoying a high level of popularity at high school and I had a lot of friends who would help me. I also remember thinking about how proud my family would be if I won. I also remembered Grandma and Grandpa Beer often speaking about church members who had been so popular and successful in various areas in their youth who then "gave it all up" or "left it all behind them" to join the church. I wanted to be like one of them one day.

The next day I picked up an application and announced my candidacy. People around me were immediately excited and offering to help. Word also came back quickly that my cousin Fred was upset about what I was doing. He was upset because he had decided to run for the office first and he was going to be a senior, while I was going to be a junior. Besides, as it was reported to me, I had no ideas about what the school needed or about how I would lead the school. I was angry about his words at the time, but looking back I know he was right. He *had* told me he was going to run before I had even conceived of the idea. The office *was* considered to be an office for a senior. Furthermore, I *did not* have any ideas about what I wanted to do or how I would do it. I just thought it would be fun to hold the office and have the high visibility and prestige it would bring. While Fred's reasons were more correct and noble, mine were certainly more typical of political aspirants. My parents' first thoughts, when they learned of my intentions, concerned potential conflict in the family. Normally I would have been very sensitive about this too, but this time I was not. As I look back, my parents and Fred's parents were the model of maturity throughout these weeks. I was very impressed by it.

The campaign lasted about two weeks. I had many classmates volunteer to help make signs and pass out literature and distribute "Vote for Spike" buttons. Wieners, Toad, and I, however, conceived the crown jewel of the campaign. At that time Wieners' father was the owner of some large trucks. We decided that we would park a semi trailer at one end of the school parking lot so that it would be in plain view of all students arriving on the morning of the voting. On the side of the trailer, in life-size letters, was "Vote For Spike." This really created a stir in the school. After lunch that day we held a "convocation" in the school gym. The three candidates, Fred, Susie Smith, and I were to give our campaign speeches before the

A Lifetime of Church

student body. I was last and was "shaking in my boots" when I got up. I do not remember a word I said, but I remember my supporters being the loudest in response. From this convocation we went to our homerooms and voted. It was during the last period of the day that one of the teachers, Bob Kitson, called me out of class and told me that I had won. It was quite a thrill when the announcement came over the public address system and I could hear cheers coming down the halls.

As I drove home I tried to comprehend what had just happened. I was so humbled and amazed by how many people had enthusiastically helped. Toad and Wieners had thrown all their political weight behind the effort and I realized that we had made a potent team. Demographically, it was not too hard to see how I had won. The senior class-to-be had two candidates. Their vote was split. I was the only candidate from my junior class-to-be. All I had to do was to get a good share of the two younger classes and I was assured of victory. It was here that my friends and volunteers made a really big difference. I had achieved what I had set out to do and I remember determining in my mind that I would work very hard to prove myself worthy of the job.

When I got home I went in the house and told Mom. She was very happy for me but was worried about Fred and her sister, Marguerite. She said I needed to go and find Dad because he had been a nervous wreck all day. As I walked out to the barn I found him in the haymow area, dying to know, but fearful to hear. He was thrilled at the news and launched into a seemingly endless series of questions. I do not remember any other adults making much of it. When I told Tammy, she was happy but I could tell she did not consider it to be a big deal because her school, NorthWood, did not even have a student body president.

It was a big deal to me, however. The school had enthusiastically taken part and had backed their chosen candidate. There were so many posters that it was hard to find room on the walls to hang them. From this point on I took school far more seriously. It was a turning point for me academically too. From this point on I was a mostly "A" student. I still wonder from time to time why I did it. I wonder whether it was God preparing me for where my life would later go or if it was simply a hasty decision that turned out well.

Perhaps it was a little of both. For sure, though, it changed the way I viewed myself and how others viewed me.

Several weeks after the election the principal told me that the school was sending me to a student leadership conference at Indiana University during the summer. When the time came to go I was apprehensive but it turned out to be an excellent week. Two memories stand out about the week. The one is an odd one, the type of memories I seem to specialize in. I passed a kid in the dorm that was heading in the opposite direction. He asked me "Where are you going?" I answered, in jest, "To heaven, I hope." He immediately replied "You better know (whether you are going to heaven or not)!" This made me instantly angry. I remember thinking that the kid did not need to be so flippant and serious when I was only kidding. Besides, I thought, "That's ridiculous, no one can know if we are going to heaven or not."

The second memory is shared with many millions of others. From the scary early days of the United States and Soviet Union's "space race" I was highly interested in our country's space program. I remember being frightened when the Soviets successfully launched the first orbiting satellite "Sputnik." I recall Ned telling me that we were "way behind" the Russians in space exploration. I was embarrassed when our first televised rocket launch resulted in the rocket blowing up on the launch pad. I remember thinking "no way" when president Kennedy set the national goal of landing a man on the moon and returning him safely to earth by the end of the decade. I remember sitting in Harry Good's barber chair watching news coverage of an unmanned camera craft crashing into the moon's surface. From the Mercury manned flights, through the Gemini program, until the Apollo program I had intently followed NASA's every move. From the tragic failure and astronaut deaths of the first Apollo mission through the fantastic successes of the late sixties, I had breathlessly followed it all. Now, in the summer of 1969, we were actually going to try a manned moon landing.

The rocket had taken off for the moon before I left for the student leadership conference. We had been informed after a morning session that Neil Armstrong and Buzz Aldrin had safely landed. That night a large group of us gathered around a TV and breathlessly watched as Neil Armstrong climbed down the ladder and stepped onto the surface of the moon. When he uttered the words "That's one small step for man, one giant leap for mankind," our group erupted in cheering and applause. We had done it! We had beaten the Russians. I was so proud to be an American. It was a desperately needed bit of good news in our country that at the time was embroiled in the Viet Nam war, race riots, and breakdown in our social and moral order. I remember thinking that such an amazing scientific and technological accomplishment would have to help restore faith in our government and quiet our critics. This evening was truly one of the proudest moments of my life.

Chapter Twenty-Two

Anyone who has played high school football knows the sense of resignation with which one approaches the "two-a-day" practices of a new season. The coaches understandably want to get the most out of these early practices. Much needs to be learned and the team needs to become physically fit. To achieve these objectives, coaches push their players to the limit. Our coaches were no exception. I never have experienced anything more physically demanding than these twice-daily practices.

As I approached my junior year in high school I was not as excited as I had been the year before. This was understandable when one considers what a year I had just come through — a new school, a new girlfriend, a new political office — how could the coming year possibly measure up? Despite my lack of zeal, I began football "two-a-days" on August 15th. It was tough, but turned out to be fun once we got started. In those days part of the "toughening up" process included fluid deprivation during practice. All we were given to drink until the end of practice was a small paper cup (about 30ml) of Gatorade and a salt tablet. This would universally be deemed to be dangerous today, but then it was the standard.

One particularly hot day I went home after the morning practice and spent the afternoon baling hay. While baling I received a sting from a bumblebee. I was not feeling well when I left for the evening practice. The practice seemed especially hard. As we were finishing up with sprints I remembered feeling numb in my arms and legs and my head was pounding. The next thing I knew I was being loaded into an ambulance. I regained my thoughts in the Goshen Hospital Emergency Room. They put me on IV fluids to treat what they called "heat prostration" and kept me for the night. By the morning I was fine. I took the day off and resumed practice the next day. I never thought much of this incident until years later. Now I realize that this was yet another time that God spared me for the future.

I was very excited as we approached the football season. Playing in the games made every minute of the "two-a-days" worth it. Our pre-season "Jamboree" was held at Wawasee that year. We were scheduled to play Dekalb High School in the second quarter. I had retained my starting corner back position from the year before. In addition, I was to play on all three special teams and back up Russ Mikel at halfback. On our first play that night, I covered a wide receiver. When the play was a running play into the line, I pivoted on my left foot to go over and help out. As I did this the flanker I was covering put a shoulder block on my left ankle. Ouch! I knew I was in trouble instantly. I managed to hobble to the sideline by myself, but it felt like I had a hot coal in the joint. When we got to the hospital an x-ray confirmed my fears. My left fibula was fractured about one inch above the ankle. The doctor put a long plaster cast on it and sent me home. That night it swelled up (of course) and was very painful. After a few days the swelling began to subside, as did the pain. I was pretty discouraged by this turn of events. I remember marveling about how I could have been so unlucky to go through the hassle of the two-a-days and to break my leg on the **first play** of the season. With this injury, football was over for the season for me. Life did go on, however. School was fun. I enjoyed being the student body president. Tammy and I had become inseparable.

In the spring of my junior year my brother Ned was married to Deb Wuethrich from the Francisville, Indiana Apostolic Christian Church. We had felt he would marry another Apostolic girl whom he had dated before they had repented, but for some months before their engagement he had hinted to me that he was more interested in Deb. He had gotten to know her through the single groups of the respective churches. Their engagement came about in the usual way: Ned — his parents — his Elder — her Elder — her parents — Deb — and back again. Once the engagement was announced in the respective churches, it was time for Ned to visit Francisville and Deb to visit Milford. When Deb came to Milford for the weekend she was understandably very nervous. On Sunday morning Dad came in from milking and yelled up the stairs that it was 9:30 (Church started at 10:00) and that everyone needed to hurry. We all knew he was teasing but Deb did not. She still laughs at the remembrance of her panic.

The next step in the wedding process was for our families to meet. According to protocol we went to meet the Wuethrichs in Francisville. We were to drive there on a Sunday afternoon for dinner. I remember my Dad fretting for weeks in advance about having to say the prayer before the meal we would share. This was customary that the visiting father says this prayer, assuming the father was a brother in the church.

To one not familiar with the Apostolic Christian Church it may seem strange that one would worry himself sick over saying a prayer aloud before a meal. Even as I was growing up, however, I understood that how a brother in the church prayed aloud was a strong indicator of at least two things. First, it was a measure of the brother's spiritual maturity. After each church service it is asked from the pulpit that a brother close in prayer. This is also asked at each noon meal on Sunday and at all church social functions. If a brother volunteers, it is assumed that his "spiritual house" is in order. If he prays eloquently it is an act worthy of honor. In a typical congregation any "good member," speaking off the record, would be able to describe the quality of any other brother's typical prayer. Grandpa and Grandma Beer often described men in the church by how they prayed. Any description of a church service would include who prayed and how they did. A "good prayer" would be long enough to include all the standard requests for blessings: the Elders, the ministers, the sick, the shut-ins, the sermon, the church. It would also include pleas for the repentance of unbelievers, for grace to overcome temptation, and for forgiveness of our "mistakes and shortcomings (not "our sin")." In addition, any "good prayer" would incorporate a number of time-honored cliches like "our precious faith," or "the sick, the suffering, the sorrowing," or "the old age, the orphans, and the widowers" to express the points. Others especially note embellishment of any of these standard facets and anything specifically prayed about. For a prayer to be a good one it must also be spoken with enough volume, with clarity, at a pleasing rate, and (especially) in "King James" English.

The second thing an ability to pray well indicated was a brother's potential for advancement. In the Apostolic Christian Church all teaching of adults, all preaching, and all church announcements are done by the Elder or one of the ministers. The only other public speaking to adults is done by the head church trustee at the annual business meeting. Non-minister or Elder brothers teach in the Sunday school classes, but they only go through high school age. Listening to public prayers, therefore, is essentially the only way for the church membership to evaluate the communicative skills of a brother for a speaking office in the church.

These factors create an atmosphere of great pressure for young and middle age brothers who are called on to pray or who volunteer to pray. Offices in the church are never to be aspired to. To do so would be viewed as prideful and seeking after vainglory. They are to be humbly accepted as God's will when they are attained. A brother should therefore be willing to pray, but not too willing. He should volunteer to pray, but not too often. It is a shame to not pray at all or to pray poorly. The sum of the matter is that public praying in the Apostolic Christian Church requires a delicate balancing of many factors to be done acceptably.

In this social and religious context it is very understandable why it was hard for my father to pray aloud in public. On the one hand, he was a member in good standing in the church. As such he was "eligible" to offer prayer. On the other hand, he had an unreasonable fear of speaking in front of others and would not do it unless he was put on the spot. Being around Grandpa and Grandma Beer and other established members a lot he was fully aware of how one's prayers were "graded." For him it was like a person who has never learned to dance being at a party where everyone else knows how to dance. Even though the individual would be fully capable of learning to dance he does not want to out of fear of being laughed at or watched. In such a case it is safer and easier to just sit it out and let others go ahead.

Nevertheless, when our family drove to Francisville to meet the Wuethrichs, Dad did his duty and said the prayer before the meal. I cannot remember a word he said, but I clearly remember thinking that he did a good job. I also remember him asking me the next day if I thought he did OK. Poor Dad — what a "fish out of water" he was in that denomination!

Deb's brother Brad and I were the same age and became friends instantly. It is a friendship that has lasted until this day. The marriage of Ned and Deb is an example of an Apostolic marriage which has worked out beautifully. It produced four special children who have always been closer to me than just nephews and nieces. In addition, our extended families have held common interests and have remained close throughout the years.

Chapter Twenty-Three

My senior year in high school is pretty much a non-event in my memory. I had been re-elected as student body president at the end of my junior year, but the campaign lacked the fervor of the first one. One classmate ran against me. Neither one of us had any dramatic campaign stunts or significant issues to debate. It basically boiled down to a popularity contest that I was fortunate enough to win.

The clear highlight of my senior year was my final football season. It was the first year that our school was a full member of the Northern Lakes Conference and our class had a goal of winning the conference in our first year. After an uneventful preseason we had our first game, which we won in a blowout. I clearly remember the Warsaw paper asking the question, "Is West Noble that bad or is Wawasee that good?" The article concluded by noting that our next game against perennial powerhouse Rochester would answer the question.

The next week we shocked everyone, including ourselves, by beating Rochester in a close game. It was the roughest game I ever played in. I was covered with bruises the next day. We were confident of achieving our goal at that point. The next two games were as bad for us as our first two were good for us. I missed both of them with a "hip pointer" injury that I had received during practice — the most painful injury I ever remember having. The team rallied, however, and our record was six wins and two losses going into our game with NorthWood. The stakes were very high for this game. Our records were the same and the winner would still have a chance to win at least a share of the NLC Championship. Greater than this, though, was the fact that NorthWood was Tammy's high school.

For me the game was one of those things in life which one wants really, really badly, but seldom gets. This one went my way. We won the game 6 to 3 and I have never forgotten the thrill. After this victory all we had to do was to beat Warsaw the following Wednesday and we would achieve our long-standing team goal. Anyone who has lived life for a while can probably guess the outcome of this story. Even though Warsaw had an average team that year, they were at the top of their game for us. They did not beat us. The problem was that we did not beat them, either. We tied 8 to 8. Our season ended with 7 wins, 2 losses, and 1 tie. We finished second in the NLC as a result of the tie. There was a locker room full of tears that night.

With the end of football came the onset of a minor, but prolonged, period of melancholy for me. Everything I had looked forward to in school was now over. I did not know what I wanted to do in the future. I was sure I would go to college but had no zeal to do it. I knew I was not right with God, but "joining the church" was something reserved for the distant future. I attended the school functions and headed the student council, but I really did not find joy in either realm. I enjoyed the wrestling season. Wieners and Toad were on the team and the team was dominant. I was the "tape-up" and injury man. I also handled the public address system at home meets.

The one truly exciting area of my life was Tammy. We had been inseparable for two years. We had long before determined we would be married after high school and were actively fantasizing about our future. Once in a while she would come to Apostolic Christian Church events with me. By this time I had already made significant progress in making her "see" the hypocrisy of all churches other than mine. I am sure I often spoke of how I would one day be a committed and sincere Christian husband. I remember her asking once why I did not just be a committed Christian now. I told her that I just "wasn't ready." I am sure she thought this did not make any sense, but we were too much in love to let such questions interfere. Looking back I see now that neither one of us had the slightest clue about the ramifications of what I had "bought into" intellectually. I know for sure that I was absolutely unaware of the magnitude of the religious and cultural forces that were slowly "pulling me in."

In the spring of my senior year I took a second shift job at Syracuse Rubber. I needed to earn more money for college than my folks could pay me to work on the farm. Working the second shift allowed me to help at home some also. I left school early to begin the 3:00 p.m. to 11:00 p.m. shift each day. The job was hot and miserable as I operated a press that made molded rubber parts. It seemed like every day I received a new burn or two on my arms. Once I started this job I quickly realized how good I had it on the farm. Perseverance and hard work were two things I had learned from my youth and after several weeks I was in a routine that was not so bad. One thing I definitely liked about the job was that I did not have to milk the cows anymore, although I really had not done much milking since football had begun the previous fall. One other thing that this job brought about was isolation from all my friends except Toad. He and I always went to church activities together. We were also of one mind regarding the merits of the Apostolic Christian Church.

In the summer following my senior year Syracuse Rubber closed for one week over the July 4th week to do inventory. That week I went canoeing with a group of friends in Wisconsin. The group was comprised of Toad, his brother Charlie, Brad Wuethrich, Phil Price, Jerry Gutwein, and me. The week began with a Sunday at the Francisville Apostolic Christian Church, where one of our friends was being baptized. Tammy had ridden there with us so we could spend the day together before I left. After church I drove her back to Milford and returned to Francisville. When I got back we all left for the Flambeau River area in Wisconsin. By the next morning we were there.

This week was one of the most fun weeks I ever had. The river was wild and the area primitive. We enjoyed ourselves as only teenage boys out on their own for the first time can. The fact that there were "beer bars" where eighteen year-olds could drink helped. Our group had a strange dynamic. While we were all "AC boys" only Phil and Jerry were "members." Brad Wuethrich had "begun repenting" the previous fall, but had "fallen away" because he was not able to quit smoking. Thus four of us smoked, drank, and frolicked while two would only frolic. This really convicted the four of us throughout the week and we discussed it more than once. On the last day I told Toad and Brad that I was never going to smoke again. Brad replied that he knew better than to make statements like that because he could never live up to them. This stabbed me in the heart because I knew Brad's inability to quit smoking was the reason he "stopped repenting." I was sure, though, that things would be different with me in the future when I repented.

For one to "start to repent" (or to decide to "join the church') is a very serious act. To make a "beginning" and to turn back is a great shame to both one's self and one's family. Individuals who "turn back" very seldom make another "beginning." Brad Wuethrich was the only person I ever knew to be an exception to this, as he did join the Apostolic Christian Church years later.

The only thing that is worse than "turning back" is to become a member and to "fall away." To many devout members, a member leaving the church is equivalent to rejecting one's salvation — even if it is to go to another church. Every person raised in the Apostolic Christian Church understands the seriousness of a decision to join the church and the life-long commitment it will require.

The living illustration of this subject in my own generation was a cousin of mine named Dave Beer. If ever there was a child of promise in an Apostolic Christian Church family it was Dave. Against all odds he was born to his polio-stricken mother while she was confined to an "iron lung." From his childhood adult Apostolic members saw him as the very definition of potential. He was handsome, articulate, bright, athletic, and respectful of authority. Farming was his passion, as were 4H and FFA. As the youngest son he was longing for the day when he could get out of school and actively begin the process of taking over and enlarging his father's farming operation. In addition to all this he was zealous for the religious traditions of his forefathers. As Dave came into his mid-teenage years it would have been hard to imagine a young man more suited for Apostolic Christian Church membership and eventual church leadership than he.

Dave began "repenting" with the same group as my brother

Ned. He had just finished his junior year in high school and had broken up with a long-term non-Apostolic girlfriend whose family was moving to another state. When young people repent they are expected to break up with any boyfriends or girlfriends they have and are to have no more contact with them. From the beginning they are to confine their social activities to church functions with church kids and "dating" is over until a proposal for marriage is accepted within the church. Having a steady girlfriend and repenting while still in high school would normally be two "red flags" within the church membership because of the multiplied social stress of the "world," but no one seemed concerned that Dave would not "remain true" to his repentance. Indeed, everything in his repentance process apparently went smoothly and he was baptized along with the rest of the converts. All that remained for Dave was to graduate from high school, get married, and start a family on his way to prominence within the church and the farming community — or so it seemed.

Only a few months had passed before the "young group" in the church noticed that Dave was not attending their functions like he should. Then the entire church (and community) was stunned when Dave "ran away" to Kentucky to see his former girlfriend. The unthinkable had happened. Dave was "falling away." He was "turning his back on God." He was "disgracing his family." He was "breaking his vows to remain true and faithful unto the end." When Peter wrote in II Peter 2:20-22 "If they have escaped the corruption of the world by knowing our Lord and Savior Jesus Christ and are again entangled in it and overcome, they are worse off at the end than they were at the beginning. It would have been better for them not to have known the way of righteousness, than to have known it and then to turn their backs on the sacred command that was passed on the them." In the minds of most of the church members, this applied to Dave.

It was not long before Dave returned home. The church did not impose formal discipline on him this first time because he maintained that he and his girlfriend did not "sin" — but the damage had been done. Dave could never again be "seen" in the eyes of the church membership and leadership apart from this failure. In the eyes of the church, however, things went from bad to worse for

Dave. It was not long until Dave's membership was revoked and he was not a part of the Apostolic Christian Church anymore. Much more could be written about Dave and his life after this era, but from his own testimony four things are notable: (1) Dave came to realize that he had never come to terms with Jesus Christ in the Apostolic Church. Rather, he had zealously "joined the church," thinking that it was the way to salvation. Later he placed his faith in Jesus Christ and was born again. (2) When he began to "fall away" he received only scolding and rejection. Compassion and encouragement were nowhere to be found. (3) When he failed as an Apostolic he lost his sense of worth to all he held dear. (4) Home, as he had known it, ceased to exist once he was out of the Apostolic Christian Church. Today Dave lives in Alaska and works in the commercial fishing industry.

There are two sides to every story. It is possible that there is much more that I was not aware of which contributed to Dave's "fall from grace" in the Apostolic Christian Church, but this was the picture before me at age eighteen in 1971. To "turn out like Dave Beer" was something that no young Milford Apostolic convert ever wanted to have happen to them. This was a frequently offered warning to any convert who showed the first sign of opposition to the ways of the church. Certainly no one wanted to shame their family and church like that! It was a warning which was very effective in controlling one's behavior — as I was soon to find out.

Chapter Twenty-Four

In late July, 1971, I had come to a crossroad in my life. I knew I needed to go to college but I did not want to. I had no idea what I wanted to study. I missed the social life I had enjoyed in high school and knew that such carefree days were behind me. I enrolled in Manchester College because Ned had gone there. He had made arrangements for me to room with Phil Price. Brad Wuethrich would be in the adjacent room. Toad would soon leave for Vincennes University. Wieners, whom I had not had contact with over the summer, was headed to Anderson College. Everything seemed to be changing as I approached the month of August. The only unquestionable right spot for me at that time was my relationship with Tammy. In my youthful exuberance I was *sure* that it was not possible for two people to be more in love and more ideally suited for one another than we were.

In the Apostolic Christian Church the most likely time for a young person to repent and join the church is the period following graduation from high school. Subtle reminders of this and covert pressures unto this end are applied to young people during this time frame. I was no exception to this. Neither was my friend Toad. We were both prime candidates in that we had both been faithful attenders of church youth activities and Sunday school. In addition, we had "member" friends and were well connected through my family.

Toad and I had spoken often of our intentions to join the church some day, but it was always in a future context. By August 1971, the "future" had come. One evening after I dropped Tammy off at the Root Beer stand in Nappanee for work, I picked up Toad and we went to my brother Ned's to play cards. He and Deb lived in a mobile home in Milford. After we had played for a while the conversation turned to matters of faith. I was not in the mood to talk about repenting, so I lay down on their couch to sleep. As I tried to go to sleep I listened to Ned and Deb encouraging Toad. He was feeling called to repent, but was afraid of the commitment. The more they talked, the more I tried to tune them out, but a spiritual battle was going on in my heart also. There was no question in my mind that I was a sinner. There was no question in my mind that I was lost and needed a Savior. I had known these facts for years. What was different at this point in time was that I knew I had run out of excuses for refusing to surrender my life to Jesus Christ. As I lay there on the couch and considered the magnitude of Jesus' sacrifice to pay the penalty for my sin the walls of my resistance began to fall down. By the time Toad and I got into my 1965 VW Bug for the drive home I was quietly sobbing. We did not say a word to each other as I drove him home. As I headed for home I knew I had to surrender my life to God. I also knew my first stop had to be at Tammy's house to tell her.

When I arrived at Tammy's house she met me at the front door. She saw that I was crying and looked scared. I simply said "I have to give my life to the Lord." She looked bewildered but said "Good, that's great." I said "You realize that it means I won't be able to see you if I do this." She said "It's OK. You need to do this." I told her that "No matter what happens remember that I love you more than anything in the world." As I drove home I prayed to God to forgive my sin. I surrendered my life to Him and asked Jesus Christ to be my Savior.

Upon arriving home I went upstairs to Dad and Mom's room. I simply said "I need to give my life to the Lord." Mom immediately walked to the phone and called Grandpa Beer. He came right over to the house. After hearing me confess all my sins and praying with me he said "I want a clean break with that girl. No strings attached." I can still feel pain in my stomach, the kind you feel when the school principal calls you out of class, when he said this. As he left he added, "That poor woman (referring to Grandma Beer) is on her knees right now praying for you." This was undoubtedly a true statement, but I'm sure it was added as an "arm twist" to keep me from wavering from the task before me.

As I lay down in my bed I began to think about the ramifications of my decision, but the thrill of feeling God's forgiveness and acceptance outweighed these thoughts and I was soon asleep.

The next morning I awakened with a pounding headache. My stomach felt like it was on fire. I felt a bit nauseated. As I lay there the reality of what I had done began to sink in. I was on the horns of a dilemma. On the one hand, I had given my life to Christ. I felt at peace with this decision. I had no thought of wavering in this commitment. I do not recall ever doubting that I was right with God after my decision to surrender my life to Him. On the other hand, I had now begun to "repent," to join the Apostolic Christian Church. There in my room, a mere few hours later I already bitterly regretted this. I cannot remember ever feeling more "trapped" than I did that first morning. Why had I acted so impulsively? Why had I not thought my decision through or allowed the announcement of it to wait until morning? How could I possibly abruptly drop Tammy like this? I did not see how doing this could in any way be the right thing to do. Warring against these thoughts was the crushing weight of knowing that my family and the church would be counting on me to see this through. What in the world was I going to do?

When I finally went downstairs Dad was sitting at the dining room table. He made some small talk before bluntly asking "Are you going to stick with this?" Not thinking I had a choice, I simply replied, "Yes." If anyone had given me an "out" I would have taken it in an instant at this point. In retrospect, I realize now that with this simple answer to Dad I missed my best opportunity to change the course of events. I know that Dad would have supported me at that point if I had decided to wait. I am sure that I would have crushing opposition from Grandpa Beer, however. I do not remember Mom being around that morning. The first order of business, in my mind, was to get some communication to Tammy. I drove to Ned and Deb's to ask Deb to call Tammy and explain the situation. When I told Deb that I had given my life to the Lord she rejoiced and hugged me. I remember being stiff as board, feeling devoid of joy. All I wanted to do was cry. Deb agreed to call Tammy. When they talked later that day, it was the first time that Tammy realized that all communication between us was cut off and that unless she became a member of the Apostolic Christian Church, we were finished.

Thus began what I now call "Dark August," 1971. I cannot find words to express the emptiness, the guilt, and the hopelessness I felt at that time. I was obsessed with finding a way to ease Tammy's heartache. I was humiliated as I imagined what Tammy's family was thinking about me. My guilt over what was happening seemed to be tearing my heart right out of my chest. Anyone who knows me knows that hurting someone, even if they are in the wrong or deserve it, is the thing that I will try the hardest to avoid. But in August 1971, I found myself in the position of causing the greatest hurt to the person I loved the most. And compounding this was the fact that I could not even speak to her and explain myself. And compounding this was the fact that I could not talk to anyone else about it, either. Whenever I even mentioned her name or openly longed for her, Grandpa Beer told me that I "was giving the devil a foothold." Thirty years later I can still feel the pain of my emotional state at that time.

I have two distinct memories from the first week of "Dark August." The first was Mom telling me that one of her AC member cousins came to her upon hearing that I was repenting. She knew about Tammy and me and admonished Mom "Don't let him do it, Mim. With that girlfriend, he will turn out just like Dave Beer!" I doubt that Mom had an agenda in telling this to me but I took it as a warning of the peril I faced if I began to waver. The second memory was from my first week in church. That morning everyone welcomed me and said they were praying for me, as they had on the previous Wednesday evening. Even though I could not speak about it to anyone I knew my only hope for a way out of my predicament was for Tammy to join the AC church also. All week long I thought Tammy would come to church and go to Sunday school with my cousin Teresa. I had no rational basis for expecting this. Her family was actively involved in their own church. While Tammy had come with me to many church youth events, she only came to Sunday school once. Her parents, rightly so, had insisted that they go to church as a family as long as she was in school and living at home. Nevertheless, I nurtured this irrational hope throughout that first week.

After the morning service I went to the church basement with the rest of the adults for the noon lunch and fellowship time. I sat in a seat that had a direct line of sight into the high school Sunday school room. When the door opened and I saw that Tammy was not there my heart sank. I had the "shock feeling" in my stomach. I had to fight hard not to cry. This was the low point, the low point of my life to this day.

Chapter Twenty-Five

After the first week of "Dark August" my head began to clear. I do not remember the exact sequence, but some facts became established in my mind. I now realize that these facts became the framework both for my behavior and for working to resolve my circumstances.

The first fact was that I was firm in my commitment to live for Christ. I never entertained a single thought of trying to walk away from my new life as a Christian. I knew that honoring God with my life meant no more smoking, drinking, profanity, and lust. I knew it also included living in a way that others would see Christ in me. This I was determined to do, with God's help, even though I was not sure what such a life consisted of. The church also stipulated that I take off my class ring, cut my hair, attend no movies or sporting events, make restitution for past wrongs, and discontinue non-church social activities. Even at this early stage, the only church stipulation that I accomplished with the heart-felt purpose of honoring God was making restitution for past wrongs. In at least two instances I received a blessing doing this because I was able to explain to the person that I was doing it because I had become a Christian. The other church stipulations I went along with because I knew it was expected of me. There was no blessing in it for me because I did it out of obligation for the purpose of pleasing other members of the Apostolic Christian Church.

Being one who loved to joke and tease and mouth off, I wondered what would be appropriate changes in my personality. I was conflicted because a sober countenance and simple practicality in one's conduct were the ideals for Apostolic Christian Church converts. I expressed my concerns about this to Mom early on. She replied, "Tom, becoming a Christian does not change who you are. You are still Tom Speicher and it would be wrong for you to try and change your personality." This was a good bit of advice. It helped a lot to be told it was OK to be happy and out-going.

The second conclusion I arrived at was that I had no one to blame but myself for my predicament. No one had forced me to "repent." I knew what the church expected of converts. I should have thought it through and not have acted so impulsively. To this day I can only attribute my sudden decision to surrender my life to Christ to God sovereignly drawing me to Himself and momentarily blinding me to my social and religious context. It took many years to begin to understand His timing.

My third conclusion was that what was happening to Tammy was not right. I could not think of a single thing in the Bible that I could use to justify it. Grandpa Beer said it was necessary because Jesus said in Matthew 6:33 to *"Seek ye first the Kingdom of God and His righteousness and all these things will be added unto you."* Grandpa also pointed out that the greatest commandment was *"...Love the Lord your God with all your heart and with all your soul and with all your mind."* He said this meant being willing to give up everything for God, including Tammy. No matter how I read these passages I could not see how it meant treating her the way we were. I refused to believe that calling this wrong was "giving Satan a foothold" or "not putting God first." It did not change my circumstances, but it helped me emotionally to stop feeling guilty for disagreeing with the church about this.

I also concluded that I would be alone in my quest to communicate with Tammy and to treat her right. I knew that no church member would help me. They would all see it as helping me "turn out like Dave Beer." I knew my older brother Ned would not help me. The system had worked for him, bringing him a good wife after he had "put God first." I knew Grandpa Beer would not help me. He remained adamant that it be a "clean break with no strings attached."

I knew that Dad and Mom would not help me either. What was

different with them was that I knew they both agreed with me that what was happening with Tammy was wrong. Early on I heard them arguing about the situation. I remember Dad shouting, "It's not right. He can't drop her like this. I like that girl!" Mom countered with "I know it's not right. But the church isn't going to change and if Tom backs off now, what will become of him?" I was glad to hear this sentiment, but I knew Dad would not prevail over Mom and that Mom would always obey Grandpa Beer. Nothing would change this dynamic.

Surrounded by an army of "warners," I warmly recall two enclaves of encouragement in these early days. One of them was my friend Dave (Toad) Baumgartner. He had begun repenting the day after I did. He and I could openly talk about anything. Not having any family in the Apostolic Christian Church, he was free to speak his mind and share his misgivings with me. He was also free to hear me out without feeling compelled to warn me about my feelings. We were in absolute agreement that giving our lives to Christ was the only thing that really mattered and the thing we needed to focus on. He was especially good at encouraging me about Tammy. He would encourage me, "God will work it out if it's meant to be, Spike. We can get through this." I do not know how I would have maintained my sanity in those days without him.

The second enclave of encouragement was my Grandma Beer. This godly woman was the embodiment of the gift of encouragement. Whatever I knew about God's mercy, His grace, and His unconditional love I had learned from her. I had learned it from her words, but much more so from her life. Grandma Beer was a staunch supporter of the Apostolic Christian Church. What made her different than most Apostolic Christian Church members I knew over the years was her selfless preoccupation to serve God by serving others. Her day-to-day life was marked by the "Fruit of the Spirit" (Galatians 5:22). Her devotion to God called her to a much higher standard than mere membership in the Apostolic Christian Church did. In those early days I could sit at her table and cry about my heartache and misgivings. She listened. She did not scold me or warn me or tell me I should not feel the way I did. Instead, she encouraged me. She reminded me about how much God loved me and that Christ was interceding for me. She reminded me of how

God had always blessed His people and cared for them. She told me God would not have called me to salvation just to make me miserable. She said she was sure God would either work it out with Tammy or He would work out something even better. She said "I know you can't imagine how this can be right now, Tommy. You just have to have faith that God wants the best for you and be willing to wait for it." A little of this and a few cookies were worth their weight in gold.

My final conclusion in those early days was that doing what was right in the sight of God would not always be doing what the Apostolic Christian Church thought was right. This sounds like an obvious fact in retrospect, but it was a fresh realization at the time. Prior to this point in my life it had never occurred to me that Grandpa Beer and his church could be wrong about anything. I know that arriving at this conclusion was good and right, but how I determined to live in the light of the conclusion was not good and right. Why? Because I should have stood up for what I believed no matter what the cost. Instead I counted the cost of not submitting to the church regarding Tammy — a stopping of the repentance process, humiliating Grandpa Beer and my family, being compared to Dave Beer — and decided I would covertly try and reach out to her. Thus began the honing of a skill that legalists universally seem to possess: an ability to "get around" the rules that are not convenient.

I spoke to Tammy three times during "Dark August." One time was sanctioned and two times were clandestine. The first time was on Sunday afternoon at the end of the second week. Mom shocked me when she suggested I do it. After listening to stern warnings not to misbehave or to give her any "false hope" I left for Tammy's house. We talked in her back yard for about an hour. Her mom came out and took some pictures. I was so embarrassed to see her mother, wondering what she must be thinking. It was so good to see Tammy again and talk with her. It was especially hard to leave. I told her how much I loved her, but I was very careful not to hug or kiss her because I knew I would be asked about it when I got home. I wanted so badly to beg her to join my so that we could still get married, but I had been warned not to even suggest this because it might interfere with God's will for my life.

The second time we talked was after I got off work one night.

Tammy had driven to Syracuse and was waiting for me in the factory parking lot. I was not expecting her. I do not remember much about this conversation, but I remember being worried that someone would see us talking. We talked a third time one night at her house. I do not remember anything about this except for the fact that her father came into the kitchen from the bedroom to talk to me. He said "I don't want you talking to Tammy about church anymore. It just upsets her and makes her miserable." As he turned to leave he asked me "What are you trying to do, Tom? This just doesn't make any sense." I must have given him some kind of an answer laced with Apostolic Christian Church cliches, because he replied "Tom, that sounds like the Amish. There isn't a Christian alive who doesn't need to ask for forgiveness for something every day." I remember I just started crying when he left because my hopelessness was now even more profound with opposition from both sides. Tammy saved the day by saying simply "It's OK. Don't worry about it. Somehow this is going to work out." It was great to hear her say this, but I sure did not see how her words could come true.

Sometime during the blurred days of "Dark August," the United States held its annual military draft lottery. Because I was eighteen, I was included. I saw Toad after work one night. He told me he had watched the lottery on TV and said "Spike, I think you got a low number." The next morning Dad told me that October 14th (my birthday) was drawn 36th. The war in Viet Nam was beginning to wind down as the South Viet Namese Army was doing more of the fighting. The draft was beginning to wind down too. Still, that year's draft went up to 150 — a lot higher than 36. And there would be no student deferments for my group. With a Presidential election looming, President Nixon had ended this politically unpopular provision in the draft system. I do not remember any feelings one way or the other about getting a low draft number. The likelihood of my getting drafted into the army seemed the least of my concerns in August 1971.

Chapter Twenty-Six

One of the traditions of the Indiana Apostolic Christian Churches is to have an annual youth fellowship day at Camp Alexander Mack in Milford. The day consists of a church service and Sunday school in the morning, followed by a meal. The afternoon is fellowship time. In the early evening there is another service in which choirs from all the churches participate. They all do several songs individually and sing several songs as a combined choir to end the evening. A preacher from one of the churches has a "short" sermon in between. The day is intended to be an opportunity for non-member high schoolers from the various churches to get to know each other better and (hopefully) form life-long friendships. Young single AC members also attend, but they usually arrive after their respective church's afternoon services. There is generally not too much interaction between the members and non-members. This fellowship day is traditionally held on the last Sunday in August, before everyone begins a new school year.

I remember this day as one of the nicer things the AC Church did. I always looked forward to it as a young person. It was a day when all the non-member boys tried to out do each other "sowing their wild oats." The summer following my junior year in high school the event was expanded to include Saturday and Sunday, with a sleepover for non-members. The young people loved this, but it was discontinued after two years. We were told the reason for discontinuing the two-day format was because the Saturday night bonfire service was too much like "worshiping the fire god." The real reason was likely because the service was deemed to be too evangelical. At the time some preachers from the Fort Wayne AC Church were taking an evangelical approach to the young people. These men (and most of their congregation) were soon no longer a part of the denomination.

In the summer of 1971, Tammy and I had both made reservations to attend the weekend. Tammy was to room with my cousin Teresa Beer. When I began repenting I could no longer attend. As the weekend approached Tammy had no intention of going, thinking she was no longer welcome. Teresa called her and invited her to come as her guest. It is likely that Teresa was encouraged to do this by my mom or her dad. Whatever the case, I heard that Tammy was going to attend and I was thrilled.

Tammy recalls that at this point in my repentance she still had no clear understanding of the AC ways. She knew she had been dumped and cut off from communication with me. Why this had happened was still obscure. She had received Jesus Christ as her Savior years before. In her mind it seemed that it was all the more right that we be together now that I had also become a Christian. The week before the Camp Mack weekend she had reached her low point. At the end of their church service an invitation was given to receive Christ as Savior or to rededicate one's life to Christ. Tammy did not "go forward" but she surrendered her life to God's will and rededicated her life to Christ. She knew that events had gone beyond her control and emptied herself for God to take over. She recalls that the heartache was still there after this, but that the frustration was diminished. If there was to be a resolution of our situation, God was going to have to bring it about.

At Camp Mack on the Saturday night of the following week, Tammy explained to my cousin Teresa what she had done the previous week at her parents' church. Being an AC young person herself, Teresa understood this to mean that Tammy had "begun to repent." Accordingly, she took Tammy to talk to one of the AC preachers who was there. The preacher was a man from the Fort Wayne AC Church named Verlin Stoller. As one who would soon be deemed by the church to be too evangelical, he was (in retrospect) the very best person she could have spoken to that night. He encouraged

Tammy. They prayed together. When they were finished, he told her it would be a good idea for her to talk to Theo Beer in the near future. Unwittingly, Tammy had begun "repenting" in the eyes of the AC Church.

When I arrived at Camp Mack that Sunday evening, someone told me that Tammy was repenting. I cannot explain how I felt upon hearing this except to say that my chest and abdomen felt like they were in the death clutch of a large reticulated python. Could this possibly be true? Two days later I drove up our lane at home and saw Tammy's orange VW Beetle parked at Grandpa Beer's house. I distinctly remember peeking through a crack in the curtains of my room, hoping to get a peek at her as she left. When Grandpa Beer confirmed to me that Tammy was joining the church I was beyond elated. Even his stern warning that I not "get my hopes up" or "try to contact her" could not diminish my joy. For the first time in a month I had reason for optimism. I was confident now that I would not "turn out like Dave Beer." His girlfriend never joined the church. Her parents were adamantly opposed to her becoming an AC. Tammy's parents (amazingly) were willing to allow her to join. Dave and his girlfriend never did get back together. I was sure from this day on that Tammy and I would get back together. Dave's circumstances and mine were now very different.

I knew now that all I had to do was to avoid "falling into sin" and I would soon be a member of the church. All the family would be so proud of me. I would be continuing the traditions of my forefathers. Other church members would view my parents as being "successful parents." But most of all Grandpa Beer would be so proud to be able to baptize another grandchild as a member of the church.

Tempering this joy, however, was a root of bitterness against the Apostolic Christian Church repentance process. Instinctively, I knew that what Tammy and I had just gone through was not right. I knew that there was no way God could have been glorified by it. I was not sure why it was not right; it would be many years before I had enough Biblical knowledge to understand it. I just knew it was not right. I was now determined to accomplish three things. First, I wanted to live for Christ. I really did. Beyond what the AC Church spelled out, I was not sure what was involved in living for Christ. But if there was more, I was open to learning what it was. Secondly, I was determined to be married to Tammy. We had planned to be married when she graduated from high school. This now appeared to be an attainable goal. The third thing I was determined to do was to get back into the good graces of Tammy's family. I was sure that they must be bitter at me for what I had put Tammy through. I know I would have been bitter at them if the tables had been turned. My family and most of the AC church members would have been bitter too.

As I entered Manchester College as a freshman in the fall of 1971, I was a very thankful young man who was full of hope.

Chapter Twenty-Seven

My college days did not start out too well. The very first day Brad Wuethrich and I had a mathematics placement test that we were late for because we were playing cards in the dorm. Such occurrences were early indicators that we desperately needed the wives we both eventually married.

I do not remember much about my classes that first year. I attended nearly all of them and I think I did pretty well. They were all required "core" courses. At that time I had no idea what I wanted to major in. Phil Price and I got along great as roommates. Every Wednesday night we would drive to Purdue University to attend the Apostolic Christian Church campus service. I do not remember a thing about the services, but I loved the food before and after. Most nights we played cards before driving to the local Dairy Queen for a bedtime snack. None of us were the definition of a dedicated student.

Once I was at college, Tammy and I began writing letters to each other. In the months of September, October, and November of that year I must have written more letters than in the thirty years since. This was technically a no-no in the eyes of the church. It would have been seen as "running ahead of God." To be doing it without telling anyone was also a no-no. "With confession, the devil flees," Grandpa Beer often reminded me. Our writing would not have been acceptable even if we had already been members. To be writing to one another while we were still repenting would have been especially frowned upon. I knew my heart and I was not convicted about it in the least. I was very careful, however, to write in such a way that the letters would be seen holy and non-presumptuous in the event that they "fell into the wrong hands." Years later Tammy showed me a boxful of these letters. I was so profoundly embarrassed by the cryptic messages and "holy talk" that I burned them all. All sorts of anger welled up in me as the feelings of those sad days came back to me. The saddest aspect of it all is that I was far more concerned about what other human beings thought about the letters than what God thought. Such is the mindset, though, of a legalist.

I had not felt any guilt for sin and separation from God from the moment I surrendered my life to Christ and after several months of repenting I knew I had done all the church required of me. I told Grandpa Beer that I thought I had peace. After a few questions he agreed. When Tammy and Toad told him the same thing, we were "announced to the church" as having found peace. This ushered in a period of time when other members of the church were free to express any concerns to me that they had about my repentance. Two people came to me during this period. One of them felt that my hair was too long. In a world context my hair was very short, but compared to other AC members it probably was a bit shaggy. I agreed to cut it shorter. The second concern was more difficult to respond to. One woman came to me and suggested that I smiled too much. I was surprised by this concern and simply told her that I would pray about it. After praying about it I talked to Grandpa Beer and Mom. Both of them felt this concern was unwarranted. They encouraged me to smile as often as I wanted to. I do not remember any concerns being expressed to Tammy or Toad.

The one possible exception to this involved Tammy. That fall she was one of the nominees for Homecoming Queen. Any other AC convert with family in the church would have flat out refused the nomination. Looser standards were applied to Tammy because "She was not of our people." In addition to this, she went to NorthWood High School. Because no other AC kids went there, very few people knew about it. This was the main reason that no objection was made. One AC member did approach Tammy about her queen candidacy. She told her she was praying for her about her "trial." Tammy, true to form, just thanked her for her concern. To no one's surprise, Tammy was elected Homecoming Queen by the student body. I was not there. It was during a football game and we were not supposed to have an attachment anyway. My Mom was especially troubled by our not being allowed to be there to support Tammy. She even went to the Sheets' to apologize and explain why. I did not know about this at the time. I have no way of proving this, but I am relatively certain that Tammy is the only AC convert in the history of the church to be crowned Homecoming Queen! I give a lot of credit to Grandpa Beer for "looking the other way." Most AC Elders would not have.

Toad, Tammy, and I were announced to the church for "proving and baptism" for the first weekend in December. On the Saturday night before we went in front of the church membership one by one and were proved. The only thing I remember about my own proving is the walk to the front of the church, hoping I would not be asked any questions I could not answer. It must have gone all right because everyone stood in support of me. It went smoothly for Tammy and Toad also. We all had wasted a lot of worry on it.

The Sunday of our baptism was a very happy day for me. In the AC Church baptisms are done during the afternoon service. I remember meeting Tammy's Grandpa Sheets in the men's room over the lunch hour. I must have apologized to him about taking Tammy out of her home church because I remember him saying, "Tom, a house divided against itself cannot stand." After the afternoon sermon, our attendants escorted the three of us to the front of the church to be baptized.

Before being baptized it is tradition that the congregation sing the hymn "Whiter Than Snow." This is traditional for two reasons. The first is because the song loosely summarizes the denomination's view of baptism. The second reason is because it is a beautiful song. As we sang this I was overwhelmed and began to sob. I am sure that most of the congregation was thinking I was crying because I was so thankful to be coming into the church. This was not what I was feeling at all. The tears I was crying were those of the joy one has when a great accomplishment has come to pass or an overwhelming burden has been lifted. I had rejoiced in forgiveness months before. What I rejoiced in at that moment was a profound sense of freedom. I was now about to become a member of the AC Church. In my Grandpa Beer's eyes nothing in my life would ever be more important than this. I now "belonged" to my heritage. I was also fully aware of the fact that the pressure on me to "act right" and to "look right" would be dramatically less as a member of the church than it had been as a convert. These feelings came pouring out of me in the form of tears at that moment in time.

Once we had been baptized we were dismissed to change into dry clothes. As we headed down the back stairs of the church to the basement I put my arm around Tammy's shoulder and whispered that I loved her. I thought no one was around but the three of us. I was wrong. Another young member saw me put my arm around her shoulder and felt it was necessary to warn me later that this was inappropriate. Having changed into dry clothes we went back to the congregation. As we knelt, Grandpa Beer and the visiting Elder placed their hands on us. Grandpa then prayed the "prayer of consecration," during which the Holy Spirit was believed to be "sealed" in us. The final act of the service was for us to be received as members of the church with the "holy kiss." We stood in the front of the church while the congregation filed by. Toad and I were greeted by the "brothers" with the holy kiss and Tammy by the "sisters." Of all the Apostolic worship customs, this one was the most embarrassing to me. I was a member of the denomination for fifteen years and never felt comfortable with it. Even this first day I wondered what Tammy's family and the other visitors were thinking about this as they went through the line.

The fellowship meal following the service was wonderful. It was a very happy occasion, during which the AC Church people tried hard to make Tammy's family feel welcome. On my way back to Manchester College that evening I stopped by Tammy's house. Her parents were very warm and told me they thought it had been a wonderful day. Even if they were just being nice, it meant a lot to me to hear them say it. I had spent the afternoon of Thanksgiving Day with them several weeks before. They had treated me like nothing had ever happened. I still marvel about how gracious they were about these events.

The next weekend was the Speicher family Christmas. Dad and Mom were hosting it. Mom suggested we have Tammy attend. This thrilled me. I remember Mom saying, "If any of them (my Dad's family) ask why Tammy is there we will just announce an early engagement." I wondered why they would think it strange that Tammy was there. None of them were familiar with the Apostolic courting customs. What really caught my attention in Mom's statement, though, was the "early engagement" part. I talked to the folks about us getting engaged that same weekend. They agreed that an early engagement was in order, but thought I should wait at least a couple of weeks.

I went to Grandpa Beer three weeks after our baptism and told him I wanted to "ask for Tammy." I requested that we leave her family out of the customary request loop, thinking that they had gone along with enough AC traditions already. To my surprise, Grandpa agreed to speak to Tammy directly. As I was leaving he told me "I knew it (the engagement) would be soon, but not this soon." I was pretty sure that Tammy would accept my proposal and she did! We were "announced to the church" before the first of the year. I distinctly remember what Grandpa Beer said. After the morning service he got up and simply announced "In Matthew 6:33 Jesus said 'But seek ye first the kingdom of God, and his righteousness; and all these things shall be added unto you.' With this in mind I announce the engagement of Brother Tom Speicher and Sister Tammy Sheets." I am sure that our early engagement raised some eyebrows but no one ever said anything about it to me.

Once Tammy and I were engaged the pressure on us decreased dramatically. It was no longer like we were living life in a "fish bowl." As long as we came to church, dressed right, wore our hair right, and did not "fall into sin" we would be fine in the eyes of the church. Grandpa Beer kept very close tabs on whether we had "fallen into sin" or not. The sad thing about this is that during the months of our engagement there was only one "sin" that anyone was worried about. Indeed, there are only a handful of "sins" that are recognized as such in the lives of AC Church members and they all require varying degrees of church discipline as punishment. Tammy and I never "fell into sin" during the time of our engagement. There were three reasons for this. First, we both sincerely wanted to honor God. Secondly, the Holy Spirit supernaturally enabled us to honor God. And thirdly, we were scared to death of what would happen to us if we did "fall into sin." How sad to think that fear of punishment by the church was considered to be the most important motivator in the minds of those who felt it was necessary to regularly warn us.

Chapter Twenty-Eight

In Luke 10:10 Jesus said, *"I tell you, there is rejoicing in the presence of the angels of God over one sinner who repents."* It is an irony that while there was rejoicing in heaven when I gave my life to Christ there was prolonged misery in my home. It also serves as a sad commentary on what men can do in local assemblies within the Church, the Body of Christ. How this must grieve the heart of God.

As I look back, it is interesting how I remember my parents during my repentance process. Two things were obvious during this time: First, neither Dad nor Mom thought what was happening with Tammy and me was right. Secondly, both Dad and Mom wanted me to "succeed" and become a member of the Apostolic Christian Church. Even this second fact, though, is complex. It was not nearly so much that they wanted me to "succeed" in becoming a member of the church, as it was that they did not want me **to fail** in the quest.

Dad's role in the early days was similar to that of a security guard. He seldom said anything about the church or my repentance. He did not need to. I knew he thought it was harsh and unnecessary. What he did was to make small talk and try to keep things lighthearted, all the time trying to determine if I was all right or not. He seemed ever-present but always on the perimeter.

Mom's role was far more complex. She was fanatical in her care and protection of us children. She would have vigorously opposed anything that hurt us — except the AC Church. While the AC Church and its social ramifications had produced only misery in her life, she felt she deserved nothing more. Believing happiness, self-worth, and her father's approval were inseparably bound to submissively enduring in the AC Church, she felt duty-bound to defend it. It was one thing, though, to endure it herself and quite another thing to see it produce misery in me. This proved to be beyond the ability of even an accomplished martyr like her to endure. In the year following my repentance Mom slowly slid down an unyielding slope into a pit of despair. Mom's own words are helpful in understanding this.

Lewie and I raised our children in the Apostolic Christian Church. I felt so inadequate to be responsible for the souls of my children. I always defended a system that I often disagreed with and questioned. It emphasized humility and self-denial. I couldn't criticize those virtues, but I knew they didn't produce joy. When I read the Bible it was full of the joy of the Lord and peace. I never felt this and it made me wonder. Whenever members got together for fellowship it seemed the time was always spent talking about others; what they were or were not doing.

There were times when I would visit with Christians from other faiths and be amazed at their spiritual conversation. We didn't do that at our church. When a select few wanted to start a Bible study at church, the leadership got very wary. It was not allowed unless led by a church leader. I would hear statements like "When people start carrying their Bible around, there's going to be conflict and trouble." I often would ask Dad or another minister why that was. They would say, "People start to interpret in their own way and this brings discord to our way." When questions were asked about the customs and traditions of the church the answers were always the same. "We have found it to be a good way." The Elders all agreed that this was necessary to be a true child of God.

Most sermons were preached on what has been found to be good as to our looks and life style. People who wore jewelry, make-up, or stylish clothes and hairdos were an offense to the Lord. Nothing was said about one's attitude compared with the outward adornment. I found myself too often being an offense to the membership because of my hair or clothing. It didn't matter that my husband wanted me to look nice. That was beside the point. It didn't matter that God made us to look one way. We should do everything we can to look worse. At least it seemed that's what they wanted.

When my boys played sports I was not supposed to go to their games. Even little league was off limits for church members. It was very hard to obey. When I went I was so scared someone would see me and tell on me. I guess because my Dad was the Elder I was watched more closely. Lewie went and no one complained about him. I felt life was very hard, but I thought it must be worth it to find favor with God. Sundays were always unhappy. I always felt like I offended someone just because I was me. My children, especially my sons, were often in trouble for being just little boys. I guess they thought, "What can you expect with a mother like her?" I nearly always cried on Sundays.

Wednesday nights were a human sacrifice. The music was sad and the sermons were always about how wayward some are and how they grieve the membership. Lewie and I kept going and hoping for the joy we were looking for. When Ned came to Christ and joined the church I thought, "Now I will be a part of it all." It wasn't long before Ned became a target for criticisms. He along with some of the other young members went to some ball games. This brought a group of concerned members to my Dad, the Elder, to chastise me for allowing it. It still amazes me that I kept trying so long. I was going to persevere and so would my family.

Meanwhile Tom had been dating Tammy for quite awhile and it was obvious they were in love. Before Tom left for college he felt the need to accept Christ as his Savior. What should have been joyous time in our lives turned into a nightmare. Tom was instructed to terminate his relationship with Tammy completely. There was no dating allowed in the church among members. Tammy was a member of another church. She was not recognized as a saved person. Tom was physically ill and so was I. The only way they could ever expect to be together again is if Tammy repented and joined the church the same as Tom. This also had to be done with no contact with Tom.

Our faith was tried to the point of breaking. How could mere men make such a judgment in the life of two souls? Tammy was so young and so alone that I was driven to despair again. I couldn't believe God would expect so much from anyone who wanted his salvation. Tammy made the effort and joined the church on her own. She came to church alone while Tom was at school. She fellowshipped with the other young members in the church and she certainly proved herself willing and worthy.

During this time, Tammy was still in high school and she was chosen Homecoming Queen. To this day I could cry that we were not there to see her receive her crown. She was so worthy of the honor and we should have celebrated with her. If the church had known they would have caused trouble. This was a time when I was overwhelmed with life. I had no joy. I had no peace and no comfort in my church. I was in a downward spiral where I felt totally out of control.

I was left to ponder my life in the church. There was never a word of encouragement. Only hints of what should be better. I knew I could never be what was expected of me. I believed that the church's expectations of me must surely be what God also expected. Why was I not able to become what God and the church wanted me to be? Was I always to be at odds with the church (God's people)? I tried so hard not to cause offense and yet even my sons were suffering for my inadequacies.

We lived right beside Dad and Mom, which was a blessing in many ways, but we also lived in a fish bowl. We could do nothing nor go anywhere that Dad didn't know. This often resulted in admonishment and disapproval. This meant if I did something to please Lewie or my children, that didn't have church approval, I had to become sneaky. At night, when I couldn't sleep, I questioned God. Am I so hopeless that I can't ever please you or your people? Other people, outside the church, seemed to like me and enjoy being with me. Was that because I had stooped to their level? The turmoil went on. There seemed to be no answer. I rededicated myself to the cause and tried harder.

For years Mom had been, as it were, at bat with "two strikes" against her. The first strike was emotional. She suffered from depression. The second strike was spiritual. She suffered from legalism and its intrinsic diminishing of her self-esteem and worth. By the spring of 1972 "strike three" was headed her way. This strike was physical. She suffered from uterine polyps that created the need of a hysterectomy. By the spring of 1972, Mom had reached a critical juncture. Physically, she was in misery and had lost a lot of weight. Her weight was around one hundred pounds. Spiritually, she was hopeless, knowing she would never "measure up" or be deemed worthy of God's love. Emotionally she was in a deep state of depression to the point that she was entertaining suicidal thoughts.

Sadly, no one but Dad knew that she was in trouble. He had seen his father in deep depression and was seeing the same signs in Mom. While I did not catch on at the time, I remember him telling me once that Mom had "the same look in her eye" that his dad used to have. He was frantic, but had no idea what to do. Even if he had known where to seek help, it is unlikely that Mom would have allowed it. Like her mother before her, Mom believed silent suffering to be a necessary part of humility and submission. A breakthrough occurred when Mom's brother Alan came home for a visit. Being a physician and not having seen Mom in many months he realized immediately that something was wrong. Alan intervened, as only a Beer is capable of doing. Within days Mom was in the hospital undergoing surgery. Her hysterectomy revealed that she had been in bad shape. While there were still no answers for her emotional and spiritual circumstances, at least we all knew that she had a significant problem. Knowing this helped us measure her needs and consider them in our words and actions. At least she was not entirely alone in her despair anymore.

All of this took place in the months just prior to two significant events in my life. Both of them undoubtedly contributed to Mom's condition. The first event was my approaching induction into the Army. In early 1972 it became apparent that I would be drafted, probably in the spring or early summer. The United States was continuing its withdrawal from Viet Nam, but there was still a lot of fighting and draftees were still being sent. This was a great concern to Dad and Mom, but it was not for me. I secretly hoped I would be sent there. It was not that I had a passion for the cause or any desire to fight. I simply observed that those who went there received a lot of attention. In small town America they were still honored and were thought of as "tough guys." Unfortunately, this is all the incentive most nineteen year-olds need to thoughtlessly place them in harm's way. It is also why young people fight wars. No way I would want such a thing at my age.

The second event that contributed to my mother's decline was my approaching wedding. Mom knew how important it was to mothers to have the privilege of planning their daughter's weddings, particularly if the mother is Pat Sheets and her only daughter is Tammy. Mom also knew that the Apostolic Christian Church performed only one kind of wedding — one that was both humble and consistent with its traditions. In this she was caught again in her life-long dilemma, wanting both to please us (and herself) and to not displease her father and the AC Church.

To his credit, Grandpa Beer tried hard to give us what we wanted. He allowed three things that most AC Elders would not have even considered. The first thing was that we held the wedding on a Sunday evening. AC weddings are traditionally held on Sunday afternoons, after a "shortened" service. Secondly, he allowed Tammy's father to walk her down the aisle. This would have been unheard of anywhere else. At first Grandpa had said no to this. He said it would cause too much offense. I knew this was important to Tammy so I simply talked to the conservative "pillars" in the church about it. They all reminded me about how worldly this was and how important it was for us to preserve the "purity of our precious faith," but when I asked them if they would be offended if Brother Theo allowed it in this special circumstance, they all said no. At this, Grandpa allowed it. The third thing he allowed was for Tammy to wear a long white veil. AC's typically wear a black veil that is about four inches wide and shoulder length. Tammy's veil was about four inches wide, but it was white and about waist length. Tammy had requested that she be allowed to wear a traditional bridal veil. Her mom had purchased one that was very modest, but it had shoulder length white lace around it. Grandpa Beer took this to the other ministers of the Milford church for examination. It was rejected as too worldly. Grandpa suggested that Tammy wear it at our wedding reception. This would have been consistent with tradition, as AC brides wear the traditional black veils during the wedding and then change into a "worldly" veil at their reception. I told Grandpa that I thought this practice was hypocritical. If the "worldly veil" was too worldly for the wedding service then it was too worldly for the reception. The long white veil was our compromise.

Tammy's family had asked if a photographer could take photos during the service. This request was denied. Photographs are never allowed in the AC services. We told the photographer this, but he stepped through a side door and took one anyway. I distinctly remember the flash as we were standing for our vows and thinking we would really be in trouble for it. When I apologized to Grandpa about it later he said he had not even noticed it. I am sure others did, though.

Before the service I remember Grandpa admonishing me for "not having any AC brothers" for my ushers. I did not know this was expected of me and tried to tell him so. He cut me off, saying "I just wanted to point it out to you because some people will be offended that you did not." My friend Wieners and my cousin Fred Hoerr did the ushering and the sky did not fall. If anyone was offended, I never heard it.

All in all, my wedding day was a very happy one. With the exception of the wedding veil, I had kept the negotiations about the wedding particulars from Tammy's parents. They had no idea that what we were doing was scandalous. The church was packed for the service. With the exception of the flash picture, I have no specific memories of it. I do remember Tammy crying as we walked out and saying, "Tom, we're married!" At that point I remember the overwhelming feeling of relief again that I had felt at our baptism. Now that we were married people would **really** leave us alone. We had made it.

The reception was held in the church basement. It went well and everyone seemed happy. After the reception Tammy's mom had some guests in her home. About half of them were members of my family, some of whom were members of the AC Church. When Tammy and I arrived we went upstairs to change clothes. As we were changing Tammy took out the wedding bands we had bought earlier. We had planned to wear them on the sly. She put hers on and handed mine to me with a "Put this on!" look. I put it on but remember being very worried that some of the "members" downstairs would see that we had them on. I think I had my hand in my pocket as much as I could. How sad.

We did not stay long before leaving for our honeymoon. As we left I felt the weight of the world off my shoulders. We had made it! Ahead of us was two weeks of bliss and then I would leave for the Army.

Chapter Twenty-Nine

Our marriage ushered in a new and distinct period in my life. The decade that followed was a very happy one for Tammy and me. In the decade we entered our life's profession, we lived in seven different places, and were blessed with three precious children. It was also a decade in which I experienced no spiritual growth. This bothered no one except God and Tammy, however, because I remained a member in good standing in the Apostolic Christian Church.

Tammy and I drove to Niagra Falls for our honeymoon. On the way we drove through Canada. On the way back we drove through the United States. I do not have many distinct memories of the week, but I do remember the overall feeling of relief. It was so fun just to be "away" and not subject to scrutiny. We thought that life could not get better as we drove around in our 1971 bright blue Chevy Vega.

Before we were married we prepared my old room to stay in before I left for the Army. It turned out that Tammy's Uncle and Aunt, Dick and Norma Rensberger were to be gone on vacation the first week we got back and they offered their house in Nappanee to us. When we arrived home from our honeymoon we stopped at my folks to pick up some things. I carried Tammy "across the threshold" of the house and up to my old room (a fete that I am confident I could still accomplish!).

On our first full day home we spent our time writing "thank you" notes for our wedding gifts. Tammy was excited to cook a special meal for our first official meal together and did so. As we sat down to eat it there was a knock at the door. It was her brother Todd. He had ridden his bicycle into town and stopped by to visit. Our romantic first meal for two thus became a meal for three. One night that week I remember Tammy entertaining for her family also — an amazing display of confidence by my young bride.

I have two other curious memories of that first week. One was that we were invited to some AC Church social activity. I remember being so upset by this. Tammy felt we had to go. I honestly do not remember if we went, but I do recall totally over-reacting to the invitation. This attitude toward church functions was an unfortunate preview of coming attractions for the decade. The second memory took place at Tammy's parents' house. She and I were there for lunch. Everyone but George was home. We all sat in the living room with TV trays. Tammy's mom asked if I would have a prayer before we ate. I agreed and began to pray. As I came to the end one of Tammy's brothers chuckled a bit. By the time I could say "amen" they were all laughing hysterically. They never said why, but I knew it was my "King James" English. I was so embarrassed. From that point on I always tried to avoid saying the prayer. It would have made a lot more sense to just discard the "thees"' and "thous" when I prayed. It has been great, however, being married into a family that has an equally sick sense of humor as my own.

One week before I was inducted into the Army President Nixon announced that there would be no more draftees sent to Viet Nam. This really eased my parents' concerns. A night or two before I left there was a farewell party at my Uncle Bob and Aunt Marguerite Hoerr's. There was a huge turnout. It was humbling to know so many had come to wish me well.

The induction day came much quicker than I expected. When it actually arrived it was not so exciting after all. I needed to be at the draft board office in Warsaw by 5:00 a.m. I remember having a pit in my stomach, as I got dressed. Before leaving I stuck my head into Dad and Mom's room and said goodby. It was very dark as we left the house and drove to Warsaw. I do not recall that we talked much. When we arrived, the Gideons gave a Bible to me. We then stood around and waited. One guy was brought there by his friends, drunk as a skunk. Before long the bus pulled up and it was time to

A Lifetime of Church

leave. It was very tough to say goodbye, but we had no choice. After a long hug Tammy left and I got on the bus. The first leg of the trip was to Wabash where we picked up some more inductees. We then left for Indianapolis. I think I slept some on the way. I know that no one felt like talking.

The induction center was somewhere in downtown Indianapolis. Once we got there we spent the rest of the day going through another physical and getting preliminary paperwork done. In the late afternoon we were all taken into a big formal-looking room for our induction into the Army. Grandpa Beer had warned me about this part. As part of our induction we were to take an oath of allegiance the United States of America. At some point in the oath we were to "swear" this allegiance. Since the Bible warns against swearing oaths (Matthew 5:33-37), we Apostolics were to say "I affirm" instead of "I swear." An AC brother who had been in the Army told me to "just mumble" this part and no one would notice. I did not understand what this was all about at the time, but I was very careful not to use the word "swear" as I took the oath. This was typical of my religious training. I knew many "do" and "do nots" but very few "whys." I was far more concerned that I not say the word "swear" than I was about knowing why Jesus addressed the subject. When the "swearing in" was over, we were all asked to take one step forward to signify that we had officially become a part of the Army. One guy in the first row did not take the step. The swearing in officer stepped over to him and asked, "Are you refusing to step forward and be inducted?" The kid nodded his head "yes." At this, the officer nodded to the military police that were present and simply told them "Take him away and begin legal proceedings." The rest of us were ordered to proceed to the door where a bus was waiting to take us to Fort Knox, Kentucky.

The day that had begun in my room at home ended in an Army barracks in Fort Knox. When we arrived we were taken into a big room full of desks. We were told to sit down. They handed out post card size note cards and told us that we all had to write a short letter to home, telling them where we were and that we were fine. No exceptions. As I lay in my bunk that first night I could hear artillery fire in the distance. I kind of had a sick stomach as I wondered what the next day would bring.

The next morning started just like the movies, with some sergeant stomping in and yelling for us to get up. Thus began a week at the processing center. The first order of business was to get our haircut. Guys with hair ranging from my "sensible" AC haircut to shoulder length all came out looking the same — bald. I remember seeing a lot of head rubbing that week. One day was spent taking tests that seemed to be like the S.A.T. I was feverishly working on my test in a quiet roomful of soldiers when I was scared to death by an unbelievably loud "Wake up!" Some guy behind me was sleeping. The sergeant had screamed this in his ear. It is funny now, but then I feared my heart would pound out of my chest. Other "highlights" of the week included getting our uniforms, personnel folders, "dog tags," and Army ID cards. When I saw my ID card I noted that my date of discharge was July 1974. This was my first real moment of sadness. In July 1972 I knew for sure that July 1974 would *never* come. Surely my life was over! Late in the first week I met a guy from Rittman, Ohio. He was an AC, but was not a member. My Grandma Beer had told me that he was being inducted about the same time as I was and that I should be on the lookout for him. His name was Leon Rufner and we got along well right off the bat. It really helped to get to know someone. Leon and I went through everything together until we landed in Germany five months later.

One specific memory of that first week says a lot about the state of race relations in 1972. It was a Sunday morning. The processing center had shut down for the day. We were allowed to spend our time in and around the barracks. There were probably sixty soldiers in our barracks and at least one third of us were African American. As I was laying my bunk reading the paper, a slow-witted country boy from southern Indiana said really loud, "Hey, did you guys see our drill sergeant? He's a great big nigger!" A long and profound silence followed. One could have heard a pin drop. I rolled over and buried my face in my pillow, desperately trying not to laugh. After what seemed like an eternity, someone at the other end of the barracks said, "How do you guys feel when someone says something stupid like that?" What followed turned out to be excellent discussion about race. It started slowly, but it was civil and very informative. Before I was out of the Army I had the privilege of being friends with guys of different races. What the slow-witted country boy had said was not much different than many of us who lived in all white communities would have said in 1972 if we had not been thinking. While such a thing might still happen today, I believe it would be much less likely. Thank God!

At the end of the first week my group of inductees had been processed. We were ready to begin eight weeks of basic training. I was one of about a half dozen soldiers in my group who had signed up as non-combatants. The Apostolic Christian Church had a policy that all of its people who were drafted go into the military as non-combatants. I did not like this policy, but this is what Grandpa Beer had insisted on when I registered for the draft. Not being one to "rock the boat," I just went along with what he wanted. At the time I never thought the policy would affect me. By the time I actually got drafted I was a member of the AC Church and had no choice in the matter. To go into the military any other way than as a non-combatant would have resulted in me being disciplined by the church. I remember taking the paperwork to request non-combatant status to Grandpa Beer's house when I received it. He filled it out for me because he said that I might not use "the correct phraseology." All I did was sign it. If I had to go to the military today, I would not go as a non-combatant. In any event, those of us who were registered as non-combatants were separated from the group and flown to San Antonio, Texas, where we would undergo modified basic training. This differed from regular basic training in that we received no weapons training. This trip to San Antonio was the first time I had ever flown. It was exciting to walk through the airports in our "dress uniforms."

When we arrived in San Antonio we were bused to Fort Sam Houston. We were taken to the modified basic training center where our leader, Drill Sergeant Martinez, greeted us. I was dismayed to learn that there were not enough soldiers to start training. This meant that we would have to undergo a "zero week." This was a week that did not count towards completing our basic training. To me it meant at least one more week until I could see Tammy. During this week we cleaned, painted, rearranged, picked up trash, scrubbed floors, and cleaned some more. What a bore. By the end of the week we had enough people to begin training.

The Apostolic Christian Church had an apartment rented in San

Antonio as a place where church kids could meet while they were stationed at Fort Sam Houston. On my first weekend in San Antonio two guys who were stationed there came to pick up Leon and me. We went out to eat and got acquainted with them. They were both AC members. One of them was from Minnesota. He had been wounded in Viet Nam while serving as a medic. He was in rehabilitation, awaiting discharge. The other guy was from Ohio. Leon and I were worried about leaving the post, but these guys assured us it would be all right as long as we were back in time for bed check. This turned out to be true. With the exception of the first three weeks of basic training, we met with the other AC soldiers every Saturday night and on Sunday, during the day. If anyone ever checked on us we did not know about it.

Grandpa Beer had warned me that I would probably meet soldiers from the AC "sister churches." He said I would need to be careful because they did some things differently than we did. In the four months I was in San Antonio I met people from both the conservative sister church and the liberal sister church. Our differences were definitely less than profound. The liberal branch allowed a piano in the church. It also allowed members to wear simple wedding bands and short moustaches. The conservative branch required members to drive black cars. Even then I thought these distinctions were silly. They were certainly not worthy of being warned about ahead of time. On Sunday morning we held a church service in the AC apartment. It was pathetic, but it was what I was supposed to do, so I took part.

Basic training turned out to be not as bad as I expected. It was tough, but not as bad as football or basketball conditioning. The hardest part for me was getting up at 4:00 a.m. The most interesting part was meeting soldiers with different beliefs than mine. This was the first time that I was really challenged in my thinking about religion. One day I met a guy from California during a break. He asked me what church I went to. When I told him, he asked me to describe it. I told him that it was a small mid-west denomination that believed the whole Bible and tried to follow all of it. He replied that his church follows the whole Bible, too. He went on to say he was a Seventh Day Adventist. Hearing the tenants of his church, I realized that he and I could not both be right in thinking our respective

A Lifetime of Church

churches followed the "whole Bible." He sure seemed sincere. I also noted that he was capable of stating what he believed and ***why*** he believed it. To my shame, I could not do the same.

Another time I met a guy who told me he was a Mormon. He really believed some strange things. I did not feel threatened by his beliefs, though. The guys who challenged me the most were the Pentecostals. They kept showing Bible passages to me to express their faith. One man who talked with me often was a big black man. He was married and had children. He also was a Pentecostal preacher. One Sunday evening he led a church service on some bleachers nearby. I could hear them singing and clapping and shouting and babbling. I thought they were crazy, but I was so ignorant of Bible doctrine that I was unable to argue with them. It was embarrassing. Even though I did not like our small, private Apostolic Sunday services, it felt good to be around people who did not challenge my thinking. I knew these other guys were wrong, but I was at a loss to say why. Conversely, I could not point to scripture to say why I thought I was right. All I had to fall back on was my family and tradition. How sad. I could not wait to get away from these radicals who were so threatening to my faith.

The nights were the loneliest times for me. Several times I had guard duty in the middle of the night. This consisted of walking around the grounds with a baseball bat. Several other times I just could not sleep. I really missed Tammy in these quiet hours. I fought it off, though, because I knew that every day brought me one day closer to the time Tammy could come to Texas and rejoin me. She was going to be driving to Texas with my Dad and Mom, my sisters Sue and Amy, and her brother Tim after my fourth week of basic training. When that weekend approached I was so excited.

Five weeks had passed when several AC friends drove me to the hotel where Tammy and the others were staying. They knew I was coming but did not know when. As a result, I was able to surprise them. By that time I had become accustomed to my short hair. They were shocked by it. We spent the evening together and then I had to return to the post. The next day was Sunday. We met them and drove to the AC apartment for church. I wanted so badly to get out of going but there was no escape. I knew Tammy's brother Tim would think it was weird. There were four others present in addition to us. After singing some songs, we listened to a taped sermon from some AC Church in Ohio. Near the end of the tape the preacher told a dramatic story about mistaken identity. The real culprit in the story turned out to be "Little Timmy!" At this my sister Sue tried to stifle a giggle. This was all it took to get us going. Mom, Tammy and the serious AC brothers were all appalled at our lack of focus. I still smile at the remembrance of it. After spending the day together they all drove north to Dallas to spend the week with my uncle Alan Beer and his family. It was hard to see them go but I knew they would be back the following weekend.

That week our basic training group did something that angered our drill sergeants. I do not remember for sure, but I think we did not do well in a company inspection. In any event, we were to be confined to the barracks for the weekend. I was devastated. When the weekend came I decided to leave anyway. Leon and I had talked about it and were pretty sure they were bluffing. After all, to confine us for the weekend was to confine themselves. He said he would keep cover for me. After Tammy and the others picked me up I told them the situation. Dad was especially worried. I was driving their car. We needed gas, so I pulled into a gas station. When the attendant came out to wait on us (this was long before self-serve) I was shocked to see that he was our assistant drill sergeant! Needless to say, this put a damper on the weekend. He did not say a word to me other than "Hi." I was pretty sure I would be in big trouble. Maybe I would even be recycled back to the beginning of basic training! But if I was upset by a factor of one, Dad was upset by a factor of ten! What an incredible lack of luck.

I decided that the best thing to do would be to go directly to the drill sergeant about what had happened. This is what I did on Sunday evening. My heart was pounding as I approached him. I simply said I was sorry and that I had no excuse to offer. To my shock and delight he simply said, "Don't worry about it. I was in basic training once myself." There is no way Drill Sergeant Martinez would have done this. I was very fortunate in that all I got out of this incident was a good story to tell. Weeks later I heard that this drill sergeant had an emotional breakdown from post Viet Nam trauma. It is likely that he was easy on me because he was simply fed up with the Army.

A Lifetime of Church

Two weeks later I graduated from basic training. I had flown to Dallas the weekend before to get Tammy. She and I drove back and she moved into an apartment, the former AC apartment. By that time there were enough AC soldiers there that the church rented a bigger apartment in the same complex. Tammy came to the post for the graduation ceremony. She looked fantastic and I was so proud of her. I was one of the few soldiers who had anyone show up for it.

The next phase of my Army training was called Advanced Individual Training (AIT). It consisted of twelve weeks of training to be a medic. During this time I was allowed to live with Tammy off post. It was fun being in our first apartment together. She got a job in a variety store while we were there.

AIT was like being in school. We spent about half the day in class and half the day was devoted to practicing what we learned. I found it very interesting. We were taught how to take vital signs, how to evaluate and stabilize the wounded, how to give shots, how to draw blood, how to stabilize fractures, how to dress and bandage wounds, how to establish sanitary conditions, and basic hospital care of patients. As we neared the end we were taken into the "field" four different times to simulate war. This turned out to be even more fun than playing war with Ted when we were little. They spent the better part of a day once having us practice loading wounded soldiers on a helicopter and flying away. This was a skill that would be used a lot by those going to Viet Nam. I thought my medic training was excellent. What strikes me as I look back is the fact that our field training all seemed so fun. Flying in helicopters, playing "hide and seek" with other units, giving signals with different colored smoke canisters, donning gas masks when tear gas was thrown at us, practicing night compass, patching up the wounded, and the like all seemed so exciting and fun. What a horror it must have been for those who went from this "fun" to the real thing in a few weeks time. No wonder so many combat veterans are so messed up emotionally. Fortunately, I never had to experience this.

In the twelve weeks of AIT Tammy and I spent much of our free time with the other AC dependants and soldiers. We got along very well with them and actually had a lot of fun. The exceptions to this were the weekends that AC preachers came to visit. They all seemed preoccupied with being sure that we were sufficiently "serious" and humble. The exception to this was when Grandpa Beer came. Uncle Bernie drove him and Grandma Beer down for a weekend about mid-way through AIT. Grandpa and Grandma enjoyed the laughter. They even joined in the games we played, like Bible Trivia. What a refreshing change.

Tammy's parents, George and Pat, came to visit one week also. We had a great time. One Saturday we drove to Mexico together. We drove just across the border from Laredo. None of us had ever been there before and we were amazed at the poverty. It was beastly hot. On the way back our Chevy Vega began to overheat. The only solution was to turn the heater up to maximum. What a five-hour long drive! Poor Pat was about beside herself. Years later she still laughed about how miserable she felt. The next day they went with us to the apartment for church. That weekend there was an especially dull and conservative visiting preacher. He did not want us to even play any of our Bible games. He said such games were too competitive. He also felt it was necessary to tell Pat that he understood all about Tammy's struggle in joining the AC church because his parents were "not believers" either. The next morning I overheard Pat asking Tammy "Do all Apostolics think they are the only ones going to heaven?" I was appalled that this minister had said something to her like this. He knew absolutely nothing about Pat Sheets, other than she was not a member of the AC Church. I suppose it is possible that Pat misunderstood him, but I doubt it. His attitude over the weekend made such a comment and attitude seem natural. How embarrassing. When George and Pat flew home later that day it was not too sad because we knew we would be home soon.

Our last week of AIT was a busy one. My brother Ted and his wife Sandy flew down the first of the week. The plan was for them to spend the week and then drive home with us. We had a great first weekend. We went to Mexico again and then drove to Houston to see the Astrodome. I laughed so much during this trip that I had a headache. I remember feeling for the first time that we were really grown up, being able to run around like we were. I have no idea why I remember thinking this, but I do. Late in the week before Ted and Sandy arrived, Tammy and I learned where I would be sent for my permanent station. We were told at "formation" one morning. They called out our names one by one. Most of the guys called before me

A Lifetime of Church

were sent to Korea, but I was sent to Germany. In our three hundred man company about a third went to Korea, a third to the Panama Canal Zone, and a third to Germany. Only two were sent to Viet Nam. Tammy and I were both excited to be going to Germany.

On Monday of our last week our company went into the field for three days. I remember three things well about this final "field" experience. The first memory was that we did a twenty- mile long forced march. This was to show us how it would be if we ever were required to move a long distance in war without vehicles. This was fun. I was in good shape at the time and it was not too hard. The second memory is that we set up a full size field hospital. It was November and a cold front moved through. This required the diesel fuel heaters in our large tent. I was impressed by how efficiently this was put up, about how the whole camp was set up and run. My third memory is of our last night in the field. It was the night that Richard Nixon was re-elected for a second term as president, a term he would not finish. As I was trying to sleep that night, at the other end of the troop tent there was a fierce argument in progress about the presidential election. It had unfortunately divided pretty much along racial lines.

In my mind, however, there was a much different conflict going on. For four months I had been in daily contact with Christians from other denominations, something I had never been exposed to before. I found most of them to be very sincere and committed to Christ. I was humbled by many of their testimonies and their knowledge of the Bible. In these last three days in the field the Pentecostal Christians worked on me to the point that I was very troubled spiritually. They must have sensed that I had very little practical Bible knowledge and that I had an open mind. Their determination caused me to start asking myself if I might be missing something. What if I was? As I lay in my bunk that night I was really troubled. I finally gave in and prayed to God about the situation. I told God that I was totally open and if there was something that I was missing, I wanted it. I was scared about what might happen and about what the implications might be for my religious context, but I was willing. I wanted to know. I lay there praying and waiting for a long time — but nothing happened. I awakened the next morning relieved, but I knew I needed to learn the Bible so I could defend my own faith. Sad to say, but it took ten more years until I got around to following up on this need of mine. One good thing came from this experience, though. I have never again been troubled or threatened by Pentecostal doctrine.

When we got back, we went through AIT graduation and headed for home. It took the four of us two days in our Vega pulling a U-Haul. It was like a dream come true to pull into Milford a full-fledged soldier who would soon be sent overseas.

Chapter Thirty

Time never flies by faster than when one is on vacation. When we left San Antonio we had a little over two weeks before I would need to leave for Germany. The time flew by like the blink of an eye. We celebrated Thanksgiving with our families and we had an early Christmas. The Sheets' came to Dad and Mom's for the early Christmas. I remember how much we laughed and joked together. I was amazed that our families had such similar sick senses of humor. No wonder Tammy has been so tolerant of me over the years!

As the day of my departure drew close I began to have a pit in my stomach. What had seemed so exciting a few weeks before now did not appeal to me at all. The day I left was a typical December day. It was overcast and humid with a light covering of wet snow. It matched my mood beautifully. After Dad finished milking we left for Chicago. Only Dad, Mom, Tammy and I made the trip. Our plans were for Tammy to join me in Germany as soon as I could make arrangements. I had no idea how long it would take, but we were hoping for no longer than a month. It was really tough to say our goodbyes and get on the plane. I knew it might be up to two years until I would see Dad and Mom again. When Dad hugged me it was the first time I had ever seen him cry. I wanted to cry also, but I choked down the tears.

The flight to Philadelphia was somewhat bumpy. I was very sick by the time we landed. I was nauseated and had a pounding headache. From Philadelphia a number of us took a limo to Fort Dix, New Jersey. We arrived around daybreak. Leon Rufner and I met again at Fort Dix. It helped to have a friend there. I only remember two things about the two days we waited there for our flight to Germany. The first memory is just sitting and waiting for hours on end. The second is that one day I was approached by a soldier who wanted to buy "some more weed" (marijuana). Apparently I resembled a local drug dealer. When I told him I did not have any and that I did not smoke it, he was miffed. I do not think he believed me.

On the third day we were notified that we would fly out that night and that we should get our gear packed. At 10:00 p.m. a semi tractor-trailer came to pick us up. We piled into the trailer, which was a large glorified cattle car and were driven to the runway. Every seat on the aircraft was filled as we took off at 11:30 p.m. We landed in Frankfurt, West Germany, in the early afternoon. As we got off the plane they were doing spot checks of our duffel bags. Of course I was one of the lucky ones who got checked. It is an extremely frustrating event to take everything out of a duffel bag for inspection and jam it all back in while others are yelling at the group to hurry. I remember being furious at the MP who obviously was amused at our frustration.

From the airport we were marched to an adjacent military air base to be transported to our final destinations. It was here that Leon Rufner and I parted ways for the first time. He went north and I went south. I was ordered to a small bus that left almost immediately for the Bavarian town of Augsburg, where I was to be stationed at the Thirtieth Field Hospital of the Third Army. The drive to Augsburg took six hours. I was beyond tired, but I was so excited to see the countryside that I fought it off. It was dark by the time we arrived in Augsburg. As soon as we were checked in they sent us to the mess hall to eat. I was starved. We then went back and reported in to the Charge of Quarters (CQ). This guy had no idea what to do with us because they were not expecting any new medics. After standing around for an hour or so a sergeant came in and decided that we could stay in the attic until Monday, when they would figure out what to do with us. As he was explaining this to us, some guy walked in to "sign in." He was in his civilian clothes

A Lifetime of Church

and the sergeant really scolded him for being out of uniform. I remember thinking how fun my stay was going to be if this was a preview of coming attractions. Turned out that this **was** a preview of coming attractions.

The CQ took the three of us to get bedding and then up to the attic. It was a very long narrow room that set atop three other floors. It was dark. It had old hospital beds and odd furniture strewn about. There was so much dust on everything that we could have written in it with our fingers. We flipped three of the mattresses over, put the bedding on, and crawled in. I was so tired that I did not care a bit how ridiculous my accommodations were. I am sure I was asleep before my head hit the pillow.

When I awakened, it was still dark. I was confused as to my whereabouts and why I had not slept longer. I got out of bed and found a restroom. As I was standing there a large, obese soldier came in. He just stood there and stared at me. After a few uneasy moments he walked straight ahead to a wall on the opposite side and violently vomited all over it. I left. On my way back to my bed I took a wrong turn and walked into a room of guys who were smoking marijuana. I am not sure who was more shocked, they or I. When I got back to the attic I heard a church bell ring. I looked at my watch and saw that it was 12:00 midnight. I had slept for twenty-four hours straight! I had never done this before and I have never done it since. What a situation. It was midnight. I was unable to go back to sleep. I was hungry. I did not know a soul. I did not have anything to do or anywhere to go. I was alone in a filthy, dark attic an ocean away from anything familiar.

I stayed in bed another hour or so trying to go back to sleep. No luck. Sometime between then and morning I walked around the compound for a while. Not even the bars were open. When daylight finally came I went to the mess hall and ate. It was a Sunday. The only other memory I have of the day is calling Tammy to tell her I had arrived safely. I had asked around and learned that I would take a taxi to a place where I could call. Someone wrote down what I was supposed to ask for. The taxi driver must have taken me right there because it did not take long. I remember that I had to pay for the call in advance then I went to a bank of phone booths. They dialed the number for me. I was very relieved when Tammy answered. We only had a few minutes and I do not remember a word we said but I do remember being careful not to tell her how miserable I was.

Monday morning finally rolled around. When we met our new commander he acted surprised to see us also. After shuffling some papers he said that he thought some of us were to be sent south to dispensaries. These were medical clinics in the smaller, outlying posts. In the next few days I learned that there were dispensaries in small posts at Bad Toeltz, Bad Ailbing, and Bershtesgaden. As I asked around and looked on maps I began to get excited about leaving Augsburg. It seemed to be a boring, non-descript town. I was told that these other places were in the Bavarian mountains. My commander also told me that I should be able to get post housing for Tammy and me. Mountains and post housing seemed too good to be true. My earliest conversations since arriving had been about the availability of housing for Tammy and me. The news, up to this point, had been all bad. The consistent answer was three-fold: There was no military housing available for any rank below sergeant, off-post housing was scarce, and the scarce off-post housing was both expensive and of poor quality. True to form, I immediately began to worry that plans would change and I would need to remain in Augsburg.

The first week passed quickly. I do not remember much of what went on. I know I was issued white medic uniforms and I think much of the week was spent cleaning the attic we were living in. The hospital wanted to turn it into a ward for an anticipated flu epidemic. Late in the week my commander confirmed that I was going to be sent south, probably to Bad Toeltz. He thought it would be at least a couple of weeks until I was sent there. This information helped because my preoccupation was to get settled as quickly as possible so that Tammy could join me. I was already feeling a bit lonely.

When I learned that I was going to be sent to Germany, Grandpa and Grandma Beer quickly informed me that there was a German family who were members of the Apostolic Christian Church that had opened their home to American AC soldiers for years. Their names were Heinz and Trudy Maurer and they lived south of Frankfurt. I had called them when I arrived in Augsburg. They invited me to come to their home the first weekend. I cannot remember how I got there, but it is likely that another soldier came and picked me up. I am sure I would remember if I had taken a train or a bus. I was warmly received when I arrived. There were several other AC soldiers there in addition to Leon Rufner and myself. Heinz and Trudy lived in a modest house in the small community of Post Neuhitten. The town was very small and lay in the rolling hills near Heilbronn. The Maurers had five children, three of whom were still at home. The children and Trudy spoke English, while Heinz did not. I was fascinated with the house, the community, and the customs. It was like stepping into the pictures of a geography book for me. The meals were great. Trudy cooked a lot like Mom and Grandma Beer. What I especially enjoyed, though, were the desserts. They were beautiful, delicious, and served in the mid-afternoon. I slept in an upstairs room with little or no heat. This was not a problem because the bed was like I was in a sandwich between two feather blankets that were about eighteen inches thick. It was quite an experience. I know it was hard to crawl out of in the morning!

When the Maurers learned that I was married they immediately offered to keep Tammy until I could find housing. This all seemed too good to be true. I promptly called Tammy and told her the situation. She seemed excited as well. Early the next week our plan was in place. Tammy would fly into Frankfurt the following weekend. I would pick her up and we would go to the Maurer's. Sounds simple, right? It was simple at the time, but looking back I am in awe of Tammy's courage. Consider the facts: Tammy was eighteen years old. We had been married a little over six months. She was to get on a plane alone to come to Germany, knowing she might be gone for two years. She was to take one large suitcase. She was coming to Germany to stay with a German family whom she had never met. She knew I was going to be sent to a new unit in a few weeks where we could look for housing. The only thing she knew for sure is that I was in Germany. What a woman! She had often reminded me that I should never doubt her love for me after this act of faith! I am equally amazed at the willingness of George and Pat Sheets to allow Tammy to do this. I have a hard time imagining that I would have been as good about the situation as they were.

The week again passed quickly. Someone drove me to Frankfurt to pick up Tammy. Again, I do not remember for sure who did this. I think it was an AC soldier who was stationed near where the Maurers lived. This was no small favor on his part, as Frankfurt was a long way from Augsburg. I clearly remember looking through a large window at the airport as the passengers on Tammy's flight came off the plane. When I saw her, her eyes were darting about, looking for a familiar face. She was pulling her one large suitcase. I finally got her attention and as I kissed her I noted that she was on the verge of tears. She later told me that if I had not been there she would have turned and got right back on the plane! After an hour or so we arrived at the Maurer's. I was so happy to have Tammy there with me. It was a very special weekend. Tammy enjoyed the company and the culture, but she was not as excited about the food as I was. She also was not impressed with the cold bathroom and bedroom. We both agreed, however, that the thick feather bed was nice. The Maurer's had a daughter who was about our age. I forget her name, but she was very nice. She had an out-of-wedlock toddler child. The two of them and Tammy seemed to get along well right away.

That Sunday we went to church with the Maurer's. It was chilly out, but the sun was bright as we all walked about a mile through what seemed like cow paths to the church. The church was a small, old, one room building. It was packed full for the service. The service was structured like American Apostolic Christian Church services. Of course I could not understand anything. I did recognize some of the melodies from the hymns, though. During the sermon I noticed that there was a marked difference in the dress of the old and young members. The old women were in black with large veils, while the young women were less conservatively dressed than Tammy. I suspected that this might be an issue in the church. Trudy Maurer confirmed this later. She said their Elder was a stern, conservative (I had noticed) bachelor who was showing very little patience with the young people.

Of course, the weekend passed too quickly and it was time for me to go. This time I went back on the train. I remember riding on a packed bus with Tammy and the Maurer's daughter to the train station.

The next week I learned that the military had a hotel in the compound. I could stay there for next to nothing if I wanted to. The only problem was that I could get "bumped" out of my room if the

A Lifetime of Church

hotel filled up and an officer wanted it. Tammy and I talked about it and decided that being together was worth the chance of getting bumped from our room at anytime. We figured in the worst case we would have to rent a German hotel room for a night. So she decided to come on the train to Augsburg. Tammy remembers this as quite an experience. The Maurer's son Peter had walked her to the bus station so early in the morning that it was pitch black out. She recalls having to hold on to his arm tightly because she could not even see her feet. The bus took her to the train station. Once on the train she had to change trains twice to get to Augsburg. All she had to go on was a note from Trudy Maurer listing the towns and track numbers. She recalls this as being far scarier than the flight to Germany. A soldier from Augsburg had driven me to the train station to pick her up. She was right on time. Our separation was over!

We probably stayed in the hotel a week. Each day we would re-register and there always seemed to be plenty of rooms. During the daytime I went to the hospital to work. Tammy spent her time reading, writing letters, and crocheting. She took walks also. In the evenings we took walks and played a lot of Yahtzee. We also had a little cassette tape player that we used for music. I remember we about wore out a "Carpenter's" tape. This sounds really boring in retrospect, but it was exciting. We were so in love and so naive that all we needed was each other's company. I remember that there were a few days that I had to work the midnight shift because there were a lot of soldiers with influenza.

We spent our first Christmas together in this Army hotel. Tammy bought a red candle and crocheted some little green and red "pretties" to put around it. She also bought herself a scarf. She gift wrapped it and was excited to have a present to open. We also celebrated the day by going out for pizza. On Christmas morning we took a taxi to the "phone place" to call home. Tammy had no sooner said "Hello" to her mom than both of them burst into tears. Her dad and I ended up chatting for our allotted minutes! While there would be some other periods of loneliness, this is the only instance that I recall when the loneliness produced tears.

Near the middle of my fourth week in Germany my orders came through that assigned me to the Fifth General Dispensary in Bad Toeltz. For some reason I picked up these orders in the hospital commander's office. He was a medical doctor with the rank of Colonel. As he was quizzing me about where I was going, I answered once with an "Uh-huh" instead of a "Yes sir." He instantly jumped on this and chewed me out, ending with "You talk that way down at Bad Toeltz, son, they will chew you out a lot worse than I am!" I remember being so shocked by his schizophrenic outburst that I made no reply except a meek "Yes sir." From this meeting I was taken to another room where I met the man who was going to take me to Bad Toeltz. His name was Sergeant Goldbaum and he was the chief non-commissioned officer at the Fifth General Dispensary. He was a Jewish man from New York. His manner was gruff but he was very competent and efficient.

We boarded a short military bus for Bad Toeltz in the early afternoon. I think it was just Sergeant Goldbaum, Tammy and me, and some supplies aboard the bus. Tammy and I were giddy about getting to our new home. It was about a three-hour drive from Augsburg to Bad Toeltz. We went through Munich on the way. It was just beginning to get dark as we approached Bad Toeltz. I was watching the countryside through the low-hanging clouds. All of a sudden I gasped as I got my first glimpse of the snow-covered mountains in front of us. I had never seen mountains before. I was so excited. Soon we drove through downtown Bad Toeltz. It looked like a movie set or page out of a history book with its brick streets and ornately painted buildings. When we pulled into Flint Kaserne we got our first look at our new home. The main part of the post was a rectangular set of two story buildings at least one hundred yards long on each side. Sergeant Goldbaum stopped here. He and I went into a building to get some sheets and blankets. We then drove to the north of the rectangular center buildings to a housing area. He took us up a flight of stairs to our new home. He told us that we were in quarters that had been used by German SS Officers before World War II. Here we were, a PFC drafted flunkie and his dependent wife, moving in to what was built for some of Hitler's best. Amazing. The door opened into a hallway. On the right there was a small narrow bedroom, then a bathroom, then a kitchen. On the left was a good-sized bedroom, then a living room. Both the bedroom and the living room opened up to a balcony. Sergeant Goldbaum soon left us, telling me to come in to the dispensary for orientation the next morning. Tammy and I then walked to the PX, which was a general store on the post. There we spent one hundred fifty dollars to set up housekeeping. As we lay down to sleep that night we were dizzy with joy. We were in Bad Toeltz, West Germany. It was our first night in a new apartment. We had spent nearly all of our money. We had no phone, no television. We did not know a soul. Our families were an ocean and half a continent away. Yet that night we could not have imagined how life could get any better.

Chapter Thirty-One

Our first morning in Bad Toeltz was exhilarating. When we stepped out onto our balcony what we saw was like an Alpine mural — green meadows leading to pine forested foothills dusted with snow leading to rocky, snow covered peaks. For two farm kids from Indiana this was quite a sight.

As I set out for the First General Dispensary that first morning, Tammy began to make our apartment a home. Sergeant Goldbaum showed me around the dispensary and introduced me to some of the soldiers. After doing some paperwork he told me that my first job would be to be cross-trained as an X-ray Technician. Heading up the X-ray department was a man named Dave Gong. I soon learned that he had been born in China and had come to the US as a child. He was a bachelor who already had over fifteen years in the Army. Before coming to Germany he had served a tour in Viet Nam. He and I got along well right off the bat. I really enjoyed learning how to take and develop X-rays. Dave was a good teacher. Over time I even got good at reading the X-rays. This was not too great of an accomplishment, though, because we only took X-rays of skeletal problems. Tougher problems like Upper and Lower GI exams and IVP's were sent to the hospital in Augsburg. There were two other jobs that I was trained to do early on. The first was to make up suture kits for the dispensary and sterilize them in an autoclave. I enjoyed this as well. I even had my own little room to work in. My second early duty was to drive the medical bus from Bad Toeltz to

Augsburg, via Munich, once a week. The purpose of this was to take people to medical appointments and to pick up supplies. The first time I went I had to drive a full sized bus. I was not sure where I was going, the roads were narrow, the traffic was bad, and I was unsure of how to read the road signs. This was frightening. After this first time I got to drive the "short-bus" and enjoyed the trips.

My fellow soldiers at the dispensary were a diverse bunch from all over the country. Steve Fugami was a pharmacist from Seattle. Poncho and Gomez were from Los Angeles. Eggie and Cacciatorie were from Philadelphia. Big Joe was from Texas. Vera Nenadovic was a physician from Yugoslavia who was employed by the U.S. Army. John Ogden was a young physician draftee from Michigan. I got along well with all of these people. We all enjoyed our work and had a lot of fun together. None of us liked the Army, but we all had to "play Army" because Bad Toeltz was home to both U.S. Special Forces and the Third Army Non-Commissioned Officer Academy. This "us against them" mentality actually helped create unity among us in the dispensary.

Our first weekend in Bad Toeltz was the New Year's weekend, 1973. On New Years Eve a guy named Steve who was a lab technician at the dispensary invited us to a party. He was married and had a baby girl. Tammy and his wife became friends right away, but they rotated back to the States soon after we came. The only thing I remember about the evening is that I drank several mugs of German beer and quickly realized that it was stronger than American beer. The next morning I awakened with a world-class headache that lasted all day. Tammy and I spent the next day touring the town of Bad Toeltz and Flint Kasern with Dave Gong. It was the first time we had seen the immediate area in the daylight. It still seemed like a fairy tale that we were there.

After the first week Tammy and I fell into a routine. I spent my days at the dispensary. She began babysitting two children, Tommy and Crissy Netzell. Their parents were an American/German couple named Dave and Regina. On some of the first weekends they took us to area guesthouses. These were family-run operations similar to our "bed and breakfast" homes. They were out in the country and reminded me of scenes from Hansel and Gretel. It helped that Regina could speak the language and explain the local points of interest. In the evenings we generally read or went to the post theater. Early on we met a couple named George and Joyce Barnett. We played cards with them but never became very close to them. In these early days we had our only period of significant homesickness. It was not that we sat around and moped, but we just had not found where we fitted in our new environment.

On one of the first Sundays in Bad Toeltz, Tammy talked me into attending church on the post. The chaplain was a Southern Baptist and the service was pretty good. I remember being shocked when they served Communion and Tammy took part. This was taboo to me. Apostolics never were to take Communion in any other church. I sat there like a zealous young Pharisee and would have no part of it. The people of the church were very warm and welcoming to us. They invited us to go with them on a bus trip to Munich. They asked us to sing in the choir. It was just the welcome we needed at the time, but I resisted it. We did go to the Munich PX with them once and we had a nice time. I dragged my heels long enough that Tammy finally gave up trying to become involved in this church. There were a number of reasons for my intransigence. First, as a member of the Apostolic Christian Church I knew that I was not to be attending another church. In addition I knew that if I started going to this church and got involved I would have no basis for insisting that we remain Apostolics when we got out of the Army. A third reason was that the Bluffton, Indiana Apostolic Christian church had begun sending tapes of their church services to us. I convinced Tammy to try listening to these on Sunday mornings instead of attending the church. She reluctantly agreed. We rarely listened to them. The main reason, however, is that I simply did not want to go to church. I was so disillusioned by what I had been through the year before that I wanted nothing to do with it. And for the first time in my life I was in a position to stay away because I had no family or other Apostolics to watch over me. How sad to think that my professed love for God was not enough to make me want to attend church. As I look back I am very ashamed about this.

Once we were settled in at Bad Toeltz we spent the first three or four months in and around the post. Things began to change with the arrival of spring. Tammy stopped babysitting and took a job at the American Express as a bank teller. We also bought a car. It was a rusty old Opal Record, but it ran well and never failed us. One of the first big excursions we undertook was to visit the Neuschwanstein, or "Walt Disney" Castle. We drove there one Saturday with Dave Gong and Steve Fugami. It was a beautiful spring day. Tammy had packed a lunch and we had a picnic when we arrived. It was a great thrill to see this castle for the first time. At least once a week we went out to one of the many local guesthouses for dinner. Tammy and I would also just drive around and see the countryside on the weekends. There was a reservoir in the nearby mountains that we enjoyed driving to for picnics. Our first long drive was over the Easter weekend. We drove to Post Neuhitten and visited the Mauers. It was about a six-hour drive. I was shocked about how recklessly the motorcyclists drove on the Autobahn. It was my first exposure to them. The weekend went well, but we were happy to be back in Bad Toeltz. It had become home to us.

In the late spring we were delighted to learn that Dad and Mom Speicher would be coming to visit. We counted the days until mid-July rolled around. The plans were for them to fly into Frankfurt. An airline strike changed their flight schedule and delayed them for nearly two days. Tammy and I had driven to Frankfurt to pick them up. We learned about the flight delay when we arrived. When we called home Mom actually answered the phone! This began an interesting two days in Frankfurt.

When we learned of the delay there was another soldier there whose parents were also to have been on the same flight. He was stationed near Frankfurt and knew the area. I do not even remember his name, but we became instant friends. He took us to a hotel where we rented a room. We then got a quick tour of the area. After supper he took us downtown. As we were walking around he said he wanted to show us something. When we got there he told us it was the biggest brothel in Frankfurt. He told us we just had to walk in and take a look. As he stood outside with Tammy I made a quick walk-through. Inside there was a huge room in which there must have been at least one hundred women. They were just standing around waiting to be chosen. My walk-through could not have taken more than a minute but it left an indelible image in my mind. As a conservative farm boy from Indiana, I could not imagine that such a place actually existed. As I look back, it was pretty dumb that I even walked in to take a look. I wonder whatever became of these women.

The next day we were told that there was a rock concert being held at a local soccer stadium. Among the groups scheduled to perform were the *Rolling Stones* and *Paul McCartney and Wings* so we thought we should check it out. When we actually got into the stadium it was announced that neither of the headline groups were going to perform. Everyone but us seemed to be either too drunk or doped up to care. After walking around for a while we decided to leave. At the exit area we encountered such a crush of people that we almost literally were carried along by them through the exit. I remember Tammy holding on my arm so tight that I thought she would pull it off. This was one of those situations in which we would have been trampled to death if we had fallen. I was glad to get out of there. We went to a movie that night and stayed in a different hotel.

Dad and Mom finally arrived early the next morning. Their plane landed in Cologne and they were bused to Frankfurt. We were so excited to see them. We started out for Bad Toeltz right away. Tammy and I tried to catch up on the previous months on the way home in addition to showing them all the sights on the way. All they wanted to do was sleep, as they had been up for twenty-four hours. Somewhere between Frankfurt and Munich I gave up trying to talk to Dad. He fell so soundly asleep that his leg kept coming over onto the gearshift and steering wheel. I do not remember Mom being able to stay awake either. Tammy and I obviously had forgotten how tiring the trans-Atlantic flight was. When we got home we took them to the third floor guestroom and left them there until morning.

Because of the flight delay I had to work the first few days that Dad and Mom were with us. After supper the first night we took them to the dispensary for a tour. I demonstrated my expertise in X-ray technology by taking an X-ray of Dad's jaw. He had a piece of steel in his cheek from an accident while working on the railroad years before. It was clearly visible on the X-ray and they were duly impressed. Once I was able to sign out for vacation we began our quest to see Bavaria. In the two weeks Dad and Mom were with us we went to Munich twice, toured the Linderhof and Neuschwanstein castles, visited the Nazi concentration camp at Dachau, spent a weekend in Salzburg and Berchtesgaden, visited Garmish-Partenkirchen and Oberammergau, and took a two day swing through Austria, Switzerland, and Italy. In addition to this we spent a number of days in and around Bad Toeltz.

Among the specific memories are Dad's pronunciation of Italy ("Itly") and Austria. In Euorpe Austria is spelled "Oesterreich." To Dad it was the country of "Ostrich," as in the bird. In Salzburg we took a tram up to the castle. While waiting we met a guy who was from Pierceton, Indiana, and had played basketball against Ned and Ted. As the tram was ascending, I teased Dad that it seemed like it was slipping and got scolded by a woman who was not amused. When we were in Berchtesgaden we took a tour of Hitler's Eagle's Nest. The trip up to it was not for the faint of heart. It required a special bus, as the road was one lane and included inclines as great as forty-five degrees and several hairpin turns. As at Salzburg I could not resist teasing Dad that the bus crashes on occasion. A portly woman a few seats ahead of us turned and snapped, "Don't say that!" in response. In Garmish we took a cable car to the top of the Zugspitz, the highest mountain in Germany. I do not know why, but I had not yet caught on that Dad was terrified of heights. Mom later confessed to us that she needed all of her skills of persuasion to get him on the cable car. On the way up we were all a bit uneasy about how high we were being taken, but poor Dad was ashen. I remember Mom "comforting" him — and herself — with the words "Now Lewie, the worst that can happen to us is that we die!" We were *all* comforted by these words. When we got back down Dad was so proud of himself and still speaks of his death-defying ride to the summit of the Zugspitz. Some of our best times, however, were our evening meals in the guesthouses around the Bavarian countryside. Mom seemed to especially enjoy the atmosphere and the people in these family-run restaurants.

It seemed that no sooner had Dad and Mom arrived than it was time for them to go. I drove them to Munich for their flight home. While it was hard to say goodbye, it was nothing compared to our farewell eight months earlier. I do not know why, but Dad and Mom's visit seemed to mark the beginning of a distinct and new phase of our Germany experience. Perhaps it was just that Tammy and I had completed a crash course in growing up. It also helped that we had just learned that Tammy's folks would be coming to Germany in a few months!

Chapter Thirty-Two

In 1973 the United States' military draft ended. This meant that the military could no longer simply draft the professionals it needed. This was first felt in the First General Dispensary in the fall of 1973 when it was time for our pharmacist, Steve Fugami, to rotate out of the service. By this time I had rotated through nearly all areas of our dispensary and had gained the favor of our leaders. They needed someone to run the pharmacy and selected me to be trained as a pharmacy technician by Steve Fugami before he left. This simple decision was to affect the rest of my life.

I loved working in the pharmacy. Fugami was a good teacher and a really funny guy. It was great to have my own little locked-off area. What was especially nice, though, was the fact that the pharmacy had a corner window with an excellent view of the mountains. In my last year I spent what had to amount to a sum of many hours staring out the window, thinking, and admiring the view. The doctors watched me pretty closely at first. Through this interaction I became friends with both of them, but especially so with John Ogden. He was a pre-maturely grey thirty- year old bachelor just out of medical school. He was especially out of place in the Army. He was brilliant, articulate, and devoted to the fine arts. He had chosen medicine as his profession but seemed to have no passion for it. The rest of us were amazed how quickly he learned German. Our friendship developed slowly because he was on officer and I was an enlisted man. When things were slow in the dispensary we talked a lot. He would show me interesting patients. He even taught me how to suture wounds. Once I had demonstrated to Dr. Ogden and Dr. Nenadovic that I could do this, they often let me go ahead, especially after hours when they did not want to come in and do it themselves. There were no other circumstances under which a farm boy like me could have had such experiences.

By the fall of 1973 Tammy and I had made quite a few friends. One couple we played cards with was Richard and Lou Spence. They were from Alabama. They both smoked like chimneys and Richard was an alcoholic, but they were really comical and fun to with. They had a sad ending, though. Before leaving Germany Richard's drinking got worse and worse and Lou left him for another soldier. Tammy and I were both shocked and hurt by this. In our sheltered existence we believed that people actually did stay together "for better or for worse." On Thanksgiving Day we had a number of people join us for dinner. There must have been at least a dozen of us. Tammy was definitely her mother's daughter that day. The food was both beautiful and delicious. The apartment was decorated like a magazine cover. Our guests were all in awe of Tammy. Of course, I swelled with pride. She repeated the feat again on Christmas Day and other times as well. Our guests were somewhat different each time, with a common core group. Tammy's fame had spread throughout the post by the time we left. What a woman!

In October of 1973, war broke out in the Middle East when Syria and Egypt attacked Israel on the Israelite holy day of Yom Kippur. In the first week of this war things went badly for Israel as Egypt took back much of the Sinai Peninsula and Syria much of the Golan Heights, areas which they had lost to Israel in 1967. The war became an international crisis when Israel threatened to use nuclear weapons to stop the advance. The United States became directly involved when we began an air re-supply of Israel. With this massive re-supply effort and some daring military moves by Israel, the tide began to turn in their favor. This, in turn, brought the United States and the Soviet Union into direct conflict because Egypt and Syria were client states of the Soviet Union. When it was learned that the Soviet Union had mobilized airborne forces for the Middle East, US armed forces went on a worldwide alert. We later learned that President Nixon gave the Soviets an ultimatum at this point:

you stop the fighting, or we will. Egypt and Syria soon called for a cease-fire and the war ended, but not before the Army of Israel had moved across the Suez Canal into Egypt and surrounded the invading Egyptian Army. Syria also lost additional territory in the end.

In Bad Toeltz our Special Forces were excited when we went on alert. Tammy said that some soldiers even came into the bank requesting Israeli currency. Nothing changed for us in the dispensary during the alert, though. One thing that did come from this war was the formation of OPEC (Organization of Petroleum Exporting Countries). In the aftermath of the war they imposed an international oil embargo upon western nations that created oil shortages and ushered in a worldwide recession in the coming years.

Tammy's parents came to Germany after Thanksgiving in 1973. We drove to Frankfurt to pick them up, but this time the plane was on time and the trip was uneventful. I do not remember anything specific about meeting them at the plane but I do remember the feeling of seeing loved ones again after a time of separation. It is a feeling I cannot describe, yet one I will never forget. When we arrived in Bad Toeltz I could see how proud they were of Tammy as they looked around our apartment. The first night there we grilled pork chops on a tiny charcoal grill that we had on our balcony. We were quite the entertainers!

One of the first conversations we had upon their arrival was about our weather. I explained to George that we had a lot of snow but that the temperatures were not as extreme as in Indiana. I added, "For example, it never gets cold enough that the snow gets crunchy." Of course, this assured us of having "crunchy snow" during their stay. George still gets mileage out of this line. It began to snow upon their arrival and continued throughout their stay. It was the most beautiful winter scenery we had during our time in Germany and no one in either of our families would have enjoyed it more than George and Pat.

We did many of the same things with George and Pat as we had done with Lewie and Mim. The day we visited Oberammergau and the Linderhof Castle with them it was snowing hard, with the most beautiful, large snowflakes I have ever seen. It was also snowing like this when we went to Salzburg and Berchtesgaden. In Berchtesgaden one night we ate dinner in a restaurant. We were seated at a corner table by a picture window. The outside light illuminated the heavy snowfall beautifully. It continued to softly settle on the shrubs outside up to two feet of thickness. It truly was a winter wonderland. Even our walks around downtown Bad Toeltz were like none others we ever took. Pat was in a "hat phase" at the time, which was perfect for the weather. On the first day downtown George bought a green Bavarian hat (with a feather) that he wore throughout the trip and for years after. What a fun time!

One very special thing we did with George and Pat was to take a three-day trip to Venice, Italy. Pat had told us when they arrived how much she hoped she would get to see "Vienna, that place with all the canals." Bless her heart. She was a touch "blond" even then. Tammy made arrangements for the trains at the American Express. The morning we drove to Munich it was still snowing. We found the right train and departed. When we arrived in Venice "guides" wanting to help us mobbed us. We followed one of them down a back street to a hotel with a vacancy without a single thought of the fact that we could have easily been mugged without anyone knowing. Our room was up a narrow, dark stairs. Once we got into the room, however, it was fine. We were all amused at the size of the bathtub. It was about one third of a normal sized one. After getting settled in we went to a restaurant and ordered pizza. When the waiter brought it to the table we were amused to find that the pizza had a fried egg "sunny side up" in the middle of it. It tasted great despite its looks. We went for a walk after supper through the narrow streets of Venice. After a while we realized we were lost. I was just starting to get nervous when we realized that we were right at our room. Apparently we had just walked in a big circle.

The next morning the weather had turned colder and it was windy. We took a water taxi to famous Saint Mark's Square, where we spent most of the day. It was historic and beautiful and huge. When we climbed the stairs to the top of the historic bell tower we about were blown away by the wind. The bells also rang while we were up there and we were thankful our hands were free to shield our ears. After an early supper of egg-centered pizza we took a water taxi tour of the city. The remainder of the day we walked around, window shopping and sightseeing. They really do have the little gondolas and the canals. Our geography books were right.

It was dark when we arrived at the train station. We waited for an hour or so for our train, drinking syrup-thick coffee and watching the people. Our plans were to sleep on the train during our return trip. Our plans were foiled by two unforeseen developments. The first was that our car had no sleeper rooms. The second was that our train had no heat! It was one of the coldest nights of my life. We had to change trains at the Brenner Pass between Italy and Austria. It was the middle of the night, there was not a soul around, and it was bitterly cold. We must have waited an hour for our train, during which time George wandered off — much to the chagrin of both his wife and daughter! The train eventually arrived and we were back in Bad Toeltz by mid-morning. We were greeted by beautiful sunshine, cold air, and "crunchy snow." It occurs to me now that the day when I was the hottest in my life and the night I was the coldest in my life were both shared with my beloved parents-in-law! The hottest day was our ride from Mexico to San Antonio with our car heater on. The coldest night was definitely our ride from Italy to Germany in a train car with no heat. George and Pat left from Munich a few days later. It was hard to see them go but we knew it would only be seven months until we saw them again — or so we thought.

Chapter Thirty-Three

As I look back over my life one thing that I have learned to do is to not plan too far ahead. I have leaned that every time I think I have things figured out that my life takes an unexpected turn. In late 1973 I had already experienced a number of these "turns" but I did not yet realize that it would be a pattern.

When George, Pat, Tammy, and I were having supper during our snowy night in Berchtesgaden, George and Pat expressed their concern about Tammy's youngest brother Trent. They said he had not been feeling well in recent months and that their family doctor did not know what to make of it. Tammy and I did not think much of it at the time but we began to be concerned when we learned in early January that George and Pat were taking him to Children's Memorial Hospital in Chicago for tests. An X-ray at a local clinic had revealed an enlargement of his heart. When they arrived at Chicago the cardiologist took a look at the X-ray and Trent's blood counts and immediately told them that they were on the wrong floor of the hospital. He sent them to hematology. There they were told the shocking news that Trent did not have a heart problem. They were told that the "enlarged heart" was a mass in his chest that would likely turn out to be something worse, perhaps even cancer. Tammy and I were stunned. Only old people got cancer. Only people we did not know. Young boys did not get cancer, and certainly not Tammy's baby brother. No way. While it would be several weeks before the family was given a definitive diagnosis we all knew that the news would be bad. Trent had a cancer called Hodgkin's disease. It had already advanced to end stage. Privately the family was told he would likely not survive beyond six months. This was about more than poor Tammy could bear. Being an ocean away made it all the worse. Those who nurture by nature need to nurture and there was no question in our minds that Tammy needed to fly home. Near the end of January, 1974, Tammy flew from Munich to Chicago to be with her family. When she arrived at the hospital and went to Trent's room she was expecting to see a sick little boy. What she saw shocked her. The energetic, happy, ornery, nine-year-old little brother she had left a year before was now barely recognizable. She is not sure she would have known him if her mother had not been at his bedside. While this was devastating, at least she was where she could now lend support to Trent and her parents.

While Tammy was gone both doctors in the dispensary spoke to me about Trent's illness. Dr. Nenadovic felt the problem should have been caught sooner than it was. "Adults often have chronic illnesses," she said, "but when a child is sickly it needs to be aggressively pursued." I remember thinking that I hoped no one would say anything like this to George and Pat because Trent's doctor was a family friend. Dr. Ogden did not give me much hope that Trent would live. He said, "Don't get philosophical or spiritual about it. Instead of living eighty years he will live ten. That's how life is." I was very offended by this. First of all I was offended by the fact that he was so blunt. I had not even entertained thoughts that Trent might die at this early stage. Secondly, I thought that doctors were supposed to be positive and offer hope. He certainly had not done so. I sure hoped that no one would talk like that to Tammy. Finally, I *was* both philosophical and spiritual about it. Why Trent? Why so young? He did not deserve this. Neither did George, Pat and the rest of the family. With thoughts like these how was one not to "get spiritual about it?" I remember spending most of the day after this conversation staring out my pharmacy window at the mountains and thinking. I had a huge knot in my stomach. I finally began to give it to God. I knew the medical picture was so bleak that it was going to require God's intervention for Trent to live. From my earliest days I had been taught that God is in control of our lives and I knew this was no time to stop believing this. It was just that I had never encountered someone as "intelligent" as a doctor who would encourage me not to "get spiritual" about a matter of life and death. No authority figure that I had ever known to this point in my life would have been that irreverent. I obviously was very naive in the ways of the world at that time.

The more I thought about what Dr. Ogden had said the more it bothered me. I brought the subject up again a few days later. We talked quite awhile about God and man and faith. He was patient with me but told me at the end of our conversation that my views were "somewhat sophomoric." I did not even realize that he had insulted me, until later that day when I looked up "sophomoric" in the dictionary. When I read that to be "sophomoric" was to be "over confident of knowledge, but poorly informed and immature," I was furious. I was no match for him intellectually at that time. My religious cliches made no impact at all. I did not doubt that I was right about the existence of a sovereign God and His operation in our lives, but again I found that I did not know enough to defend my faith. Dr. Ogden must have been somewhat curious about what motivated me to live as I did, though, because he later wanted to know why I acted so "messianic" toward my fellow soldiers. I took this as a compliment. And I did not have to look up the word this time. John Ogden was a young man when he offered his counsel to me. It would be interesting to know if he was as calculating when his parents or other loved ones faced death. I rather doubt it. I am sure I am not the only one who had a lot to learn in 1974.

Tammy stayed in the states about two weeks before returning to Germany. She was happy to be back but I found her to be quite melancholy in the weeks that followed. Trent was gravely ill. They had operated to remove his spleen and to stage the cancer. Chemotherapy was to begin as soon as he was sufficiently healed from the surgery. The doctors told the family that they were going to give Trent as much chemotherapy as he could take and continue as long as he could take it. He had his first treatment soon after Tammy got back to Germany. It was awful. In addition to prolonged nausea and vomiting, he ran such a high fever that he required cool baths to bring it down. There were a lot of lumps in a lot of throats in those days. Subsequent chemotherapy treatments were not quite as bad as the initial one. The worst part was the nausea and vomiting. Poor

Trent would begin to vomit when he entered the room for his injections. He continued vomiting for at least another twenty-four hours. The treatments were generally on Monday and he usually would get back to school for a half day on Thursday. Tammy's folks said he never complained once. When I remember how difficult this was for us as a brother-in-law and a sister, I can scarcely imagine what it must have been like for George and Pat. One evening after receiving Trent's grim diagnosis, George was seated with his Bible open on his lap. As one might expect, his heart was breaking with sorrow. He recalls looking down at his Bible through his tears and seeing only the words "Thy son liveth." It is likely that his Bible was open to John 4:50 where Jesus made this promise to a nobleman whose son was sick at Capernaum. Skeptics might attribute this to chance, but we have always believed this was a miracle. While Trent continued his chemotherapy for five years, his cancer went into remission immediately and never came back. Of the ten juvenile cancer patients in Chicago's Children's Hospital with Trent, he was the only one to survive beyond five years. The scripture "Thy son liveth" did in fact apply to George and Trent.

Chapter Thirty-Four

As I look back on my Army experience in Germany I am reminded that in many ways my day to day life was not dramatically different than life has been at any given location or time period. There are, however, a set of memories from the Fifth General Dispensary that are precious and distinct, like the morning I walked into the dispensary and was told to rush to the emergency room. When I entered I saw a young man on the floor. The doctors were frantically working on him trying to restore his heartbeat. After CPR, chest thumps, and electro-shocks failed Dr. Nenadovic administered an intra-cardiac injection of epinephrine. When this failed he was pronounced dead. I had never seen anything like this before. This twenty-six year old man had walked into the dispensary moments earlier complaining of chest pains. As he was explaining that he had been in a drunken fight the night before and had been kicked in the chest, he collapsed. As he lay there dead we could see the abrasion on his chest. Apart from this he looked like the picture of health. As we moved the body into another room I was told to remove his wedding ring. His wife had not yet joined him in Germany. This really upset me as I imagined the grief that this news would bring his wife and family. It was very quiet at work the rest of the day. We later learned that an autopsy determined the cause of death to be a heart attack. Even then I wondered if this was a cover-up. My best guess now is that the kick to his chest led to a cardiac or large vessel bleed.

About once a month I had to spend the night at the dispensary as CQ (Charge of Quarters). There was an office area with a desk and a bed in it. If no one came in we could sleep — but only after the chores were done and the floors were buffed. Sometimes all this CQ amounted to was a night away from Tammy. Other times there was some real excitement. It was during these CQ nights that I would get to do X-rays, suturing, and wound bandaging more than during the daytime hours. Usually the patients were soldiers who had been injured in scuffles with other drunken soldiers. Sometimes the patients were military dependents. The doctors were much more conservative about what they let me do with the dependents. Four CQ nights stand out in my memory. One night a call came in from a German community hospital that an American dependent teenage girl had been injured in a car accident. They wanted us to come to get her. Another soldier and I drove around the Bavarian countryside for hours looking for the hospital. We finally found it around daybreak. It turned out that this girl was riding in a van that had the side door open. She had been drinking and when they rounded a corner she fell out onto the pavement. She was wearing a bathing suit and had lost a lot of skin. I can still remember the smell of the dried and oozing blood and the stale alcohol on the way back. Quite unpleasant! I am sure this girl healed up fine, but she was quite a mess at the time.

Flint Kaserne was home to a U.S. Green Berets unit. Being an airborne unit they often took part in parachuting exercises. One night they had a "night jump" while I was on CQ. I had just fallen asleep when some soldiers came shouting up the stairs that there would be some wounded soldiers coming in soon. It turned out that the plane was too low when the soldiers jumped. They got their parachutes open but hit the ground before they were expecting to. Three of them had one broken leg and one soldier broke both legs. After taking X-rays they were all transported to the hospital at Augsburg.

Another night a baby was brought in screaming in pain. The baby was a beautiful, chubby boy about one year old. X-rays showed that he had a fractured femur (thigh bone). Today there would certainly be a child abuse investigation over an incident like this. I think the doctors were suspicious but nothing was ever done, as far at I know. When daylight came the doctors arranged a helicopter transfer to the hospital at Augsburg. They had me ride along to watch the baby. The ride up and the transfer were uneventful. On the trip back I was dozing when I was seized with horror as I realized I was falling. The fall stopped as quickly as it began. When I looked up at the pilots they were both laughing hysterically. I do not know what they did to produce the falling sensation, but it was a great joke. I just wished I could have been on the other end of it.

My most curious CQ memory happened around mid-night one night. I had just fallen asleep when two soldiers who were outside the office area awakened me. When I went to see what they wanted I realized that they were in a heated argument. Apparently they had already been in a fight and had come to the dispensary to get patched up. I tried to get in the middle of it to see what was going on. As I was trying to get a word in edgewise, the guy who was the angriest sucker-punched the other guy, breaking his jaw. This was such a cheap shot that I was instantly enraged. As soon as the guy threw the punch he turned to leave. Without thinking I grabbed him. He tried to get away and the two of us rolled down the steps, first to the landing and then around the corner and then down another flight of stairs to the entryway. This entryway was shared with the Non-Commissioned Officer's Club. A few of the drunks peeked out the door to see what was going on. I had the guy subdued by this time and I asked for help holding him until the Military Police came. When no one would help, I let the guy up and he ran away. I was foaming at the mouth mad at the drunks who refused to help and told them so before going back up to the dispensary. The other guy was at the top of the stairs, holding his jaw in agony. He told me that he knew the other guy and would file a complaint.

The next morning the guy was transported to Augsburg to have his broken jaw wired. I never heard another word about the incident so I doubt the MP's ever did anything about it. As I look back I cannot imagine why I went after this guy to restrain him. He was not much bigger than me, but he was drunk and obviously violent. The only explanation I have, in retrospect, is that it was purely an impulsive response to the "cheap shot." It is also interesting as I look back that neither of us was injured as we wrestled down two flights of concrete steps. I remember thinking at the time that I would need to be careful whom I told this story to, as 'brothers" in the Apostolic Christian Church were supposed to refrain from violence. I am left to wonder, also, if either of these two guys today could remember a thing about why they were fighting. I would wager, however, that neither of them has forgotten the senseless act of violence between them.

Apart from our concern for Tammy's brother Trent our last seven months in Germany were some of the best of our lives. We both loved our jobs. At the dispensary I had learned every department. The doctors liked me because I could help them from the pharmacy to the X-ray to the emergency room to the lab, where I had learned to draw blood, take cultures, and to perform basic blood counts and urinalyses. It was not that I was so brilliant; I just found it all fascinating. The doctors loved Tammy. She was the Belle of every Ball.

Tammy and I had a number of friends, but we spent most of our social time with a couple named Jerry and Deb Wall. They had moved into an apartment directly across the hall from us. They were both from Joliet, Illinois. We were about the same age and shared many common interests. Deb worked on post as a secretary and Jerry was an MP (Military Policeman). At first we just went back and forth to play cards in the evenings but later went on several trips together.

In our last seven months we rarely spent a weekend at home. By that time we were aware of how fortunate we were to be where we were. I found myself often encouraging my fellow soldiers to get out and see the country, but most spent their entire tour around the Post, drinking and doing drugs. In the late winter of 1974 Tammy and I and two friends from the dispensary, Dave Gong and Edward Driver, drove to Berlin. To make this drive required special orders from the Allied Command Center in Frankfurt. Part of the post-World War II Four Power Agreement provided for air, rail, and ground corridors through East Germany to West Berlin. The one road to Berlin in 1974 was the Berlin-Helmstadt Autobahn. One could not go to Berlin this way without special orders approved and stamped by representatives of the United States, France, Great Britain, and the Soviet Union. They were required to pass through the West German - East German border. Most soldiers wanting to visit Berlin took a special train or flew there via one of the three air corridors. I was determined to experience Cold War politics and

A Lifetime of Church

relentlessly pursued these special orders to drive there until I received them. I am so thankful that I did because this trip was probably the most interesting one I have ever taken.

Dave Gong had a 1972 VW Beetle and the four of us set out for Berlin. We arrived at the Helmstadt border crossing by late morning. There we were given special instructions for our drive to West Berlin. We were told that when we passed through the American checkpoint we would encounter an East German checkpoint that would have a gate like a railroad crossing across half the road. We were to ignore the East German guards and drive around their gate. Once past this checkpoint we would come to a Russian checkpoint. There we were to stop the car. Our driver was to get out with our orders, approach the Russian checkpoint office, salute the Russian attendant, and hand him the orders. He would then stamp them and send us on our way. The drive to West Berlin, driving the speed limit, was to take three hours. We were told that if we were late arriving, the US Military Police would come looking for us. If we arrived too soon, we were told we would be given a speeding ticket. As we entered West Berlin we would need to check in with the Russians, ignore and drive around the East Germans, and check in with the Americans. During this drive we could not be in military uniform and if we were seen taking pictures we were old that our cameras would be confiscated. We were told lastly that if anything happened to us between Helmstadt and Berlin we were to demand to speak to a Russian Authority. Under no circumstances were we to cooperate with East German authorities. For anyone too young to remember the Cold War it is hard to imagine the tension that existed between the East and West in 1974 that would make such instructions necessary.

All of this was a bit frightening, as we made sure the car was full of gas and prepared to leave. I clearly remember looking up at the guard towers, one American and one East German. Both were high, surrounded with barbed wire, and manned by armed guards as they faced each other. We drove through the American checkpoint and around the East German checkpoint as instructed. When we stopped at the Russian checkpoint Dave Gong was so nervous that he did not put the car in neutral as he started to get out. After a tension-breaking laugh, he went to the office and had our orders stamped. The drive through East German was uneventful. The countryside was flat and nondescript. I recall that the road, while four-lane, was in very poor shape compared to the West German roads. The first reason for this was likely the fact that the East German people owned very few vehicles privately. In addition, maintaining a road to West Germany would have been a very low priority for the East German government. They concentrated on walls and fences to keep their people in, not roads to help them drive to the border.

It was early evening when we arrived in West Berlin. After checking into our hotel and eating supper we spent the evening walking around sightseeing. In the heart of the old city the only building not leveled during the war was the Kaiser Wilhelm Cathedral. The West Berlin people kept the scarred shell of the old cathedral and built new around it. The result was a beautiful picture of the past and the present. We all enjoyed our tour of this. Beside the cathedral was a new set of buildings that the locals called the "Lipstick and the Compact." The "Compact" was an opera house and the "Lipstick" a memorial to the suffering of World War II. After the war Berlin had built an excellent mass transit system of subways and trams. This made our getting around very easy.

The next morning we set out for "Checkpoint Charlie." Part of the post-war Four Power Agreement allowed for the free movement of allied soldiers throughout Berlin. Soon after the war all Soviet and East German soldiers were restricted to the Soviet zone of occupation. The United States, Great Britain, and France, refused to restrict their soldiers and insisted that the "free movement" provision of the Agreement be honored. "Checkpoint Charlie" was the crossing point where this provision for free movement was honored. It was made famous in 1947 when American and Soviet tanks faced each other down there during the Berlin blockade and subsequent Berlin Airlift that preserved the freedom of West Berlin. The building of the "Berlin Wall" in 1963 formally divided the city and prohibited free movement, but Checkpoint Charlie remained open.

We all planned on walking across the border to East Berlin, but when we arrived at the checkpoint we were told that only soldiers who were in uniform could cross there. If Tammy wanted to see East Berlin she would need to sign up for a civilian bus trip which would cross at another place. There was a waiting list for these bus tours, so poor Tammy was out of luck. On the American side we were given instructions before walking across. We were told that there was an East German check zone on the other side of the gate where they checked any cars trying to cross over. If we were seen taking pictures within one hundred feet of this zone our cameras would be confiscated. We were again reminded to demand to speak with a Russian if we got into any trouble. They also told us to expect to encounter an East German guard as soon as we entered the check zone. We were to ignore him and walk on.

Before we left to enter East Berlin we walked Tammy to a waiting area. It was a room inside a Checkpoint Charlie museum. It was so sad to view the pictures and read the accounts of the poor East Germans who had died trying to get across to West Berlin at Checkpoint Charlie. Even being right there it was to hard to imagine that people often risked their lives to flee to the freedom that we had grown up with and took for granted. There was also an exhibit of people who had successfully made it across and this was encouraging. I remember noting one exhibit in particular. It was a picture of an East German border guard with the note "The worst shooters in the world." The note of explanation pointed out the number of escapees who had been shot at versus the number who were hit. The implication was clearly that these soldiers were sympathetic to the escapees. We were all sobered by the time we left this museum. Tammy was especially nervous and made me repeatedly promise that I would be careful and "not do anything stupid." I was a bit nervous myself. I had no intention of doing anything except what was allowed.

As we approached the checkpoint I noted that there was a wall that came right up to each side of a one-lane road that passed through. Across this one-lane road was a steel barrier to prevent unauthorized drive-through. On the right side of this was a small entryway for soldiers to walk through. It was U-shaped so we could not see what was on the other side. I walked through first. When I came out on the other side I encountered a large, menacing East German guard who was standing directly in my path. If I had not been warned about this in advance I am sure I would have turned around and gone back. With my heart pounding I simply looked straight ahead and stepped around him. After walking a few blocks we stopped and talked about what we wanted to do. We had been told that the Kaiser Wilhelm street would be straight ahead and that there we would find "the sights." We could see the Berlin Wall several blocks to our left so we thought we would walk to it and follow it to the Kaiser Wilhelm Street. When we walked to the wall it did not look like a side street that we should be on. We turned to go back to where we had started from and saw two uniformed soldiers standing back there staring at us. At this point we decided to go back and stay on the major streets.

In all we spent several hours walking around East Berlin. I found it to be very drab. There were no street vendors and few storefronts that were attractive. One thing that stood out to me was the fact there were many churches that had been bombed out and not rebuilt. These were the only buildings we saw that were still in ruins. The East German war memorial was interesting. There were several groups of East Block soldiers there viewing it. They also had an impressive changing of the guard. As we were standing there the guards snapped their weapons to begin the ceremony. Ed Driver jumped when they did this, scared to death. I thought this was very funny, but it made me flinch too. After this changing of the guard we headed back for West Berlin. As we passed the check zone we saw a sad sight. The East German border guards had a car stopped. The occupants had been ordered out. As they were standing by watching, the guards were meticulously searching the car. The front hood and the trunk were open. The back seat was taken out. There were four guards with mirrors searching under and throughout for stowaways. We had often heard that this happened, but to see it was another matter. It was hard to imagine that all this effort was put forth just to keep citizens from escaping to the west. Such was the mentality of the Cold War. No wonder cameras were forbidden in the check zone.

Tammy was just starting to worry when we arrived back. She listened patiently to our tales but I saw even then that one had to experience "the other side" to fully appreciate it. In the afternoon we took a bus tour of West Berlin. We also visited several famous sites at the Berlin Wall, including the western side of the Brandenburg Gate, where both President Kennedy and President Reagan had given famous speeches that elucidated the foundational differences in personal liberties between the East and West. At every stop along the Wall there were crosses and memorials to those who had died trying to escape. I found this all to be quite sobering. In 1974 no one in his wildest dreams would have envisioned that the political situation in Berlin would be a relic of history within twenty years. No one!

The next morning we drove back to West Germany. I got brave and took a roll of pictures as we went. This was the only roll of pictures I never got back while in Germany. I have always felt that they were confiscated by the military. Once back in West Germany we headed to Bad Toeltz. It was good to be home. Of all the things that we did while in the military, I found this to be the most interesting. There were a number of years in the late 1980's that I was invited to our local middle school to share slides and accounts of the experience. I doubt that many middle school students today would have any idea of what I was talking about if I were to share the experience with them.

As the Easter weekend approached in 1974, Tammy and I thought we should drive to Paris. Dave Gong said we could use his VW Beetle and we headed out. This trip was as unplanned and spontaneous as our trip to Berlin had been well planned and deliberate. We left early one morning and by late afternoon we were there. The drive through the French countryside was beautiful, but not all that different from the farming areas of middle Germany. After we ate some supper we started looking around for a place to stay. It was at this point we realized we had not planned well. There were no rooms available. We were about resigned to sleeping in the car when we found a room at the Charles DeGaul Airport.

The next day we were determined to see everything Paris had to offer. After touring the Eiffel Tower and the Notre Dame Cathedral I had a brainstorm. The traffic was unlike anything I had ever seen so I suggested we hire cabs to get us around. To get around the language barrier I bought a postcard with the main sights of Paris on it. From then on we simply hailed a cab and pointed to where we wanted to go. I suppose that they could have driven us wherever they wanted to before taking us to our destination and we would have not known the difference, but none of the trips seemed too long. They certainly were intense, though.

After supper we checked a few places for a room. When we

were unsuccessful we decided to head for home. In retrospect, this was so foolish. We were exhausted from a short night and a frantic day. Tammy fell asleep around the German border. The next four to five hours were a monumental struggle to stay awake. With the accelerator to the floor we sped along the autobahn. I sang every song I ever knew and started over again several times. I also variously employed pinching, squirming, and slapping techniques to keep me awake. Occasionally Tammy would awaken and tell me I was being too loud. Of course I sarcastically replied that I was sorry for disturbing her sleep. God evidently was with us, though, because we arrived home safely around 4:00 a.m. What a trip!

The last significant trip we took during our time in Germany was with our friends Jerry and Deb Wall. They owned a little "pop-up" camper and a bright orange VW Bug. We headed south and east through Austria and Switzerland. We spent a night in Berne and continued on to Lucerne. From there we headed to Lake Geneva, where we stayed several nights in Montreux. We had a great time on this trip, but we were so close to leaving Germany that some of the former thrill of being in Europe had begun to fade.

Soon after returning from Lake Geneva we began making arrangements to be discharged from the Army. The Army allowed us a given amount of weight and cubic feet to send things home at their expense. This was a cubic container about five feet on a side. In Tammy's last week she carefully packed everything we wanted to take in this single container. One night during Tammy's last week there the staff of the dispensary held a farewell party in our honor. I was really touched by this. It was the only farewell party our group held for anyone in my two years there. The highlight of the evening was when our commanding officer presented me with the Army Commendation Medal. The award itself was not all that uncommon, but what meant a lot to me were the words that went with it. They were especially flattering. In late June 1974 I drove Tammy to the Munich airport for her flight home. It was not hard to say farewell this time because I knew I would follow in a week or two. After Tammy left I lived in the dispensary barracks for a few days. I was there when I received my orders for discharge. When my orders came through John Ogden offered to drive me to Frankfurt. His suggestion was that we leave a few days early and travel there on the historic "Romantic Road." After some final good-byes we started out for Frankfurt. We took two days driving there, staying one night in the famous walled city of Rothenburg. On my final day in Germany we toured the castle in Heidelburg and headed for Frankfurt. That same evening I boarded a soldier plane for my flight back to the United States. Every seat was full as we rolled down the runway. As the plane lifted off there was a spontaneous cheer. We were headed home.

Chapter Thirty-Five

Oftentimes in my life I have experienced what I now call endogenous melancholy, or melancholy "without an apparent cause." It is hard to describe to anyone who has not experienced it or something similar. When it hits me I have an inability to concentrate, my chest feels slightly tight, my stomach feels a touch icy, and I am somewhat anxious or sad. I also find that I do not want to be around other people. Most of the time when I deal with this I come to a point that I realize something must be bothering me for me to feel this way. I then try to determine what that "something" might be. The "big hurts" of life do not cause it. I am able to easily identify them and generally can deal with them pretty well. The cause tends to be the subtle, little hurts or the chronic little irritations or the impending little "what ifs" that get me feeling this way. As I try to think of what the source might be, I sometimes discover that the reason is something obvious that I have pushed out of my mind, like an unkind comment or an unmet expectation or withdrawn loyalty or seeing someone I love hurting. Many other times the reasons remain undefined or obscure. These forebodings are the toughest times for me. Making these times worse is the fact that I do not like for anyone to know that I am struggling. This is not smart because Tammy can *always* tell that something is wrong. So can my mom, my sister Sue, and my daughters. Despite my efforts to the contrary I apparently am transparent. My efforts to hide my occasional melancholy are also not smart because "talking it out" always helps. I am still learning this.

As I flew home from Germany in 1974 I was filled with a mix of conflicting emotions. On the one hand I was longing for home. I missed my family. Tammy was already there. I would soon be returning to school, to really get started with life. On the other hand I was feeling the endogenous melancholy. I would be returning to school, but those I had started with would be seniors and I would be a sophomore. It did not seem fair. In addition I knew I was returning home to the Apostolic Christian Church. I knew that the pre-army pressures would no longer be there, but I did not look forward to getting involved in it again. I suppose that I was a bit bitter yet, or perhaps I simply did not want to submit to the ways of the AC Church again after being out of it for twenty months. On the balance, however, my joy and expectation far outweighed my melancholy as I approached home.

When we landed we were taken to the Army discharge center at Fort Dix, New Jersey. It was late Friday afternoon when I arrived there and no sooner had I arrived than the discharge center closed for the weekend. We were told that it would reopen Monday morning and that we were on free time until then. This did not help my mood at all. When I called home to tell Tammy that I had arrived safely back in the States she told me that my Uncle Bob and Aunt Marguerite Hoerr were in New York City on business for the weekend. When she learned that I was delayed until Monday, Tammy suggested that I try to hook up with them. She said that my mom had the details of where they were staying. When I called Mom she also encouraged me to call them. She said that they were staying at the Plaza Hotel in New York. I did not really want to go to New York, but there was absolutely nothing going on at Fort Dix and I did not know anyone even if there had been. I made a call to the bus station and found out that I could take a bus to New York within the hour, so I took a taxi and headed out. Once on the bus I fell fast asleep and the bus ended up in New York's Grand Central Station around midnight. Surrounded by a host of scary people, I stumbled out into the street and hailed a taxi. I had no idea where the Plaza Hotel was, so this cab driver could have taken me anywhere. It did not take us long to get there so I assumed the driver had taken a direct route. When he left me off at the Plaza Hotel I was shocked. I

A Lifetime of Church

was expecting the garden-variety Holiday Inn type hotel, not the opulent grand old structure I was standing in front of. I went in and explained the situation to the desk clerk. He was going to call Bob and Marguerite's room, but I asked if I could just sleep on one of the sofas in the lobby rather than bother them. Seems hard to imagine it today but this idea was fine with them and I curled up on a corner love seat. In an instant I was asleep.

Uncle Bob woke me up the next morning. He and Marguerite were appalled that I had not come up to their room. After cleaning up and having breakfast, Uncle Bob left for a business meeting. Aunt Marguerite and I headed out to see the town. Once Bob rejoined us I was given the royal tour of New York City. What a day! Among the sights I was taken to see were Central Park, the Statue of Liberty, and the Empire State Building. I recall being surprised and a bit disappointed when we reached the top of the Empire State Building and I saw the new twin towers of the World Trade Center. I had expected the Empire State Building to be the tallest building on the skyline. The weather for the day was beautiful and the company was even better. After seeing some major European cities I did not expect to be impressed by New York. I was wrong. In the evening we went to a special restaurant where I had my first steamed oysters. Interesting. That night I slept on a roll away bed in their room.

The next morning Bob and Marguerite left for the airport and I took a taxi back to the bus station. It was a Sunday morning. My bus did not leave for a while so I took a walk. I came to Times Square and remember thinking "This is a famous place. I better check it out." I was shocked by what was in the blocks around it. There were street preachers, people sleeping on the sidewalk, beggars, hung-over drunks, and pornography shops. This was all very depressing to me so I soon returned to the bus stop and just waited. On the way back to Fort Dix I reflected on the weekend. It was really good that I had gone to New York. Not only had I seen the city and its sights, I was reminded by being with Bob and Marguerite how much I had missed my extended family while away. In addition the weekend had allowed me some time to adjust to the fact that my life was changing to a new and very different phase. Tammy and I had been very content with our lives in Bad

Toeltz. The prospect of starting over was unsettling. However, I was now more mentally prepared to face it than if I had jetted directly home from Germany.

When I arrived back at Fort Dix I just sat around until bedtime. The next morning I was discharged before lunch. The last item in my discharge was to get my final pay. When the discharge officer peeled off over three hundred dollars in cash I thought I was a wealthy man! I then waited for hours until I was taken to the airport for my flight back to Chicago. While I waited I remember watching huge transport planes endlessly circle, doing "touch and go" exercises on the adjacent airfield. The oil embargo by OPEC had created fuel shortages in many areas in the country. It was the news of the day, yet the military training went on unabated.

In the late afternoon I boarded a flight for Chicago. By this time all my previous melancholy was gone and I could not wait to get home. On the flight I was seated next to a little girl with long pigtails who was very chatty. I remember her asking me if I thought President Nixon was guilty of crimes in the Watergate Scandal. My view was that he probably was involved in the cover-up but that I did not believe he had done anything bad enough to be impeached. I also believed that he had not done anything that was worse than most of his predecessors, but that he had just gotten caught by the liberal media, who especially hated him. The little girl and I were in agreement about President Nixon. We both thought he would finish his term in office. In less than two months, though, we were both proven wrong. The Watergate Scandal, combined with the war in Viet Nam, changed America. They created a deep mistrust of both the government and the military. This, in turn, contributed to a general breakdown in respect for authority in all areas of society that we are still feeling the effects of today.

When the plane landed in Chicago Tammy, Dad and Mom, and Ted and Sandy were there to greet me. It was strange as we drove home. Dad and Mom chatted about things that seemed foreign to me, things like what was happening on the farm, in the family, in the church — little, everyday things that were never included in the letters and the brief, infrequent phone calls that we had exchanged in the previous two years. By the time we made it back to Milford I felt like I had "caught up." That night, as I got ready for bed, I took off my Army uniform for the last time. My military experience was officially over. In July 1972 I had looked at my new Army ID and seen that my date of discharge was July 1974. At that time I had a sick feeling in my stomach, wondering if 1974 would ever come. 1974 had in fact arrived, and I was now back to where I had started: In Milford, a college sophomore-to-be, and a member of the Apostolic Christian Church. At this realization my stomach again began to feel a touch sick.

Chapter Thirty-Six

After I had been in Germany about one year I received my weekly letter from Dad. Usually they contained an update of goings on at home. In this letter, though, he addressed the issue of my future plans. At the time there were two Milford kids who had gone to college, graduated, and come back home. One of them was working as a carpenter and the other as a gas station attendant. It greatly bothered him that these two had invested so much time and money and had come away with unusable degrees. Dad challenged me to carefully consider what I wanted to do before I returned to college and then to go for "something I could use" when I graduated. This advice got me to thinking about what I wanted to do. It did not take long for me to decide that my interests were in the medical field. My experiences in the Army had convinced me of this. My first thought was that I would go to medical school. I knew that this would be an uphill fight, though, because I already had one year of less than adequate grades on my academic record. I guess that a "B" average was not bad, but it would never get anyone into medical school. I knew I would be a more dedicated student when I returned to college but I was not sure of what results this would bring. I also knew that I loved my work in the pharmacy at Bad Toeltz. This would definitely be an achievable goal. Dr. John Ogden really encouraged me to give medicine a try and this was my intention when I was discharged. I had re-enrolled in Manchester College for the fall of 1974 but this was still about two months away when I got home from Germany.

My first few days home were spent making the rounds and catching up. Tammy and I loved our little mobile home. The first day home I went to Goshen Hospital to see my brother Ned. He was in charge of the summer recreation program and had been hit in the eye with a baseball the night before. I saw my sisters also. Sue was sick with strep throat. When I saw Tammy's brother Trent I was taken back by how thin and pale he was, but he was as energetic and personable as I had remembered him. It was great to see Grandpa and Grandma Beer, too. I remember Grandpa telling me that my haircut "was wonderful." No doubt it pleased him that my appearance would be acceptable to the church members on Sunday.

My brother Ned was running a summer home improvement business in 1974 and asked if I wanted to work for him until I went back to school. This was convenient and I enjoyed doing this. We did a lot of roofing. It was hot, hard work but the constant banter made it fun. Tammy wanted to try something in the medical field and took a job as a nurse's aid in a North Manchester nursing home. They were willing to wait until we moved. This job did not turn out to be the kind of work she was suited for, however, and it was not too long before she was working at a local bank as a teller.

In a few weeks it was time to move our mobile home to North Manchester and start back to college. We moved into a lot next to my cousin Dan Doll and his wife Beth. We were best friends during our year there. Dan and I rode to class together, took many of the same classes, and studied together. We both were mouthy and had the same sick sense of humor. In addition we hunted together and canoed on the river behind our trailer park — oftentimes when we should have been studying.

I had no sooner gotten back into the flow of school than I began to rethink my college plans. It occurred to me that if I finished at Manchester College in pre-med and did not go to medical school I would be left with a useless degree. I decided to apply to pharmacy school for the following fall. I figured that if I still wanted to try and go to medical school after graduation I could do so as a pharmacist. If not, then I would have a profession to pursue. By the end of the first semester I applied to the pharmacy schools at Butler and Purdue. By spring break I had been accepted to both schools. At the time I would have preferred to go to Purdue, but it would have taken me four more years to graduate from there. With a term of summer school I could graduate from Butler in three more years. This made our choice easy. As we neared the end of the school year, Tammy and I were busy making plans for another move.

Returning from Germany I was wondering what it would be like to re-involve myself in the Milford Apostolic Christian Church. I had worried that we would be under a microscope again, but this proved not to be the case. We were only around for Sunday services. The other members received us back warmly and treated us well. It was a time of transition in the Milford Church. Grandpa Theo Beer, Great Uncle Henry Beer, Elmer Hartter, and Walt Steffen were the four ministers and three of them were getting older. With the encouragement of the congregation the leadership decided to put in another minister soon after we returned from Germany. I hoped it would be my uncle Phil Beer. It was quite a scene on Election Day. Following the afternoon service Grandpa Beer asked the membership to stay for a members-only meeting. Everyone was then asked to submit one name on a ballot. While the ministers counted the votes, the congregation sang. Grandpa then announced the top four vote getters and we voted for one of them. This was repeated again until there were only two names remaining. As people's names were left off the new slate there were audible and dramatic sighs of relief. What a scene. When a vote was held between these the final two, one of Grandpa Beer's nephews was selected as the church's next minister. I remember thinking that he was a good choice as it gave the Ezra Beer family, by then the largest in the church, representation on the pulpit.

Tammy and I made our move to Indianapolis in late May 1975. Our little mobile home made the trip to West Glen Village on West 10th Street just fine. Tammy took a job with Indiana National Bank. On her first day I drove her downtown for training. We arrived well ahead of time, but, as Tammy said "I would sooner be one hour early than one minute late!" Once she was trained she worked as a relief teller, traveling to different branch banks around the city. She really liked doing this. A few days after the move I began pharmacy school. In order to complete the schooling in three years I needed to take two terms of organic chemistry that summer. My professor was great and I enjoyed the class. I felt it was a major accomplishment when I received an "A." This really boosted my confidence for what was to follow.

With the move we began attending the Indianapolis Apostolic Christian Church. They received us warmly. It was not long before we had friends there also. The congregation was largely made up of people in the 30-40 year age range who were professionals. While the church maintained the teachings and customs of other Apostolic Christian Churches, little effort was made to scrutinize the activities and attire of each other throughout the week as in the rural and small town congregations. This was in part because we did not see each other except on Sundays and in part because the people in this Indianapolis congregation placed a lesser emphasis on activities and attire than did other congregations. For a "nominal member" like me, this was ideal. I could live like I wanted to during the week and play the role of Apostolic Christian Church member on Sunday. I was happy. The family was happy. The sad problem, though, was that God could not have been happy with me. While I was glad to accept God's grace in Christ I was only giving back a moral life — no meaningful service, no evangelism, no offerings, no spiritual growth. This was not the fault of the Apostolic Christian Church. It was my fault. I knew better.

I continued to do well academically in the fall of 1975. I was fascinated by the subject matter they were teaching. I had met a young man from Germany during the summer named Stephen Flasha. He and I became friends and study partners. We complimented each other very well. I was better at chemistry than he was and he was better at mathematics. We kept one another on track and had a lot of fun doing it. Our cooperation continued until we graduated. I also began working as a pharmacy technician between the summer and fall terms at Saint Vincent Hospital. I learned about the job from a fellow Apostolic Christian Church member who worked at the hospital. While in school I worked one night per week and every other weekend. When we were not in school I worked full time. This was a perfect job for me throughout school. I learned a lot about pharmacy, I had a lot of fun with my co-workers, and even made a little money.

At the end of this first term I ended up with four "A's" and one

"B". This was the best report card I ever had. At the end of the spring term I ended up with another excellent set of grades. I thought that maybe I would have the grades to enter medical school after all. John Ogden had kept in touch with me and had kept up the encouragement unto this end. I had created a win-win situation in my schooling. I loved pharmacy and my grades were now good enough to have a reasonable chance of pursuing a second option if I chose to. Everything was working out according to plan. But this was all about to change.

Chapter Thirty-Seven

Historians generally agree that the social upheaval that blossomed in the 1960's was fueled in part by the introduction of the first widely available oral contraceptives. By 1976 the medical community had begun to question the safety of these agents for long-term use. After studies revealed that there were better and safer hormone combinations most of the early oral contraceptive brands were replaced by lower estrogen and phasic agents.

By early 1976 Tammy had been on the "pill" for nearly four years. As members of the Apostolic Christian Church we were not supposed to be practicing birth control but this was an issue we were not convicted about and except in Apostolic Congregations with conservative Elders birth control was essentially a "Don't ask, don't tell" issue. As the reports calling into question the long term safety of oral contraceptives became known, Tammy began to worry. No dream of her youth was more precious than her desire to be a mother. With the consent of her doctor she decided to stop the pill for a while until the long-term safety could be more firmly established.

One does not need be a prophet to guess what happened next. In June of 1976 we learned that we were going to be parents, most likely in December. I did not believe it at first. I was sure the test was wrong. When Tammy went for her first doctor's appointment and heard the heartbeat I became a believer. Before this appointment I remember her passionately, but quietly telling me "Tom, I desperately want this baby." I am sure that I was not the first prospective father to not know how to feel about such news. My brain was awash with concerns. There were economic concerns. We had no medical insurance that covered pregnancy. Also, how would we pay the bills once the baby came and Tammy could not work full time? There were relational concerns. Tammy and I had each other full time for four years. How would a baby affect us? I also had a physical concern. Tammy was born with one of her hands smaller than the other and the fingers of this smaller hand were webbed. Several surgeries fixed the problem and it never caused her any problem but we wondered if our children might inherit the problem — or something worse. It was certainly a prayer concern. I also had concerns about the future. Where to live? What to do?

All my life I knew that someday I would be a father. This was a given. Beyond this basic fact, though, I had never given the subject any thought. Was I up to this? After a few days of shock I began to share Tammy's excitement. It occurred to me that children were God's greatest blessing to a marriage and that if we were going to have a baby that I could count on God to make a way for us. Making a living as a pharmacist would be just fine. Wherever we lived would be OK. I figured that becoming parents would not be as tough as several things we had already been through. One thing I noticed from the very beginning was how my prayers changed. Bringing a child into the world opened up a whole new realm of petitions. And once I caught the excitement one of my biggest concerns was quickly eliminated — the lack of medical insurance. When I spoke to the Pharmacy Director at Saint Vincent about the problem, he bent the rules a bit and included us in the hospital's insurance.

I started my fourth of five years of pharmacy school in the fall of 1976 with exuberance. I loved the schooling. I liked my job at St. Vincent. I liked the Apostolic Christian Church in Indianapolis. I loved the prospect of becoming a father. Life was great. In this fall term I was inducted into the Rho Chi Pharmacy Honor Society. Dad and Mom came down for the induction ceremony. I never received anything for this except the honor, but it was nice anyway.

Our baby was due in late December. There was a touch of irony in this. Being born on December 26th, Tammy had often proclaimed to her mother as a child that she would ***never*** have a baby on or near

Christmas. Pat Sheets had some fun with this as the day approached. Tammy's doctor would not let us go home for Christmas so we planned to celebrate it ourselves. Tammy's family was planning on driving to Indianapolis on Christmas day in the afternoon so we had this to look forward to. We went to bed early on Christmas Eve. We were sound asleep when we heard some very off-tune, but passionate Christmas carolers outside our window. George, Pat, Tim, Todd, and Trent had come to surprise us! And what a surprise it was. This began one of the most special Christmases of my life. We stayed up late, got up early, and ate all day.

When December passed and January arrived we knew Tammy was overdue. We were not concerned, though, because first pregnancies often go over. When two more weeks passed with no labor we began to worry. The doctor reassured us that everything was fine. If the fourth week came and went without any action he would consider inducing labor. In the middle of the fourth week I called Tammy when I got to work after school and she told me she had been having contractions all day, that they were getting both harder and closer together. I called again before I left at 11:00 p.m. and she was still in labor. There was a nasty snowstorm as I drove home. When I got there I felt relief. The roads were bad and more snow was forecast.

That night Tammy woke me up around 2:00 a.m. She said the contractions were within the parameters they had given us for going to the hospital. She called our doctor and he agreed. When I went out to warm up the car I was shocked about how much more it had snowed. It was also blowing hard and bitterly cold. I got in the better of our cars only to find that it would not start. I then got into my car, a 1965 "beater," and it started. Whew! Tammy and I soon got in the car to leave. When we backed out of our drive, the car stalled. We were at the panic stage when it started again. The roads were very bad, but we made it safely. Once safely inside, they hooked Tammy up to the fetal monitor and we waited. And waited. And waited. Tammy had reached a point where her contractions were not getting any harder, but they were not getting any less either. By 10:00 a.m. the next morning the doctor was tired of waiting and decided to induce labor. I was amazed by what followed. No sooner had the Pitocin begun to drip into the IV line than

Tammy's contractions became dramatically harder.

In several hours it was time to move into the delivery room. I still cannot express how I felt as I sat by Tammy's side watching the birth. It was like a dream. With one final push, Trischa Lynn Speicher came into the world. When the doctor laid her on Tammy's stomach her arm stretched out and her left hand opened up not a foot from my face, tiny but perfect. I was speechless. I was overwhelmed with a torrent of feelings — gratitude, love, awe, relief — all I wanted to do was cry. And I am sure I would have if I had uttered a word. She was the most beautiful baby I had ever seen. She was tiny, fine featured. She had a nose that looked like Tammy's. How anyone can see such a thing and not both acknowledge and praise God is beyond me. At that moment I was absolutely certain that life could not get any better.

Trischa was soon in the nursery with a pink nametag and Tammy was in a post-delivery room. We found out at that point that the blizzard had shut down the city. Butler University announced that there would be no classes on Friday, the next day. This was great news for me as I had no intention of going anyway. Since there was no way I could get home it was decided that I would spend the night with some friends from church who lived near the hospital. I remember that before I left they brought Trischa in for a late feeding. A basketball game between Indiana University and Wisconsin was just concluding as she was wheeled in. Tammy instructed her,

"Trischa, this is a basketball game. You will need to learn that this is very important in our family." I was amused that this was her mother's first admonition to her.

A day later we took Trischa home for the first time. I had gone there to clear a path to the door earlier in the day. When we were all safely inside I remember a feeling of "Now what?" The blizzard was even worse in our parents' area than in ours. Tammy's folks were stuck at home for nearly a week before pay loaders came and opened their road. Tammy's mom, however, was not to be denied. One day after we had Trischa home Tammy's dad took Pat to the end of their road on a snowmobile. They were picked up there by my bother Ted, who had borrowed a four-wheel drive vehicle. They arrived safely in Indianapolis in the late afternoon. We could not have been more proud as we introduced Trischa to Ted, Sandy, and her two grandmothers.

When Monday came I figured out the answer to "Now what?" The answer was "Continue with life." Tammy's mom had stayed for the week to help Tammy adjust. I went back to school and work. But life for me was never again the same. School and work were now just necessary diversions until I could get home to enjoy Tammy and Trischa. Academics and professional pursuits now took a back seat to being the best father the world had ever seen. Even then I wondered how seven pounds of beautiful, wiggly, fussy humanity could make such a difference in what was important to me. I clearly remember the pride I felt when Grandma Pat called her sister Jean to report on Trischa with bravado and passion that only Pat Sheets could display. I remember her exclaiming "Oh Jean! You have to see this baby! She's the most beautiful baby I've ever seen!" When we took Trischa to church for the first time I remember an older man telling me as I was holding her "You think you could not love her or enjoy her more than you do right now, but you will find it only gets better and better." I did not believe him at the time, but I now know what he said was very true.

After one week Grandma Pat went back home. As soon as she left Tammy set out to get everything organized. She began by doing a load of wash. We had a portable washing machine at the time that filled at the kitchen faucet and emptied into the kitchen sink. Tammy got the washer started and began on something else. When she returned to the kitchen she sat down and started to cry. It turned out that when she started the washing machine she forgot to take the stopper out of the sink. When the machine emptied it filled the sink and overflowed onto the floor. By the time I got back home the mess was cleaned up and the crisis was over. Just a little lesson in life!

In a few weeks we were in a new routine. Tammy was amazing. The first time Trischa had a fever Tammy took a pillow and a blanket into her room and slept on the floor all night. After a month or two she went back to work two days a week. We traded babysitting with a pharmacist whom I worked with. This was tough at first but we got used to it. The rest of the school year went well for me and I worked a second summer full time at St. Vincent Hospital. My fifth and final year of pharmacy school went quickly. Most of the academics were done after the fourth year. What remained were externships and various clinical projects. I just wanted to get out and get on with life. Our plans were to remain in Indianapolis after graduation. The management at the hospital told me early on that they wanted to hire me to work as a staff pharmacist. We both thought we would want to be out of the city and closer to our families by the time Trischa went to school, but this was a long way off in 1977.

The highlight of my final year had nothing to do with school. It had to do with football. Notre Dame had a great season that year, led by quarterback Joe Montana. When the bowl games were announced Notre Dame was matched with number one ranked Texas in the Cotton Bowl. Bob Gann, Tammy's brother Todd's father-in-law, offered us tickets to the game. We jumped on the opportunity. Our quest began a few days after Christmas in 1977. Grandma Pat watched Trischa and Tammy, Tim, Todd, Trent, Sharon, and I left for Texas. Our first stop was Conway, Arkansas, where Sharon Sheets' parents lived. We stayed with the Ganns a day and a half and then headed for Dallas. Our plans were to watch the game and spend the night with my uncle Alan Beer and his family.

The game exceeded our wildest expectations as Notre Dame demolished Texas to win the national championship. That evening we were at Uncle Alan and Aunt Dorothy Beer's eating supper when I noticed that I was chilling. Alan, a physician, was watching Trent and began quizzing him about how he felt. Turns out that Trent had spiked a fever. When we checked we found that Tammy and I were feverish too. Alan was really concerned about Trent because of his on-going chemotherapy and admitted him to the hospital. By the time we got back from the hospital Tammy and I felt awful. We loaded up on medication and went to bed. The night was filled with aches, alternating sweating and chilling, and weird dreams. By morning we felt better. Alan told us that Trent's fever went as high as one hundred and five through the night. He wanted him to stay until the next day to be sure he was all right. At this news it was decided that Todd, Sharon, and Tim would head for home. Tammy and I were to stay and fly home with Trent. When we got home a few days later we learned that Todd, Sharon, and Tim all got sick on their way home also. What a trip! We have laughed about it for years.

On Trischa's first birthday another blizzard came. I was very fortunate to make it home from work the night it came. Blizzards were fitting for Trischa's birth and first birthday. She was a very spirited child who rolled over at three weeks and walked at nine months. She also talked early, clearly, and often. Her demolition of her first birthday cake is legendary in our family. She became progressively more content as she could do things and express herself. Everyone told us that she was fussy but we had no basis of comparison. We did not wish for anything other than what she was and could not have been happier with her than what we were. Before we could imagine it was possible my final semester in college came and was nearly finished. At the yearend pharmacy awards ceremony I received an honor when I was named co-recipient of the Merck, Sharp, and Dohme award for being the top student in our class in the subjects of Pharmacology and Medicinal Chemistry. The prize was only a copy of the Merck Manual with my name on it, but I was very proud to be the co-recipient. Before going to the Army and growing up a lot, receiving an award like this would have been unthinkable for me.

By the spring of 1978 our plans were set. After graduation we were going to stay in Indianapolis. I was going to take a pharmacist position at St. Vincent Hospital. We were both relieved to be so close to being finished with school and getting on with life. But once again the road we were on was about to round another corner and lead us to an unplanned destination.

Chapter Thirty-Eight

When my career in Little League was in full swing Dad or Mom would often take me to town for games or practices. Later on I would stay after school for them. After I was done with the scheduled event the routine was to walk to Walter Drugs uptown. There my friends and I would treat ourselves at the soda fountain and hang out before calling for someone to come and get us. Over the years this had been the routine for many classes of students. In one of the booths at the soda fountain my innocence was shattered when an older boy showed a nude centerfold to me one day. In these same booths I often tried to impress local girls and laughed hysterically at the antics of local bad boys. It was at the unattended counter where I once stole a five-cent Pay Day candy bar — one I paid for years later — while using the store phone to call home. In many ways this downtown drug store served as the community youth center. A man named John Perry owned the store. He had grown up as a poor boy in Warsaw, Indiana. With the help of the GI Bill he became a pharmacist. He came to Milford in 1954 and bought the store several years later. With hard work and an acute sense of business John soon had the store making money. We were all scared to death of John as kids. He ran a tight ship and many kids over the years had been scolded or shown the door when they did not behave. John was fair, however. If one treated him with respect, respect was shown in return.

In early April of my last term in pharmacy school I came home from working a Saturday shift at St. Vincent Hospital. Upon my arrival Tammy told me that my dad had called. He had run into John Perry that morning in town and John had asked him about what I was planning to do after graduation. He told Dad to have me call him if I was interested in a job. My first reaction to this news was excitement, as was Tammy's. I had grown up in Walter Drugs but it had never once crossed my mind that I might work there. We both hoped to be nearer to our families one day but until this moment this was only a future prospect. I called John Perry right away and we made an appointment for later in the week. If you had asked either Tammy or me what we would choose that night it would have been to move to Milford and take the job.

The next morning I began to think about all of the implications of taking a job in Milford. In 1978 pharmacy was a rapidly changing profession. The emphasis was changing from getting the right medicine to the right patient to patient education about their medications and medication monitoring, two disciplines formerly left exclusively to physicians. Pharmacy Colleges and pharmacy professional organizations had begun to successfully promote the pharmacist as an available, valuable member of the health care delivery system. Hospitals were the first institutions to begin incorporating pharmacists directly in patient care. St Vincent Hospital, where I worked, was especially pro-active in this. By 1978 pharmacists were sitting on their therapeutics and formulary committees. A pharmacist was making "rounds" with the physician intern teams and a pharmacist was a permanent member of their "code team" or medical emergency team. Pharmacy Colleges across the country had begun to offer a new six-year degree called the Doctor of Pharmacy, or PharmD degree, to meet the demands of these evolving clinical services. It was an exciting time to be a graduating pharmacist.

Because I was excelling in pharmacology the leadership at St. Vincent planned on using me in their clinical work. In my pharmacy class there was a clear division between those who planned on going in to retail pharmacy and those of us who "planned on using our education" in hospital pharmacy. Those of us in this latter group no doubt had an element of intellectual arrogance that was clear to everyone but us in those days. My mentor at the hospital flat out told me "You're too good for retail." The sum of this in

April, 1978, was that I felt good about my education, my potential, and my up-coming career in hospital pharmacy. As I imagined working at Walter Drugs in Milford, Indiana, a primitive image came up in my mind. Would there be enough prescriptions to keep me busy? Would the patients or the doctors be interested in my professional input? Would we even be able to get the drugs we needed quickly? Would John Perry be willing to pay the going rate? How would I explain my sudden change of mind to my hospital superiors? They would think I was crazy. And what would it be like to live in a small town again — a small town where everyone knew me? I loved everything about living in Indianapolis except the prospect of sending Trischa to school there. Wrapped around all these questions was whether I was prepared to become a part of the Milford Apostolic Christian Church again.

When Tammy, Trischa, and I drove to Milford for my meeting with John Perry I was conflicted. If you had asked me on the ride to Milford what I was going to do I would have said I would be staying in Indianapolis. Arriving in Milford, however, the balance began to tilt the opposite way. There was one simple reason for this: everyone on both sides of the family was so excited about the prospect of us moving home. Tammy's folks suggested that we could fix up the little house on their farm and live there. This sounded great to both of us. My heart was pounding as I drove to Milford to meet with John Perry. He was not at the store when I arrived. The pharmacist who was leaving Walter Drugs was on duty. He and I chatted a while before John came in. It was general chitchat except for one statement. He told me "Be sure you get these weekends straight before you take the job." Before I could follow up on the admonition John Perry came in. John and I walked across the street to the EMS building where there was an office. John was very pleasant, but all business. His offer to me was $16,800 in salary. This was several thousand less than retail chain stores were offering. The rest of the package was similar to what others were offering. His offer had two advantages. Instead of discounts on store merchandise he said I could buy anything at cost. The second advantage was that I could have anything from the soda fountain for free. This would undoubtedly amount to some significant savings as I could eat there each day for free. A third advantage was even better yet. John would pay pharmacist's pay from day one. This was three months sooner than anywhere else, as they all required that their employees pass their board exams first. He told me that if I took the job I would need to work every Saturday and every other Sunday from 9:00 a.m. to 12:00 noon. He quickly added that this would only be for one year until he hired a second pharmacist, a young man who was already working summers for him. When John was finished he added, "This might be a great opportunity for you. Someone will need to take this over when I retire." As we were walking across the street back to the store John encouraged me to accept the job. He said, "Milford is a good community. As a pharmacist you will be respected and reached out to a lot."

I could tell that Tammy really desired to move home. Deep inside I knew that I really wanted to also. Neither one of us relished the thought of working every Saturday for a year but we knew we would tolerate it if necessary. As for the nature of the work and whether it would be challenging or not, I remembered speaking to a retail chain store pharmacist who was filling in at the hospital several days before. He reminded me that I could talk to people as much or as little as I wanted to about their medication in retail pharmacy. It would be entirely up to me. It hit me that he was right about this. As we talked we realized that John Perry had been in Milford since 1954. He had one pharmacist employee during the recent years. What were the odds that this man would leave Walter Drugs at the exact time I was graduating? Tammy and I were convinced God had opened this door for us and that we needed to walk through it. Our families were thrilled. My dad had been so nervous that I might not take the job that he looked physically sick. Obviously, he was happy too.

With the decision made the wheels of change were set in motion. Tammy's parents began making the little house on their farm livable. We put our trailer up for sale. I broke the news to my boss at St. Vincent Hospital. He was nice but I knew how he really felt. With what seemed like incredible swiftness, my college education and our time spent in Indianapolis came to an end. It was a very proud day for us when both of our parents attended my graduation. Ahead of us lay life. If you had asked me at that time what I expected I would have likely foreseen only work, more children, enjoying family, and a quiet existence from that point on. And in many respects this is what came to pass. I planned to remain a member of the Apostolic Christian Church. This was an integral part of my heritage and who I was. I retained my cultural affinity for the organization despite my disagreement with many of its practices. I knew that I was a nominal member, but this was all I wanted to be. I also knew that if I was to rear my children in the system that I would need to walk a fine line between promoting it as the only "sincere" church and not agreeing with many of its practices. To do otherwise would be to ensure that they would never "repent" and join the church. This approach was the one my parents had used. It had worked for me so I assumed it would work for my own children.

As I drove the blue 1965 Oldsmobile home from Indianapolis with the last of our belongings I was filled to the brim with hope. George and Pat had fixed the little house up really cute. Between Tammy and her mother it could have been no other way. We awakened from the first night in our new little home to the sound of an Amish horse and buggy passing by on the gravel road that we now lived on. It was a drizzly, foggy, Sunday morning. Except for the horse and buggy, it was intensely quiet. I remember thinking "Man, what a change!"

Chapter Thirty-Nine

The old saying "You can take the boy out of the country, but you can't take the country out of the boy" was dramatically true of me. I did not realize how much I missed the farm until I got back. When I was not working as a pharmacist, I was busy on the farm. I helped my father-in-law with odd jobs. I helped my dad. I planted a garden and loved it. The new realm of joy, however, was enjoying it all with Trischa. Nearly every day we did something outside together. We would walk to the drain ditch to throw stones in the water. We worked in the garden together. We took tractor rides through the woods. We would drive to see Grandpa Lewie's cows. She was an especially fun child to play with — a non-stop talker who was always ready to go and do something. When we could not go outside, we read books. Trischa never saw a book she did not like. All my life I had heard older people say how quickly life passed by and how they wished they had spent more time with their families. I was determined to not be this way and became obsessed with making the most of every moment with Trischa.

Whenever I was not working, Tammy and Trischa and I were on the move, visiting someone in the family or one set of parents or the other. When we were not visiting them, they were visiting us. The first summer home, Mom and Dad were busy preparing for my sister Sue's wedding. She married Glen Losee that September. Glen was a man of a few words who came into a family of many words. An expert mechanic, Glen kept the family autos in peak condition.

When Tammy began working part-time that fall, Sue watched Trischa. Life was great.

I enjoyed my work at Walter Drugs. I had much to learn about the actual practice of pharmacy, but my boss, John Perry, was patient. Brent Kaiser was also there as a student pharmacy technician that first summer. He had worked there the summer before and was a help to me as I got started. Some viewed John Perry as a grouch. Some even wondered aloud if I would be able to get along with him. From the beginning, though, I found John to be an easy man to work for. If anything, he did too little "bossing." Professionally, I was satisfied. I soon learned to tell people what was necessary for them to know. I soon learned to detect who was interested in more information and who was not. Standing all day long took some getting used to at first. It was not long until I was wearing shoes that were both bigger and softer. I came to realize before long that my work would never be my passion in life. I enjoyed my work. I knew it was necessary. But even in 1978, I knew that work was just something I did until I got home to Tammy and Trischa.

The Milford Apostolic Christian Church congregation was somewhat different from what I had grown up in. There were a number of young families there who were not there when we left. This made our coming back less difficult. There had also been a change in leadership during our absence. My Grandpa Beer had retired from the Eldership and was replaced by a younger man. The new Elder was generally enjoying the support of the congregation when we moved back. This would change dramatically in the next few years as he would attempt to change the Milford congregation into the likeness of more conservative Apostolic Christian Church congregations. The new Elder was from one of the largest families in the church, a branch that had not been previously represented in the leadership. On the positive side, he was a better than average preacher. He was also a good conversationalist. He was at his best when he could help someone who had a genuine physical or material need. He was a wealthy farmer with a young, compliant family who were all church members. On the negative side, he was a very insecure man. He only understood obedience and support. Anyone who held a different opinion than his own was viewed as non-

A Lifetime of Church

supportive or divisive. His manner, in conflict, was marked by quick, sharp, defensive responses that were invariably followed by him asking for forgiveness. This flaw was compounded by his inability to let go of the past. If anyone was ever at odds with him, he struggled to see him or her in any other light from that point on. The new Elder's weaknesses had not yet manifested themselves to the general congregation when we moved back to Milford.

In the Apostolic Christian Church, singing is a very important part of church activity. There is congregational singing before, between, and after church services. The social gatherings of young members are often called "Singings." When Sunday school groups visit one another there is singing. For Vacation Bible School sessions, Christmas, Thanksgiving, and Easter programs, there is singing. All of this singing is done a Capella. When one can carry a tune, this singing atmosphere is very gratifying. Those who cannot carry a tune are also expected to sing. I always thought that it would have been tough to be an AC and not be able to sing on tune. Because of the prominence of singing there are two jobs in the AC church that are very important: song leader and choir director. Being blessed with an ability to sing well, it was logical that my first job in the AC church was director of the youth choir.

I was asked to take this job during my first year back. The new Elder himself asked me. His son had been doing the job and wanted a break. I did not want to do this. I could sing, but I had never directed a choir. Everyone I talked to seemed to think that I should take the job so I reluctantly did. My Uncle Bob Hoerr helped me get started. My sister-in-law Deb helped me pick out music and played the piano whenever I asked. I learned two things right away. The first was that directing a choir was natural for me. The second thing I learned was that the job was a lot more work than I had anticipated. It seemed that I was constantly getting the choir ready for something. While the performances almost always went well it was nerve wracking to get people to practice. As I look back I realize I learned much about adolescents during these years. I got along great with the kids and felt I established a lot of good relationships. I also learned patience. This was good for me.

After our first winter in the little house I began thinking about getting a wood-burning stove. The effects of the 1973 OPEC oil embargo were still being felt in the United States. The high oil prices had ushered in a worldwide economic recession that would continue for some years yet. Because of the high energy prices many people were looking into alternate heating sources. Our decision to begin burning wood was hastened by an incident that took place one day while I was at work. In our little house was a freestanding oil-burning stove. One spring day Tammy laid some of Trischa's wet clothes on it to dry. Forgetting they were there, she walked over to her mom's house. When she got back there was smoke in the house. The clothes had ignited and fallen on the floor. Other than the smoke and some carpet damage, though, the house was undamaged. We were fortunate. After this we bought a wood-burning stove. My dad bought one too. Beginning then and continuing for years to come we cut wood together. It was a special activity we shared. A year later my father-in-law George also bought a wood-burning furnace add-on and began burning wood. He and I worked together cutting wood also. The old saying was that firewood warms one three times: when it is cut, when it is split and stacked, and when it is burned. I found this to be true. As time passed I discovered there was a fourth "warmth" that came from burning wood — the warmth of the fellowship we had as we cut the wood together.

In 1979, Mount Saint Helens, a dormant volcano in the State of Washington, began to rumble and quake as pressure within the cone began to increase. This would continue with ever-increasing frequency and power until 1980 when there was a massive eruption, an eruption so powerful that one whole side of the mountain was blown away. In the year leading up to this eruption there were many warnings issued by those watching the mountain. Despite these repeated warnings and continued tremors, some of the people on the mountain refused to listen or make changes or take precautions. When the eruption finally came it was far worse than anyone had anticipated. Some near the mountain perished instantly. Hundreds of square miles of surrounding forests were flattened like toothpicks. Many western states were plagued for months to come by the volcanic ash. Life would spring up from the devastation in and around Mount Saint Helens, but things would never again be quite the same for those involved in the upheaval.

In early 1979 pressure began to build up in the Milford

A Lifetime of Church

Apostolic Christian Church. The "rumble" which caused this was the voting at the annual church business meeting. Among other things that evening was the selection of two new Sunday school teachers. Those nominated were two men from conservative, "good member" families and my brother Ned and me. Ned had begun a new job as Principal of the Milford Elementary School the previous fall. He was an extremely popular teacher prior to this. In the previous years he was in charge of the youth summer recreation program in Milford. The number of children involved in the program was unprecedented, and the program's administration was a model of efficiency. Ned was even named Milford's "Citizen of the Year" for his efforts. In addition to these activities he was a successful middle school football coach and he continued to operate his home improvement company in his "free time." Ned was as popular as he could have been in every area of his life except the AC Church. The members of the church were sharply divided over his sports activities. The "good members" supported the official church position, which deemed all sports to be worldly and something that members of the church were to have no part in. While the "good members" would not have advocated church discipline for Ned, they were united in their belief that he should hold no office in the church until such a time that he conformed to the church's position on sports participation and attendance. The "nominal members" largely felt that Ned's activities were good but they understood the church's position and knew he would eventually be called into account for them. The "bad members" thought what he was doing was good and that it was none of the church's business. The debate about Ned's sports activities generally went as follows: "Do your kids take part in the summer recreation program? Yes. Wouldn't you sooner have a Christian coach and leader for them? Yes. Then why do you object to Ned's work? Because Apostolic Christian Church members are not supposed to be involved in sports."

Grandpa Beer tended to be a tolerant Elder during his tenure. He allowed Ned to serve several terms in the Sunday school during Ned's sports-involvement years. He received nagging criticism for this leniency from the "good members." To these people he encouraged patience, pointing out that these activities were part of Ned's livelihood. He also would note that Ned's long-term plan was to be in school administration, where he would no longer be taking part in his present controversial activities. Ned's detractors did not limit their complaining to Grandpa Beer. They also made their concerns known to Elders of other AC congregations, Elders who were more conservative than Grandpa Beer.

When Grandpa Beer was put in as an Elder several Elders from other AC congregations came on a Sunday, had the church vote, and ordained him into the office. By the time he retired the process had changed. Once the church had chosen Grandpa's successor, he had to be examined by the national Elder body before he could be ordained. One might think that this was a simple procedural change, but the ramifications of this change were dramatic. The essence of the change was that only staunchly conservative candidates were approved for the office of Elder. Those who were approved agreed in advance to preserve the denomination's teachings, customs, and traditions. This essentially precluded any future change in denomination's thinking and practices as the lowest common denominator, the "status quo," became the ideal. Milford's new Elder had long been a conservative traditionalist in the church, but even his ordination was delayed for a period of time until all could agree that he was "ready." It followed logically then that Grandpa's successor came into office committed to restoring conservative uniformity in the Milford congregation. Part of this was undoubtedly his own desire, but part of it was an obligation to the national Elder body also.

On the night of the 1979 Sunday school election involving Ned and me the new Elder had only been in office a year or so. When the votes were counted, Ned and I were chosen to teach Sunday school ahead of the conservative brothers. In addition, an uncle of mine was elected to an office ahead of a conservative brother. The "nominal members" and "bad members" were delighted. The "good members" however, were stunned. Not only had their candidates been defeated in a vote by the congregation, they had been beaten by a man like Ned Speicher. What did this say about the future purity of the church? There were even rumblings that Ned's and my supporters had stuffed the ballot box. Indeed, the following Sunday the new Elder scolded the church for these voting irregularities and made it clear that there would be changes in the future. As we left for home the night of the election the new Elder told Ned the evening had given him "much to think about" as he left for the Elder conference. We did not know what he meant at the time, but the years to come would show that the events of this evening were pivotal in bringing about some leadership initiatives that would greatly increase the rumblings and internal pressure in the congregation.

Chapter Forty

It was not long after Tammy and I moved back to Milford that we decided we wanted another baby. After our experience with Trischa we figured we would be expecting in no time at all. Wrong. It was not until we had been through over a year of waiting, months of doctor visits, and two courses of the fertility drug Clomiphene that we finally learned that we would be expecting a baby in October, 1980. In my zeal to be the best father and husband in the history of the world I began a daily journal in June of that year.

In those days Trischa and I were having so much fun in the woods on the farm that I had the idea to reforest it. The State of Indiana provided very inexpensive nursery stock for this purpose. In the spring of 1980 I planted six hundred trees in the woods. They were maples, poplars, walnuts, sycamores, and red oaks. I had prepared for the trees arrival by preparing planting sites in the open areas of the woods. At three-pace intervals I scalped the sod away. With this done ahead of time, the planting went quickly. That spring and summer I spent many, many hours planting them and caring for them. For many of these hours Trischa was right at my side. What a privilege.

In the summer of 1980 there were rumblings in the congregation of the Milford Apostolic Christian Church that the church needed another minister. Grandpa Beer and two other ministers were getting older. Grandpa would have been eighty-two and the two others were not far behind. Some in the congregation felt strongly that these men should retire in order to make room for younger replacements. Unfortunately, many of these people were not too kind in the way they made their feelings known. Others in the congregation urged patience, reasoning that the older ministers had served so faithfully over the years. On Sunday, June 15, 1980 there was a vote taken about whether the church should elect a new minister or not. My journal entry of that day follows.

At the member meeting we learned that the vote as to whether another minister should be elected did not carry when all the "qualified yes" votes were considered as "no" votes. I cannot honestly feel that now is the proper time. I would much sooner wait a while and let the spirit of the church improve. As for Grandpa, Henry, and Elmer, I pray that we show much patience with those who over the years have given so much. A little golden rule and brotherly love now will save us all a lot of guilt later. I'm so glad that Grandpa admonished the church about the nature of the attacks on Elmer...certainly wish (the new Elder) would have had the wisdom to do the same. People who can make such caustic comments cannot be filled with Christian love. (The new Elder) is the key. For things to improve he must begin to be less dictatorial and begin to show more loving, conciliatory leadership.

Grandpa Beer later explained to me that many of the "yes" votes were qualified with the basic message that they were "yes" only if some of the old ministers retired first. Other ballots contained some hurtful personal notes. The result of the vote was that the issue was tabled for ten months.

In the fall of 1980 three events took place. One of them was very sad and one very joyous. I was not sure what to think about the third event at the time. The sad event unfolded in the church. For as long as I could remember I was proud of the fact that our church denomination had its own personal property insurance. The congregations within the denomination funded this insurance. Those wishing to be a part of the program paid an annual assessment based on the previous year's needs. Time had proven this program to be trustworthy to the point that secular lenders accepted it to cover their loans. Each congregation had an elected local insurance representative. The

A Lifetime of Church

beauty of the system over the years was that it was founded on trust and operated on trust. When there was a claim, it was paid. There was congregational pride in the fact that there were seldom any questions asked. In all my years in the AC church I heard of only two claims that were disputed. Both of them happened in my first year after college. The one claim was relatively small and it was paid after a Milford AC member wrote a letter of appeal to another church representative subsequent to being denied by Milford's representative.

The second claim was much larger. The same Milford representative made the denial. It was never paid. The situation arose in the fall during the chopping of corn silage. A family in the church filled a silo that year which had not been filled in several previous years. Prior to filling it the family had the silo checked out and were told it would be fine. Once the silo had been filled, however, it fell over, crushing a farm tractor. No one was hurt, but the silo, the silage, and the tractor were destroyed. The family turned the claim into the church insurance representative without a thought that it might be questioned.

Following a church service weeks later the Elder informed the family that the claim was denied. The denial was because the accident was not deemed to be "an act of God" by the church insurance representative and whomever else he might have spoken to. The family was devastated. They pleaded with the representative to just "turn the claim in" as had always been done in the past, but their pleas were to no avail. The family's children were not members of the church and were furious. I learned about the situation through one of these children while at work. It soon became apparent what was really behind the claim's denial. Just as there were "good members" and "nominal members" in the church, there were also "good farmers" and "nominal farmers." Everyone in the congregation knew who fit into which category, too. In this case it was the "good farmers" who were making the decision. I soon heard their side of the story through the talk around town — things like "Everyone knew that silo was no good...They had no business putting silage in that silo...There was no wind that day, the old thing just crumbled." The defenders of the church leadership's action went on the offensive by pointing out that if the parents of this family would act more mature and support the leadership, their children would settle down. The issue at hand — whether an insurance claim was legitimate or not — soon disintegrated into an argument about who had the power to make a decision and the necessity of supporting the church leadership.

Working at the pharmacy I began to see that the townspeople were amused by the trouble among the AC church members. They also generally felt the family was being treated unfairly. Some even suggested to my family member co-worker that they hire a lawyer to fight the injustice. I found this very embarrassing. I could not imagine why this family and this incident had been singled out for denial after a lifetime of seeing claims paid without question. One day on the way home from work I stopped at the Elder's house to speak to him about it. I explained how this was being perceived in the community, that it was casting our church in a very negative light. I informed him that outsiders looking at this were simply concluding that those they trusted were cheating this family. I explained my concern that this would produce lasting bitterness in this family and especially among their non-member children. I suggested that if it was the church's desire to be tougher in paying claims that it would be wise to pay this one and then make the new restrictions clear for the future. This way people would have a choice whether to be a part of the more restrictive program or not. My conclusion to him was that I believed there was nothing to be gained by denying this claim and much to be lost.

To my surprise and dismay my words made no impact at all. The Elder was clearly more concerned about how all this was affecting him and how it was making his job harder than he was about whether the decision was correct or not. I remember only two things that he said during our visit and both of them seemed strange. After hearing me out he asked if the people would be satisfied with a replacement tractor. "I have one just like it," he said. He added "Maybe there was a wind over there that day that we didn't have here." The family lived across a field from him. I felt worse when I left the Elder's house than I had felt when I came. It was obvious that the decision would not be altered. This was the first time I remember being concerned about the survival of the Milford AC congregation. A partial payment of the claim was eventually made, but not from the insurance fund. It would come from the "poor relief" fund as a result of some behind the scenes efforts of another Milford minister. For this family, however, it was too little, too late. The damage had been done. It also increased tension among the church members. Some sided with the leadership. Others sided with the family. While the insurance representative and his supporters had their way in the matter, no one "won." Because the fruit of this incident included bitterness, pride, and mistrust, the Milford AC congregation "lost" in a big way.

The second event of 1980 was the birth of our second daughter, Traci. The pregnancy was uneventful, as Tammy's pregnancy with Trischa had been. As in all other areas of her life, I found Tammy to be amazing as a bearer and rearer of children. The week before Traci's birth one of Tammy's first cousins gave birth to a microcephalic baby. This was very sad and very sobering as we awaited our own baby. My journal entries of Traci's birth follow.

Tuesday, October 7, 1980. Still no baby! I mowed the lawn this morning, first thing. Hopefully this will be the last time before spring! Tammy was feeling energetic so she picked up all the potatoes which we dug Sunday and put them in baskets. Trischa helped, of course! Trischa and I then decided to plant some beechnuts. Following Uncle Henry's advice I dug a depression in the garden first. Then we started planting the nuts in 25 little clay pots. She handed the nuts and I planted. When we finished planting we nestled the pots into the loose dirt and watered them. When the leaves fall I'll cover them for the winter. If anything grows we will plant them next spring in the woods.

Before dinner and work, Tammy was still feeling energetic so we toured the trees. I think the walnuts were nipped by the frost two nights ago.

Work was going as usual when "Suddenly, the phone rang!" It was Tammy and she thought she was starting labor. This was about 4:30pm. At 7pm she called again and wanted me to come home. I was in the middle of filling a prescription and I called Brent (my coworker) to come in. I was finishing the prescription when the phone rang again and the other party simply exclaimed, "You get home!" The other party, of course, was my mother-in-law.

So, we made it to the hospital at 7:35pm and settled in to some serious labor.

Wednesday, October 8, 1980. The labor had continued about the same until about 1:30am. Then the contractions suddenly got much harder. Tammy got a shot for the pain and in four contractions went from 4cm to complete dilation. The doctor was called and they took us to delivery. Tammy had to work hard not to push. Then when she could push and the doctor was in place it only took about three pushes — and — at 2:36am 10/08/80 TRACI LEIGH came into the world!! As with Trischa the first thing I noticed was the "Tammy" nose. She was anatomically perfect. I felt the strongest urge to cry when they put her on Tammy's stomach and I realized what a God-sent miracle had just taken place. What greater blessing can be bestowed on a person than to see a precious innocent continuation of one's self ushered into the world? My one wish for her, as it has been and will continue to be for both Trischa and her is that they do not die unsaved. Anything else is inconsequential. What a lucky individual I am!

So, now you start life, Traci. I am going to try my best to spoil you rotten with love and attention. I can't do it with material things and hopefully never will try to. Welcome, girlie, I love you!

Traci was not as fussy a baby as Trischa was but she did not sleep too well. Early on I remember taking my turn with her through the middle of the night as she kicked and cooed. She was such a beautiful baby that it was hard to be very angry with her. Even though she looked strikingly like Trischa did as a baby it soon became apparent that she would have blue eyes. To this day their differing eye colors are their most distinguishing features. It took several months after Traci's birth until I had a clear mind again. I was so in awe of the miracle of birth and God's handiwork.

The third significant event that took place in 1980 was in the political realm. Ronald Reagan was elected President of the United States. It was a time of deep economic recession. Inflation and unemployment were soaring. Interest rates were in the mid-teens. The Cold War tensions were high between the United States and the Soviet Union. The country was struggling for optimism in the wake of the Viet Nam war and the Watergate scandal. In the midst of these challenges along came Ronald Reagan with a new, radical set of ideas. In the middle of budget deficits, he advocated deep tax cuts. In response to the Cold War tensions he proposed a massive military build-up. Rather than wallowing in our national woes, he extolled our national virtues, reminding us that we were the greatest nation in history, that our future was bright, and that we were the beacon of freedom to the world. As he continued to speak this way our national pride began to be restored and people began to expect a brighter future. His most stunning declaration was that Communism would "end up on the ash heap of history." I remember being embarrassed by this declaration. In my mind there was no way this could happen. History, however, proved him to be right.

Chapter Forty-One

The "little house" at 900 N 625 W was bustling with activity, as 1980 became 1981. The warmth generated by our wood-burning stove that winter was exceeded only by the warmth in our hearts. My typical day consisted of work, then home — then holding, playing with, and reading to the girls until bedtime. Tammy was a natural as a mother. The little, square, four room house was transformed by her touch to feel like a palace. Except for the occasional mouse that we needed to trap, we did not think life could get much better.

In the spring of 1981, the issue of needing another minister in the Milford Apostolic Christian Church was revisited. I anticipated the election in my journal entry of March 1981.

Sunday, March 1, 1981. Where did February go? It seems impossible that March is here. What changes will the next several months bring? Last Sunday it was announced that we will choose a new minister on April 26th. I suppose that the main contenders are (my brother Ned and two others). Poor Ned, I really feel it will fall on him. I share Mom's concern that it will alter our now excellent family relationship. If this does come to pass he and Deb will need our special support.

Poor Mom was like a cat in a cage as the day approached. It was the opinion of everyone in our family and of many others who expressed their feelings that my brother Ned would be chosen.

Having been in the AC Church her whole life Mom knew full well that Ned's selection would subject us all to increased scrutiny. We would no longer have the liberty to be at odds with the church in the future should Ned be a minister. The church leaders in general and our Elder in particular demanded full support from their ministers and their ministers' families. Having suffered under such pressure her whole life, Mom wanted no part of this for a child of hers. It was during this time frame that I first heard her say something that would be repeated many times in the coming years: "I feel like God is asking me to sacrifice one of my children." Dad was so competitive by nature that he wanted Ned to get the job. I felt it would be the best thing for the church. Ned was a natural teacher. I was confident that he would be a great preacher, too. I was sure that the young, non-member "friends of the truth" would be more inclined to join the church if he was elected. In addition, I felt that Ned's popularity in the community would help the church's community image.

Everything seemed to be moving in this direction as the "big day" approached. I remember cutting wood with Dad and him obsessively speculating about who "so and so" would vote for, undoubtedly covering the entire church membership several times over. But even if we only counted those who had openly said they planned to vote for Ned we approached a number close to a majority. There was a big surprise coming, however, as my journal entry of April 26, 1981 points out.

Sunday, April 26, 1981. I could have used about four more hours of sleep this morning, but Traci saw to it that we made it to church on time. We read about Pentecost in Sunday school. (The visiting elder) had the afternoon service and did a great job. I was miserable throughout, however. We had the minister vote as scheduled. We sang 45 minutes before they returned with what we presumed would be some information. However, they simply announced that the church needed more time. The Elders' words were carefully chosen: "The church needs more time. We do not know how much. We will not say more." I was stunned, as was everyone else. I think the whole church felt they deserved some sort of an explanation. Anyone who inquired was simply instructed to pray for patience. I hope this period of "time" isn't too long because the church presently is in no mood for it. My heart really goes out to those who were in contention. For them it must have been like having a stillborn baby.

This produced some significant, easily detectable rumblings within the church. The "internal pressure" was definitely rising. Having made the stunning announcement, the visiting Elder announced a closing song from the hymnal entitled "Wait, and Murmur Not." Not many people knew the tune and the sound of the singing matched the mood of many people. The title of the song was appropriate for the Elders' wishes, but it definitely did not achieve the desired result. The congregation had no choice about the "Wait" part, but the "Murmur Not" part was another matter. As I left the church that afternoon I was disappointed. I became angry when a brother of our Elder, who had carried the Elder's briefcase to his car, was on the sidewalk outside the church explaining that "no one had any clear support," that the vote was "too scattered" for the Elders to proceed. This upset me because he was speaking as one who was sure of what he knew. I reasoned that if the congregation had been refused an explanation, then the Elder's brother should not know what happened either, and if he did know, he certainly should not be openly telling people.

Later that day I drove to the Elder's house. By that time my anger had passed and I simply wanted to know if any individual in the congregation had been told more than what the congregation had been told from the pulpit. The Elder received me warmly and confirmed that everyone in the congregation had been told the same thing. He then wanted to know why I was asking. I answered that I had heard an explanation after church by one who spoke as if he knew. Upon further questioning I reluctantly told him who had given the explanation. Hearing that it was his brother he immediately walked into the house and called his brother, despite my plea that he not call. I had told him that his word was fine with me — and it was. He soon came back with an assurance from his brother that he had not opened the briefcase as he walked it from the church to the Elder's car. This was embarrassing to me because I never thought for a minute that he had "peeked" in the briefcase. I had simply wanted to confirm that everyone in the congregation was on equal footing concerning what they had been told. Before I left, the Elder encouraged patience, saying, "Just give this thing a little time, Tom. It will all work out." In retrospect, this is a visit that I wish I never had made. I did not accomplish anything, and given a few more years of maturity, I would have known before the fact that nothing would be accomplished.

In the next few days I thought about what might have happened to bring abut the need for "more time." Either many people did not vote for whom they said they were going to vote for or my brother Ned had significant support. Also, if the problem had been that the vote was "too scattered" and "no one had any clear support," the Elders could have told this to the church. This would have been a reasonable explanation that people would have accepted. While only the two Elders will ever know exactly what happened, it is my conviction that the problem was not that "no one had any clear support." I believe the problem was that my brother Ned had significant support, but his involvement in sports and coaching in the recent past would have made him unacceptable to many in the church and to most AC Elders. I believe they were unwilling to allow the vote to proceed because he might be the one chosen. Grandpa Beer later told me that this was what he thought happened also.

It was not too long before the shock of the "need more time" announcement wore off and people put it on the "back burner." It was clear, however, that the "murmur not" request was not going to be honored. Slowly, but surely, a resentment towards the Elders was growing among the thirty-something "nominal members." We could see that the leadership of the denomination was becoming more and more conservative. With this trend we saw less and less trust of the membership by the leadership. There were three clear signs to us that operations in the AC Church leadership had changed. The first sign was in a sermon our new Elder preached one Sunday afternoon. In this sermon he laid out his view of what his responsibility was as the new Elder. The essence of his vision was that it was his job to preserve the customs, traditions, and teachings of the denomination by "building fences." This farming metaphor of "building fences," or erecting clear boundaries, would serve two purposes. It would keep the membership in harmony with the denomination's "historical ways." It would also keep the "world" out. The second sign was that our new Elder no longer made decisions about our congregation on his own. Decisions were now made with the input and consent from outside Elders. This new practice was consistent with the national Elder body's preoccupation with "holding the line" and uniformity. The new practice was a big change from the leadership of Grandpa Beer, who relied heavily on the advice and consent of his local ministers.

The third sign that things were going to be forever changed in the Milford AC Church was the new voting restrictions. As he had promised after the election that placed Ned and me in Sunday school, our new Elder made changes in how votes were conducted. The first change was that all elections were now preceded by nomination votes. Candidates with sufficient support were then interviewed by the Elder to determine if they were sufficiently supportive of the ways of the church and the leadership. Only "approved" candidates were presented to the congregation for a final vote. Questionable candidates were simply screened out. The second change was that absentee voting was no longer allowed. Even spouses could not vote for spouses. No exceptions. At elections the number of ballots were matched with the number of members in attendance. In my mind this was so sad because it clearly demonstrated that the leadership did not trust the congregation anymore. It should have been clear that only "good members" had any future in the denomination, but I still held out hope the trend would moderate at that time.

A new minister was finally chosen in December of 1981. The church was informed that we would address the issue in October. I noted this in my journal entry of October 4, 1981.

Sunday, October 4, 1981. Tammy kept the girls home today so they wouldn't expose the rest of the church (to chicken pox). *(Our elder) announced that* (visiting elders) *will be coming back this December 6th. Perhaps I shouldn't be but I'm optimistic that we will get it taken care of this time. Grandpa Beer announced to the church today that he intends to retire when we elect a new minister. What a life of service he has lived. I love him like a father.*

Grandpa Beer decided to retire from preaching when he realized that his continuing might be impeding the election of another preacher. His decision to retire was not made lightly, but once the decision was made he never looked back. This was typical of Grandpa. Grandpa was very careful to publicly support the new Elder and the church in general. Privately, however, he would at times express his concerns about what was happening. He was concerned about the "need more time" result of the last vote, telling me "everything had been left to people's imaginations." He was also concerned about the message the new voting procedures were sending to the congregation. He often had said over the years "A healthy church will naturally produce the leaders it needs." But mainly he kept his opinions to himself. It had to hurt a bit that the new Elder did not consult with him, but he never spoke of it. Grandma Beer was even more troubled than Grandpa, but she tried even harder to hide her feelings.

On Sunday, November 22, 1981, the Elder interviewed Ned and Deb. I wrote about this in my journal.

Sunday, November 22, 1981. We had quite a night last night. We had just gotten to sleep when Traci started jabbering. She finally started crying. Tammy found she was feverish. Since our last episode we were both more worried than we should have been. She went back to sleep about an hour later but I didn't get back to sleep until about 2:30. I felt like a zombie in the morning.

Our Thanksgiving program went very well. Afterwards we went home and had dinner with George and Pat. We napped throughout the afternoon and then went to visit Mom and Dad. When we got there we went with them to Ned's to babysit so they could go talk to (the Elder) — they were "summoned" earlier in the day. They got home about three hours later. They really didn't know much more than before they went, but they encouraged (the Elder) and they feel it will be handled properly. I must admit that I feel better too.

The minister election was held on the first weekend in December. My journal entries record how I saw it unfold.

Saturday, December 5, 1981. No work today. The day was cold but beautiful. Dad and I had planned to cut wood but I went to help

Ned fix his water heater. The last six months have been hard on us all, but exceptionally so for him and Deb. He needed to keep busy today. Tonight we had a special church session. The memorandum was read first and then we voted again for a minister prior to being dismissed. Afterwards we went to Warsaw for pizza with (some friends). Ned obviously was in misery. Hopefully tomorrow we can put an end to this.

Sunday, December 6, 1981. Today was an important day — only the years to come will tell how important. This afternoon, Ned and Dale's (Strassheim) names were put to a vote. About 35 minutes later they returned and announced that Dale will be our new minister. I didn't vote for him but I wish the very best for him — the welfare and future of the church will depend on him more now than ever.

Dale Strassheim turned out to be an excellent minister. He was a hospital administrator by profession. His people skills and public speaking skills were very good. The fact that he had no extended family in the Milford AC congregation helped him to be objective and even-handed in his dealings in the church. I hardly knew Dale when he was placed in the ministry, but we were destined to become good friends and mutual supporters. With the election of Dale the "rumblings" in the church quieted for a while. The internal pressure leveled off. It may have even lessened a bit. This period of quiet, however, ultimately turned out to be only the calm before the storm.

The harmony in the little house in the country was interrupted for a bit in late 1981. Traci was progressing nicely, but was sick more than normal with ear and upper respiratory infections. Other than the nights of inadequate sleep we were not bothered much by them. We figured it was all a part of rearing children. On November 6, 1981, however, Traci gave us a big scare, as my journal indicates.

Friday, November 6, 1981. Today was a day I'll remember as long as I'll live. Work was very hectic again. We are finally getting the EOM stuff done. Plus I was worried about the choirs, the house, and my future at work. Tammy called at 4:00 p.m. and asked me to bring a bunch of stuff home. She said Traci had a 103 degree fever and had been screaming since her nap. So by the time I stopped at the grocery store, the nursing home, and the gas station I was heading home late and feeling sorry for myself. I had plans for the night and intended to cut wood tomorrow morning and thought we could look for wood stove add-ons in the afternoon. I thought all my plans wouldn't work out now. In about one hour I was to feel like a fool for these ridiculous thoughts.

    When I got home Traci was crying. I was shocked when I felt her — she was burning up. Tammy had given her a baby aspirin at 1:00 p.m. and some Tylenol at 5:00 p.m. We decided to put her in some cool water. However, she fought it so that we soon took her out — too soon as we were to find out. We got her dressed and I gave her 1 grain Tylenol rectally. While Tammy started supper I held her. She was so hot and her breathing was labored. I asked Tammy if she had been breathing like that all afternoon and she seemed to think so. I took her into the living room and sat down with her in my chair. Trischa was walking up to us when Traci's hands started to quiver. I saw in Trischa's eyes that she noticed it and I told her to go to her room. Right at that time Traci's eyes rolled back, she stopped breathing, and her whole body started quivering. Tammy rushed in and frantically tried to help before running across to get her mom. At first I just kept her airway open, but as seconds passed I saw she was turning red and blue. I was horror stricken as I started mouth to mouth breathing for her — still she didn't respond. I kept thinking, "I'm losing her! Please Lord please!" I soon realized Trent was in the house calling the ambulance and Tammy came back into the room. She was hysterical and I told her to leave. Finally after another breath I turned her on her stomach and patted her back twice — she coughed and started to whimper — I knew she was okay. I held her and wept. In a minute or less I was absolutely shaken to my foundation. Ironically my first thoughts were how foolish I had been to have been so concerned about such meaningless things a few minutes earlier. I also thought about how much God loved me to sacrifice his Son's life — this one minute revealed this in a way previously unknown to me.

    Traci continued to whimper and I gave her to Tammy. Pat had called Dr. Hinton and he said he was on his way, so I called the ambulance off. Soon a State Cop who had heard the ambulance call stopped to see if he could help. We immediately began bathing Traci and continued until Dr. Hinton came. He put a bag of ice on her head to get the heat away from her brain. He said her lungs and ears were clear. He though it must be a virus. I went to town to get some Phenobarb elixir and when I got back she was sleeping. I was still so upset that I wept most of the way there and back.

My folks came around 8:00 p.m. and Traci woke up about half an hour later. She was burning up again. I gave her the Phenobarb and we began sponging again. About 20 minutes later we had made no progress so we gave her a cool water enema. While we were putting it in she started another convulsion, but screamed and came out of it. So I had Tammy call Dr. Yoder. While she was on the phone Traci started yet another one. Dr. Yoder told us to take her to the emergency room. My folks took Trischa and Tammy's folks came along.

When we got there poor babes started another convulsion — just a beginning of one — so we began sponging (her with cool water). She had another short one before the doctor came. He also said her lungs were clear. However he ordered blood work, throat and nose cultures and a chest X-ray. He came in soon after and told us that she had pneumonia in her left lower lobe. I saw the X-ray and it was prominent.

So they admitted her and started Ceclor 125mg every six hours, Phenobarb 10mg every six hours, and Tylenol. By the time we got to her room we could feel the "rattle" in the lower left lung — obviously it was coming on rapidly. When I left for home Traci was able to manage a half smile and even tried to touch my nose to beep it. This was like a flower in the desert. Tammy stayed and George, Pat, and I went home.

I always thought that my girls were so precious and meant the world to me. However tonight I realized I must do more to savor each moment. Even though Traci may not have been close to death — **I thought** she was and it was an experience I shall never forget — may it never happen again.

This incident ushered in a very nerve-racking year and a half for Tammy and me. It was the first of Traci's four incidents of febrile seizures, but it was also the first of many more times that we sat frozen beside her waiting for them. She could spike a fever without warning. The years have dulled the memories some, but I can still get chills at the remembrance of the anticipation. We took Traci to several specialists during this time frame. The neurologist put her on Dilantin after the fourth episode. More importantly, however, he ran tests that ruled out any epilepsy. He pointed out that 95% of febrile seizures occur between the ages of six months and two and one half years. This was exactly true of Traci.

Part of the "American Dream" is home ownership. Tammy and I started our quest for our "piece of the pie" in late 1981. Ever since we came back to Milford realtors had been trying to match us with a house to buy. We resisted because we were so happy in the little house in the country. We also were afraid of the high mortgage interest rates, which at the time were in the upper teens. With the arrival of Traci the little house was getting "smaller" all the time. My drive to work was ten miles one way. I did not mind the drive, but fuel prices were very high at the time. We also started to look in earnest as it came time for Trischa to start school. This would have been a long bus ride from where we were, but for me Trischa starting school presented a more compelling reason to move to Milford. Grandpa Beer and others had cautioned me that it was important she go to school where other AC Church kids went to school. Doing this would provide her with group support and ultimately increase the likelihood that she would "repent" and join the church. This admonition had an impact on me because I had grown up with the understanding that the measure of one's success as a parent was whether their children became members of the AC Church or not. I never spoke about this reason much with Tammy. While she was as understanding of the AC ways as an "outsider" could have been, I was sure she would have pointed out to me (quite correctly) that this was a silly reason to relocate.

We had looked at a number of houses since moving back home, but none of them ever captured our interest. This changed when one of the members of the AC Church bought a farm from an estate about one mile east of town. On this farm was a really cute two story white house. When we expressed an interest in the house, the owner of the farm, Carlton Beer, went out of his way to make it possible for us to have it. We fell in love with the place right away. When we learned that the best mortgage rates available would be nineteen per cent we began to get "cold feet." Carlton Beer again went out of his way to help us, offering to finance it himself until we could do better than his Federal Land Bank rate, which was fourteen per cent. In addition to this he wanted no money down. When my uncle Phil Beer offered to do the closing for free we had the very best house available to us for the very best deal possible at the time. Carlton Beer's treatment of Tammy and me represented the very best of the Apostolic Christian Church, the aspect of the church I had been most proud of growing up. He chose to be charitable to us and this was an act of Christian love that I have never forgotten and for which I am still grateful.

The move to our new house was beyond exciting, as my journal entries indicate.

Friday, January 1, 1982. Another year. For us it was a most eventful one. A new minister in church, a new home, a new brother-in-law, a new "sister-sister" in faith (my sister Amy, who had joined the AC Church) *and most of all more loving experiences with my wonderful frau* (wife) *and girlies. Trischa has become so inquisitive and so feeling and prettier every day. Traci is truly my little peanut. Even though she and Trishca look so much alike they are so different. Whereas Trischa was high strung and constantly driving at age one, Traci is simply an imp! She is such a tease — my little blue-eyed dream baby. Her illness* (in November) *helped me realize how truly precious my girlies are. I'm so hopeful that the insertion of ear tubes will eliminate her chronic illnesses.*

This morning Traci woke up promptly at 7:00 a.m. It did not mean a thing to her that it was New Years Day. Poor Tammy was nearly dead with exhaustion, but she took the first shift from 7:00 to 10:00 a.m. Then I took a turn until 11:30 when Traci took her nap. Poor Trischa got up but I couldn't stay awake to entertain her. Tammy, Traci, and I finally got up at 1:30 p.m. This afternoon while Tammy packed I moved our clothes to the house. Dad and Tom Kroh went with me on the second trip and we took a whole truckload.

We ate supper at Mom's. Tammy was to join us but she slid in the ditch at the end of the road — poor Maw. We all turned in early to get a good start for tomorrow.

Saturday, January 2, 1982. We had our last load loaded by 12:30p.m. today. Morrie (Beer) *and Pat* (Speicher) *and George provided trucks and Ted brought Yoder's step-van. In addition we had Tom, Glen, Rich, Trent, Lynn, Andy, Sue, Amy, Pat, Sandy, and of course, Tammy and me.*

Grandma Beer made a feast for dinner — just a "little something" as she said. We really had a nice time. My mom kept the girlies. On the way back to the house after lunch we took two big truckloads of wood. It was quite a day.

As I sit here this evening I can't believe it has really happened. Trischa is so excited that she is running about ten notches above maximum!

As I look back on this I am still astonished about how hard our families worked to make this possible. In the month following the move my brother Ned must have been at the house every other day helping us with something. In the years since I have tried to help others as I was helped. Having been on the receiving end of this I had an extra incentive to try and help "make someone else's day." I guess that is how it is supposed to work.

The final significant happening of 1981 involved my Grandpa Beer. As mentioned earlier, many days in my youth were spent riding with Grandpa on his feed route, producing many precious memories. One day in July of 1981 Grandpa Beer came in to the pharmacy. He often came in to chat, but this day he had an idea he wanted to run by me. Over the years he had built up a good business selling twine to farmers. He had a particularly loyal following among the Amish and other conservative people. With his special gifts of remembering names and chatting he could generally sell them anything he had. On this particular day he was thinking about the future, and at age eighty-three it was probably about time for him to be doing this. He told me that he thought I could be a salesman and wondered if I would be interested in "working into" his business. He added that he hated to see it die with him. "I made over six thousand dollars last year in a few months," he said.

When Tammy and I talked over the idea we decided the extra income potential would be worth giving it a try. Thus began my "twining" days, which were to continue for the next five years. In the spring and early summer of this period many Wednesdays (my day off) and Saturdays were spent riding around the northern Indiana countryside in Grandpa's twine-laden blue Chevy truck. As I look back I remember every trip as an adventure, beginning or ending with a Grandma Beer feast. Grandpa Beer was a non-stop chatterer, either with the occupants of his truck or whoever's house we were stopped at. I learned a lot about a lot of subjects on these trips and more about some things than I needed to know or wanted to know.

By the time the first twine season rolled around, my brother Ned was in on the deal and he began "administrating." Since Grandpa had all his customer information stored in his brain this initial organization was a challenge. By the second twine season we had accumulated names and addresses of customers. With this information we sent out letters in advance of the season and took orders. This made the operation a lot more efficient. One year we even had enough volume to bypass the wholesaler and buy directly from the twine manufacturer in Mexico. Through Ned's brothers-in-law we were able to arrange transportation of the twine from New Orleans to Milford as they returned from a grain run. In two of these five years Grandpa Beer was laid up with injuries. In these years Ned, my Dad, and I basically did it all — with Grandpa's supervision, of course!

These were challenging days for Ned's wife Deb and for Tammy, as they were often left alone with young children while we delivered twine. They were patient, however, because the extra money came in handy. We also tried to take the children whenever there was room for them. One year we made a special deal with the children. We told them that if they were patient and helped out at home while we were gone that we would use some of the extra money to take them to a hotel with swimming pool for a weekend. This was a time in our lives when neither Ned nor I had any extra money to do a lot of special things like this so everyone was thrilled with the deal. When the twine season wound down that year the time came for Ned and me to get paid. We were expecting to get fifty cents each for every bale of twine we sold, amounting to about $750. This was a lot of money at that time. As if it was yesterday, I remember Ned and I sitting in Grandpa's living room on the "big day" when he told us that rather than pay us what we had earned, he was applying that amount to what we owed him! As we were picking our jaws up out of our laps Grandma Beer said, "Boys, I want you to know, that this is **not** my idea!" To this she added a hard blink of her brown eyes for emphasis. It is a rare thing for Ned or me to be speechless, but this is one time that we were so stunned that neither of us had anything to say. When we regained our wits we mentioned that we had promised our families some time away with our earnings. We even added that we wished we had known before the fact that he was planning to do this. It was all to no avail, however. Grandpa had made up his mind.

We have often laughed about this over the years, but it was not a bit funny at the time. With Grandpa laid up with a broken hip, we had kept his business going that year. And we had spent many hours away from our families to do it. I remember feeling angry and hurt. Poor Mom was so angry that all she could do was cry. There was nothing we could do about it, though. We had both borrowed about a thousand dollars from Grandpa the year before, so I guess it was his right to collect on the loans. He should have told us before the fact, however. Thanks to credit cards, we took the kids away for a weekend anyway.

In retrospect I realize that his incident put a damper on the whole arrangement. Ned and I no longer felt compelled to please Grandpa by being available whenever it suited him. We both knew we could make a lot more money by working extra in our professions if we needed to. It was also obvious that Grandpa was not ready or willing to allow us to "take over." The next year Grandpa was healthy and I noticed that be began hiring Amish boys to help him whenever possible. He could hire them much cheaper than Ned and me. As our lives got busier, we were eventually not involved at all. Grandpa's original vision of passing the business on was not fulfilled. As his ability to work diminished, so did the business. Looking back, I realize that what I missed most when we were no longer involved were Grandma Beer's meals. Grandpa Beer was a great man — but he was not perfect!

Chapter Forty-Two

Those growing up in the mid-west knew the meaning of the phrase "the calm before the storm." As thunderstorms approach there is a true calm before the wind blows and the rain falls. I cannot say if it is a scientific fact or not but it seems that the more intense the storm is, the more pronounced is the calm before it. Those who are wise will listen to the weather reports, sense wind and temperature variations, and watch the sky as the storms approach. To do otherwise is to risk being caught unaware and even place one's self in harm's way. Like the people in Washington State who ignored the rumblings from Mount Saint Helens, each year there are those in the mid-west who ignore "the calm before the storm" and are unprepared for what follows.

I remember the years of 1982 and 1983 as "the calm before the storm" in the Milford Apostolic Christian Church. There were no ministers to elect, no questionable nominees to church offices who needed to be "screened out" of the elections at the annual business meetings, no major issues before the congregation. People were getting along well. By this time frame I had begun to direct the adult choir in addition to the youth choir. Our adult choir took two weekend trips to other AC Churches in my tenure. One was to Mansfield, Ohio in 1982 and another was to Goodfield, Illinois in 1983. It would have been hard to find anything more acceptable to the church leadership than singing, choir, and visiting other AC congregations. Because of this, the groups involved in these trips represented a good cross-section of the Milford AC Church. Our common interest in these trips allowed us to get to know each other better and to enjoy each other's company. The preparation for these trips and the trips themselves were the high points of Christian fellowship in my years in the AC Church. Indeed, I remember this period of time as the only time that I was content as an AC member. It was the only time I remember enjoying good fellowship outside of my family. It was the only time I involved myself in activities because I wanted to instead of out of a sense of obligation.

It was also during this "calm before the storm" period that the first signs of a coming personal spiritual renaissance began to appear in me. There were six factors involved in the "birth pangs" of this renaissance. The first factor was surely the sovereignty of God through the Holy Spirit who created the desire in me to know Him better. This factor undoubtedly ushered the other factors into the picture. For years I observed Tammy quietly, but faithfully doing her daily devotions. This second factor began to convict me to emulate her. I did not yield to this conviction for few years but it definitely bothered me. A third factor was teaching Sunday school. As I tried to make the lessons interesting for the kids I found myself being drawn to God's Word more and more. Teaching with my older brother Ned helped me to see that there were many excellent outside sources of information that helped illustrate Biblical teachings. Ned was also very good at relating world events to scripture. This sparked a personal interest in Biblical prophecy in me. I may have been one of the teachers, but I found I was the one learning the most. A fourth factor was sacred music. The more I worked with choirs, the more I was touched by the music and its message. Singing became an act of worship instead of simply something I did as a part of church activities. This first experience of worship added fuel to the spiritual sparks within me.

The fifth factor in the seeds of my spiritual renaissance was a friend named Rich Stoller. Whenever I spoke to him he drew me into a spiritual conversation. Rich was the first person in my life that challenged me consistently in sound Biblical doctrine outside of the context of the Apostolic Christian Church. Even though he was an AC member, he did not like to talk about the AC Church much with me. He preferred to talk about the Bible. It bothered me that he always did this because I had so little usable knowledge that I could not participate in the conversations on an equal footing. But Rich's manner with me was so unassuming that I kept coming back. If he had not been a fellow AC I am sure I would not have. One time he gave me an audiocassette series from the Friends of Israel Gospel Ministries on prophecy from Matthew 24. If I had to point to an "official" starting point of my spiritual renaissance it would be this audiocassette series. The material was presented in a clear, concise, sequential, passionate manner. I had never heard preaching like that before and I was captivated by it. Despite my best listening I was unable to find any "questionable" teaching in the series. All my life others had placed before me a mental picture of all preaching outside the AC Church as shallow and compromising. This whole paradigm of only the AC Church preaching the "pure word," as they said, began to be called into question in my mind from this point on.

The sixth and final factor in the beginning of my spiritual renaissance was the inquisitive nature of my daughter Trischa. The more Bible stories we taught her, the more she wanted to know. Whatever we gave her, she learned. She was virtually a non-stop question-asker also. Many of the questions were not easy ones to answer. More than once I was convicted about the fact that I knew my answers were less than adequate. Other times they were just plain evasive.

With all these forces working on me one would think that I became a serious Bible student. Sadly, this was not the case. During this period of time I learned a lot about the Bible from Christian radio, Christian para-church organizations, and Christian friends, but I did not learn it from studying the Bible myself. Becoming a serious Bible student was still a ways off. In retrospect this is very sad. Often I have wondered what would have happened in my life if I had been obedient to the Holy Spirit's prompting sooner. I believe it is likely that I could have saved myself a lot of heartache if I had been.

In the winter of 1982 Tammy had a prolonged bout of not feeling well. Despite a lot of testing we never did figure out what the problem was. One of the things the doctor suggested, however, was that she discontinue oral contraceptives for several months. That's right. You guessed it. We learned we were expecting a third child in May of 1982. We were thrilled. We hoped for a boy, but as the pregnancy progressed all the "signs" — how Tammy was "carrying" the baby, the baby's heart rate, our gut "feelings" — pointed to a third girl. My journal entry of July 16, 1982 records a bizarre and humorous dream that I had about our upcoming baby.

*Friday, July 16, 1982. Last night I had a really funny dream. It started out that I was out home helping Dad milk. Next I was in the house having choir practice and the kids were all on the stairs. Oddly, Lynn Klophenstein and Candy Wuethrich (*Two AC women whom I had not seen in years*) were among the choir members. Next Barb Ray (*an employee of Walter Drugs*) came out of Dad's Indian room (*where he displayed his artifacts*) and told me that Tammy had gone to the hospital and had a baby girl. I was really upset and wanted to get there. I remember seeing Traci as a baby and wondering if the new one looked like her. However, all I had on was a pair of gym trunks and I couldn't get through the kids to get upstairs to change. When I finally did get dressed and came back downstairs, Barb was there to show me the birth certificate. We had named her Toni. I was really upset that I had missed so much as I went outside to leave. But as I got to the car there was Tammy with a load of laundry. She said, "I left the baby in the nursery. I just have too much to do!"*
What a dream. It's how our lives have been going lately — busy, busy. I wonder how true the dream will be with regard to the baby.

The "big day" turned out to be December 16, 1982. My journal entries tell the tale.

Wednesday, December 15, 1982. When I came home tonight, the girls both came running to the door to meet me. After kisses and hugs, Traci insisted that I kiss Mommy!
Thursday, December 16, 1982. Fortunately, we didn't have to wait long for things to get rolling last night. We had just gotten asleep when Tammy's water really broke at 12:25 a.m. Almost immediately she started labor. We soon called George and Pat and we were on our way through Milford at 2:21 a.m. Tammy told me on the way that she had gone up to check Trischa and had found her lying sideways in her bed. When she turned her, she kind of stirred and Tammy whispered "Goodbye". I'm gong to the hospital to get

the baby." Tammy said her eyes got as big as golf balls, she smiled, and rolled over, again fast asleep.

When we arrived at the hospital Tammy was dilated 4 cm and didn't make a whole lot of progress until around 4:00 a.m. By 5:00 a.m. she was starting to hurt. Dr Petersen was in delivering another baby so he performed a peri-cervical block on her around 5:30 or 6:00 a.m. This really made a big difference and Tammy was able to relax again. By 7:00 a.m. she felt that she needed to push. Dr. Petersen came in to check her and told me to go get changed. By the time I got changed they already had her in the delivery room. When Dr. Petersen came in to do the delivery, he sat down and said, "It's going to be a girl." Much to my surprise Tammy replied "Not this time. It's going to be a boy." She does not remember saying this. The thing that surprised me about it was that all along we both felt we would have a third girl. It seemed to be over with as quickly as it had begun. After three pushes, at 7:22 a.m. I witnessed the third miracle of my life — Travis Alan Speicher came into the world!!! I was so stunned, thankful, and overwhelmed that I just broke down. How could a person be more blessed? After two beautiful perfect little girls to have a perfect baby boy! All through the pregnancy I didn't allow myself to hope for a boy for fear of disappointment. I honestly never expected anything but another girl. Now it seems as if we are a family — if he can survive the affections of his big sisters!

Tammy and I both noticed right away that he looks a little different than the girls (they were nearly identical). His nose is longer and less "Georgish" and his mouth is different, more like I remember Ned and Deb's kids, with the small recessed chin and big cheeks. He even has a dimple on the right side! He weighs 7 pounds, 2 1/2 ounces and is 19 inches long.

It took about an hour before Tammy and I could talk to each other without crying. By about 9:30 a.m. I was walking close enough to the ground that I thought it was safe to leave for work. I had left the delivery room almost immediately after the birth to call Pat so Trischa could know before school. Pat caught her as she was about half way to the bus. I got a hold of Mom at Sandy's. As the news hit the beauty shop it sounded like a screaming madhouse!

When I got to work, I was so excited that the first several hours went well. However, by noon and throughout the afternoon I was *really dragging. I felt like I was in a fog. I was elated when John came in and sent me home at 4:30p.m. I got to the hospital in time to hold Travis. He is such a fine-featured little doll!*

By the time I got home I was really beat. George and Pat were staying overnight so I told Trischa that I would sleep upstairs with her in the trundle bed. She disappeared and awhile later she came and said, "Dad, I don't know who did it but the trundle bed has sheets and blankets on it and it is all ready for you." Her face was shining like the sun she was so proud of herself. Before we went to sleep we snuggled and talked about how lucky we are to have each other and Traci and Travis. She is such a little lady anymore. I'll probably have to wait for heaven to have a day much better than today!

It took months for my feet to hit the ground after the addition of Travis to the family. Our home life was like living in a fairytale book in those days. No matter how bizarre our lives outside the home became, our home and family was the ultimate refuge. My journal entry of November 24, 1983 describes my heart.

Thursday, November 24, 1983. Thanksgiving Day. It seems impossible that another year has gone by. I was thinking about what I am thankful for tonight. In terms of family, I honestly don't know how I could have done better. I feel like an integral part of both my own and my in-laws. With rare exceptions there is only joy and happiness when we are in one another's presence.

As for Tammy and the children, yesterday and today have exemplified Tammy. With a fussy, sick, clinging baby and a gimp husband (I was down with a back injury) *the household went forward without missing a stroke. Her mood was upbeat and she, the kids, and I left this morning looking ready for church — and the house looked ready for company. Even after eleven years I'm still amazed at her ability to cope, to organize, and to make the best out of any situation. I'm also amazed that after eleven years and three children she is more beautiful than the day I first laid eyes on her that night at the Root Beer Stand.*

The children are another matter. I don't know that I ever tried to sit down and imagine what our children would be like, but if I could have chosen them characteristic by characteristic I couldn't have possibly done as well as what I have. All three could have been designed by Mattel for dolls. Trischa, with her voracious mind and tender heart, trying to be an adult at age six. Trying to reason with and guide her little sister in the "paths of righteousness" one moment and deviously provoking her the next. Playing in her dollhouse one moment and playing the piano and reading fifth grade books the next — with Traci always one step behind.

If Trischa's beauty is matched by anyone it has to be Traci. Only big brown eyes and big blue eyes separate the two from being twins three years apart. At her tender age Traci has become a master aggravator of her older sister. An avid watcher of "Sesame Street," she has quickly picked up which is "different," "bigger," and "smaller." I predict that she will always be a very persuasive girl because she is an expert at talking and expressing herself with her eyes. I'm hoping and praying that her thermostat is now properly functioning forever and that the winter of '83 won't ever be repeated. I kind of hate to see her learn to say "R's" because then there will be no more "Tisha," "Taci," and "Tabus."

And Travis — one year ago I would never have dreamt that I'd ever have a baby boy. I was certain he would be a girl. His chief talents at this point are "speed-crawling" and plant and dirt eating. He also loves to play with a ball, much more so that the girls ever did. Perhaps this is just coincidental, however. He is almost to the stage to be considered a "walker." He is so proud of himself when he does.

Of course the thing for which I'm most thankful for is Christ and my salvation. My faith is unwavering that from day one He has had His hand on me and has so richly blessed me with my salvation and my family, not to mention my material well-being. Everything else rates such a distant 3rd to God and family that they don't even warrant mentioning.

It was a time of personal contentment in every area of my life. My work was reasonably satisfying. My marriage and family could not have been better. My activities in the church were acceptable. Even as I describe this period of time as "calm" in the church, it was a relative calm. There remained a constant tension between our

Elder and all of us whom he perceived as less than fully supportive. Even though the congregational rumblings were barely perceptible, it was clear to me that the internal pressure was slowly rising as 1983 neared an end. The voting for offices at the annual business meeting always increased tensions, but this year there was an added feature. I noted this feature in a journal entry October 2, 1983.

Sunday, October 2, 1983. After church we had a member meeting at which Elmer Hartter announced his retirement (from being a minister), effective January first. Elmer has been on the pulpit longer than I have been alive. He is a wonderful Christian and has contributed immensely to the church...of course this means another minister election...which I hope and pray goes more smoothly than the last one!

For some time I had been thinking about talking to the Elder about his insecurities and how they manifested themselves in his dealings with the church members. I believed that unless he changed, things would be very difficult for Ned when he became a minister and, if for Ned, then the whole family. I do not remember what circumstances prompted me, but I wrote the Elder a letter in January 1984. I mention this letter in my journal entry of January 9, 1984.

January 9, 1984. I spent most of my time tonight writing a letter to (the Elder). I feel that I just have to try to reach him somehow to make him see that he is being his own worst enemy. I felt better, having written it, but I'm not sure I'll send it. Even though everything I wrote is true and well intentioned, I'm not certain he will view it as such.

I sent the letter a few days after writing it. I kept a copy of the letter and include it here:

Dear (Elder):
One week ago I said that I would love to get together with you and talk. I've been burdened a long time to express my support, love, and wishes for you and the church. This burden has been growing a long time as I see you becoming more and more defensive and less

self-assured in you leadership of the church. I want in my own weak way to try to encourage and uplift you, to help make your job more enjoyable and less of a burden. I decided that I would try to express myself in the form of a letter since time factors and personalities and preconceived ideas often compromise true expression when individuals speak one on one. I love you, support you, and want you to continue to grow as the spiritual leader of our wonderful church. I therefore offer this letter in humble Christian love.

First of all, I voted for you to be our Elder. My entire family voted for you. You received our support because of your powerful ministry of God's word. As a minister you were relaxed and fed us a practical, everyday ministry of God's love in our Christian lives. As a minister you gave us a lot of hope for the future of the church. I recall being elated at your selection to be our Elder. I remember telling some brothers in Indianapolis soon afterwards that we had been blessed with a dynamic young Elder who I was sure would provide the church with positive, forceful leadership.

*The first several years my expectations were met. You seemed to be growing into the position very nicely. Your zeal, your smile, and your self-confidence were in tact. Things seemed to change, however, with the election that put me in to the Sunday school. In retrospect, it would have been far better for the church if (*the three conservative brothers*) had been put in (*elected to the offices*) that night instead of Flip (*my uncle Phil Beer*), Ned and me. I honestly believe that the absentee voting would never have become an issue if they had.*

I understand the position you were in. Undoubtedly absentee votes influenced what must have been tight races. Perhaps they even determined the outcome. Without having voter's names on those ballots, we can never be absolutely sure. In any event, I would agree that the system of absentee voting had gotten somewhat out of hand. However, I would stake my life that none of our brothers and sisters willfully and knowingly cheated. If there were not more votes than there were members in the church, we as Christians should have trusted one another and not have assumed the worst. Even assuming that some willful cheating occurred, which I'm certain didn't, the individual responsible had a problem far greater than changing the process alone is going to cure. If the heart and intent of the people casting the "questionable" absentee ballots was unchristian, then I also suggest that the wrong spirit was present in the hearts of the brothers and sisters who were so suspicious of the number of ballots cast and so outraged by the outcome of the election.

I concede that it created a tough situation for you as our Elder. I agree that it was best that as much as possible people willing to be present should have done the voting. However, the problem should have been addressed only after tempers were returned to normal. It should have been addressed in a proper forum such as a special member meeting. Finally, we the elected deserved either a vote of confidence (or word of confidence) or the election should have been done over. As it was I never was sure that I enjoyed your support and blessing during my tenure in the Sunday school.

Your decision was that henceforth only those present would vote. No exceptions. Why couldn't it have been: henceforth there will be no absentee voting without prior approval? You could have legitimately insisted that only unavoidable absences be honored. Still, I could support your system if it were not for the fact that it was conceived and instituted in mistrust of the membership. I would trust my every possession and even my life with any of my brothers and sisters. Why then are our heads counted and matched against ballots at every business meeting? Even if we try to not think about it each time the essence of the act is to say, "I don't trust you to be honest." In return Satan has a rich soil into which he can plant "If he doesn't trust us, why trust him?" I suggest that the heartache over delaying the last minister election would have been avoided if the system had not been sown in mistrust. Had the membership been made to feel trusted they would have given you reciprocal trusting support.

I honestly believe that you always have and always will trust your membership. I honestly believe in the whole membership that there is no genuine mistrust of you. I'm certain that there isn't. However, the aforementioned election, its aftermath, and the rigid new system have fostered and continues to nurture that small mutual seed of doubt which works on our subconscious. It is robbing us of our unity and unqualified Christian love. It makes us refer to one another as "us and they," "camps," "liberal and conservative," etc. These things have no place in the church and in our Christian lives. I believe the situation can be cured, and if it can be, it must be. We are a church crying out for your renewed leadership.

Since I was a boy I respected you. I loved to bale hay for you. I have fond remembrances of you teaching my high school Sunday school class. I have always enjoyed and appreciated your ministry of the Word. As one who has been and continues to be a supporter of you, I would like to make some suggestions in love.

First, for every time you admonish the church or an individual, try to compliment them and encourage them another time. We all need to be loved and approved of at one time or another.

Secondly, try not to view every issue as black and white. Most issues, especially among people, are the result of misconceptions and misunderstandings and are therefore gray. It has been my experience that very seldom is one person all right and the other all wrong.

If you have a dispute with someone, please try not to let it enter into your preaching. Not only is it unfair to the individual, it detracts from the preaching of the Word. As much as possible try to separate your person from the Spirit on the pulpit. I know that often you must contend with weighty problems and personal hurts before you preach. I'll pray that God will give you grace to let the Spirit prevail.

Fourth, try to be the type of Elder who exudes warmth that people will want to counsel with. A good shepherd must be a good listener and seek out the sick of heart and the lost. If an individual tells you a problem or concern, try to address yourself to them and not counter with a problem or pressure of your own. Even though your cares and concerns as our Elder probably are greater than those of the rest of us, each individual esteems his or her own problems greater than anyone else's. It's not necessarily right but it's human nature. As the anointed of the Lord, you have the promise of an extra measure of grace to draw upon.

Fifth, I encourage you to continue to seek the counsel of your ministers and as many of the segments of the church as possible on issues that require your discretion. Very seldom will you please everyone. With human beings 100% agreement is virtually impossible. Try not to take every disagreement or dissension as an attack on you personally. I would suggest that nearly always it is not directed at you but at authority in general. This is not the proper spirit regarding authority but we as humans all have a dark nature which tends to make us seek after our own wants and needs instead of the wants and needs of the whole. I will pray that you will find grace to not view most disagreements as attacks on you but rather that you will use your position to assure that the resolution of the disagreements brings us back to the needs of the church instead of the needs of individuals. Bear in mind always that in every group, on every issue, that those who are at the extremes of each side make the most fuss. Try to not lose sight of the large "silent majority" in the middle who want to support you in assuring that common sense and moderation prevail. Once an issue is settled strive to leave old wounds healed. To bring them up time and time again only serves to make the scars bigger and therefore the previous healing less strong. Encourage us not only to forgive but to forget as our Father has forgiven us.

Above all try not to respond in anger. Just as I have a terrible problem with being a continuous worrier, you have a tendency to be quick to anger. Anger is seldom, if ever, an appropriate vehicle of response. Not only does one not respond as well in word and thought, the listener receives no benefit because he or she sees the anger and not the response. Hence the wedge is driven deeper. On the other hand, while the wedge remains in place if anger is allowed to cool before responding, it can be more easily removed once anger is no longer a factor in the response. The scriptures are clear that anger serves no useful function in dealings among Christians. I will pray that God will give you grace to war against anger, just as I pray He will grant me grace to worry less and have more faith.

*Finally, fully use the abundant talents that God has blessed you with. He has blessed you with the gift of ministry. He has blessed you with the ability to conduct the church services in an organized manner. He has blessed you with the gift of being a master conversationalist. Use this gift of communication to seek out those in need for encouragement and counsel. In general, use your many talents to develop people skills, to communicate, to listen, to exhort, to encourage, to direct, to **lead**. In so doing, the membership will grow to want to support, obey, and follow you.*

You are my Elder. You are our Elder. We freely elected you to the job and want you to lead us. God has given you the requisite talents. I'll continue to pray that you will receive grace that your spirit might be continually renewed and refreshed. I can only imagine the pressures that go with the job. Please accept this in the spirit with which it was intended. I love you and I love the church and our precious faith. I want nothing more in life than to see it preserved and for my family to follow me on this pathway. Therefore I want desperately for you to succeed and flourish as our Elder.

If the Elder ever responded to this I do not remember, although there may have been an oblique reference to it once. Eighteen years after the fact I am somewhat embarrassed by some of the phrases and terminology in the letter, being reminded that the way we spoke to each other in the Apostolic Christian Church basically amounted to an English dialect. Terms like "have the grace," and "my weak way," and "humble," and "our wonderful church," and "preserve the way," and "I support," and "I love," and "heavy burden," etc, are requisite for acceptable conversations between AC members and their leaders.

Chapter Forty-Three

On February 22, 1984, my boss John Perry left for a ten-day vacation. When he went on vacation I covered his hours at the store. This made a seventy-hour workweek, but Tammy and I were glad for the extra income. John never paid me cash for these extra hours, but he allowed me to take store merchandise to cover my hourly rate. It was a pretty good deal. Nothing could have prepared me for what I encountered as I drove to work three days after John left. I write of that day in my journal entry of February 25, 1984.

Saturday, February 25, 1984. This morning we were awakened by Trischa coming down the stairs crying. As soon as she got in bed with us I could feel that she was burning up and she was chilling too. She complained of a horrible headache too. Poor Babes — we got some Tylenol into her and by the time I left for work her fever had come down some. Tammy called in and took off work.

As I drove to work, I was disgusted. With the Morton choir (an Apostolic Christian Church congregation from Illinois) coming for a weekend visit, Trischa sick, Tammy off work, and a twelve hour day ahead of me I thought I really had it tough. I passed Carlton and MaryAnn (Beer) and (their son) Steve (Beer) as I came to town. I wondered what they would have had going that early in the day. As I approached Milford I saw that a train was stopped across the road. I was again irritated to have to detour around it, as I was already late for work. As I crossed the tracks at the mill I could see down the tracks that the train had hit a vehicle. A chill went through me for an instant as I considered whom the unlucky individual(s) might be. As I entered the store I asked Raymond Pinkerton (a man who worked for the local mortician) whose vehicle had been hit and he replied "Ronn Beer." I then asked if it hurt him. He replied, "Killed him!" I then knew where Steve and Carlton and MaryAnn had been and where they were headed — to Shari's house (Ronn's wife).

*I felt like I had been socked in the gut with brute force. I was so stunned. And I thought **I** had problems.*

Ronn, I learned, had been on his way to pick up a hired man who had failed to show up for the day. Ronn and the wreck scene were such a mess that they weren't even sure for a while if he had been alone in the truck or not. Shari had helped him milk and later said how grateful she was to have had the extra, final time together.

What a tragedy. Shari had just seen her father die and be buried earlier in the week. She is due to have their second baby next week.

I worked all day in a fog as I tried to sort out my thoughts. For sure, something like this puts things into perspective. It poignantly reminds one to live each day and each moment to the fullest; that we really do have no promise of tomorrow. If only some who are unconverted can draw these same conclusions and be born again! If Ronn had been unconverted the tragedy would have been compounded a million fold.

On the way home from work I stopped at Shari's. The whole (extended) family was there. I embraced and sobbed with them all one by one as we expressed what we really mean and have meant to one another over the years. Why did it take this to bring forth this sharing?

When I got home I found that Trischa was quite a bit better. (Doctor) Percy felt that she was a victim of both the flu and strep and put her on Amoxil. I was grateful to be home and fade off to sleep.

This tragic accident touched the whole community. Tammy and I were deeply saddened. Carlton and Mary Ann Beer had been so kind to us in obtaining our house. Their sons Steve and Ronn and their families lived on either side of us. They were friends, fellow AC members and great neighbors. Ronn's death was the first time Tammy and I had experienced the loss of someone who was both young and close to us. We were especially sorry for Carlton and MaryAnn in that Ronn was the second son they had tragically lost.

Several weeks after the death of Ronn Beer Tammy and I went to Minneapolis, Minnesota to visit Tammy's brother Todd, his wife Sharon, and their daughter Sylvia. They had moved there several months before. Tammy's brother Trent and his wife Lynn drove with us. It was the first time that we had gone anywhere without the children for more than a day. Even though the trip lasted less than a week, I remember it very fondly. We lounged, watched movies, and shopped. I remember noting how quiet and relaxed Tammy was without three little children to attend to. When the time was up we headed for home. Our trip up had been snowy, but it was a beautiful drive back. If we had known what awaited us upon our return we likely would have stayed and sent for the children.

We had been back from Minneapolis a few days when I had a morning off. As I often did, I spent the morning moving wood into our basement for use in our furnace. As I was doing this, (the Elder) pulled into our driveway and wanted to chat. He had never done this before. At first I was a bit apprehensive, but he was in a great mood. We sat in his car and had a long cordial conversation. I do not remember anything about the conversation other than its pleasant tone. The next day I figured out why he had stopped. My journal entry of March 15th tells why.

Thursday, March 15, 1984. The day started simply enough. I went to work and was nearly done reading the newspapers when Tammy called. She said that Deb (Speicher) *had called and asked if she could drop Kasee off for the day. She also asked if the older ones could come after school. She said that she would send their PJ's because it might be late.*

All day long I stewed about what might have happened. I knew it had to be something bad and I assumed that they must have gone to Francesville so therefore the trouble had something to do with Deb's family. When I got home for supper it was quite a scene. Grandma Pat and Jennifer (a niece) *had come over so we all had a hearty supper shared by eight children and three adults! It was a lot of fun.*

Around 11:30 p.m. Ned and Deb arrived. They looked terrible. They had gone to Francesville to see Wendell (the Francesville AC

Elder). They realized that something wasn't right in their life and had decided to set it straight. It was very moving to hear of their courage. In all my life I have never been prouder of Ned.

Ned and Deb had been married for fourteen years. Their four children ranged in age from eighth grade to pre-kindergarten. During the months they were engaged to be married they had been intimate several times. They had privately brought this sin before God at the time and had been forgiven. Now, fourteen years later, this sin was to be brought before the church. Why? There were three reasons. The first reason was the church's stand on fornication. They classified fornication as a **sin,** not a mistake or a shortcoming. Because it was considered a sin, it required church discipline as punishment — even if it was fourteen years later. The second reason Ned and Deb were bringing the sin before the church was because of the upcoming minister election in the Milford AC Church. Ned knew if he were to be elected to the job that he would need to sit in judgement of others who might come forward with this sin in the future and knew he could not do this in good conscience. Compounding this reason was the fact that another couple from a nearby Apostolic Christian Church congregation had come forward with the same confession two weeks before and was accepting their punishment. Undoubtedly, the stunning and tragic death of Ronn Beer had tweaked the consciences of many people about being ready to die.

The third reason that Ned and Deb came forward was more personal. It was silently rumored over the years that some Elders and ministers in the AC church were willing to hear such confessions and not take them before the church. With this in mind they first went to Grandpa Beer. When he refused to hear the confession, they were stuck with no option except to come forth with it. They made their confession to the Milford Elder, who sent them to the Francesville, Indiana, AC Elder who had married them. Our Elder had stopped by my house "just to chat" the morning after they made their confession to him. Apparently this was to see if I knew and to gauge my response.

The evening Ned and Deb told Tammy and me I was stunned. I was in awe of their courage. Ned explained that the Francesville

Elder had told them that the minister election would be stopped "until this was taken care of." I understood this to mean that nothing would happen until Ned was eligible again. So did Ned.

I remember thinking that an act of humility and honesty like this would exalt him the rest of his life as an AC minister. Ned then explained what the process was. First they would be excommunicated. For a month or so a "ban" would be placed upon them, during which they were to come to church as usual but no one was to greet them or speak to them. During the lunch time between services they were to remain in their pews while everyone else went for lunch and fellowship. During this time no one was to visit their home or invite them to their homes. This tradition of the "ban" was based on the AC church's interpretation of I Corinthians 5. Following the "ban" they would no longer be considered members of the church for a while and then eventually be restored. They told us that when they were officially excommunicated the congregation would be asked to stand in support of the Elders. At this Tammy immediately exclaimed, "I won't do that. This isn't right!" This sort of response was so uncharacteristic of Tammy that we were all stunned. I know now that because she was not raised in the AC church she saw instantly that this was intrinsically wrong. At the time I did not think it was right either, but I did not know enough scripture to refute it. In any case, Ned and Deb said they wanted us to support the church's action for their sake. In the end Tammy did go along with it, but it definitely was done under duress.

Ned and Deb's action really convicted me, as my journal entries of the next two days indicate.

Friday, March 16, 1984. We had a busy day at work today. When I got home I was pretty bushed. Ned and Deb's courage had me going over my own spiritual life and I wasn't liking what I was seeing. Tammy and I talked a long while before going to sleep.

The excommunication was scheduled to take place after a woman's "proving" for baptism the next day, on a Saturday night. My journal records my struggle that day.

Saturday, March 17, 1984. I worked 8:00 a.m. to 8:00 p.m.

today. Business wasn't too good and the day seemed to go on forever. I had some struggle getting to sleep last night and I was troubled most of the day. Around 5:00 p.m. I decided to wipe my own slate clean and not give Satan any leverage niche on me.

I figured if Ned was courageous enough to confess his sin that I needed to follow his example. All day long I tried to list all the sins I had committed since I had given my life to the Lord in 1971. Once I had everything I could think of I called the Elder. His wife told me that he and a visiting Elder were at the church. I called the church and they told me to come right over. With my list in hand I left the store in the care of a clerk. The Elders listened intently as I went through my list. When I was done they looked at each other. The one Elder simply said to the other, "I'm free. How about you?" Our Elder simply nodded in agreement, adding that he thought one thing on my list needed "to be made right." Apparently my list did not include anything that the AC Church deemed to be a "sin." Rather, my list must have been full of "mistakes and shortcomings." I went back to the store relieved, but confused. When I got back the clerk asked me "What's wrong with you today? You look like death warmed over!" I suppose I did. Part of me did die that day — my spiritual innocence. In the months to come my head would clear and I would embark on a quest to study the Bible in earnest. At this point I began to be no longer content to go along with things just because this was "the way we have always done it." I became determined to understand what the Bible had to say about issues of faith. In the Milford AC church Ned and Deb's excommunication produced the equivalent of the first eruptions of Mount Saint Helens. The big eruption was yet to come, but "the calm before the storm" had definitely ended.

When the actual excommunication was pronounced on Ned and Deb that night the floodgates of my emotions broke. As I stood in a "prayer of support" I began to cry. I felt guilty for standing "in support." I felt like the "punishment" was unnecessary and grossly disproportionate to the "crime." I felt like something precious was ending, but I did not know for sure what it was. It was probably just the end of innocence.

The church was nearly empty by the time I walked out that

night. I had cried as I never had before or since. Unknown to me that night was the fact that the biggest change in my life was now on the horizon.

Chapter Forty-Four

After the excommunication of Ned and Deb there were six weeks of relative calm in the church. During the noon hour between Sunday services while the "ban" was in place, Dad and Mom and Tammy and I sat upstairs in the pews with Ned and Deb. Most of the congregation honored the "ban" and did not speak to them, although some ignored it. It was a scene dripping with irony. There sat Ned and Deb, prominent and beloved by the community, accepting the shunning of their own church for something which had taken place fourteen years before, something they had years before repented of and sought forgiveness for. In addition to this, there were members of the congregation sincerely supporting this action, members "fearful" that they would ever sin so grievously and so "thankful" that they never had. All of this began to trouble me more and more as each Sunday passed. Deep down I knew that Ned and Deb's sin was no worse than many of the "mistakes and shortcomings" that were committed by nearly everyone there at one time or another. Ned and Deb's sin dishonored God, but only they were harmed by it. Many of the "mistakes and shortcomings" injured other people as well as dishonoring God. Even then I was well aware of the teaching of Galatians 5:19-21a, where we are told *"The acts of the sinful nature are obvious: sexual immorality, impurity and debauchery; idolatry and witchcraft; hatred, discord, jealousy, fits of rage, selfish ambition, dissensions, factions and envy; drunkenness, orgies, and the like."* In this passage I saw no distinction made between "sexual immorality" and sins like "hatred, discord, jealousy, fits of rage, selfish ambition, dissensions, factions and envy." I was also well aware that Galatians 6:1 instructed Christians *"Brothers, if someone is caught in a sin, you who are spiritual should restore him gently. But watch yourself, or you also may be tempted."* What was happening to Ned and Deb was anything but "gentle." Instead of being "restored" they were now excommunicated and being shunned. Something was definitely not right.

As a family we were trapped. If we questioned what was happening it would have only made it worse for Ned and Deb. Grandpa Beer, our patriarch, was solidly behind the church's stand. All we knew to do was to "take it" and to encourage Ned and Deb as much as we could. What an awful period of time.

There was a great sense of relief when the "ban" was lifted. Ned and Deb were not considered members of the church anymore and they were not to be referred to as "brother" and "sister." They could not take communion and were not allowed to "greet" with the "holy kiss." For all practical purposes they were now like "friends of the truth." We assumed that this stage of their discipline would quickly pass. We were wrong. It soon became apparent that it might take years for them to be restored

As the month of May approached Grandpa Beer heard that the Elder would soon take up the issue of electing a minister again. This really troubled me. There were two reasons. First, Ned had been told, regarding the minister election, "nothing would happen until this (the discipline) was taken care of." If the Elder was now to go ahead with the election, Ned had obviously misunderstood what "taken care of" meant. I asked the Elder if it was true that we would soon be going ahead with the election. When he said that we were going ahead I asked if we could please wait until Ned's discipline was over. To this he frankly replied, "Tom, Ned is not a candidate."

The second reason I was troubled was because Grandpa Beer had told me "Tom, you know that it (the office of minister) might now fall on you." I had replied to him that I did not want any part of it. At this he sternly warned me not to "try and run from God like Jonah." He had continued, "If God wants you to do this He will make it possible to do it." He added that I had better be praying about it. If I was sick a factor of ten at the thought of this, Tammy was sick a factor of one hundred.

The official news came on May 6th. I spoke about it in my journal.

Sunday, May 6, 1984. We had a nice day at church today. There was a member meeting afterwards and (the Elder) announced that we are going to vote again for a minister in two weeks. I had expected him to go ahead, but not this soon. With Ned ineligible for the time being, the possibilities are sobering. I don't really feel that it will fall on me, but one never knows. As bizarre as this year has been not too much would surprise me. I so hope that it isn't in God's plan for me. As for now I can't decide whom to support. Poor Ned and Deb. They feel total isolation. Today was especially hard for them. I hope and pray that all this will pass quickly.

This devastated Ned. He felt the Elders had deliberately misled him in order that he would go along with the discipline quietly. He felt alone, hopeless, and impotent to change his lot. I am sure I would have felt the same way if I had been in his shoes.

One night during this period of time something happened that would lead to a profound change in my life. I remember it as clearly as yesterday. As I crawled into bed one night it occurred to me that I needed to begin studying the Bible. There was no opening of the heavens or prior struggle about this. It just hit me that I needed to begin studying. For no particular reason I opened to the Book of Romans and began to read it. After reading the first few chapters I realized that I did not understand what I was reading. I started over. When I read through chapter three the third time I realized that I still did not understand it. I remember thinking "You are a college graduate. You can understand this!" But other than a few phrases, it was not making sense to me. This greatly bothered me. I even had difficulty falling asleep.

I had been reading the Bible for years. A few years before I had read straight through it. My pattern was to open it and read whatever it opened to. This method of Bible reading was encouraged in the AC Church because in so doing "God will give you what he wants you to have." Over the years I had learned the stories of the Bible very well, but I knew no systematic Bible doctrine. For doctrine I had relied on the church. Now things were different. Having become confused greatly humbled in my initial readings, I now felt compelled to understand the Book of Romans. It occurred to me at this point that if — heaven forbid — I was made a minister, I would need to be able to open to any passage in the Bible and preach from it. How could I possibly do this? I thought how humiliating it would be to open to a passage and not know anything about it.

The result of this experience was that I devoted myself to studying the Book of Romans. I approached it academically. I took notes. I bought a Bible dictionary. I even bought a Wycliff Bible Commentary. This was especially helpful. I was particularly interested in the Wycliff Introduction to Romans. There I found historical notes, authorship notes, major themes, and a detailed outline. I had never seen anything like this before for a book of the Bible. By the fall of 1984 I had come to understand two critical doctrines. The first was the doctrine of "Justification by Faith." All my life I had understood the facts that Jesus Christ had died for the sin of all mankind on the Cross of Calvary, that He had been buried, and that He had literally, physically arisen from the dead on the third day. I had understood that salvation was a free gift by God's grace through faith in Jesus Christ. I also had been taught that God gives believers the grace to live for Jesus Christ after conversion. I never doubted any of these facts. I also never remember doubting my salvation after placing my faith in Jesus Christ as my Savior from sin. Never once do I remember wondering if I had "lost it" or if I was in danger of "losing it," although there were many years that I routinely prayed to God that He would protect me from sin which would cause me to "lose it." What had always been murky in my mind were two seemingly mutually exclusive AC teachings. On the one hand I was taught that salvation is a fee gift that comes by grace through faith in Jesus Christ. On the other hand I was taught that one does not receive the gift until one **works** his way through the AC "repentance and conversion" process. Compounding my confusion were two more AC salvation teachings: that one can never **know** they have salvation. It is always a future prospect. One can only "hope they make it." In addition, God might take the "gift" of salvation back if we do not do enough good works. Of course "good" AC members understand that one's chances of attaining the gift or keeping the gift depend on "remaining true and faithful unto the end" and are increased in direct proportion to which they submit to the teachings, customs, and traditions of the denomination.

The doctrine of "Justification by Faith" cleared up the issue of how one becomes acceptable to God. After studying the issue for months I understood that when we believe in Jesus Christ as our Savior from sin God judicially pronounces us to be acceptable to Him. It is a legal declaration from the highest court in the universe. I understood that this is not based on our merits or our works, but on the merits and finished work of Jesus Christ. Understanding that God legally declared me acceptable because I was trusting His Son as my Savior was like lifting a window blind in a dark room. It was like the last line of a Sunday school song from my childhood, "Open up your heart and let the sun shine in." Having come to understand the doctrine of Justification by Faith, I then began to understand how the precious promises of Romans chapter 8 could be true and how they could apply to me.

The second critical doctrine I came to understand was the "Righteousness from God" that comes through faith in Jesus Christ. (Romans 1:16,17; 3:21; 5:21; II Corinthians 5:17-21). This really took a long time to sink in. Once it did, however, I began to understand how God could declare a sinner just and acceptable when the person placed his faith in Jesus. I had always wondered how God could accept me because I knew I needed forgiveness even on my best days. The Apostle Paul's writings to the Philippians in Philippians 3:1-9 became clear to me — and precious, especially verses 8 and 9: *"Finally, my brothers, rejoice in the Lord! It is no trouble for me to write the same things to you again, and it is a safeguard for you. Watch out for those dogs, those men who do evil, those mutilators of the flesh. For it is we who are the circumcision, we who worship by the Spirit of God, who glory in Christ Jesus, and who put no confidence in the flesh — though I myself have reasons for such confidence. If anyone else thinks he has reasons to put confidence in the flesh, I have more: circumcised on the eighth day, of the people of Israel, of the tribe of Benjamin, a Hebrew of Hebrews; in regard to the law, a Pharisee; as for zeal, persecuting the church; as for legalistic righteousness, faultless. But whatever was to my profit I now consider loss for the sake of Christ. What is more, I consider everything a loss compared to the surpassing greatness of knowing Christ Jesus my Lord, for whose sake I have lost all things. I consider them rubbish, that I may gain Christ and be found in him, not having a righteousness of my own that comes from the law, but that which is through faith in Christ — the righteousness that comes from God and is by faith."* By the fall of 1984 I was rejoicing in Romans chapter eight. I still had much to learn at that point in my spiritual renaissance, but these first two doctrines had become the key to unlocking the New Testament to my understanding. Studying the Bible in the light of these two doctrines helped to make sense out of what had formerly appeared to be contradictory passages. It also greatly helped me to understand the difference between **becoming** a child of God and **living** as a child of God. At that time Bible study for me was like being a child on Christmas morning, opening one gift after another.

Running parallel to my spiritual renaissance were events beyond my control, events that would ultimately bring me to where I find myself today. In retrospect these events seem so melodramatic and unlikely that if I had not lived through them I would suspect they were the product of an aspiring fiction writer.

The Milford Apostolic Christian Church conducted a nomination vote for a new minister in mid-May, 1984. On May 29th the dreaded call came. I speak of it in my journal entries of the 29th and 30th.

Tuesday, May 29 1984. This morning we were all having a nice time getting around for the day when the phone rang. I answered it and found it to be a call I was afraid would come. It was (the Elder) *on the line wondering if we could make ourselves available tomorrow to talk to he* (and two visiting Elders.) *He said I had "some support" in our recent balloting.*

I soon left to spend the morning helping Trent (Tammy's brother) *clean up from the hog roast. We had a nice time and got a lot done.*

Tonight I had a sick feeling in my stomach as Tammy and I talked over how we would respond to questions that we were sure would come.

Wednesday, May 30, 1984. At 3:30 p.m. today Tammy and I

arrived at (the Elder's). The three of them (our Elder and two visiting Elders) talked to us until 4:45 p.m. It was a cordial meeting with no surprises. We answered as honestly as we could and there seemed to be no objection to what we said.

We left feeling pretty good but throughout the remainder of the day and evening I felt a sense of foreboding. I can't believe how things have changed in a few short months. Suddenly nothing is the same anymore. It seems like a dream that we are now faced with this imminent prospect when three months ago I gave it hardly a passing thought. It weights so heavily on me that I can get almost sick if I allow myself to think about it too much. I want God's will to be done in my life. I really do. But I can't yet bear to consider what a change might be imminent in my life. Why me, when there appear to be others who would want the job and probably be more qualified? How would it affect the kids, Tammy's family, my work, and Ned and Deb? I've always tried to live by faith but I'm so lacking at this moment. My wish and desire is that it will fall on another brother. I want this desperately but I'm afraid to pray for it because I know God's ways are above mine. If ever I've needed to trust, it's now.

Tammy and I were both mildly surprised about how general the questions were that the Elders asked us. It all boiled down to three issues. The first was "Do you support the church?" We could answer "Yes" to this. It was our church. The second was "Will you support (the Elder)?" We could honestly answer "Yes" to this also. After some discussion on this point I remember stating that I would support the Elder's decisions if I knew in advance what they were. To this the visiting Elders reminded me "Sometimes an Elder needs to make a decision based on what only he knows. Will you support him in these times?" I remember replying, "I will do my best to support him all the time." I do not think they were completely satisfied with this but they accepted it. The third issue was television. It was a "given" that an AC minister could not have a television in their home. Would we be willing to give it up if we were placed into the ministry? After some discussion we agreed that we would take our television out of our home if I became a minister. Even as this discussion was in progress I remember thinking that ministers "who have older children at home" were allowed to have a television.

This was frowned upon, but was tolerated. I knew that soon our daughter Trischa would be considered an "older child." After the meeting Tammy was upset that I had agreed to do this.

For one not growing up in the Apostolic Christian Church it is hard to imagine why Tammy and I even entertained a thought of subjecting ourselves to the prospect of me becoming an AC minister. Indeed, it is hard for me to recall the mind set that produced this willingness. There were multiple factors, the first of which was a strong life-long teaching of the necessity of one being willing to accept God's will for one's life. To "run from God" was to invite His wrath. No matter how much I feared the prospect of becoming an AC minister and the certain changes it would bring to my life, how could I possibly know if this was God's will for my life if I did not allow the process to proceed? Another factor was the example of others over the years. My fear of becoming a minister was the standard feeling. All the AC ministers I knew spoke as if they were dragged kicking and screaming into the job, but they did it because they believed it was God's will for their lives. I doubt that this was true of everyone, but it was the only acceptable stand to take. For an AC to openly aspire to such an office would have been viewed by others as prideful and as selfish ambition. The biggest factor for me, however, was the influence of Grandpa and Grandma Beer and "the family." How could I honor Grandpa Beer and be true to my heritage if I did not allow my name to be considered? It is hard to overstate how important it was to me in those days to be assured of my Grandpa Beer's approval. And what about "the family?" Grandpa Beer openly told me that I was their "last hope." Others in the family insinuated the same. All of this also needs to be seen in the context of the stunning events of Ronn Beer's death and Neb and Deb's excommunication. To say the least, in the mind of an AC it was not a time frame in which one wanted to trifle with what God's will may have been for one's life.

As Tammy and I wrestled with these feelings, the month of May turned into June. Ahead of us lay the most bizarre event to date. It concerned my sister Sue and her husband Glen Losee. Glen was a dear brother-in-law. He was a master mechanic who would do anything for you and expect nothing in return. He was an extraordinarily quiet man who must have marveled at the excessive verbiage in our family. He and Sue had their son Joey the summer before, about six months after Tammy and I had our son Travis. Several years before this Glen had been diagnosed with Marfan's Syndrome, a genetic disorder that historians believe Abraham Lincoln also had. In addition to this, Glen was an alcoholic. He drank every day, but we seldom saw him drunk. In mid-June of 1984 Glen had fallen asleep on his way home from work late one night, narrowly missing a tree and probable death. He was drunk when this happened and it was the first time that we siblings were made aware of his significant problem with alcohol.

The last weekend of June 1984, was scheduled to be a busy one. The plan was as follows: On Saturday evening there would be a communion service at church. After this service the church membership would vote for a minister from a list of Elder-approved nominees, of whom I was one. On Sunday there would be a member meeting after church, during which either the new minister would be announced or there would be a final vote. If I think about it, I can still feel the ache in my stomach as that weekend approached. Everything seemed set. For our immediate family, however, the weekend would unfold dramatically different, in a way that we could never have imagined, as my journal entries point out.

Friday, June 22, 1984. It looked rather overcast this morning as I did my (Bible) reading. I thought that perhaps it would rain before Dad and I could get any wood out. However, the morning went well and we got a lot done. Most of our time was spent cleaning up a top of a huge oak tree that had fallen over the fence onto Fred Beer's beans. Dad and I had a super talk about what Sunday might bring. I was still really warring within myself, wanting God's will to be done but only if my being a minister wasn't a part of it. By the time we made it to Grandma Beer's for a "little something" to eat I was feeling pretty well resigned to whatever the weekend might bring. In my wildest dreams I couldn't have imagined what actually was before us in the next forthy-eight!

I was at work for only a half hour or so when (my Aunt) *Beck came in to ask where Dad was. She said that* (my brother-in-law) *Glen* (Losee) *had collapsed at work and had been taken to Goshen hospital. She said that* (my sister) *Sue needed Dad to come and be* with her. The only information regarding Glen was that they thought he must have hurt his back again. About an hour later they called from the hospital and said that they thought he had a kidney stone but they couldn't explain the numbness in his right leg and arm. Still later in the afternoon the news was that they had attached a catheter directly to his right ureter but that the kidney still was not functioning properly. I talked to Dad around 6:30pm and he said that they were thinking of transferring (Glen) to South Bend for further evaluation about his non-functioning kidney. At this point we also discussed whether to cut wood or not in the morning. Neither of us felt that the problem would prove to be serious enough to require us to alter our routines. Little did we know what lay ahead!

When I got home I had just settled in for some serious book reading with the girls when the phone rang. It was Sue. She had been at the hospital when she got a sudden frantic urge to get home and see (her son) Joey. Now she was about to go back and she wanted me to know that she had written a card for me and was leaving it at the house and that I should get it before Sunday. Tammy and I could tell that she was scared to death and so I offered to drive her back to Goshen. I could then bring Mom back home from Goshen or South Bend, whatever the case might be.

On the way to Goshen she reflected about how much she loved Glen and how she had often wondered in past years why God had brought him into her life. I encouraged her that she might not fully understand what God has in mind for them as a couple or for Glen personally for years to come but to commit it to God in faith because He does have a plan.

When we arrived at Goshen they were just wheeling Glen out for transfer to South Bend. Sue rode in the ambulance with him and I drove with Mom. Mom said that they decided to transfer him tonight because they were troubled about why the kidney wasn't working. As we drove to South Bend we contemplated that perhaps he would be in for some surgery to unblock or remove it. We discussed that any time one enters a major organ system like the renal system that there is some risk but we were confident that in a few days everything would be back to normal. Most of our discussion, however, was what the next several days would bring for the family. The context was the upcoming minister vote and *our relationships with one another in its aftermath.*

Saturday, June 23, 1984. We pulled in to South Bend Memorial ER at 1:00am. It was raining so hard that I got soaked running 100 feet from the parking lot to the entrance. We waited only about twenty minutes before they called us back to the room. The doctor on duty was very sober as he informed us that Glen had a dissected aorta. My gut turned to ice when I heard it but I could see that Sue and Mom were unsure what this meant. Sue asked "Well, what about the kidney?" He looked down for a moment before saying grimly "Quite frankly, the kidney is the least of our concern at this point." I could see the fear and disbelief in Sue's eyes but before she could respond the chief cardiovascular surgeon of the hospital came and asked us to step out so that he could examine Glen. While we waited a few long moments in the waiting room, I explained to Sue and Mom what the aorta was and what its function was in the body. There was no describing it without conveying the gravity of the situation. By this time poor Sue was sobbing with her head on Mom's shoulder.

The cardiovascular surgeon called us back and informed us that the other physician's diagnosis was correct. He said that they do all open-heart procedures at South Bend except something like this. His recommendation was that Glen be transferred to Indianapolis or Chicago immediately. He asked if we had any preference and I replied that we knew John Isch. (John Isch was a cardiovascular surgeon who was also an AC minister in the Indianapolis congregation.) *He said "Good, that's who I had in mind anyway." He then left to make arrangements. I went out to use the bathroom and get a blanket for Sue, who was shaking violently. When I came back there was a nice looking man standing quietly in the corner of the room. Mom told me that he was a chaplain. I then tried to comfort Sue a bit. Mom told me how the chaplain had knelt with them and had such a comforting prayer. I saw now that he was gone. Until we left the hospital he appeared whenever there was a lull and then was gone as quickly as he came. He was quiet and gentle in his manner. He really seemed to bring some peace to the situation. We all felt that God sent him to us.*

Sue soon left to make some calls and the chaplain suggested that I go to her. When I found her she broke down and asked me to continue with the calls. She then asked me to pray with her. Once we finished Mom and Sue went to the waiting room and I went to ask the chaplain for advice as to how I might approach Glen. Instead I found the surgeon, who informed me just how serious the situation was. He said that we might not even make it to Indianapolis and even if we did, Glen might not survive the operation.

Sue and Mom soon came back. It was beginning to sink in that we were facing a life and death situation. Sue begged me to talk to Glen. I was reluctant but knew I had to. With Sue embracing him I said "Glen, if you have ever learned how to pray you must now. If you want to be saved please pray and ask Christ to come in to your life. You are facing a life and death situation." He opened his eyes for an instant and muttered, "I know" very distinctly. Mom then asked that I have a prayer. When I finished I felt frantic about what to do next. I turned around to find that the chaplain was back. I said, "You are experienced in these sort of situations. What else needs to be done?" He said, "Nothing. I feel that he responded very positively." As the time of departure for Indianapolis drew near things were reaching a hysterical level. Sue was pleading with Glen "Honey, I love you! Have I taught you anything? I want to be in heaven with you! Please pray, please pray." As they wheeled him out the chaplain was suddenly there again. He put his arm around me and confidently whispered, "Go with courage. The Lord will go with you."

(I will never know for sure this side of heaven, but I have always wondered if this chaplain was an Angel. Days later we contacted the emergency room, hoping to thank him, but no one there knew of any chaplain who was there that night. His ministry to us and his manner was certainly godly, if not angelic.)

It was now 2:00 a.m. as we embarked on our high-speed chase to Indianapolis. Sue rode in the ambulance with Glen. Mom and I followed. We picked up (my brother) Ted at US 6 and 31. He and (his wife) Sandy were shaken, having seen the ambulance scream by moments before. For the next two hours Ted, Mom, and I had a spiritual discussion as lively as our 75 mph drive. It was lovely and very constructive. I was so thankful that we were afforded the opportunity to have it. It was an answer to many past prayers.

We arrived in Indianapolis at 4:00am. The ambulance had arrived 15 minutes before us. Poor Sue had gotten so violently motion-sick that they gave her a shot on the way. It proved to be a great blessing as she was able to sleep several hours during our four-hour wait. Around 5:30am I called John Isch. When I told him what had happened, he just replied "Oh no." He then continued on to say that of the acute afflictions that can come upon a human being there is nothing more difficult to deal with from a medical standpoint than a dissected aorta. I told him that we didn't expect him to do the surgery but that if he got in the area we would love a moment of his time for spiritual support. He said he would call (his associate) *Dr. Fess* (who had been in surgery since 1:00am when we called from South Bend and who would later do Glen's surgery) *and be in touch later.*

As we waited the next agonizing hours a wonderful Catholic Nun came on the scene and ministered to our needs. Around 8:00am Glen's arteriogram was done and the surgeon (Dr. Fess) called us into the ER room for consultation. We all gathered around Glen's bed and Dr. Fess gave us the grim news. The arteriogram showed a severe dissection. His aortic valve would need to be replaced and a double coronary bypass would follow before repairing the dissection could even be attempted. The odds of a successful repair were slim at best, but the worst news was yet to come. The arteriogram showed no blood flow to the bowel, right kidney, liver, pancreas and spleen. If the bowel were dead (due to lack of blood flow to it) *they would close him up and not go on. He said quite frankly "It couldn't be worse." As we all stood there sobbing the Nun had a very nice prayer with us. I left to make calls to home. When I got back John Isch was there. He had really talked to Glen. He told him that he probably wouldn't be here tomorrow and that if he wanted to be saved to ask Jesus to come into his life now.* (My brother) *Ted was roaming the area like a caged cat, sobbing and frantic that Glen might go into this surgery and not have this commitment* (to Christ) *made. It was such a scene of despair as we were told to say our "good-byes" that I just couldn't believe it was actually happening. As Sue stood by Glen sobbing I held her and tried to comfort her. She turned to me and confessed to me that she was lost and wanted Jesus to come into her life. She said that she knew I wasn't in any official capacity but that she wanted me to know. I told her that this is all God wants. From that point on Sue had an unbelievable strength.*

(Many years later I am struck by several facts. On the eve of possibly becoming a minister in my church, I was not sure how to lead my dying brother-in-law into a saving relationship with Jesus Christ. From my journal entries I see that I gave him the right advice, but I had no confidence in the advice, nor would I have been capable of showing him scripture to back up my advice. Furthermore, having encouraged him to ask Jesus for forgiveness of his sin, I felt I needed to turn to the chaplain for advice and reassurance. In addition, I note that my sister Sue told me that she "knew I was not in any official capacity, but that she wanted me to know" that she had asked Jesus Christ to become her Savior. These observations show the training we had received in our church and our confusion about salvation. At that time we both thought we needed to talk to someone in an "official capacity" in addition to surrendering our lives to Christ. In our minds, asking Christ to forgive our sin and surrendering our lives to Him was only the first step in the repentance and conversion process of the Apostolic Christian Church.)

The last few moments before they took him to surgery were the most touching of my life. One by one we said our goodbyes to Glen. I told him that his folks were on their way down and that they told me to tell him that they were praying for him and that they loved him — very precious terms coming from a home where prior to this moment they were seldom, if ever, expressed. Glen told me to tell them that the loved them. Sue was last. She asked him if he had anything that he wanted to tell her. He feebly moved his big, rough mechanic's hand and patted her arm. He said "Love you...see you in heaven." Then they took him away. We all knew that it was forever, barring a miracle. In the back of my mind I hadn't discounted that possibility. After all, we had just witnessed two: Sue and Glen were now in the family of God.

Where we ended up was probably indicative of the gravity of our situation, as we were taken not to the surgical waiting room but to the pastoral care office. John Isch and the Nun accompanied us. Once there we were all given a wonderful spiritual challenge from John. He then prayed with us, served us coffee, rolls, Tylenol, and words of comfort. All this from a man who was expecting fifty guests at his house for the afternoon.

Soon (my Uncle and Aunt) *Bob & Marguerite (Hoerr)* appeared on the scene. It was a Godsend for us. I then privately talked with (three physicians from our extended family). All three had the same message. It couldn't be a worse situation for Glen. They all fully expected us to soon hear that the surgeon had found his bowel to be dead and had closed him back up. Death would probably follow in one to three days.

We had all momentarily forgotten, however, that God was still on His throne. Around 11:00am the phone rang and was answered by a priest. He soon appeared with a smile and miraculous news. The bowel was fine and the surgeons were moving on to the heart! A tidal wave of emotion immediately swept over the room! Sue asked for and I gladly offered a heartfelt prayer of thanksgiving. We then settled in for a long day. Around noon Ned, Deb, Tammy, Sandy, Nikki, Missy, and Dad arrived. Soon behind them followed George and Marilyn Losee. We all gathered in the room and Ned offered a beautiful prayer committing our wait unto the Lord's care. Throughout the afternoon we waited. We chatted, napped, ate, and prayed. Tim Sheets *(Tammy's brother, who worked at the hospital as a pharmacist)* provided us with bits of good new on several occasions when we were getting anxious about a lack of news. Late in the afternoon came the news that we thought we would never hear. One of the surgeons came out and told us that Dr. Fess was closing Glen back up and soon he would be transferred to cardiac recovery. We would soon be able to all see him! With joyful hearts we all gathered around and Ned offered another prayer of thanksgiving.

They soon came and asked that a few family representatives come up to cardiac recovery. Mom, Dad, George, Marilyn (Glen's parents), Sue, and I went. Dr. Fess met with us in a private room and explained what had taken place. He had been in surgery since at least 1:00am and had spent nine hours working on Glen but he looked chipper. He explained that he first opened the abdomen and to his surprise found the bowel to be alive. He said, "I don't know why." He then paused, turned around and looked us in the eye and repeated, "*I **don't** know why!*" We all knew why and I felt that he did too. He was giving God the credit without verbalizing it.

The explanation then proceeded on about the surgery. He gave us some statistics. His group does 1000 or so open-heart surgeries a year with a 90% plus success rate. They get cases like Glen's from all over the mid-west and see from 6-16 a year with a 90% plus **failure** rate. He concluded by saying that Glen is definitely beating the odds, but that he is not out of the woods yet. The first 24 hours would be critical. Glen's chances were now 50-50 for survival. We felt that was great considering nine hours before we had all given him up for dead.

I was sent downstairs to get the rest of the family. We all went in to see Glen together. I was shocked how good he looked. He was on the respirator and had every imaginable body function monitored. Sue went up and squeezed his hand and told him that she loved him. She was sure that he moved his fingers in response.

We weren't allowed to stay long and we all left with sober minds as we considered the day's events. God had demonstrated his power to us all. Yet for God, restoring Glen had been a small matter. I left the hospital resolved to try and never again underestimate His awesome power and majesty. My mind also went back to the mysterious chaplain in the South Bend ER. He had been right when he confidently admonished me to "Go with courage. The Lord will go with you." He was right. The Lord went with us all!

Sunday, June 24, 1984. Last night we went to Tim & Beth's (Tammy's brother) after leaving the hospital. I knew that after communion last night that the church had voted again for a minister. So that I might make plans for today I called (the Elder) to see if my name had been dropped or retained. He informed me that there would be a final vote today between (another man) and me. He wanted me to attend if it was at all possible. We woke up feeling drained and resigned to another trying day.

After checking in at this hospital and finding that things were going better than we possibly could have expected, Tammy and I left for Milford. Before we left Dad pulled Tammy aside and pleaded with her to do what was best for the family. (We understood this to mean

A Lifetime of Church

that we should go along with whatever might happen at church.)

We arrived at church at 11:45am. Everyone was very loving and interested in Glen but my stomach was in knots. After the service (conducted by a visiting Elder) *we held the vote. As the ballots came down my row we were one short and* (the man next to me) *didn't get one. He looked for a moment and then leaned back. He then whispered to me, "I can support either of you. I don't need to vote." These words rang in my ears as we waited for what seemed to be an eternity for the Elders to return. In about fifteen minutes the Elder returned and asked the ministers, Grandpa Beer, and Elmer* (Hartter, the minister who was being replaced) *to come down. For another "eternity" (probably fifteen to twenty minutes) we waited. Then they returned and announced that the vote was a **tie**!*

We were then given a choice. If we wanted, we could have two ministers. Otherwise we would put the two names in the Bible and Grandpa Beer would draw one out. We then voted and the vote was sixty nine per cent for one minister. We then had a prayer and Grandpa walked slowly up to pick the name out. He had a short silent prayer. He handed the slip to (the Elder) *and he announced "Tom Speicher!"*

It was if an electric shock went through my body. Me?! Even though I had thought that after Saturday I could face anything, I had warred within myself right up to the time that the lot was announced. I thought at that time that I had a complete peace. But now I was stunned. I heard Tammy start to sob and (the Elder's brother) *told me to go and sit with her. (A visiting Elder) then gave some words of encouragement from the Book of Timothy. (The other two visiting Elders) then, in turn, had some words of comfort and encouragement. We then stood at the entrance and met the church. It was an emotional time of love and support. Everyone was positive. I could tell from the comments that some people were a bit concerned about my commitment to the church, though.*

Following this we had a church supper. Tammy and I didn't get a chance to eat much because everyone wanted to talk. I remember one of the visiting Elders admonishing me "Don't think that being a college graduate is going to help you in this." This seemed strange, but I accepted it. When the supper was over we went to George and Pat's and recounted the events of the weekend to them. As we expected, they were wonderful and completely supportive. Tammy's dad said "I told Pat (her mother) that one day they would put you in as a minister there."

As I consider the recent past I realize that this has been a six months to remember. I never would have dreamt at Christmas that I would be minister. I knew it would be Ned. The way things unfolded and then came back together I have to take courage in the knowledge that God has had his hand on us all. While I cannot imagine myself attempting to preach a sermon I have to have faith that God didn't select me to be an unprofitable servant. Tonight I feel certain that in the days and weeks to come that I will truly learn the meaning of taking "one day at a time."

Monday, June 25, 1984. I woke up this morning with a splitting headache (small wonder). However, after some medication and some time I arrived at work by 8:00am. The day went well. We were busy and my headache didn't return in full force. The news of my new job was already spreading rapidly around town. Quite a few people mentioned it and offered encouragement.

*When we got home at 5:00pm I realized that I had, for the most part, forgotten that today was our 12th wedding anniversary — **12 years**. Who would have ever dreamt twelve years ago that we would be in the position wherein we now find ourselves? Last week we had planned to go out to eat at the Moonraker. But since we had been away from the kids so much we settled for a family outing at McDonalds. We ended up having a special time together.*

Reading these entries eighteen years after the fact I am struck by how dramatic they seem. I believe that it would be impossible to over-dramatize that weekend. When Glen was released from the hospital a week later he and Sue came home. A month later Glen was able to return to work. In all my years I have never personally witnessed as clear a demonstration of God's sovereign healing power as I did that day.

My sister Sue continued in her "repentance" process. She was later baptized and became member of the AC Church. Glen testified that he had sincerely trusted Jesus Christ as his Savior but he did not become a member of the AC Church. Our Milford Elder never came to visit Glen. My mother was deeply hurt by this. The most likely reason for this was because John Isch had been involved in Glen's profession of faith. John was already out of favor with the AC Elders by that time and before long would no longer be with the denomination. But perhaps it was simply because our Elder was too busy. There could have been other reasons, too. I guess only he would know for sure. Glen lived eleven more years and endured two more major vascular surgeries before he died suddenly and without warning from a ruptured aorta. He maintained that he was trusting Christ as his Savior unto the end but he never was victorious over alcohol. God definitely used Glen as an instrument in compelling me into His service.

Chapter Forty-Five

As Ronald Reagan was nearing the end of his first term as President, the United States was winning the approval of Western European governments to deploy a new generation of American intermediate range nuclear missiles on their soil to counter a perceived advantage held by the former Soviet Union. At this same time we were modernizing the nuclear missiles based in our own country. Tensions were very high between the East and West in those days and the specter of nuclear war haunted all of us to some degree or another. In the middle of all this there was a made-for-television movie released entitled "The Day After." This movie depicted a nuclear exchange between the United States and Soviet Union and what the aftermath might be. The message of the movie was essentially that from one day to the next life, as we know it, could cease to exist. It was a frightening and depressing movie, one that sought to remind the country of the dangers of nuclear proliferation. The degree of consequence was infinitesimally smaller, but in a tiny way I believe I felt somewhat like the people in the movie on the day after I was chosen to be an Apostolic Christian Church minister. "What is life going to be like now? How will it be at work? How will I act around my friends, around Tammy's family, around my own family? What will everyone expect from me from now on? Will I ever have a private life again? How will all of this affect my children? Will they grow up to resent me? Will they become rebellious like so many other preachers' kids? How will I find the time to be the best father that I possibly can be to them? And Tammy – how will all of this affect her over the long run? Will our relationship be affected?" These were just a few of the questions that were flying around in my mind. The biggest question of all, however, was whether I would be able to preach a sermon or not. If I was going to allow this profound change in my life I thought how incredibly sad it would be if I would turn out to be a "flop" as a preacher. I knew the answer to this question would soon be answered because I would likely be called on to preach within the week. My journal entries describe how I was feeling as the big moment arrived.

Saturday June 30, 1984. I worked 8-8 today. We had decent store business but the pharmacy wasn't too great. I had a pit in my stomach most of the day as the tension was starting to build for tomorrow. I just have to keep faith and let God calm me and provide. I can't believe what is facing me. News from the home front: Travis got a haircut this morning and was very naughty!

Sunday July 1, 1984. Well, another month is past. I sure hope that this month is not as tumultuous as June was! Knowing what was before me I awakened with my stomach in knots today. I tried to do my (Bible) reading as usual but I had a difficult time concentrating. Thoughts kept racing through my mind. What if I fail miserably? Why has this happened? Etc, etc. Around the time that I left for work (In those days I worked every other Sunday morning from 8:00am to 11:00am) I decided that my fretting would be to no avail. I was going to have to give it (preaching) a try whether I wanted to or not. Work lasted forever as I now just wanted to get the "maiden voyage" over. When I got to church I saw that (two visiting ministers) were there. At first there was a great feeling of relief but then mixed feelings, as at some point or another I was going to have to do the job. Waiting would only prolong my agony. (One of the visitors) had the afternoon service from 1 John 3. I had a few comments and then the closing prayer. Afterwards I had a few words of thanks and reassurance for the church and thanked the church in behalf of the family for their support of Glen and Sue. The first words were nearly impossible but thereafter it wasn't nearly as bad as I had anticipated. In retrospect, it seems like a dream. The last time that I had looked out from the pulpit was when I was a little boy, pretending to preach over the noon hour.

We came home from church terribly exhausted and devoid of emotion. Neither of us could express how we felt. We just lay around for awhile and felt blank.

The first sermon I ever preached was on a Wednesday evening the following week. It was from Mark, chapter seven, in which Jesus was teaching the religious leaders that what defiles a man is not what he eats or what ceremonies he observes, but what comes forth from within a man, these things show the condition of an individual's heart. In light of what the future eventually brought, there is a touch of irony that this text was my first sermon. In any event, the sermon seemed to go very well. It actually was not too bad once I got started.

Tammy and I crossed our first hurdle very soon after being placed in the ministry. One Sunday I was seated by our Elder over the noon lunch hour and he asked me if I had removed the television from our home yet. When I asked him if we could please wait and see if it becomes an issue, he sternly replied "It is an issue with me right now." I had naively hoped that there would be some "give" on this issue, but I was wrong. We fulfilled the Elder's wishes and removed the television from our home the following day. We took it to my Dad and Mom's house and stored it in an upstairs closet, thinking that when our children met the AC church's definition of being "older children in the home" that we would bring it back. This was a difficult thing to do because we did it against our own convictions, in deference to the convictions of others. I was especially concerned that our older daughter Trischa would object and become bitter. She was seven at the time and showed an amazing degree of maturity when we explained the situation to her. We bought her a sound system to make up for it.

In mid-August of 1984 I attended the annual Elder conference in Lester, Iowa. I flew there on a small, chartered aircraft with five other AC ministers. On the way there I had a long conversation on the subject of church discipline with one of the Indianapolis ministers, whom I had been a friend with when we lived there. At the time I instinctively knew that the church's handling of Ned and Deb's confession was not right, but as of yet I did not know enough scripture to argue against it. Before the plane landed in Lester, Iowa, however, I had been given a very clear and reasonable scriptural outline of the doctrine of church discipline. What I remember most clearly was this man's explanation of the **purpose** of church discipline: for the **restoration** of sinning Christians. This was the opposite of what was happening to Ned and Deb. The purpose of their discipline, according to the AC church, was to punish them for sin in their past. The more I thought about it, the more the injustice being done to Ned and Deb bothered me. In the weeks following this teaching about church discipline I began to study the doctrine myself. The more I studied the issue, the clearer and simpler it became. I began to wonder how the AC Elders could hold to their view in light of the scripture. This was a dangerous thing to start asking myself, because it soon occurred to me that if the Elders could be so wrong about church discipline, they could be wrong on other doctrines as well.

The Elder conference itself was a sight to behold. There were no new teachings or issues put forth, so I was free to mindlessly observe the proceedings. Everything was done to portray a clear hierarchy in the organization. The non-office holding brothers in attendance were seated first. Behind them, in any remaining areas, were seated the sisters in attendance. We ministers then walked to the rows in the front that were reserved for us. Finally, the church Elders walked in two by two. All eyes were fixed on them as they were seated at the very front. From among the Elders, five were selected to be "Corresponding Elders" for the group. They were the ones who were seated on the pulpit. It would be difficult for anyone to not feel some degree of exaltation being paraded in like this and I remember seeing some countenances on faces that bothered me. Of course, I could not look into these men's hearts, but I remember being troubled by it. It was just a "feeling," but this was at a time in my AC experience when I was looking for all the good I could find to hold onto. I only remember two other things about this Elder conference. The first memory was the music. It was very beautiful to hear hundreds of men singing hymns acapella. The second memory was speaking to the Elder from my sister-in-law Deb Speicher's home church. I asked him if Ned and Deb were going to be restored after the conference. He replied that he and several others had "spoken forcefully" for their restoration, but that it was not going to happen soon. Having told me this, he quickly moved away.

In the months that followed, Tammy and I settled into our new routine. After the initial shock and curiosity, the townspeople soon forgot that their local pharmacist was also a preacher. The "sky had not fallen" as I initially feared. Tammy and I still loved each other and the kids still loved us (most of the time!). I found that preaching God's Word came naturally to me. My stomach was still in knots before each service, but each time, once I began, I was fine. I understood the Bible more and more each day. I began listening to Christian radio all the time. I was also buying audiocassette tape series from "The Friends Of Israel Gospel Ministries" and from "Grace To You." All of the materials from both of these organizations were reaffirming what I was learning from the Book of Romans on a daily basis. It was during this time that the Elder first cautioned me to be careful about "bringing outside sources" into my preaching. It was also during this time that Tammy and I became good friends with (fellow minister) Dale Strassheim and his wife Carol. We enjoyed each other's companionship from the beginning. The more I got to know Dale, the more he opened up to me and shared his own misgivings about some of the denomination's teachings. He was particularly troubled about our Elder's leadership methods. Dale was a very bright and articulate man who was the head administrator of a large local hospital. As such he was concerned about our Elder's insecurities and his intolerance of any opposing views to even a greater degree than I was. He had been severely rebuked by our Elder in my presence once. We were at the Elder's home for a minister's meeting. Dale had requested the meeting so that we could help our Elder shoulder some of the responsibility of running the church. This meeting was the first of only two I ever remember being held. It was during this meeting that another minister asked our Elder about the status of Ned and Deb's restoration. Our Elder replied that the issue would be discussed at the next Elder conference. Upon hearing this Dale Strassheim began to wonder aloud about how the church was handling this. He was speaking very carefully when he expressed that he wondered if a sin like Ned and Deb's — one in which no one was harmed, one which had been repented of, one which was not on-going even needed to go beyond the local Elder. Our Elder listened to this point, then jumped to his feet and shouted at Dale, "To things like this I just have to say 'Get thee behind me, Satan!'" He continued, "The disciples asked our Lord 'How can these things be?' and He told them 'God's ways are not man's ways!'" I was shocked. The only other times I had witnessed such an angry outburst was when I was in the Army. There was then dead silence in the room until another minister timidly uttered a smooth-over statement or two. The meeting was a disaster. I rode home with Dale that night. He was devastated and wondered if he could ever get back into our Elder's good graces. I do not think he ever did.

As 1984 came to end we approached the annual church business meeting and annual church elections. Our Elder had made it clear that his voting methods would not be altered. There would first be a nomination ballot for all offices. He would then only allow people on the final ballot who passed an interview with him and were found to be sufficiently supportive of both him and the church. At the actual meeting, only those present would be allowed to vote. This annual business meeting, held in the early days of 1985, would bring about a profound increase in the "internal pressure" within the congregation and produce "rumblings" heralding the coming massive eruption. The drama began to unfold for me one night after work. Tammy and I and our two older children were going with her family in a huge motor home to visit her Aunt and Uncle in Colorado the week after Christmas that year. On the evening we left I closed the store at 9pm, excited to be leaving. As I turned from locking the front door of the store, I found our Elder there. It was dark and he startled me. Apparently, he had been waiting there until I came out so he could talk to me. He wanted to speak to me about two people who had been nominated for Sunday school teachers. The men were both cousins to me and the one was a nephew of the Elder. His nephew had been nominated the year before and had given his support to the Elder. The Elder told me that this year his nephew told him that he "had changed his mind" and could not give his "full support" anymore. The other cousin had not been a member of the AC church very long. His wife was a believer, but not an AC member. Apparently the Elder had noticed that my cousin attended his wife's church on occasion and that he sat with her in the balcony of the church sometimes rather than sitting on the "men's side" in the auditorium downstairs. The Elder had shared his concern with my cousin about these two issues. According to Elder, my cousin did not share his concerns and had told him that he intended to continue on as before. The Elder added that my cousin told him that he would teach if he was elected, but that he did not feel "called" to do so. Our Elder viewed this response as not being supportive and told me that my cousin's name was being left off the ballot. He wanted to know if I would support him in this action. I should have plainly said that I did not think my cousin's "issues" warranted his removal from consideration, but I did not. Instead I simply replied, in the context of him requiring "total support," that he had "no choice" other than to only allow those "in full support" to be considered. The Elder was satisfied with this response from me. He obviously thought that I agreed with what he was doing; when all I meant by what I said was that I recognized the rules of the system he had set up. In retrospect, this "politically correct" answer was a terrible mistake on my part. I knew that the Elder's nephew had "changed his mind" about supporting the church because of the church's beliefs on church discipline. I did not support the church on this issue anymore either. As for my cousin, I thought these were silly reasons to remove his name from consideration. As I look back, I guess I assumed at the time that neither of these men really wanted to be on the ballot or they would have told the Elder what he wanted to hear. It had been my experience at that point that the Elder's questions about support were asked in such a way that one had to go out of their way to answer unacceptably. I have no excuse for my answer except to say that I was scared to tell him otherwise. In addition to this, the Elder had caught me so by surprise that I did not think before I talked. I guess I just wanted to be on my way to Colorado.

The week in Colorado was wonderful. Eighteen years later we still refer to it and laugh about it often when we get together with Tammy's family. I had no idea that back home there was a firestorm in the church over the removal of these two men's names from the Sunday school ballot. Coming home to the fallout of the Elder's voting policy was the first instance in what would become a pattern in future years of having vacations tainted by bizarre happenings. I wrote about the days after my return from Colorado in my 1985 journal entries.

Monday January 7, 1985. This morning I drove to Goshen and visited Ida Graff & Lucille Davenport. Tillie Rassi was sleeping so I didn't see her. I came home encouraged and happy that I had gone.

I ate dinner with Grandpa and Grandma Beer. They were depressed about (my two cousins) *being left off the ballot and about Ned & Deb. I was, too. Later in the day I found just how wounded these people are and I learned that* (the Elder) *had used us ministers as being in complete agreement. To my amazement, I found as the day went on that many of my own family thought that I was sitting in judgment of* (my two cousins). *I spent a lot of time on the phone and went home* **totally** *depressed. For a brief time playing with kids brought me some relief. Tammy & I marveled at what has taken place in our lives as we tried to go to sleep. It looks like this will be a* (sleeping pill) *night.*

Tuesday January 8, 1985. All day long I worked in a fog as my depression deepened. I am not cut out for this work. I know now that God has given me a talent to preach the word but I simply can't bear to sit in judgment of people on non-sin issues. Tammy and I both felt today that there is no way that we can continue to be in the ministry. If (the Elder) *expects me to rubber stamp his every move in the name of "support" my prospects of longevity in the ministry are slim.*

Why has this all happened? Why? My life was simple and happy a year ago. I've had a lot of spiritual growth this past year and I'm very thankful for it but I'm not cut out to be a rule enforcer. What am I going to do?

Tonight we even called my old boss in Indy about job prospects and money. The job would sure be there but there is no way we could survive financially. Plus I don't want to move and uproot the children. This isn't an answer. Tammy & I love these people. It looks like another (sleeping pill) *night.*

Wednesday January 9, 1985. Today everyone is over their

hysteria and common sense is reigning once again but my depression is continuing. I realize (the Elder) used me but it was my fault because I was too reticent. He called me at noon to check on my "support" and our conversation didn't go well. I was so upset going back to work that after I'd been there awhile Rita (a clerk at the store) asked me if I knew that my white coat was on inside out!

When I came home Tammy had a wonderful supper but I couldn't be the happy, grateful husband & father that I should have been. I love the Lord and want to serve Him, but can I sacrifice my principles in order to function in the church? I've just been pleading with God to show me what to do but I don't even know at this point what to ask for except that His will be done.

Surprisingly, the (church business) meeting went very smoothly and peacefully. Afterwards we went out for pizza with Grandpa and Grandma Beer and the Aunt/Uncles & Dad & Mom. All is well between us. I'm left knowing that henceforth I must be clear and precise with my answers when speaking with (the Elder). I hope and pray that nothing like this happens again. I want to be a good servant of the Lord but at this point I'll be surprised if I'm still preaching in our church five years from now. But who knows? I just plead that the Spirit will guide me and that the Lord's will be done.

After the business meeting I presumed that the crisis was over. I was wrong. Three days later I received a very angry phone call from the Elder on a Saturday morning.

Saturday January 12, 1985. I staggered out of bed this morning to get ready for my twelve-hour day. As I was building the fire I heard the phone ring. My gut turned to ice when Tammy told me that it was (the Elder). The conversation met my worst expectations. Among the insinuations: lack of honesty in my commitment to him, to the church, and Tammy's hair not "up" at work. I was flabbergasted. For twenty-five minutes I tried to figure out specifically what he wanted or expected of me and what he thinks I promised him. Tammy was on the extension and was equally stunned. I told him that I will gladly sit down from the pulpit if he isn't satisfied with me but I think that everything I said went unheard. I left for work empty – totally empty. Tammy and I see no way that this can work if things *like this are going to continue to take place. We thought that we **were** supporting him and **were** measuring up. If he comes back again I'm going to have to insist that he specifies exactly what he wants of us and I want (the other two ministers) to be present.*

Needless to say, it was a rotten day. I called (an AC uncle of mine) and asked his advice. He said to do nothing for the time being. I just can't believe that this is all happening. I can't believe that the Lord wants it to be this difficult.

Sunday January 13, 1985. After work it was difficult to leave for church. I was scared to death that (the Elder) would want to take up where we left off yesterday. However, he acted as if it never occurred.

After these incidents I learned that (fellow minister) Dale Strassheim had also received similar calls and scoldings. Dale was particularly concerned. As a professional administrator he knew that he needed to find a way to rationally communicate with the Elder when in disagreement. We decided that we would try to approach the Elder when he was not angry and ask him for ways to express our minds to him, ways in which he would not automatically see us as not supportive and become angry. Dale may have eventually spoken to the Elder about this, but I have no recollection of ever having done so. These conflicts ushered in a year that was pivotal in my life. During this year I continued to study the Bible diligently. I preached with all the zeal I could muster. The church seemed to be receptive to my preaching. With the exception of intermittent, subtle warnings from the Elder that I "stick to the scriptures" everything seemed fine between the church and me — on the surface.

During 1985, four significant things took place. The first thing was rooted in my Bible studying. It began to come clear to me that the doctrines I was learning in the Bible were different than what the Apostolic Christian Church held to. Nowhere was I finding salvation to be a result of the "repentance and conversion process" that I had been taught my whole life. A minister friend from the Indianapolis AC congregation told me early on that I should not stop studying the Book of Romans until I thoroughly understood it, because, as he said, "You will not have a systematic understanding of the rest of the New Testament until you do." When I had reached the point that I felt comfortable with Romans, I bought an audiocassette series about it from "The Friends Of Israel Gospel Ministries." I also ordered a study guide about the first eight chapters of Romans from "Grace To You." Both of these resources confirmed what I had come to believe, namely: (1) God is the Author and Finisher of our faith. (2) Salvation is purely by Grace alone, through Faith alone, in Christ, alone. (3) The only merit a human being can ever have before God is by believing in the Person and finished work of The Lord Jesus Christ. (4) We are "justified" (or saved) the moment we acknowledge our lost state and place our faith in Jesus Christ as our Savior from Sin. (5) Our "good works," or the service we render to God are a result (or fruit) of our salvation, not the basis of it. (6) We are secure in Christ. Perhaps because of my legalistic upbringing, the teaching by "The Friends Of Israel Gospel Ministries" deeply influenced my thinking. No teachers before or since have been as influential as they were to me on the subjects of law and grace. The single most influential teaching that I ever received was from an audiocassette series on the Book of Galatians by a man from the "Friends Of Israel Gospel Ministries" named Marvin Rosenthal. So clear was his teaching on the differences between law and grace that I could still teach a lesson about it at a moment's notice. By the middle of 1985 I knew that I had beliefs about salvation that were different than the church in which I was preaching. I did not know what I was going to do about these beliefs at the time, but they were already precious and liberating to me. I remember speaking to my Mom about what I had come to believe. She listened very carefully and replied "I talked to Flip (her AC brother) about this before and this is what he believes, too."

The second thing that began to become clear to me in 1985 was that I was in an on-going struggle against bitterness toward some of my extended family and the non-family "nominal" members who were my "supporters." Many of them initially expressed their support for me and expressed delight in the fact that I had been elected to the office of minister. At the onset of the problems with the church elections this year, however, most of them were angry with me instantly, without even asking what my role had been in the fiasco. This hurt me deeply. In addition to this, many of my "supporters" rarely heard me preach. The reason for this was that I worked every other Sunday morning. As a result, I seldom preached on Sunday mornings. Most of my sermons were on Sunday afternoons and Wednesday nights, times when the "nominal" members did not attend. Many of these "nominal" members expressed delight at my election because now their "friends of the truth" loved ones would have someone on the pulpit with whom they could identify, but by 1985 it had become clear to me that neither they nor their "friends of the truth" loved ones cared enough to be there. There were two specific thoughts which I warred against: The first was "Why did they vote for me if they were not willing to get involved and try to make it work?" The second was "If they don't care about the future of the church, why should I? Why should I put myself and my family through this?" The answers to these questions were always the same: Only God could have brought about the circumstances that had placed me in the ministry. Love for God and obedience to Him are reasons enough to continue. I believed that He had gotten me into this and that He will get me out if He wanted to. -AND- I knew Grandpa and Grandma Beer were depending on me. At that point I still could not even entertain a thought of letting them down. So I continued to forge ahead.

The third significant thing that happened in 1985 was that my friend and fellow minister Dale Strassheim lost his job and had to move to find equivalent employment. This discouraged me greatly. I did not see how I could continue on in the ministry without his support and encouragement. That summer we attended the annual Elder conference in Morton, Illinois. While we were there I was able to speak at length with some other ministers who were in trouble with the Elders for their beliefs. Two of them were ministers from Indianapolis and the other was from Bluffton, Indiana. It was clear to me, after speaking to them, that I would soon be in trouble with the Elders also, as I held the same beliefs. The conference was very troubling to me. All the speaking was a general re-hash of what was spoken about every year. I remember one Elder speaking forcefully against all Christian colleges and universities. The conference's conclusion was that no members of the Apostolic Christian Church were to attend any of them, as they all held "at least" one erroneous doctrine. I remember thinking that it was very ironic that a church denomination would openly advocate attending secular educational institutions instead of any Christian institution. I have one more peculiar memory from this conference. During one of the breaks, I needed to use the restroom. The Morton church was an older building and had inadequate facilities for such a large group. The restroom nearest me was down a long, narrow, winding stairway. There was a long line of men going down on one side of the stairway and another line coming up on the other side. As I descended, I had to "greet" every brother who passed me with a "holy kiss" and tell them my name. Having used the bathroom, it was necessary to repeat the process on the way up. I never felt comfortable with the custom of the "holy kiss" and so for me this was a most unpleasant experience. Everyone else seemed to be enjoying this bizarre scene, but I certainly was not. I guess that this incident was illustrative of my general feelings toward this entire conference. Dale Strassheim and I discussed the conference at length on our return home. He did not feel any better about it than I did.

The fourth significant event of 1985 was the restoration of Ned and Deb to full membership in the church. At the Morton Elder Conference the matter had been turned back to the Indiana Elders to handle as they saw fit. In October of 1985, there was a member meeting after church one Sunday. During this meeting Ned and Deb were required to apologize to the congregation for their sin and for the shame it had caused the church. While Deb was apologizing, she added an apology for the length of her hair, which had recently been cut shorter than she had wanted it to be. After the apologies the membership was asked to stand in support of their restoration to membership. Everyone stood and the matter was closed. I was concerned that some of the more conservative members would not stand in support because of a conversation I had a month before with a woman in the church fellowship hall. During this conversation the woman frankly told me that she and her husband were opposed to Ned and Deb's restoration. After all, she said, "What if (her son) gets engaged in a year or two and thinks 'Ned and Deb only got a year and a half. I guess I'll just go ahead (and sin).'" I tried to make her see how harsh her attitude was and how much they had suffered, but my words fell on deaf ears. I was relieved to have Ned and Deb's discipline over with, as was the entire family. But ending the discipline did not change the fact in my mind that it had been wrong to begin with. Tammy and I had both decided that we would never go along with such a thing again, no matter what the cost. At the annual business meeting several months later Ned was elected by the church to teach the High School Sunday School class, to begin the following summer. I was mildly surprised the Elder allowed him to be considered, but not at all surprised that the church elected him to the position. He was, undoubtedly, the most qualified man for the position and the church recognized this. Those who were encouraged by Ned's election to Sunday School would have their enthusiasm dashed in a few short months, however, as Ned's lack of favor with the Elder was far from over.

The sum of these four factors was that by the fall of 1985 I had determined that I needed to step down from the ministry in the Apostolic Christian Church. I had no idea how I was going to do this. Any scenario I came up with had drawbacks. There were two things that I most wanted to avoid. The first was to disappoint Grandpa and Grandma Beer. At that point I still would have endured a lot to avoid hurting them. The second thing I wanted to avoid was to split the Milford AC church. In September of 1985 Tammy and I drove to Kokomo, Indiana, to investigate taking a different job, thinking that if we took a job so far away that it would be an adequate excuse to retire from the ministry. The job was good and the money was better than I was getting, but we simply could not bring ourselves to move away from our families and our home, which we loved.

In November of 1985 the Elder had several converts who had "found peace" and were ready to be "announced to the church" for proving and baptism. The other ministers and I attended a meeting to hear their testimonies before their "announcement." I remember as clearly as yesterday the testimony of the first convert. When the Elder told her to tell us "what happened," she began "I have always wanted to do it and I knew all my life that one day I would. One Sunday during the noon hour I was at (another AC church) and was thinking about doing it. I knew how happy my grandparents would be if I did it, so I decided to go ahead and do it." The three of us were silent for an awkward moment before Dale Strassheim asked, "Did you go ahead just to please your grandparents?" To this she answered "Oh no," and, upon questioning told us that "doing it" meant repenting and asking for forgiveness and joining the church. I was very troubled by this exchange. After we had questioned her, I believed that she really had given her life to Christ. But if this was all the clearer she could be about what had taken place in her life, how could she ever be obedient to scripture and share her faith with others? As far as I could determine from her testimony all she would be able to tell a lost soul would be to "come and join her church" if the person wanted to be forgiven. Shortly after this I decided to seek counsel from some outside sources about my predicament. In seeking this counsel I wrote a letter to the counselor staffs of both "Grace To You (John MacArthur)" and "Insight For Living (Chuck Swindoll)." Both ministries had contributed greatly to my spiritual renaissance and I knew they would give me sound Biblical advice. The following is what I wrote:

November 26, 1985.
Grace To You.
Dr. John McArthur Jr.
And/Or Counselor Staff.

Dear John:

My name is Tom Speicher and I live in the small Mid-western town of Milford, Indiana. Milford is the town of my birth and except for the seven years that I spent away in the Army and at college, I have lived my entire life here. Next month I will be thirty-three years old. My thirty-third year is significant to me in that I will be the same age as my Savior was when He offered Himself for me, and also because my life seems to be at crossroads in the two of its most critical areas: my work and my church.

I will first write of my background. I was reared on a small dairy farm. Our family lived in a house side by side with the home of my maternal grandparents. They were like a second set of parents to us. My grandfather was the Elder (head pastor and leader) of our local church congregation for nearly fifty years. Between my parents and my grandparents I witnessed sanctified lives in action all my life. Because of a lack of wealth on my father's part remaining on the farm was not possible for me. In the summer following my graduation from high school I bought the "Pearl of Great Price" in giving my life to the Lord. The following fall I enrolled in a local private college without any specific professional goals.

After my freshman year, with student deferments ended, I was drafted into the U.S. Army. Two weeks prior to this I was married to my high school sweetheart, Tammy (Sheets). The Army proved to be a blessing for us. We were stationed in southern West Germany. Not only did we have an "extended honeymoon," I was also put to work in a pharmacy. When I was discharged in 1974 I went back to college and became a pharmacist. During college I worked at a hospital and had fully intended to continue working there as a pharmacist. However, one month before I graduated I received a job offer from my present employer in my hometown of Milford. Tammy and I both felt that the Lord made the opening for us so we took it. That was seven and one-half years ago. It was also three beautiful little children ago.

The move back to Milford was a very good one for the most part. I quickly gained the confidence of the townspeople and presently enjoy a great deal of professional satisfaction. The move also brought me back to my home church congregation. This proved to be blessing too for the first six years. I first taught three years in the Sunday school. I was soon in charge of the Jr. High/High School choir and later of the adult choir. I also served as a church song leader. The most recent step for me was in June of 1984 when I was elected to be minister in the church (Our denomination uses entirely lay ministers. I am one of four and we rotate services). The Lord has blessed me in this work too and my ministry has been well received.

At this point the obvious conclusion is that I am a fulfilled, fruitful Christian servant. Such, however, is not the case. Enclosed you will find the Statement of Faith of our church. In order to come to an understanding of my frustrations I must give you a background on the set of deeply entrenched "customs and traditions" upon which we operate. They have become unwritten addenda to out Statement of Faith and in recent years have become the "measuring stick" for righteousness among many of our members both locally and across the land. Bear with me while I give some examples.

1. Our Sisters are to have their hair "long." This has been amplified in recent years to include that it be "up" as well (i.e., In a "bun"). Sisters who don't conform are made to "feel it" in conference memoranda and often in sermons by our Elders. For a minister's wife conforming is not optional. We have received a lot of pressure regarding this lately (and for the sake of unity we conform, for the most part). This is an area of emphasis with our converts, in particular.
2. We are not to wear jewelry, including even a simple wedding band. It is OK, however, to wear the finest of modest contemporary apparel. Watches, dress pins, and hairpins are OK too.
3. We are not to participate in or attend organized athletic events. This is true for all ages. If a high school athlete comes to Christ, he or she must "give this up." Even parents are not to attend the athletic events of their children. Depending on the local Elder, doing so can result in being barred from holding a church office. Other youth activities, such as 4-H, choir, drama, and band, however, are permissible.
4. We practice church discipline, but only "sex sins" are punished (with rare exceptions). Recently a couple in our congregation was "banned" for two weeks and excommunicated for one and one-half years for having intercourse twice during their engagement fourteen years before. This one and one-half year loss of church membership was unprecedented for brevity. They have since been restored to full fellowship but it has nearly destroyed their family and spiritual lives. Adulterers are never restored to full membership. Discipline is exercised upon confession of sin to the local Elder. In recent years our Elder has required the congregation to stand in support of disciplinary actions. Failure to do so would be "not supporting the church" and could bar one from holding a church office. Sins other than "sex sins" are generally termed "shortcomings" and "mistakes." This had become a terrible struggle for me. I believe that God

does not differentiate between sins, as we do, and while I do believe in the doctrine of church discipline, I believe that it is for the sole purpose of restoration of the member who is continuing in sin. I do not believe that it is to be a punitive legal system as we often make it to be.
5. In church we have separate seating; men on one side, women on the other. We have no piano or organ in the church. All singing is done acappella.
6. Television is strongly discouraged. Ministers are not allowed one at all, except if there are "older children" at home.
7. We greet one another (men/men and women/women) with a "holy kiss" (on the lips) within the church. Needless to say, this is a stumbling block for many.
8. Our Sisters are to be covered during worship. Tradition has brought us six-inch shoulder length veil.

One of the strongest aspects of our church is our fellowship and family closeness.

We are reared in such a way that our church becomes a part of our heritage. If one could poll our membership on the above eight points, I'm sure that a large majority would have serious reservations about at least some of them. However, nearly all go along because "this is the way we've always done it." Only a small percentage of people reared in our church ever are converted in other churches. The other side of this coin is that only about one fourth of the people reared in our church ever join it. Most just attend their whole lives or do not go anywhere. Converts from the "outside" are rare, generally being the result of one of our young people marrying "outside the faith" prior to being converted. Tammy and I are a case in point. She was "not of our people." From these facts it is apparent that our people have a strong affinity for the church but are not willing to join it. A common expression is "I'll never join that church, but I sure don't wanna go anywhere else."

As may be apparent from the Statement of Faith, the body of church Elders guides the church. These leaders are elected from the church ministry by vote and generally serve until late in life. Only those ministers who are in one hundred percent support of the church doctrine, structure, customs, and traditions are even considered for the Eldership, regardless of local church sentiment. In the last fifteen to twenty years there has been a trend to centralize authority in the Elder body. When my grandfather was our Elder, there was a lot of local autonomy. Questions and concerns were settled locally or after consultation with an Elder from a neighboring church that was familiar with the people and the situation at hand. Now nearly everything must be taken to the full Elder body and unanimity must be achieved before any word is forthcoming or any decisions are made. The most conservative voices nearly always prevail and everyone "goes along for the sake of unity." The result of this procedural change has been that the church is becoming more and more conservative and Elder oriented.

One issue in particular which concerns me is that the Elder body has of late been inferring that individual church members cannot properly discern the Holy Spirit's directions and that they are to yield to the local Elder's higher level of discernment. Hebrews 13:17 is being heard more and more and being applied to this issue in particular.

Our present Elder is a complex man. He is a wealthy farmer by profession. He is a good conversationalist and a better than average preacher. As a leader he is very stern and the thrust of his leadership is to "preserve the way." Our relationship is good as long as I don't make any waves. "Support" is all that he wants from me and questioning any practice or belief of the church is simply not tolerated. He was reared in a home with a strict authoritarian father, he reared his own family that way, and consequently he can't understand why everyone won't obey him unquestioningly. He is a man of quick temper and equally quick apology. More than one person has cited him as the reason for not coming to the Lord ("joining the church"). I genuinely want to respect him as a brother and as a leader but am finding it so difficult to do. I pray daily that God will give him compassion and teach him people skills and I also pray that no roots of bitterness will spring up in me. Prior to his Eldership he was a good "love of God" and "repentance" preacher but this all seems to be lost now in his overriding concern for submission and methodology.

If I were you I would be wondering at this point "Why did Tom allow himself to get into this situation, knowing the system as he did?" Tammy and I have asked ourselves that question hundreds of times the past year and a half. There were many factors that led up to it and I shall endeavor to name a few. For several years prior to this I had felt the Holy Spirit's prompting to be more diligent in the Word. In my choir work there was fruit as we had many in the church active and excited. We were traveling and enjoying fellowship with other churches. We seemed to be breaking down walls between factions within the church. We also seemed to be experiencing a unity among us that had been absent for many years. When one of our older ministers retired and we prepared to elect another one, people began suggesting that I would be their choice. I honestly didn't see how it could happen but I did not want to go out of my way to work against myself in case the Lord had the ministry in store for me. In the several months that I knew I was one of three nominees I was overwhelmed at the prospect. I was honored to think that others would consider me. I felt the slight thrill of the challenge. I knew that my grandparents would be exhilarated and see it in part as a reward to them for their diligence over the years. When Tammy and I were interviewed by three Elders prior to the final vote they basically wanted to know only two things: would I support our Elder and would I get rid of our television.

As I write this I find that I am embarrassed to relate it to you. In retrospect I can see that we were **so** naive. I should have known how it would be in the ministry. However, I got caught up in the emotion of the events and didn't take time to count the cost. My prime conviction at that time was that if the Lord wanted me to preach the Word I would do it and that if He didn't I wouldn't be elected. I failed to realize that it is one thing to be a member of the church and to "go along" with its customs and traditions (when I would be seen by others) and quite another thing to be (by position) an advocate and defender of them. For me it has become a monumental difference. The more that I grow in the Word and in the Spirit the less important they become. As they are applied and viewed presently, I see them as a definite detriment to the winning of souls for the kingdom.

Tammy and I are very happy and abounding in the Lord. We are growing spiritually and feel His guiding hand day by day. I want to state unequivocally that preaching the Word is not the issue. I count that a privilege. The options before us all look unattractive at the present time. Let's consider:

1. We continue on as we are.

    Soon our children will begin to participate in school sports activities. If we attend we will be at odds with both our Elder and certain segments of the church. I feel that when one properly conducts himself that there is nothing wrong in attending athletic events. I also feel that it is important to support my children's worthwhile activities. I also feel that I could no longer "stand in support" of severe church discipline as in the case that I related earlier.

    These are just two possible instances of open conflict that could occur any day. Many in the church would agree with my stance. If I stood fast on each issue I would most likely be silenced (dismissed from the ministry). This could lead to a split in the church or leave us a bitter, unfruitful church. I don't want peace at any price but I want to be absolutely sure that I stand on the Word before something that I do or say becomes the focal point of controversy.

2. I step down from the ministry and continue as before.

    Many people (both members and unconverted souls) see in me a ray of hope for the future of the church. My ministry has been well received and for these people (and especially my parents and grandparents) my stepping down would be a severe blow. Also, I would need to offer some explanation as to why. If I was honest (which of course I would have to be) the explanation itself could have unwanted consequences. For example only those who are supportive of the church doctrine, customs and traditions can hold church offices. In all probability this would exclude me. Knowing our local Elder, I would never be trusted again.

3. I could leave the church.

    I would then need to either find another church or start out on my own. (Incidentally, two of our general area's most growing vibrant churches were started by people of our denomination who selected option # 3). As I analyze myself I don't feel that I would be one to strike out on my own. However, I don't know of any local church that I would want to be a part of. For me to leave the church would be like pulling my arm off. The church seems to be an ingrained part of my heritage and my family ties in it are strong. I was a boy of ten when it split once before and I vividly remember the heartache and misery that it caused. Those who left are still "bad guys" in the eyes of many who remain, despite the fact that they know it is wrong to feel that way.

If I could be absolutely sure that it was what the Lord wanted me to do, I would consent to option # 3. I am sure that His grace would be sufficient, but I would need all of it to avoid dying of guilt.

Despite my best effort I am not sure that I have fairly related my situation to you. Perhaps one has to "live it" to fully understand. I have turned to you for counsel because your ministry has played a major part in my "spiritual renaissance." I try to feed on your daily messages, your tapes, and your study guides as often as I have time to. I have yet to find an issue upon which you and I differ theologically. As the Lord gives me guidance I plan to continue to support your ministry in prayer and financial support. I want nothing more than to be a faithful, fruitful servant of my Lord Jesus Christ. I am willing to do whatever He wants me to do if I can only discern it. This includes any of the above options and any others that you may offer. Until I hear from you I will continue to serve, pray, and "wait upon the Lord."

In Christ,

Tom A. Speicher

In December of 1985 it became known that Dale and Carol Strassheim would soon be moving away to take another job. They had exhausted all options in our area and they now had no choice but to move. I wrote my thoughts about this impending change in my journal.

Wednesday January 11, 1985. After church Dale & Carol came out to visit. They have job offers, one from Phoenix and one from Minneapolis. Next week they are going to visit both places. They are really torn about what to do. Neither can believe that they are being led away from Milford. It was a wonderful evening of sharing. They left at 12:30am.

Tammy and I both realize that if they in fact do leave that it will have profound effects on both the Milford church and us. I anticipate that (the Elder) will try harder to "work me into shape." I also anticipate that he will ensure that a "supportive brother" will succeed Dale. I believe also that I will not last long in the ministry. If I do stay on I'll have to either learn how to stand firm and handle adversity or I'll have to "fall into line." My prediction is that I won't last long. I am praying hard that the Lord will show me what to do. I am praying for Grace to do whatever, even if it is "staying on." I know one thing though; there is no going back to my former state of spiritual dormancy.

Tammy and I were also making a big decision during this time. It seems silly in retrospect, but we agonized over whether to bring our television back home or not. There is no question that there is much that is bad on television. There is, however, much good also. My thoughts about this decision follow:

Thursday, December 19, 1985. Tammy went shopping all day with her Mom and (her cousin) Jill so I kept the two little Spikes (my two younger children). It was bitterly cold all day again. After we had played for a while we visited Grandpa and Grandma Beer. While we were there, I walked over to Mom and Dad's and put our TV into the back of the car. I covered it because I didn't want the kids to know yet. For the last six months Tammy & I have agonized over whether to get it back or not. In a lot of respects it has been good for us. We are no longer bound to it and we spend our time a lot more constructively together as a family. However, lately the kids have been pushing as to why they can't watch specials,

"Sesame Street," cartoons, etc. I have no good answer to give them. To tell them the "church" doesn't allow us to have it would only create bitterness. They know better than to believe that it is all bad. Furthermore, everyone we socialize with (except Dale & Carol) has one and we are constantly running them places to watch this and that. After much thought and prayer Tammy and I have decided that children have enough forces working at them (that might cause them) to rebel. They don't need us to provide any. Bringing the TV back, putting it in the basement, and carefully monitoring its use seems to be the best option. This had been one of the most agonizing decisions that I've ever made. If this gets to certain people in the church, there are bound to be fireworks. I pleadingly pray that the Lord will give me grace, courage and the wisdom to know when to submit and when to stand.

In retrospect it seems very silly that I would refer to bringing back a television into our home as "one of the most agonizing decisions" that I had ever made. It is not so silly when I think about the decision in the context of those days. The agony had nothing to do with the television. Tammy and I had both grown up with television and were not harmed by it. The agony had to do with the consequences of bringing it back. I did not tell the Elder what I had done. I reasoned that if it came to his attention that I would admit to it and accept the consequences, whatever they may be. I knew that it was only a matter of time until I would no longer be a minister, anyway, so what did it matter? At this point I decided I needed to inform Dad and Mom about my convictions and intentions. I assumed that they would understand and I was not disappointed. I wrote about my conversation with them in my journal.

Sunday, December 29, 1985. Today (the Elder) *arranged for me to come and talk tomorrow morning. He has been after me for quite awhile to come alone so he can check with me about how I feel about some things. This time there was no putting it off. I know that sooner or later I need to level with him about my convictions but up to now I haven't had the courage to. I was really melancholy about it most of the day. However, tonight Tammy and I talked to Dad and Mom and we explained that if he* (the Elder) *can't be satisfied with* us we will step down and let him get a replacement who can support him as he feels he needs to be supported. They gave us their blessing and assured us that Grandpa and Grandma Beer feel the same way. We went home feeling apprehensive but a lot better.

I slept well that night and awakened with a sense of resignation about what I was about to do. My journal entry of that visit follows:

Monday, December 30, 1985. I arrived at (the Elder's) around 8:40am. He was quiet, peaceful, and seemed to be very down. I didn't say much for a long while but once I got started I spoke my heart in such a manner that I surprised myself. I was able to say exactly what I wanted to. I also explained forcefully and often that I am ready to peacefully step down anytime that he can't be satisfied with my convictions or me. This morning he took it all very well and we parted peacefully but I expect him to mull it over and be back at me soon. I left feeling free as a bird, but apprehensive about what may be ahead.

During this meeting I expressed my views on a number of issues. I first told the Elder that I did not support the church's stand on church discipline. I explained why and told him what I believed about the doctrine. I also explained that I saw nothing wrong with parents attending their children's athletic activities or coaching their teams. Rather, I saw these activities as both worthwhile and commendable. I also told him that I felt the national Elder Body's focus was not on the right things. Instead of being preoccupied with "preserving the way" I felt they should address issues such as why so few children raised in the AC church ever join it and also evangelistic outreach. I spoke of my concern that our denomination spends so much time warning members about what they are not to be doing and so little time teaching us what the Bible says we should be doing. I also told him that I could not go along anymore with excluding people from consideration for church offices for non-Biblical reasons. On these issues he could no longer depend on my "full support." My hope in leveling with him like this was that he would simply allow me to step down from the pulpit and quietly fade away. I thought this was an easy way out of the situation that we both found ourselves in. I would have been willing to tell the congregation what I had told him. There would have been an uproar, but it would have been an uproar that would have passed quickly if I took responsibility for my actions and did not "feed" the discontentment.

As I think back on these days, sometimes it is hard to remember anything happy. I am so thankful that I kept a daily journal. Most days were routine: going to work, coming home, and playing with the children. With the exception of the church situation, it was a happy time in our home. My journals bear this out. One entry during this period of time warms my heart. I would have never remembered it if I had not written it down.

Saturday, January 4, 1986. Poor Travie had a tough night. He was up several times, burning up (with fever), and he vomited too. The little rascal won't take any medicine but children's aspirin, which is what I prefer he not take. Anything else (except Amoxil, which he loves) he spits up.

After he was up and vomited at 2:00am. I couldn't sleep. I was reading the Bible at the kitchen table (I was reading in Exodus – the description of the Tabernacle- excellent cure for insomnia!) when he peeked around the corner and said "Dad, will you wock-a-by me?" I said "Go to bed, Travie. Its late and Daddy's reading the Bible." He tilted his head, put his hands on his hips, and looked so forlorn as he said, "Come on Dad, pweeze?" I rocked him to sleep!

Chapter Forty-Six

In January 1986, I received replies to my letter from both "Grace To You" and "Insight For Living." The letter from "Grace To You" was simple and straightforward. They simply suggested that I find a new church home for my family and offered some advice about what to look for in a church. The letter from "Insight For Living" was written by a man named Cyril J. Barber. It was a lengthy letter that contained the information that I had been longing for. Instead of offering specific advice, Mr. Barber challenged me to think the matter through in the light of the Word of God. After listing some qualities to look for in a church, he turned to the matters of the basic needs of man and provision of God to meet those needs. The letter read as follows:

Insight For Living

January 3, 1986

Mr. Tom A. Speicher
Rural Route 1, Box 10
Milford, In 46542

Dear Tom:

I trust that during the past couple of weeks you have had the opportunity to weigh carefully the information I shared with you in my earlier letter. (*I never did receive this letter and have always wondered what it said.*)

At this time I would like to point out some of the criteria of a healthy church.

1. A healthy church is one where Christ is regarded as the Head, and where the members acknowledge this not only in their doctrinal statement, but also in the manner in which they conduct the services of the church and its business affairs (Ephesians 1:22; 4:15; 5:23; Colossians 1:18; 2:19).
2. A healthy church is one in which the Word of God is taught in its fullness (Acts 20:27) and applied in practical ways to every area of daily life. The message of the Gospel is seen as involving the totality of all that Jesus Christ preached and came to accomplish. This extends beyond the preaching of the message of salvation to take in the needs of each and every believer, as well as the community in which they live (Ephesians 1:7-12; Colossians 2:8-12, noting v. 10a).
3. A further evidence of a healthy church is its emphasis upon grace, as opposed to either legalism (arising out of man-made rules or requirements) or license (growing out of a false emphasis on love), so that each believer may enjoy true liberty in Christ (Romans 8:1; 2 Corinthians 3:17; Galatians 5:1, 13).
4. Ideally, a healthy church should also be characterized by the warmth of its fellowship, which in turn forms the basis of a caring community (John 13:34-35; 15:9-10; Romans 12:9).
5. The genuineness of a healthy church will be evidenced in the quality of its worship (John 4:24). This is essentially internal, as opposed to external. It arises out of true love for the Lord and a commitment of ourselves to walk in reverential awe of Him. Such worship is quite apart from gimmicks (designed to draw in

outsiders) or programs that entertain (Matthew 15:7-9; Philippians 3:3; Colossians 2:20-23).

Your gifts are obvious, Tom, and I am sure that the Lord can and will use you to His glory in some way. Whether this is in your present church or some other remains to be seen. Enclosed with this letter you will find a copy of Chuck's booklet entitled God's Will. I would urge you and Tammy to read it carefully.

We can always discern the truth, Tom, by looking carefully at the source of power. Pseudo-Christians and false religions derive their source of authority from the power to curse. By contrast, in Judaism and Christianity (as revealed in the Bible), there lies inherent in the message God communicated to his people the power to bless.

In false forms of religion, the attraction is to a group. Adherents to this group are given feelings of belongingness, worth, and competence. Should they ever wish to leave the group, however, these assurances are hastily withdrawn. The result is a feeling of loneliness, isolation, and vulnerability. Oftentimes the need for these psychological assurances is so great that the defector will rejoin the group he or she has left.

Only through a unique and lasting relationship with each Member of the Godhead can these needs be truly and permanently met. So that you may have a clear understanding of what is involved, Tom, I invite you to weigh carefully what the Bible teaches.

When God made Adam and Eve, He made them in His image (Genesis 1:26-27). They were His special creation. They drew their identity from their relationship with Him. In a very real sense, they belonged to Him.

Adam and Eve were also made for each other (Genesis 2:18). This gave them a unique sense of oneness (Genesis 2:23). They belonged to each other.

In addition, God prepared a beautiful garden in which Adam and

Eve were to live (Genesis 2:8,15). This completed their sense of <u>belongingness</u>—vertically, horizontally, environmentally.

Adam and Eve were also the apex of God's creative handiwork (Genesis 2:7). He fellowshipped with them in the cool of the day (Genesis 3:8). In a very real sense, Adam and Eve knew they were unique. They enjoyed true <u>worth.</u>

God also gave Adam and Eve work to do. They were to "rule" or "have dominion over" the earth that He had created (Genesis 1:26,28; 2:15). All of creation was benign so that the work could be done easily and without strain (contra. Genesis 3:17-19). Adam and Eve enjoyed a sense of <u>competence.</u>

When sin entered the world, however, all of this was lost. Sin separated Adam and Eve from God. They hid from Him (Genesis 3:8). They were later expelled from the garden (Genesis 3:23-24). Gone now was their feeling of <u>belongingness</u>.

As a result of sin, Adam and Eve had a new sensation of shame. Their thoughts turned inward upon themselves (Genesis 3:10). They became conscious of self, and with this came an awareness of their nakedness. They no longer possessed feelings of true worth.

Furthermore, the ground was cursed and would no longer be conducive to sustaining life. Hardship and toil were to be the legacy of disobedience (Genesis 3:17-19). Gone now was their feeling of competence.

Fortunately for Adam and Eve, God bridged the gap and in grace provided for their spiritual and physical needs (Genesis 3:15,21).

All of us, however, have continuing needs for feelings of <u>belongingness</u>, <u>worth</u>, and <u>competence.</u>

In the plan and purpose of God, provision has been made whereby all believers in Jesus Christ can have these basic needs met. The solution lies in the development of a unique relationship with each

Member of the Godhead.

As Christians, we have been brought into a new and vital relationship with God the Father. We have been made members of His family. We are accepted by Him and have access into His presence (Ephesians 1:3-6; Hebrews 4:16; 1 John 3:1-2; 4:16,18). We call Him "Father." In a very real sense, therefore, we <u>belong</u> to Him.

This relationship with God the Father serves as an antidote to feelings of anxiety (see 1 Peter 5:7; compare Proverbs 3:5-6).

A realization of our true worth is derived from our relationship with Christ the Son (1 John 4:9,17). As we meditate on the price He paid for our redemption (1 Peter 1:18-19; compare Psalm 49:7-9) and realize that we have been made heirs of all the glories of His kingdom (Romans 5:7-8,11; 8:17), we come to realize our true <u>worth</u>. This is quite apart from any work which we may perform.

This relationship with the Lord Jesus Christ satisfactorily takes care of feelings of guilt (2 Corinthians 7:9-11) through confession (1 John 1:9), which leads to restoration.

Finally, our ability to cope with the harsh realities of life is restored as we allow God the Holy Spirit to control our lives (Ephesians 5:18). He indwells us and enables us to deal with each situation as it arises (John 14:16-17; 1 John 2:20). Through our relationship with Him, we again experience a feeling of <u>competence</u>.

This relationship with the Holy Spirit satisfactorily takes care of feelings of anger (arising out of our frustrations over things we cannot control, or circumstances causing us to feel rejected and/or humiliated).

In a very real sense, therefore, God graciously meets our basic needs through a vital relationship with each Member of the Trinity. Feelings of <u>security</u>, <u>significance</u>, and <u>satisfaction</u> can be ours as we avail ourselves of the resources He has given us.

So you see, Tom, your true security and the meeting of these needs comes from the Lord, and not from any group of which you may be a member.

I know that the decision facing you and Tammy is a weighty one. We are concerned for you and your family. Do let me know if we can be of further service to you.

>Warmly in Christ,
>Dr. Cyril J. Barber
>Counseling Associate

PS: Years ago when God spoke to His people through Hosea, He lamented that His people were perishing for lack of knowledge (Hosea 4:6). They had neglected the teaching of His Word. The same is true today. People are suffering mentally and emotionally, relationally and spiritually because they have been deprived of the counsel of Scripture (cf., Amos 8:11). I trust that as you commit yourself to reading good books, the Lord will bring new meaning to your life.

It would be hard to overstate the importance of this letter to me when I received it in 1986. It "hit the nail on the head," so to speak, regarding what held me back from being bold for what I had come to believe as truth. Taking an honest inventory of my life, it was necessary I acknowledge that my belongingness, worth, and competence were derived from my heritage, which were centered on my maternal family and church denomination. This explained why I so greatly feared not pleasing Grandpa Beer, why I viewed "leaving the church" as such a monumental decision. It also made it so clear to me why my mother was so fiercely determined to "measure up" in the eyes of her father and the church, why she had endured a life of misery to remain in her circumstances. Realizing that God had so totally provided for my fulfillment through a relationship with Him was the most liberating, blessed truth I have ever learned. I long ago lost track of how many times I have used the concepts of belongingness, worth, and competence in personal evangelism. They are concepts that everyone can identify with because they are permanent, ongoing needs that everyone has. At this time I rejoiced in these concepts, but I had no idea how critical they would be in preserving my mental, physical, and spiritual well being throughout the massive eruption that was coming.

I predicted that the Elder would mull over what I had told him and ask for another meeting. I was not disappointed. My journal entry records some of my thoughts that day.

Friday, January 17, 1986. After I took Travis and Traci to Sonya's (their sitter) this a.m. I headed to the (church) fellowship hall for a second meeting with (the Elder). We find that we have a lot of differences as we talk. As I knew would happen, he misinterpreted me on a lot of the things I said in our first meeting. He also pinned me down on my feelings regarding Christian involvement in and attendance at sports events. Once I admitted my feelings on this he didn't try to pin me down on anything else. When we were done he said that he felt a lot better, but I definitely felt worse. I feel that the two of us are worlds apart in our Christian priorities. I just don't see how I am going to last in the ministry. But how do I get out without provoking a "blood bath?" The only answer that I can see is to totally give it to God and let come what may. I am sure of one thing, though. I must be true to my convictions from now on.

The whole rest of the day was kind of a cloud. Even work was slow and dreary.

When I arrived at the meeting that day the Elder began by explaining why he wanted to meet me there instead of at his home. "I wanted to meet you here today," he said, "because when (my son) sees me walking around with my head down it upsets him." I have met very few people in my life who were as good at using guilt and intimidation as motivating techniques as the Elder was. At one point in the discussion that morning I asked, "Why can't I just peacefully step down and allow you to find a replacement?" I clearly remember his reply. "If you would step down there would be half these people wanting to go and set up a church somewhere," he said. This statement really surprised me. I replied instantly, "I don't want any part of anything like that." And I sincerely meant it. The Elder's statement was the first time I heard anyone mention splitting the church and starting another one. I was aware that several groups before me had done this, but I had never envisioned it as a part of my future. Ten days later this prospect surfaced again, this time during a visit by Grandpa Beer to my house.

Monday, January 27, 1986. I dropped Traci and Travis off at Sonya's and headed home. Grandpa Beer soon stopped by (this was very unusual). *He...was concerned about* (the Elder's) *service yesterday morning. He is very concerned for the future of the church. The only problem is that he thinks I'm the key to holding it together. I share his concerns — probably more so. I'm committed to doing the best I can for as long as I can, but I don't share his confidence that I can hold it together. I'm trying to put it in God's hands. Time will tell.*

My lack of favor with the Elder began to become common knowledge the following Sunday. My journal entry that day explains what took place.

Sunday, February 2, 1986. After work I went to church. I had a nice chat with (my uncle) *Flip over the noon hour. He had a lot of timely advice.*
I was very apprehensive about preaching this afternoon. It seems like it is harder after it goes well like on Wednesday night. My texts were Psalm 111 and Colossians 2. I felt very inspired as I went through them. As I was preaching I noticed that more than usual people's eyes were darting to (the Elder) *off and on. What I was saying (actually, what the Word was saying – I tried to stick right to it) was evidently provoking him or people were looking to see if it was. It was very uncomfortable. When I was done he got up and really drew a sharp contrast, saying that salvation by Grace through Faith was only part of the story and that there are other books in the Bible and that we are to consider the whole counsel of God and that faith without works is dead – etc, etc. I felt like a fool. I could hardly look up.*
When we were off the pulpit he excused (the other minister) *and began talking to me* (in front of everyone). *He said that he knows I asked to keep our differences private but since I "don't support"*

him and "hold up his arms" and since he and I can't come to an agreement, that he needs to follow scripture and take it to two or three others as per Matthew 18. He said that he was going to talk to (two other brothers) about me and wanted to know if I wanted to be present. I replied that I felt it didn't matter whether I was (there) or not since they would believe him anyway. I pleaded to just let me quietly sit down in the course of time. He replied that he was going to try and get me back in line. When I told him that he must be prepared for what may come if he takes this public, he didn't answer. I did tell him, however, that if he was going to contradict me in front of the church that he would better off to declare questionable scriptures off limits. He replied that he felt he added to my message. As I found out later, if he really felt he added, he was the only one who felt he did.

I left church devastated. I don't know when I left feeling worse. I just felt dirty, like I needed to go home and take a bath. If he begins rallying his forces against me, I'm done. I feel like an outcast; like I'm the little boy on the playground about whom a group of kids is whispering. As near as I can figure out, I stand accused of three things: (1) I expressed that I felt the focus of the national elder body is on the wrong things: customs, traditions, and preserving the way instead of salvation and sanctified lives. (2) I expressed that I feel parents have an obligation to support their children's worthwhile activities, to include sports, and (3) I expressed that I didn't feel it was right to keep people off ballots for non-scriptural reasons. This boils down to me "not supporting him and the church's doctrine."
(That evening we visited Dad and Mom. Ned and Deb were there, as were an Uncle and Aunt.) *I wished later that I hadn't been as open with them as I was but I tried to convey above all else that I don't want to fight and I don't want anyone fighting for me.*

The truth of the matter is that I was guilty of all three charges. I did not dispute this. In my opinion, there were far more important issues that the Elder and I disagreed about, but these were the ones he was focusing on. This was fine with me. In the last few years I had seen the heartache suffered by those who had been judged acceptable or unacceptable in the church according to their stand on these issues and it was very wrong. In my opinion, by using these three criteria as the acceptability "screen" the Elder had conferred upon those people deemed "acceptable" a false sense of righteousness and upon those deemed "unacceptable" a false sense of unrighteousness. The issues had become incredibly divisive. They had taken the church's focus off the Biblical imperatives of Christian love, of measuring all things by Christ, of producing Spiritual Fruit, of living as the Light of Christ in the world, and had placed the focus on our relative "goodness" or "badness" as adherent's to the customs and traditions of the Apostolic Christian Church. It was fine with me if the Elder wished to take his stand against me on these issues.

Some time after this sad Sunday I was spending a typical day at work when Otto Beer, Junior came into the store. Otto had been a member of the AC church years before and was one of the leaders of the church split when I was a young boy. It had been an ugly, angry division. I had grown up believing he was a dangerous man who espoused false doctrine. As I got to know him as an adult, however, I had found him to be a very nice person who truly loved the Lord. I knew some of the people who attended the church where he was the Pastor. I found them to be devout believers who lived lives that I could not fault. From time to time Otto came into the store to ask me how things were going in my life and in my ministry. When I had first been placed into the ministry he reminded me that salvation was in Jesus Christ alone, not Jesus Christ "plus" something. Even then I had no disagreement with him on that statement. On this particular day I was not busy and we were able to talk a lot. Before I knew it I was expressing some of my frustration with the issues before the church. He asked me if Tammy and I would like to get together and share sometime. I replied that I would and before the week was over we had accepted an invitation to their home. As Tammy and I drove there after work one night, I was fearful that we would be seen. I knew that the Elder would deeply disapprove of our visiting Otto and his wife Joan. After being welcomed into their home, Otto surprised me by asking me if I was "saved." Tammy and I both testified that we had believed in Jesus Christ as our Savior from sin years before and had been "born again." I was taken back by this question, but it made sense when I considered Otto's own testimony. He had grown up much as I had. His father was my Grandpa Beer's older brother. After serving in the Navy he had "joined the church." For years he was a zealous defender of the faith, until he heard the preaching of Billy Sunday and Billy Graham. Upon hearing them preach the Gospel, he realized that he had never placed his faith in Jesus Christ. Rather, he had "joined the church," believing membership in the AC church was how one became right with God. He soon left the AC church and had spent the next twenty years helping found two Independent Bible Churches and Pastoring one of them. In my forty-nine years, I have yet to see a more tireless and effective one-on-one evangelist than Otto.

It was good that we spent the evening together. He understood first-hand the frustrations I was dealing with. He tried to make me understand that leaving the AC church is a monumental, frightening step to take before the fact, but a very small event as one looks back on it. He also made a thought-provoking point in reminding us that Jesus called on people to leave the legalistic religious system of the day and to "follow Him," rather than to work from within it. To help with our feelings of isolation he suggested that we become involved in a home Bible study with some couples from the church that are interested in spiritual growth. I knew the AC Elders frowned on Bible studies that were not held under the supervision of the church, but I could not see anything but good coming as a result of studying the Bible. In the past several years the church leaders had tried twice to sponsor Bible studies. Both failed after a few meetings because people felt compelled to only say the "right" things. At least this was my opinion of what happened. I wrote about my decision to start a home Bible study in my journal.

Friday, April 18, 1986. This morning I drove to Zondervan's in Warsaw to look at some Bible study materials. I had a nice time browsing and found a very interesting looking one that had also been recommended to me by (a minister-friend from Indianapolis). After much thought and prayer about what could be done to turn up the "spiritual thermostat" in the Milford church I suggested to Ned that we start a private Bible study. He enthusiastically agreed and we are going ahead. I am certain that (the Elder) *won't approve, but I want to begin it to add to my spiritual and church activities, not to detract from them. I want to establish some more spiritual relationships in church. In any event, I am convinced that the benefits of the study far outweigh the risks of* (the Elder's) *disapproval. We have tried it twice under the auspices of the church and it has not been successful, largely because of restriction and intimidation. I have faith that if the Lord is behind this it will prosper and if He isn't it will fail.*

This Bible study proved to be a blessing. It was the first time I had ever been in a private study. I found it very interesting to share with other believers and to wrestle through difficult passages. Tammy and I were one of six couples who enthusiastically took part in it.

Meanwhile things continued to become more and more tense in the church. The Elder had obviously spoken to his brothers about my "lack of support," because two of them approached me on different occasions wanting to know if I was "going to disappoint them?" I tried to reassure them that I only wanted to quietly "step down" from the ministry and that I did not want to be divisive. Once during these weeks I stopped at Grandpa and Grandma Beer's house for dinner, only to find them discouraged about the future of the Milford church and wondering aloud if all the trouble was because they had not been good stewards while Grandpa was Elder. This hurt me deeply and caused me to search my heart anew. Having done so I still could not come up with any reasons why I would be doing the "right thing" to go along with what I believed were the "wrong things" in order to preserve my continued activity in a "system" which I believed the leaders saw as more important than the Savior. It was a good thing I had thought the issues through afresh, because I would need all my wits about me in the coming month of May 1986.

Sunday, May 4, 1986. It was kind of a tough morning for two reasons: I know I would have to have the morning service and be alone with (the Elder) *all day. By the time we reached church I had reached an inner peace, knowing that God's will is that His people be fed. I felt that the service went well. My texts were from II Kings and I Corinthians 15:1-25.*

Over noon (the Elder) was friendly and upbeat. I thought that it was going to be a great day until after the afternoon service. He started inquiring about my support and whether I would meet with other Elders. When I asked what he hoped to accomplish by me meeting with them it set him off. I spent the next forty-five minutes trying to calm him down. At one point he got up and said that he was going home with a heavy heart. He proceeded to say with a glare and a voice of utter contempt "I hope the Lord condemns your heart for what you've done to me!" He kept referring to a list of "sayings" which he had from our last meeting. I was stunned as to how they were out of context and misinterpreted. When I tried to explain it only made matters worse because he viewed it as double talk on my part. He did inform me in no uncertain terms that if I can't come around that I would be sat down. Furthermore, I can't be useful in the ministry if I don't support the church's stand on sports. As he left I told him I would like to know what he had on his list of my sayings. No sooner had I arrived home than he called and rambled them off to me. I was so amazed that I didn't even respond. One of us has a terrible memory.

Devastated as I was, I was able to pull myself together and help host Mom's birthday party. Our whole family came and it really was a special evening. Trischa, David, Kasee, and Traci spent hours at the ditch and in Gilbert's woods. They were so thrilled and felt so grown up when they got back. Travie and Joey got so filthy playing in the dirt that I had to take a picture!

After they all left and we got cleaned up, reality set in again. I called Dale and had a long talk with him. He and Carol had a tough day, too. It was their first Sunday since moving. We didn't arrive at any answers but it was good to talk.

The move to Minneapolis was very difficult for Dale Strassheim and his family. There were many logistical and professional reasons for this, but among the things that hurt most was the fact that his office of minister did not "follow him" to the new AC congregation. In years past it was routine for the office to follow the minister when moving from one congregation to another, unless there were too many ministers in the new congregation already. Such was not the case in Dale's new congregation. There were not too many ministers. The reason the office did not follow Dale was because he did not receive "a good report" from his previous Elder. This was very unfair. Dale was an excellent minister and his preaching was widely appreciated. He had some reservations about the same issues that I did, but Dale was solidly committed to the denomination. Silencing Dale Strassheim, in my opinion, was a severe, self-inflicted wound by the AC Elders.

The day after the Elder and I had our unpleasant conversation after church I went "on offense" to be sure he and I understood each other.

Monday, May 5, 1986. I spent a very restless night. I awoke with determination to set the record straight. I decided that if am going to go down at least my words must be accurately recorded. This was the one piece of advice Mom had for me yesterday, too. At 7:30am. I called (the Elder) and asked for the "list of sayings" so that I could respond in writing. He was in kind of a sobby, angry mindset. He informed me that he "just couldn't take anymore" and was going to call a meeting of his brothers and his sons to seek advice regarding his "stewardship." I responded that I thought it would be the worst move that he could make because even if he mentioned no names everyone would know exactly the source of his discouragement. They would then characteristically lash out at me and "my people" would then respond in kind, in all probability. After this route for a while he calmed down and finally agreed to read the list to me again. After talking for a while more we parted peacefully. I spent the remainder of the morning typing out my recollections of what I actually said, including elaboration regarding context and my full position. All the while I kept thinking how absurd it was that the response was even necessary. The issues are hardly worthy of debate. At this point I am convinced that my days as an Apostolic Christian Church minister are numbered. I am daily pleading with the Lord to stop me and turn me around if this is not His will for me. I mean it from the depths of my heart.

I kept a copy of this list of responses to the "list of sayings" attributed to me by the Elder. I include it here for the record. Next to each number on the list is word for word what the Elder had on his list. Following each "saying" is my response. As I read this many years later I am again reminded that acceptable "official" talk in the Apostolic Christian Church was somewhat akin to speaking in an English dialect.

May 5, 1986

Dear Bro. (Elder):

With our meetings of 1986 as background and with our conversation of this morning particularly in view, I am offering the following written response in the sincere hope that you and I can more clearly understand one another. In each case below I will first list what you had in your notes from our conversation of Monday morning, April 7, 1986. I will then list my response according to my best recollection and the present feeling of my heart.

1. *"Preach blood of Christ...can't support rules, customs and traditions..."*

    I believe that the entirety of the scripture revolves around the Person of the Lord Jesus Christ, whether it is in history, prophecy, types, or doctrine. For me to say that I only feel led to preach the blood of Christ is to embrace the Word fully. I feel that the redemptive work of Jesus in the saving of souls is the paramount issue, overriding all others. I can't support rules, customs, and traditions of the church, as a part of my **pulpit** ministry because I believe that would detract from the lifting up of the Name of Jesus.

2. *"No screening of ballots for teaching positions... (Ministry?)"*

    I do not support the removal of names from ballots for non-scriptural reasons. I believe if the church is healthy spiritually that unfit members will not be elected to the positions for which they are nominated. I believe furthermore that if the church is perceived to be unhealthy and therefore incapable of making a responsible choice that elimination of names will serve only to intensify the problem. I feel that this practice has served to create enmity among our brethren in that for some it nurtures a bitterness for not being considered trustworthy and acceptable while for others it nurtures a feeling of righteousness and acceptability which is based on improper criteria.

3. *"You were advised to keep feelings to self..."*

I was advised by a brother whom I consider to be godly not to use phrases and expressions that irritate you. Examples are "commitment," "come to Christ," "make a decision," "accept Christ," "forgive us when we sin," etc. He suggested that I substitute more traditional words such as "repent," "mistakes," and "shortcomings."

4. *"He doesn't feel it would help to talk to other Elders (Will if he has to)..."*

I believe that other Elders would have little interest in hearing anything other than an affirmation of unqualified support from me. The very fact that they would be asked to speak with me would indicate to them that I am unsupportive and unable to be handled by you, regardless of what you might tell them. Furthermore, they do not know me like you do, nor can they in a short period of time and they may very well force your hand to take action which you do not wish to take. If this is prayerfully taken into account, I will meet with them at your request.

5. *"Just dreaming about Indy..."*

Despite nearly 24 hours of soul and memory searching, I have absolutely no recollection of having made such a statement. It would be out of character for me to make an inflammatory remark like that. In addition, I would have no basis in fact for making the statement because I don't know how the Indianapolis brethren will respond. If I made such a remark, it was uninformed, presumptuous, and inflammatory and I ask your forgiveness.

6. *"Refer to teaching of our kids by those who feel sports are wrong..."*

When this point came up we were discussing barring those from teaching positions that are involved in coaching little league. As I recall, you asked me if I thought it was fair to the brethren who supported the church's stand on sports to have brethren teaching their children in Sunday School who saw nothing wrong with that activity. I observed that the question could be (and often is) turned around by those brethren who don't want their children taught that it is wrong for parents to be involved in little league. I believe that the Bible should be taught in Sunday school and that merit or lack of merit of parental involvement in little league and other activities such as 4-H shouldn't be discussed.

7. *"He offered to sit down and explain to church..."*

If 100% support of the church's customs and traditions is necessary to enjoy your confidence and if I need to give unquestioning obedience to your office, I will step down and explain why to the church.

8. *"He is sorry that he didn't keep his promise, but I question if this is the feeling of his heart."* (Reference #7 above).

When I was approved for the ministry I told you on several occasions that I would uphold the church and that I would support you as Elder. On one occasion I said that sometimes it would be out of conviction and other times out of duty. On the first Sunday in church after being elected I stood before the church and stated that I was reared, baptized, and married in the church. I said that it was part of my heritage and I supported it as my church home. I further stated that I support you as our Elder. I made these statements in good faith.

As I settled into my new role I soon realized that it was one thing to be a member of the church and to "go along" with the customs and traditions and quite another to be, by position, an advocate and defender of them. I saw how people were categorized and set at odds against one another over how well they did or did not support them. I have come to believe that Christian fruit bearing and charity among the brethren is suffering because of an over-emphasis on our church's customs and traditions.

As for supporting you, I thought that I promised to become a valued informed partner, working with your leadership for the common goal of winning souls for the Lord. What I have found is that I am to support and not ask questions. I have found that an alternate point of view is seldom sought and never appreciated.

If I knew two years ago what I know now I wouldn't have made the commitments that I did. You knew what would be expected of me and your suspicions that I didn't have what it would take were therefore correct. I am very sorry about that. I made my "promises" (I never remember once using the term "I promise" nor being asked "Do you promise?") in good faith, but as it turned out, in ignorance.

9. *"If everyone in the church had his feelings and attitude we wouldn't have any trouble..."*

I made this statement in response to your question "What would happen if everyone felt the way you do?" It goes without saying that in any group if everyone had the same attitude and the same feelings on issues that there would be little chance for trouble. I in no way meant to suggest or imply perfection on my part.

10. "I feel he is critical of Elders" (The Elder's personal note — not a statement of mine)

I recall making only two general observations about the national Elder body in our conversations. I am concerned that our focus is so heavily oriented towards "preserving the way." I feel that salvation and exhortation of Christian fruit bearing are much more important issues. Secondly, while the Elders ask for (and deserve) the complete trust of the membership, the membership in turn is not counted trustworthy to conduct open elections (Note: with regard to this I refer both to #2 above and our practice of not allowing spouses to cast absentee ballots).

11. "Feel parents should attend sports activities of children..."

I have stated that I feel parents have a responsibility to support the worthwhile activities of their children. When asked if I was including sports activities, I replied yes.

12. "If I would convince you, I'd have a terrible time convincing Tammy..."

Tammy and I are one flesh and nearly always of one mind. If the term "terrible time" was used, it was too emphatic.

13. "Love (the Elder) more than I ever did before and I'll do anything I can to help him but there are just some areas I can't support..."

True. I feel this way because after two years in the ministry I better understand (the Elder's) background, emotional makeup, and office.

14. "Feels (Elder) is too worried about conformity..."

True. See part (#1) of #10 above.

After finishing my "official" responses to this "list of sayings," I gave a copy to the Elder, the other Milford minister, and to the Elder's most reasonable brother. I was not ashamed of what I believed and I wanted to stand on my own words rather than what others "said" I was saying. To this day I do not understand why the Elder simply did not allow me to publicly state that I no longer could support the church on some issues and voluntarily retire from the ministry. Around this time I asked the Elder this very question. His reply to me was that he was going "to try one more time to bring me back into line."

Just when I thought the situation could not get any more complicated, it did. The previous fall my brother Ned had been elevated to the position of Principal of Wawasee High School. That same fall the football team made a dramatic run all the way to the Indiana 3A State Championship game. It was part of Ned's professional responsibility to provide leadership for this. In the spring of 1986 Milford's local newspaper ran a feature article on the football team's dramatic season. The occasion of this article was the awarding of the State Runner-Up Championship Rings. The article had many photographs, but two of them ignited a firestorm in the Milford Apostolic Christian Church. In one of the photos Ned was seated at his desk wearing the Championship Ring that had just been awarded to him. In another picture he was "leading a cheer" by the student body after the team won the Semi-State Championship game. After the publishing of this feature article, Ned was called to a meeting with the Elder and the other minister. I was not invited, nor did I know about the meeting. I wrote about the meeting after the fact in my journal.

Monday, May 12, 1986. Ned was called to a meeting with (the Elder) tonight. (The other minister) was there, too. The result of the meeting was that unless Ned goes to (the Elder) with a "changed attitude" by week's end he will be removed from Sunday school. When Ned pressed him for specifics he would only reply "you know." Two things that I know of specifically are that Ned had a ring (the state football championship ring) on in a newspaper photo and in another newspaper photo he was "leading a cheer" when Wawasee won the football semi-state. Serious charges! The official charge, though, was "bad attitude." He was really down tonight as we talked. I know one thing for sure: (the Elder) will have to be a lot more specific than this to hope for any support from me!

How does one define a "bad attitude?" It is a difficult notion to "get a handle on." In my own experience I think I know one when I see one, but often the problem with the person whom I see as having a "bad attitude" is simply that he or she does not agree with me. And simply not agreeing with me does not necessarily mean the individual has a "bad attitude." In characterizing a truly "bad attitude" I would say first of all that it is rooted in bitterness. A bitter individual has no desire to accurately assess conflicts or to work for their resolution. A bitter individual wishes to hold on to the hurt of injustice. The anger and separation "feel" justified and good. Furthermore, people or institutions that might wish to make amends and seek peace are "punished" by being denied resolution. In the absence of a desire on the part of "offenders" to seek peace, it is absolutely true that bitterness only hurts the individual who is bitter. Even when "offending" parties want to seek peace, denying them the opportunity to do so does not hurt them nearly as much as it hurts the bitter individual. I guess a "bad attitude" is rooted in bitterness from real or perceived injustices and it is characterized by one being oppositional just for the sake of being oppositional. Did Ned have a "bad attitude?" Well — Was he bitter? Did he have reason to be? Would we have been bitter if we were in his circumstances? I believe the honest answer to the last three of these questions is "yes." Was there any effort on the part of the institution or the leadership to seek peace with him, to convey to him that he had "belongingness," or "worth" in the organization? Was the institution or the leadership giving him the opportunity to demonstrate "competence" as a part of the group? I believe the answer to these two questions is "no." The tone of Ned's restoration had been one of "we are graciously allowing you back in" as opposed to "we are welcoming you back as a valued member of our church." Was Ned being oppositional? The answer to this depended on whom you talked to. Was he oppositional just for the sake of being oppositional? Same answer. Only Ned knew for sure the condition of his attitude. Regarding this, though, I am confident of two things. The first is that (the Elder) viewed everyone who did not agree with him to have a "bad attitude" or its equivalent, to be "non-supportive." The second thing I am confident of is that a wounded person tends to be a bitter person and our responsibility as Christians is to reach out to such individuals and seek their restoration – not to reinforce their hurts, as the church had done (and was doing) with Ned and Deb.

Ned defended himself by pointing out that these activities were a necessary part of his profession. He had used the same argument in earlier years to defend himself against his critics when he was involved in coaching athletic teams while teaching elementary school. This defense had two subplots. One was the unspoken understanding in the denomination that only farmers could live ideal AC lifestyles and involve themselves in absolutely acceptable activities related to their profession, like 4-H, county and state fairs, and farm-progress shows. Members of the denomination who were not farmers were aware that farming and farm-related activities were the "ideal" and many of them did not like it, including Ned and me.

The second sub-plot in Ned's self-defense was to challenge the denomination's thinking to acknowledge that we were in a changing world and a changing economy. The clear fact of the matter was that the future AC church would have less and less farmer-members and more and more non-farmer members. In the future there would need to be acceptable activities that were not farm-related. During the heat of this controversy a visiting (non-farmer) Elder told a story while preaching. The story was that his boss at work asked him to become involved in an activity that the AC church did not approve of. When he protested, his boss told him "The choice is yours, your church or your job!" The Elder replied, "I choose my church!" I told this Elder later that I felt his story was an inappropriate public slap at Ned. He acted surprised and said he had not meant it that way. Right. Ned's self-defense tactics fell on deaf ears.

In any event, the conservative members of the church were furious about these photographs of Ned. Not attending sporting events and not wearing rings were two dearly held AC "customs and traditions." To involve one's self in either activity was not to be done. To allow one's self to be photographed while involved in either of these two activities was unthinkable – even for "nominal" members. For a controversial, newly elected Sunday school teacher, recently "punished" brother like Ned Speicher to be photographed while participating in these activities required intervention by the Elder. There is no doubt in my mind that the Elder needed no urging to pursue this matter, but I am sure that many "good members" would have insisted if he had not pursued it. News of the Elder's plans prompted a most unlikely intervention.

Saturday May 17, 1986. Early this morning Deb called. Ned received a call from Grandma Beer this morning around 6:30. She was crying (an extremely rare occurrence) and pleading with Ned to placate (the Elder). Understandably, Ned was very upset. I soon called back and suggested that he and I both go and talk to them. I think that Grandma just couldn't bear it by herself. (Mom had told her, but no one had told Grandpa).

He soon came over and we drove out and spent the morning talking with them (and Mom). Grandpa felt that Ned should capitulate this one additional time. He also admonished me to "be careful" and not to get myself "into trouble." We parted not in complete agreement, but with a clear understanding and mutual support.

This was a painful meeting but one which was inevitable. I think we all came away perhaps knowing for the first time that the ultimate resolution for our church will be a separation of fellowship. I know that God is still on his throne and I remain prayerfully willing to be turned around but with the dictatorial and regressive trends within the Elder body apparent I now feel that this is the probable outcome.

As had been the case with Mount Saint Helens a few years before, the "internal pressure" within the Milford Apostolic Christian church had now risen to a crisis level, but despite repeated "rumblings" that should have prepared everyone for the imminent "eruption," no one anticipated how soon and how dramatic it would be. The "rumble" which produced the eruption that blew apart the Milford AC church congregation came from a most unexpected conflict, which occurred the day after Grandma Beer's plea to Ned.

Sunday May 18, 1986. If I may be so bold as to predict, I feel that the events of today mark a turning point in my life. We had a normal Sunday morning and left for church apprehensive, but resigned. I didn't feel that (the Elder) would try and remove Ned on a busy weekend like this. (A visiting minister) was with us and had the morning service. My part was to read a thank-you from Dale and Carol. I had no sooner sat at the lunch table than (the Sunday School Superintendent) came and informed me that there would be a minister/Sunday school teacher meeting in five minutes to elect three new women Sunday school teachers. He was "sorry that he didn't get to me sooner." Prior to going I told (the other minister) that I would insist (the Elder) be more specific about Ned before I would even consider supporting the decision. He then told me that I should agree that Ned has a "chip on his shoulder." I asked him how he made that determination. He soon saw that I wasn't going to accept his opinion in lieu of supporting evidence and we dropped it.

I went to the meeting not even knowing who was presently teaching, let alone who might be good with the kids. (One woman) suggested (my sister-in-law) Deb to me right away when I asked her (who she thought might be good for the job). With Ned's situation I didn't feel I wanted to put that on her so I didn't vote for her. I voted for (One person) and someone else instead (I couldn't think of a third person). (The Elder) then gathered up the ballots and told (other the minister) & me to come across the hall. When we finished counting, Deb had eight votes (which constituted a majority) and the next closest was five (maybe six). At this point (the Elder) set his jaw and said, "I don't enjoy support in that household. I'm not allowing her name to be accepted." I then asked if he had talked to her or any of the others receiving votes. He replied "I told Ned to come to me with a change of heart and he didn't." I then told him that I couldn't support this action. In anger he replied, "I know you don't support me or the church. You already told me that. It's a burden which I must bear!" He and (the other minister) then took the six names below Deb and went back for a second vote. Once collected we went back again (I didn't vote).

I was sitting there silently boiling when (the Elder) said, "Tom, I know this hurts you, but I don't enjoy support in their house." I then asked if he had talked with the others (being voted on) and their spouses. How does he know that he has their support? I then told him that what he had just done was discriminatory and wrong! He glared at me and snapped at (the other minister) "You can *support him if you want!" To which* (the other minister) *replied "Oh no,* (Elder), *whatever you say." At this point I nearly had to pick myself up off the floor. We went back and announced the "winners."*

Travie was sick this morning (his chest – we started him on Amoxil) so I took the girls home to pick up Tammy. I was so angry at what had just taken place that I was afraid of a stroke. On the way home I decided that there was no way that I could go on the pulpit (for the afternoon service). *Tammy was stunned by what had taken place and she totally agreed.*

I went back in (to the church auditorium) *and sat down by Grandpa* (Beer) *and briefly told him what happened and that I was not going onto the pulpit.* (What I told him was that something had happened over the noon hour that I could not go along with in good conscience. He replied "Are you sure that this is what you want to do? You know this could be the beginning of the end, don't you?" I replied "yes" and added, "I will understand if you don't want me to sit by you." At this he looked at me and sternly said "You sit right here!")

I sobbed a lot of tears of sorrow during the early part of the service but by the end I came to realize that the Lord had abundantly showed me the course to take. The incident over noon was totally unexpected. In addition it was clearly a case of corruption and prejudice (in my mind). *There were zero questions in my mind that it had to be opposed. It is an issue upon which I can firmly stand.* (The Elder) *came to me afterwards and said, "Try to understand." I replied that I understood perfectly and thanked him for clearing up in my mind what I should do. Up until this incident I was still uncertain and the issues somewhat cloudy. I thanked him and told him that now he can get other brothers to support him like he feels he needs to be supported. With this I said "Lord bless you" and walked away.*

Once home I had a tender talk with Trischa and told her what I had done in response to something that wasn't right. In tears I told her that one must do what is right no matter what and that this decision would hurt Grandpa and Grandma Beer very much. I feel that if I had not taken a stand today that I would have no right to expect my children to be upright in their lives. She was quiet but she understood.

Where do we go from here? I believe God alone knows. I feel the best course of action is to be quiet and allow the church's response to develop.

The thing that was unique about this incident was that it involved my sister-in-law Deb. Ned had always had his detractors, but no one ever had a bad thing to say about Deb. She was (and continues to be) one of the sweetest, most accommodating people in the world. Even people whom she does not like are seldom aware of it. It would have been difficult to find anything that I would have more likely instantly opposed than seeing her judged without trial like this. One could have given me a hundred guesses and I would not have guessed Deb as being the focal point of the controversy that would prove to the "straw that broke the camel's back" in my stepping down from the pulpit in the AC church.

Surprisingly, it was a rather quiet week after such a dramatic weekend. I do not recall
any specific feelings, other than feeling determined to stay the course and a slight sense of relief that I had something concrete to take a stand on. I knew I would be required to meet with the Elder and some visiting Elders to assess the situation and the arrangements were made to do so mid-week.

Wednesday May 21, 1986. I had just arrived at work this morning when (the Elder) *called. He wanted me to meet with "some Elders" Friday. He was really low and said, "They might just turn me* (the Elder) *out to pasture." Sure. When he said that they wanted to have Grandpa* (Beer) *talk to them I protested. I said, "I wish they would just leave him alone. He hasn't been used in years, his wounds have healed, and he is an old man." He said, "Can I leave it up to him?" If he* (Grandpa Beer) *wants to, I suppose that it's OK with me, but I feel the only reason that they* (the Elders) *want him is to "lean" on Ned and me. Before he hung up I told him that I would not be on the pulpit tonight. He asked me if I was sure if that's what I wanted to do. I replied that it's what I have to do.*

The remainder of the day was very melancholy for me. At church it was as if nothing had happened. (One man) *was the only person to say anything to me. He told me to "keep the faith."*

*Friday May 23, 1986. I was really calm about meeting with the Elders until about half an hour before I left. Once we got going everything was fine. (*Four visiting Elders*) were present. (*Our Elder*) didn't come in and I thought he was really acting (*immature*) outside. He wouldn't even go to the door and tell them I was present because they might think he was "eavesdropping." I told the Elders exactly what I thought about what had transpired. They wanted to discuss other issues but I really tried to confine the discussion to those at hand.*

My discussion with these Elders was very civil. After some small talk one of them asked me if I had any problem with the church's practice of repentance, confession, restitution, and conversion process. The question was phrased like "You don't have any problem with this, do you?" I replied that I supported these practices as long as they were done as a fruit of salvation rather than as a way to attain salvation. I was very surprised that none of them pursued this statement. If they had pursued it they would have had a way to avoid addressing any of the issues that had produced our meeting. It is also possible, however, that none of them had any problem with my answer. My other memory of this first meeting is that they were shocked that I did not intend to continue in the ministry. In answer to what I "wanted," I said, "I want to quietly sit down and for the church to quickly find a replacement who can support (the Elder) to the degree he requires." At this, one of them leaned forward in his seat, looked me in the face, and asked "Do you mean to tell me that you have no intention of continuing in the ministry!?" When I affirmed this, I think they knew they had a much bigger problem than what they had previously thought. I met again the next evening with two of these men and our Elder.

*Saturday May 24, 1986. I worked 8-8 today. We were slow and the day seemed to take forever. Right after I got to work (*the Elder*) called and asked if I could come out for another visit at 8:00pm. I agreed and had that to ponder all day too.*
*After work I drove out to (*the Elder's*). (*Two Elders from the day before and our Elder*) met with me. I found that they had asked Grandpa to come too! Before Grandpa came in I asked them why*

he was invited. They replied *"for valued input."* I then questioned them as to why his input was desired now after having been **totally** unused for eight years. I continued that (the Elder) was told **not** to counsel with him. At this both (of the visiting Elders) seemed stunned and spent the rest of the evening saying that they never told him that. I know that it embarrassed (the Elder) but it had to be stated. Grandpa came in later and expressed everything that he had pent up for eight years.

Conclusions of the night: (1) Ned out (2) Deb out (3) Tom wrong to have sat down – but – since I'm down I should stay there for awhile! They asked me to write out a statement for the church and let them see it tomorrow. I also went abundantly on record as opposing their decisions and in warning them that they will have to pay a high price to pull this off.

This was a most interesting evening. The meeting went on for hours. The two visiting Elders truly were stunned when I told them that our Elder had told me he had been told not to counsel with Grandpa Beer. The response of the visiting Elders and their repeated protests that they had not told him this convinced me that they loved and highly respected Grandpa Beer. They even asked the Elder "Who told you not to counsel with Brother Theo?" The Elder hung his head and gave a name of a then-retired, conservative Elder from Ohio. It was obvious that these two men were sorry that the Elder had not consulted Grandpa Beer since his retirement. From their reaction to this news it was obvious to me that the Elder had personally welcomed this advice not to consult with Grandpa Beer. As I look back, this is very sad for two reasons. First, because Grandpa Beer had been deeply hurt by being abruptly cut off by the new Elder, and, secondly, because the new Elder could have saved himself a boatload of heartache in the Milford congregation if he had sought some seasoned advice from Grandpa.

There was another very significant fact I learned that night. While explaining why Ned was being removed from the Sunday school, one of the Elders told me that our Elder had made a big mistake in allowing Ned to be considered in the first place. "This took place far too soon after his discipline," he said. He then continued, "There has never been a case where a disciplined brother has been allowed into such a high position, particularly so soon." I had suspected that the discipline played a role in deeming Ned to be in possession of a "bad attitude," but I had no idea that "being fully restored" did not *really* mean, "fully restored." One of the visiting Elders went on to explain how he handles controversial nominees in his church elections, no doubt insinuating how our Elder should have handled Ned. "It does not happen often," he said, "But when I have a candidate who is not acceptable, I just quietly remove his name. Only I know about it and it does not create a problem."

In the end, I was pleased that Grandpa Beer was given a chance to express his hurts and frustrations to two men who loved him and were glad to hear what he had to say. I think this helped him rest in the fact that he had done a good job leading the Milford congregation in years past. While I was pleased with this aspect of the meeting I was very troubled to learn that the church had not fully restored Ned and that they never would restore him to the extent that he could hold an office of high responsibility in the denomination. This seemed to be deceitful to me. If this was to be his standing, they should have told him so. In addition, I thought it was both deceitful and unfair to tell him he could not teach Sunday school because of a "bad attitude," when in reality the reason was that he was not eligible – and never would be. This last fact was to figure heavily in the meeting that would take place at church the next day. When I arrived home that evening I called Ned and told him what I had been told. He had suspected the same.

*Sunday May 25, 1986. I left work very apprehensive this afternoon. Ned called this morning to inform me that (*one of the visiting Elders who had been present the night before*) had called (*the Elder from Deb's home church*) very upset and insisted that he come to Milford for the day.*

*The Elders met with Ned and Deb at 11:30am. (*Our Elder*) asked me to come down at 12:00 noon. Once they reached an impasse with the three of us they asked Ned and Deb to leave and started on me about my statement (*to the church*). After about twenty minutes of inconclusive censoring we went into church at 12:30.*

*The member meeting lasted two hours and they never **once** mentioned the issues. The only definite statement was that I was* *wrong; that I had no right to sit down. This was repeated about a dozen times! If I hadn't mentioned Ned and Deb's names in my censored statement they would have never been mentioned! The **only reason** that I agreed to read a censored statement was with the assumption that **they** would address the issues.*

When I entered the Sunday school room where the meeting was taking place I encountered a surreal scene. In the corner were Ned and Deb. Deb was holding on to his arm. Elders who had been questioning them flanked them on either side. When I sat down, one of the Elders (who had not been present the night before) looked at me and said "Brother Tom, Brother Ned and Sister Deb feel that their recent discipline had something to do with his removal from Sunday school. We have told them that it (the discipline) had nothing to do with it." I was absolutely dumbfounded by this statement. I looked at the Elder who had told me the discipline was the chief reason the night before and asked, "Nothing to do with it?" The Elder who had spoken the night before did not look at me. The Elder who had asked me the question replied "Nothing." Again I said, "Nothing at all?" The same Elder replied "Nothing." I was so surprised by this that I did not pursue the matter. Two of the Elders in that room knew full well what I had been told the night before and they remained silent. It was the first time in my life that I had ever had the first tiny doubt regarding the integrity of the Elders of my denomination. There had always been issues that I disagreed with them on, but I had never doubted their integrity. Prior to this moment it had never once occurred to me that they would be willing to shade truth or withhold truth for the sake of expediency. Yet on this day and on this issue it happened. To this day this remains a hurtful memory.

I wrote a statement for the church as the Elders had asked. When Ned and Deb were dismissed from the meeting, they read it. They were not satisfied with the statement because it raised several issues they wanted to address themselves. The meeting had run way too long already, so they asked me to change one line of the statement that dealt with what I thought they felt about my decision to step down from the pulpit. Later I read the statement before the church with their inserted line. I include the statement here for the record.

May 25, 1986

In the past two weeks two events took place in the administration of our church. The subject nature, the circumstances, and the timing of the actions that were taken are such that I cannot in good faith continue to serve the church in the ministry. I want you all to clearly understand that I view these two events as symptoms of an underlying problem. In the past two days the Elder brothers and I have openly and honestly investigated what has transpired. Decisions made by (the Elder) *regarding the events have been upheld and the changes instituted in our church election processes by* (the Elder) *have been affirmed. It must be noted that while having Bro Ned and Sis Deb be the souls involved made the events more personally painful to me, I would have taken the same stance for any brother or sister in the church.*

(Three visiting Elders are named) *could not have been more kind and more attentive to my concerns than what they were. I will be forever grateful to them that they allowed me to speak my heartfelt concerns without fear of recrimination. Their conclusion regarding my decision to be silent is that it is correct, but only for the time being.* (This line was stricken and replaced by the Elders with "They feel it was an error on my part to refuse to minister and have pleaded with me to prayerfully reconsider.") *They have pleaded with me to be very prayerful and reflective and to allow Jesus to work in my heart. This I readily agree to do in that it will be a continuation of what I have been doing for the last one and a half years.*

From the innermost depths of my being I want to convey to each member of our household of faith that I love you with the love that the Apostle Paul describes in I Corinthians 13. You have all been very kind to me and I fully recognize that my ministry to date would not have been possible without your intercessory prayerful support. My greatest desire is for heaven where the issues which divide us presently will be remembered no more.

In the name, the attributes, and love of Jesus
I remain your loving brother, Tom

The week following this meeting was a quiet one for me, but it was not for Ned. The man who had been a finalist for minister when my name was drawn from the lot asked to meet with Ned and was pretty hard on him. This was he same man whose wife had expressed to me that they opposed Ned and Deb's restoration "so soon." This greatly upset Grandpa Beer.

Thursday, June 19, 1986. Day off! I talked with Mom for quite awhile this a.m. She is having a tough time fighting bitterness lately, particularly after hearing how self-righteously (the conservative brother) talked to Ned this week. She is really feeling no attachment to the church anymore, but sees no option open to her as long as Grandpa and Grandma Beer are living. It is pretty evident that they are the glue holding things together at this point. From my human perspective I think that it is too bad they couldn't have been spared this. At this moment I need another dose of Romans 8:28.

Mom was fiercely determined to devote her life to caring for her parents in their old age. This is something she sincerely wanted to do, but there was undoubtedly a factor of "wanting to pay them back for all they had done for her over the years and for all the hurt she had caused them when she was young." Grandpa and Grandma Beer adored Mom and I am certain they never loved her or appreciated her any less than the rest of their children. I believe they were oblivious to the fact that Mom felt she needed to work at gaining (or retaining) their favor. In their minds she always had it.

This determination to "see it through" with her folks in the AC Church had become a real source of conflict between my parents by the summer of 1986. Dad was done with the AC Church. For months he had been going to church with Mom and then taking our Travis and my nephew Joey to the playground at the school until church was over. He has expressed many times over the years that he is glad he did this, because if he had expressed his feelings to the Elder or the Elder's supporters, it would have been ugly. Dad was also committed to the care of Grandpa and Grandma Beer. This was not the issue. The issue in his mind was that their care and remaining in the AC Church did not have to be a package deal.

When Grandpa Beer learned that the self-righteous, conservative brother was harsh in his conversation with Ned, he was very upset – so upset that he came to my house to tell me to not allow it to happen to me.

Friday June 20, 1986. I was off this morning and watched the Spikes. Travie and I were lying in bed playing "snake" when Grandpa Beer arrived. He wanted to chat about church. He obviously was very upset about the way (the conservative brother) *talked to Ned and he told me not to go to* (this man's) *house. I am to have him come to my house if he wants to talk. Evidently* (this man) *was a real thorn is Grandpa's flesh while he was Elder and I feel that he knows more about* (this man) *than what he is saying. He also wanted reassurance about my convictions and intentions... The poor man sobbed and shook as he hugged me and left. Why must he be subjected to this in his twilight years?! He is just tormented that all of this is his fault because he was too liberal. The fact of the matter is that the church was immensely better off (and bigger) when he was in charge.* **Why** *can't* (the Elder) *and the other Elders see what is happening and be a bit more conciliatory? I sure pray that I don't get bitter.*

Melancholia was beginning to set in but the kids quickly perked me up.

Several weeks passed before the visiting Elders returned to Milford. During these weeks I went to the church services and carried on with life. I found it very strange that virtually no one outside of my family asked me about why I had sat down from the pulpit. During the church services everyone acted as if nothing had happened. Did they care? I honestly did not know. I do know, however, that it was becoming increasingly more difficult to attend the services and feel the isolation. When July arrived the Elders returned.

Wednesday, July 2, 1986. At 6:45am (the Elder) *called and told Tammy the Elders would want to meet with me at 10:30am. Tammy and I talked about it and decided that she should come along. We had been very prayerful about my inactive status all along and I had to admit in all honesty that I hadn't felt a single twinge of inclination to go back.*

When we got there, after we exchanged a few platitudes their first question really clinched it for me. They asked, "Tom, we know that one time we had your complete support. How do you feel now?" We were back to square one: I either give them the one-hundred percent support they want or stay where I am. We proceeded to talk over the same issues as before for the next one and a half hours and parted peacefully. It was so frustrating! In private they are open, reasonable men. In public it is as if they are different people altogether.

The results of the member meeting (that night): 1. Ned out. 2. Deb given opportunity to go in (to Sunday school), but refuses because of Ned's rejection. 3. Tom just won't serve. 4. (One visiting Elder) apologizes to the church for not telling them the issues last meeting – then states "I should have told you that Brother Tom was sitting down from the pulpit" and sits down, thus restating the only thing that everyone did know. 5. (Another visiting Elder) states, (with a forlorn look) "We tried to find a solution but we failed. What can we do?" 6. Not one issue stated or one reason given for any action taken...the meeting was a total waste of time.

Ned and Deb were devastated as were Tammy and I. For us it was the final nail in the coffin.

As I look back I realize that after this meeting it hit me for the first time that not only was I finished as an AC minister, I was also finished as a member of the AC church. The Elders had obviously decided to "cut their losses" and move on. They were not going to admonish one of their fellow Elders, no matter how misguided his actions. I do not know why it took so long for me to come to this realization. The night after this meeting was a long one for me.

Thursday, July 3, 1986. I didn't sleep well last night. I awoke this a.m. feeling numb. Empty. Alone. I sat at the kitchen table and wrote a letter to the church announcing my permanent resignation and the reasons why. As soon as I finished I felt better...

Tonight we hosted Bible study. It was really a rich, rewarding evening. I was somewhat surprised in that everyone was completely supportive with the vision of a new church. That scares me too but I went to bed with some hope again.

This was the first time I remember discussing the idea of starting a new church with anyone other than Ned. He had a vision for this long before I did. The next day we went to my uncle Phil

Beer's for the annual July 4th family get together. As we were waiting to eat a discussion started about the trouble in the church. One of my uncles stated, "I don't think that going out and starting another church is the answer!" I was taken back by the tone of his statement and by the fact that he assumed I was going to undertake a project that I had just begun to think about the night before. Apparently there were others thinking about the idea a lot more than I was. I replied to him "What do you think is the answer, then?" He did not reply. Looking back I now understand why it was difficult for him to even consider changing churches. He had raised his family in the AC church and they were now adults. It was easier for him to take the good of the denomination and overlook the bad than it was for me because I had little children at home. It was a future prospect for me to decide if I wanted to subject them to the same frustrations that I had grown up with and to try and convince them that "the good outweighed the bad" in the denomination, all the while hoping that they would one day do as I had done and join it. For my uncle, these decisions were already in his past. At his stage in life it was very easy to be an AC member. Just do not cause any waves, involve yourself when it is convenient, be absent when there are things you do not want to be involved with, and you will get along fine. There will be no expectations of you as long as you mind your own business.

In the next several weeks I revised my resignation letter four different times, hoping to make it more meaningful. I did not submit it because of pressure from Grandpa and Grandma Beer. I could not bear the thought of hurting them but the only reasons they could give me to wait were "It's going to get better" and "Something is going to work out." Nevertheless, I waited and continued to attend services. As the weeks went by it was becoming more and more clear to me that it would be wrong for me to continue in the AC Church. I no longer had any confidence in the leadership. The past months had demonstrated to me that all of their interests were secondary to the "preservation of the way." But more critically, I now acknowledged to myself that I no longer believed the same things as the AC Church, particularly the doctrines of Salvation. In previous months I had tried to convince myself that the beliefs I held were not all that different than the AC Church, but they were different and I needed to face this fact. My study of the Bible lead me to the conclusion that above all else Christians are to be witnesses for Jesus Christ and actively propagate the Gospel. I could no longer "hide my head in the sand" and pretend that it was not wrong that the AC Church was not obedient to these clear commands. "But what about Grandpa and Grandma Beer?" This question was always there to complicate my intentions. I began to think about a statement my friend Rich Stoller had made once made during a discussion about hurting our parents by leaving the AC Church. He had asked the rhetorical question "Hey, at what point do we stop being our parents' children and start becoming our children's parents?" I do not know if this was an original thought of his, but it was the first time I had heard it. I had to conclude that it was past time for Tammy and me to be first and foremost "our children's parents."

In late July and early August of 1986 three significant events took place in our lives. The first event was that my brother Ned, Tim Steffen, I, and our wives began working on a "Statement of Faith." We reasoned that if we were to start a new church we would need a Statement of Faith and that if we did not start a new church it was still important to determine exactly what we believed. To begin this task we went to area churches that we thought were sound in their teaching and obtained copies of their Statements of Faith. I also had copies of the Statements of Faith from Grace Community Church (John MacArthur) and First Evangelical Free Church (Chuck Swindoll). We spent at least two long evenings comparing and contrasting these documents and researching the Bible. The result was a compilation of what we believed. This was a very beneficial endeavor. It demonstrated to us how much different our beliefs were than the Apostolic Christian Church. This, in turn, helped free us from guilt over leaving it.

The second event was a very traumatic one for Tammy and Me. It occurred at some AC friends' house. I recorded it in my journal.

Sunday July 20, 1986. We were invited to (some AC friends') house for an evening of fellowship. There was a big group there. After supper some of us went outside to walk around. As we passed by their garage I noticed their big dog lying on the car hood. (The host), Traci, Travis and I then walked out to look at his farm equipment. He and I talked while the kids climbed around. We had been there about half an hour when I heard some screaming up by the house. Or was it Traci doing one of her "scream songs?" I wasn't sure and I hadn't realized that she left for the house. The next thing I knew Tim Steffen came out and told me to come to the house because the dog had bitten Traci. My gut just turned to ice when I saw Tammy carrying her out, her dress already blood-soaked. I took a quick peek and saw a deep one-inch gash under her left eye as we got into the car and left. It wasn't until we got to the first corner that we took the handkerchief away and saw the other bad gashes in the mouth-nose area. Tammy about "lost it" at that point and I was just sick.

Poor Traci was just hysterical all the way to the hospital. She kept saying, "I wanna see me!" "Why did that doggie bite me?" "Am I going to die?" After what seemed like an eternity we made it the ER at Goshen. Once we were in a room I called Mom and Dad and asked them to get the kids.

I was prepared for two fights: (1) Neither Tammy nor I had our insurance information with us and, (2) I wasn't going to let the local ER hack sew her up. Neither happened. Traci was in their computer already and they had already called a plastic surgeon by the time I got back.

Dr. Leuz arrived in about half an hour and decided to go ahead (the OR had been standing by). He was very calm and gentle. He told her that he didn't care how much noise she made, but she could not move. She had three lacerations: one under the eye, one between the nostril and the lip, and one on the lip. There were many other scrapes and seeing them I shuddered to think how bad it might have been.

I don't remember ever praying so hard as I did when they started. She was scared to death (understandably) and cried whenever they touched her. After they finished the one under her eye she began to settle down. By the time they were finishing she nearly fell asleep. In all she had twenty-six stitches, three of which were beneath the skin on the lip cuts.

It was a quiet, reflective ride home. Satan was trying really hard to convince me that this was a punishment for the trouble in church. I was really heartsick as I considered how that must have terrified poor Spikie. When we got home I could see how surprised Mom, Dad, Trischa and Travis were. Having seen her before, Tammy and I thought she looked great. Travis took one look, backed off, and said, "I don't want to look at that!"

As we settled down for the night I did a lot of reflecting. I realized that I learned new meanings for two old phrases: (1) "I wish that it would have been me," and (2) "Its a lot worse when it happens to one of your children!" I also learned anew what a "fervent prayer" is. This event clearly brought back to me the fact that I spend a lot of time and energy fretting about things that are insignificant in the overall life picture. I need a greater orientation of my eyes heavenward!

Traci was very swollen for several days and looked very bad. Our hearts about broke for her. Gradually, though, she began to heal. Over the years she has had two additional surgeries to revise the scars and today one cannot even notice them without looking very closely. My Dad and Mom took this very hard. Upon hearing the news Dad threw a coffee cup across the kitchen, shattering it on the opposite wall. This very atypical reaction on his part no doubt was an expression of the long-term frustration he had felt at seeing his children under stress. If I had been in his shoes during this time frame I probably would have thrown a cup across the kitchen too.

The third significant event was as joyous for Tammy and Me as Traci's dog bite was traumatic. Tammy's parents had spent the evening with us this day.

Saturday, August 9, 1986. (After supper) Tammy and I sat at the kitchen table with George and Pat and discussed the church situation. They seemed to think that a new church might be an answer. It is hard for me to explain it to someone outside the AC Church even yet. Nor matter how hard you try, it all sounds so cultish to anyone not really familiar with "our way" that it is embarrassing.

They left around 10pm and we then got the kids to bed. I read stories to Traci and Travis. Tammy then put the "Dude" (Travis) into bed while I took the girls up. I then read some Bible stories to Traci. Trischa and I then studied Matthew chapter 11. It was an excellent chapter and we had quite a discussion.

Tammy was in bed asleep and I was reading when Trisha came in. One look at her face and I knew what she wanted to talk about. She came over to my side of the bed and said "Dad, I've got to talk to you. I've been really bothered lately that if I died or if Jesus came back that I would not go to heaven. I want to ask Jesus into my heart." At this point we saw that Traci had followed her down and was listening. I woke Tammy and while she took Traci back up (to bed) *Trischa and I talked some more. I asked her why she thought that she wouldn't go to heaven. She replied that sin in her life would keep her from Jesus and that she had never asked for forgiveness or for Jesus to come into her heart. I asked her whom she thought put this conviction in her heart and she correctly replied "God." She said "I've been really thinking about it for the last four days, especially that one night at the hotel when Travis kept rolling on me and I was awake a long time. Jesus kept calling me but I kept saying, "you're too young, this is ridiculous." Kerri and David and I talked about it a long time, too. Kerri said that it's not hard at all. Dad, it is time. I want to give my heart to Jesus!" I said "OK, honey. Do you know what it is when you turn from your sins to God and ask Jesus to be your Savior?" She thought for a second. "Do you remember what we studied in the Bible in Matthew?" She quickly replied, "repent." I asked her then "do you believe than if you repent of your sin and ask God to forgive you and ask Jesus to come into your heart that He will?" "Yes," she replied. "And Trischa, what is it on your part that makes this possible?" She replied (beautifully) "faith that Jesus died on the cross for me." And with a slight pause "I want to ask Him into my heart." I asked Tammy "What do you think, Mom?" She said, "I think we should pray together." So we knelt together beside our bed. I told Trischa in her own words to confess to Jesus that she feels lost and ask Him to forgive her and become her Savior. She asked me to pray first. We all clasped hands. I prayed a little bit and then she had the purest, most sincere little "sinner's prayer" that I could imagine. Tammy then prayed and I finished up. Trischa's face just glowed with excitement as she told us "Oh, I feel so much better. I'm so happy!" We then shared some scripture about the joy of salvation and about her security in Jesus. She told us that for days the Sunday school song "turn, turn from sin and doubting, look to God on high" had* been running through her mind and said "I'm so glad that I listened! This is the neatest time of my life!"

By this time Traci was seated on the bed with us listening with a countenance that said, "What's going on here?" We talked a little more about how excited she is to tell everyone and then everyone went to bed (again). Tammy went and checked her a little later. She was still awake and still bubbling.

Soon I was the only one left awake. I finished an article in "Israel My Glory" entitled "Faith." It was exactly what I needed. I reflected about how my gut "turned to ice" for an instant when I realized that Trischa wanted to talk about her soul. I realized (to my shame) that even though I now know better I am still somewhat trapped by my indoctrination by the church on methodologies of salvation. In a long reflective period I concluded two things: (1) There was absolutely no question that what I had just experienced was pure, simple, and one hundred percent right. I'm sure the angels rejoiced. (2) We must now move on and find a suitable congregational environment for our children.

On the last weekend of August 1986, some visiting Elders came and interviewed the entire Milford Apostolic Christian Church congregation. Ned and Deb and Tammy and I met with them on Saturday night for about one and a half hours. It was a cordial meeting. We discussed the same issues we had been discussing all along, including the denomination's position on church discipline, sports involvement, and the Elder's handling of the conflict of the last several months. We finished our discussion on the topic of whether Christians sin or not and what the differences where, if any, between a "sin" and a "mistake or shortcoming." It was very clear that their preoccupation continued to be the "preservation of the way." It was also very clear that they had no intention of taking any action against one of their fellow Elders. We had reached an impasse and there was no reason to talk further. My final words to them that night were "Brothers, I fear you have made the system bigger than the Savior." With this we parted in peace.

Sunday, August 31, 1986. I hardly slept at all last night. I finally added some more to my resignation letter (written in early July) *and decided to give it to them* (the Elders) *tomorrow.*

They accepted my letter and (during the member meeting) *asked me to read it from the pulpit. I was surprised, but I did* (read it) *and elaborated some along the way. The remainder of the meeting was touching as we apologized to each other, cried together, and greeted one another farewell.*

For the record, I am including a copy of what I read to the church. Before I read the letter I offered a copy of it to anyone who wanted one. One of our Milford Elder's sons was the only person who ever asked for a copy. For years I wondered why the Elders allowed me to read the letter from the pulpit. Allowing one openly at odds with the Elders to speak to the congregation from the pulpit was an act I had never heard of before in the Apostolic Christian Church. In the years since I have come to understand that allowing me to speak was a brilliant tactical move on their part. I openly incriminated myself against the denomination. In addition to this, because I was allowed to read the letter publicly I felt no need to mail it to the membership. Without a copy of the letter in their possession, it is likely that the congregation soon forgot what all the fuss was about. Would I have mailed the letter to the membership? I cannot know for sure, but I doubt it. At that time I was just glad to be moving on and putting the conflict behind me.

July 3, 1986

Dear Brothers and Sisters:

In the past months it has become clear to me that my uncertain status in the church has been the focus of much confusion and speculation. I sense uneasiness within the church when we come together. I feel that we as a congregation are beginning to align ourselves according to "man" as did the church at Corinth in the Apostle Paul's day (I Corinthians 1:11-13; 3:22-23). This situation, I fear, is providing fertile soil upon which Satan is exercising his devices and therefore a remedy must be found. If the church is paralyzed because of me, I believe that it is my responsibility to try and resolve the problem. Out of love for the church and my Savior, I have concluded that each of you needs to know (officially) that I will not be ministering in our church anymore. Perhaps knowing this, the church will feel free to move ahead.

As I have visited with you over the last several months, I have learned that most of you have little or no idea as to why I am no longer on the pulpit. I have tried to the best of my abilities to explain my concerns to the Elder brothers who have visited us. For the record, there are four main areas of concern that preclude me from serving.

1. To continue in the ministry, I must support our current system of church elections. I cannot. I can only support one person - one vote majority rule among brothers and sisters in good standing. I cannot support the screening out of individuals from nomination ballots for non-scriptural reasons. Going along with this practice convicts me that I am sitting in judgment on my brother or sister for whom Christ also died. I believe that this practice is not in harmony with principles set forth in the Word regarding judging and Christian forbearance (I Corinthians 4:2-5; Matthew 7:1-5; John 7:2-4; Romans Chapter 14). I believe that a healthy, praying church will not elect those brothers or sisters who are unsuitable for service. I believe furthermore that if the church is perceived to be unhealthy and therefore incapable of making a responsible choice that elimination of names from ballots will only make matters worse. It would seem that the time and energy that we have spent on this issue would better have been spent trying to resolve the issues which (presumably) make the church unhealthy in the first place. I am sure that there are instances when the local Elder alone knows of ongoing sin in a member's life that is unrepented of. In these cases, I fully support his responsibility to confront and counsel. If no repentance is forthcoming, I can then fully support the removal of that individual's name from consideration. I cannot support "head counts" matched against "the number of ballots" in our church business meetings. I also cannot support not allowing a brother or sister to

A Lifetime of Church

vote for his or her spouse when the one cannot be at the meeting. It is intolerable to me that we as born-again Christians are counted worthy on one hand to be ambassadors for Jesus and possessors of the Holy Spirit while on the other hand we are not trusted enough to conduct a fair and open election.

2. I believe that the New Testament Church is a body of all born-again believers. I believe that the church's head and one supreme authority is Jesus Christ (I Corinthians 11:3; Ephesians 1:22; Colossians 1:18). I believe that Elders are biblically designated officers serving under Christ and over the local congregation as leaders. In this capacity they are to fit biblical qualifications (I Timothy 3:1-7; Titus 1:5-9; I Peter 5:1-5). When Elders perform according to these criteria and act in the light of the Word, I believe that they are worthy not only of honor (I Timothy 5:17), but also of the flock's support and following.

   If I am to be a minister in the church, I must give my complete support (in advance) to all the Elder's decisions and actions. For me to do this in good conscience, I would have to believe in my heart that it would not be possible for them ever to be wrong. While I view our Elder brothers as men of God who are doing their best, I believe that Bible teaches that flesh and blood only achieved perfection in the person of our Lord Jesus Christ and that the rest of us will only see it in a glorified state. I could pledge complete support only with the qualifications that in each instance (A) the Elder is acting according to the attributes of his office and (B) that he is acting in the light of the Word. I have learned that a qualified pledge of support is not acceptable for service in the ministry.

3. I believe that nearly all Apostolic Christians involve themselves in some non-church activities that are not one hundred percent pure. I view these as "gray areas" in our Christian walk in which we need the Holy Spirit's direction

to balance involvement on the one hand with consideration of our brethren on the other (I Corinthians 8:1 thru 11:1; Romans chapter 14). I cannot support declaring some "gray areas" wrong and off limits and other "gray areas" acceptable and approved when they are in reality both equally "gray." The prime example cited here is our denomination's stance that all viewing of and participation in "organized" sports must cease before a convert may be baptized and before a brother or sister can be used in church offices. Certainly organized sports are not **all** good. They are not **all** bad either. I believe that this practice creates an opportunity for Satan to divide Jesus' redeemed by causing some to feel rejected and causing some to feel acceptable and to feel a righteousness that is based upon improper criteria. I believe that the old Christian dictum "unity in essentials, liberty in non-essentials, love in all things" is well applied to these "gray areas" of our lives.

4. I wholeheartedly support the doctrine of church discipline. The church's responsibility to discipline members who are unrepentant of ongoing sin is a clear Biblical teaching. I cannot, however, totally support the way our denomination carries out this responsibility. Specifically, I cannot support lifelong separation for sin that has been repented of and overcome (I Corinthians 5, compare with II Corinthians 2:3-11). I believe that the sole purpose of church discipline is to bring the sinning Christian to repentance and thus to restore him to fellowship and fruit bearing within the Church.

As much as is in me, I want to convey to you that I took my position in the ministry with great hopes and the best of intentions. In retrospect, I realize that I was ignorant as to what would be expected of me administratively. As much as I would like to change what has transpired, I realize that I cannot. We all are left only with the present and perhaps the future. Please forgive me for any division and heartache that my involvement in the church ministry has caused. On the other hand, please know that I am eternally grateful if I have touched any lives while I had the privilege of preaching

God's Word. Regardless of what the future may hold, I will continue to love you and esteem you all as my brothers and sisters until my dying day. It is my sincere hope that you (the church) will put the issue of "Tom Speicher" behind you, that you will quickly elect my replacement, and that you will turn your attention to the fields white unto harvest.

        Sincerely in Jesus,

        Tom

Chapter Forty-Seven

I spent nearly thirty-four years of my life in the Apostolic Christian Church denomination. I was a member of the denomination for fourteen of those years. In all these years my affiliation with the denomination constituted a critical part of the definition of who Tom Speicher was. Less than one year before I left the denomination I wrote in a letter that leaving the church would be "like pulling off an arm" for me. Yet in August 1986, I left the denomination. Why? Those who know me and still are in the Apostolic Christian Church would likely offer one or several of the following reasons: Tom left because he wanted an easier way. Tom left because he fell into false doctrine. Tom left because his brother Ned unduly influenced him. Tom left because he could not get along with the Elder.

I did not leave because I wanted "an easier way." The expression "an easier way" is understood in the AC Church to mean "I want to join a church which has no rules" or one which "has no expectations" of its members. In my life I have observed two general mental approaches to living the Christian life. One approach is to say, "I am a Christian. The evidences I offer for this are my church membership and the things of the world that I deny myself. My motivations for living life as I do are fear of God's judgment and my obligation to God." The second general approach is to say, "I am a Christian. The evidences I offer for this are my activities in the church and my witness for Christ from day to day.

My motivations for living life as I do are my love of God and my gratitude for what He has done for me." Having lived life both ways I can say with confidence the first approach is far easier than the second approach. In the first approach the standards for "success" are the rules of one's church and how one lives relative to other human beings. In the second approach the standard is Jesus Christ. In the first approach one can reach a point where he or she knows the expectations have been met. In the second approach one is aware that sufficient gratitude can never be shown to God. In the first approach one primarily fears God's punishment for sin. In the second approach one fears grieving God's heart for not choosing to honor Him with a fruitful life. I did not leave the Apostolic Christian church for an "easier way." The truth of the matter is that there is only one Way — Jesus Christ (John 14:6) — and I believe we dishonor Him when we presume we can add anything to the work He accomplished for us at Calvary other than a life of love and gratitude in His service.

Did I leave the denomination because I fell into false doctrine? From the AC doctrinal viewpoint, the answer to this question is "yes." Did I fall into false doctrine? No. Did I leave because my brother Ned unduly influenced me? The answer is "No," although the trauma of Ned's troubles in the denomination drove me into the Word of God where I came to believe that the actions against him were not Biblical.

Did I leave the denomination because I could not get along with the Milford Elder? Absolutely not. Apart from the two years I was a minister in his congregation, we got along very well, and even during these two years we got along reasonably well, given the tension. Never once did I doubt that he was doing what he sincerely thought was in the best interest of the denomination. We just did not agree on what this was. My nature is to be upbeat and compliant. I generally respond well to reason. If one makes requests of me on the basis of need and in the spirit of cooperation, I find it almost impossible to say no. As a rule, I will first work overtime to avoid conflict. If this fails my next strategy is to work overtime to make peace. Only rarely and usually as a last resort will I initiate conflict or become a part of it. And when I do this is almost always the result of something I see as mean-spirited or unjust. If the Elder had used any motivational techniques on me other than guilt and intimidation, I undoubtedly would have lasted longer as an AC minister. Who knows? I might not have been driven by despair into the Word of God and still be in the denomination.

The reason I left the Apostolic Christian Church denomination is because I came to hold different beliefs. All my other experiences were simply cumulative factors that caused me to study the Bible with an open mind. My first area of disagreement is Salvation. I believe one enters into salvation (or is "born again") the moment he or she places their faith in Jesus Christ as their Savior from sin. I believe this a gracious gift of God that comes through faith alone in the Person and finished work of Jesus Christ. I believe this salvation is a present possession of every true believer. (John 1:12,13; 3:14-18; 5:24; 11:25,26; 14:6; 16:7-11; 20:31; Acts 2:36-39; 4:12; 16:29-31; Romans 1:16,17; 10:9,10; II Corinthians 5:17-21; Ephesians 2:8-10; Colossians 2:1-15; 3:1-4; I John 3:1-3; 5:11-13). I believe that salvation is a sovereign, gracious work of God in an individual from beginning to end. I believe that God's sovereign work in salvation includes man's free will and that He justly holds individuals responsible for refusing to believe in Jesus Christ. I believe this apparent paradox is perfectly resolved in the mind of God and is taught in scripture (John 3:14,15; compare 12:32; John 6:44,64,65; Romans 8:27-30; Romans 9; Ephesians 1). I believe, furthermore, that the true believer in Jesus Christ is secure in his or her salvation. (John 3:14-18; 5:24; 20:27-30; Romans 8:1,28-39; Ephesians 1:3-14; 4:30; I Peter 1:3-5; 6:37-39; Hebrews 7:23-25; Jude 24,25; I John 5:11-13). I believe that every true believer will do good works (Matthew 5:16-17; Ephesians 2:10; 4:20-24; Titus 3:3-8) and that these good works are a fruit of salvation, not a route to attain salvation or maintenance of it. (Romans 4:1-5; Ephesians 2:8,9; II Timothy 1:8-10; Titus 3:4,5a). I believe that God sets one free from the curse of sin and death at the moment of salvation, free to serve Him out of love and gratitude. (John 8:31,32,36; Romans 6:18; 8:12; 8:20,21; Galatians 5:1).

Do I believe members of the Apostolic Christian Church are true believers? I know that I was when I was a member. I believe the only true believers in any denomination are those individuals whose faith is in the Person and finished work of the Lord Jesus Christ alone, not Jesus Christ plus the church or Jesus Christ plus the church plus good works or Jesus Christ plus anything else. Do I have a problem with elements of the Apostolic Christian Church repentance process? I believe that confession of sin, restitution for past wrongs, and seeking peace with other people are all good things to do, but only if they are done as a fruit of salvation rather than a route to attain salvation. When demanded of an individual as a route to attain salvation, I believe they form the basis of salvation by works, which I believe is clearly not in harmony with scripture.

My second area of disagreement is the doctrine of church discipline. I believe there are two purposes of church discipline. The first purpose is to preserve the witness of the Church, the Body of Christ, before the unbelieving world. The second purpose is to restore Christians in on-going sin back to fellowship in the church and harmony with God. I believe church discipline is appropriately applied only when an individual still refuses to repent after Jesus' instruction in Matthew 18:15-17 is followed. I believe it is wrong to deny a repentant believer fellowship.

My third area of disagreement is with the general approach to scripture. I believe God desires that the Bible be systematically studied. I believe that God desires the Bible be systematically preached. I believe scripture provides the sole basis for authority in life and in the Church. I believe it is always wrong to elevate customs and traditions and religious systems to an equal or greater importance than the Word of God. This is a line that I felt the denomination crossed at times.

My fourth area of disagreement with the Apostolic Christian Church relates directly to the first area. It is the area of evangelism. It is my belief that the spread of the Gospel through evangelism and missions is the clearest command to the Church by Jesus Christ. It was also the clear teaching and example of Christ's Apostles. The Gospel was to be preached throughout the world (Matthew 28:18-20; Mark 16:15; Luke 24:46-48; Acts 1:7,8). What the Gospel, or "Good News," is and the message to be preached was clearly spelled out by the Apostle Paul in First Corinthians 15:1-4 *Now, brothers, I want to remind you of the gospel I preached to you, which you received and on which you have taken your stand. By this gospel you are saved, if you hold firmly to the word I preached to you. Otherwise, you have believed in vain. For what I received I passed on the you as of first importance: that Christ died for our sins according to the scriptures, that he was buried, that he was raised on the third day according to the Scriptures.* Romans 10:8-10 *But what does it say? "The word is near you; it is in your mouth and in your heart," that is, the word of faith we are proclaiming: That if you confess with your mouth, "Jesus is Lord," and believe in you heart that God raised him from the dead, you will be saved. For it is with your heart that you believe and are justified, and it is with your mouth that you confess and are saved.*

Jesus unveiled the master plan for the spread of the Gospel to the entire world in Acts 1:8. The Book of Acts bears out that this is exactly what happened. The Gospel spread from Jerusalem, to Judea, to Samaria. From there it went through Crete, Lebanon, Syria, Turkey, Greece, and Italy. We also know it spread to Egypt and North Africa. To be accepted by so many diverse cultures and races, the message had to be simple. It had to be Christ-centered. It had to have addressed the universal problem of sin and the universal needs of forgiveness and reconciliation. To gain so many diverse adherents it could not have made demands on things such as hair length and styles, apparel, jewelry, and methods of worship. It had to have been the message of Romans 10:9,10. I believe we have no right in our present era to preach a different message than the Apostles of Christ did.

In my last two years in the Apostolic Christian Church I came to hold these beliefs. By the end of August 1986, I knew I could no longer remain a part of the denomination and be true to my convictions. The decision to leave was a simple and natural progression at the time. It is a decision that I have never questioned. Did I forsake my heritage in leaving? If my heritage was only membership in the AC Church, then I did forsake it. If, however, my heritage was a deep faith in God, a life committed to His service, and a willingness to contend for what I believed was right, regardless of the cost, then I did not forsake it. I affirmed it.

Chapter Forty-Eight

On June 25, 1972, Tammy and I walked out of the Apostolic Christian Church in Milford. The previous eleven months had tested us in ways we had never imagined. Having negotiated a narrow path between faith in God and fear of man we had achieved our goal of becoming husband and wife. Pursuit of this goal had required delicate balancing of competing interests on our lives. The goal of our marriage had seemed like a distant light at the end of a dark tunnel filled with pitfalls. It is hard to describe the overwhelming feeling of relief and freedom I felt that evening. I had given very little thought to life beyond that evening the previous eleven months until Tammy and I were driving to Niagra Falls the next day. It then began to occur to me, "Now what? Where do we go from here?" Apart from the US Army, I had no idea. But I knew we would go together. And this is all that mattered to me.

The same two questions would be before me on the last Sunday in August 1986. On that hot afternoon I had walked out of the apostolic Christian Church in Milford for what would be the last time. I was crying. Before I got into my car to drive away, I encountered six people. The first was a woman who was a member of the church, but whose husband was not. She said, "My husband agrees with you, Tom. My family does not. And I'm right in the middle. I don't know what I'm going to do!" The second was a woman who hugged me and said, "I am so proud of you!" The third was a man who shook my hand and simply said "Thank you for your honesty." The fourth was a woman who shook my hand and said "Thank you for all you have done." The fifth was a man who hugged me and said, "It will be alright." The sixth was my brother Ned. He calmly walked up to me and confidently said, "Well, we launch next week." The first four people remained in the denomination. The last two did not.

My tears were a strange combination of joy and sorrow. I was greatly relieved and happy the conflict was over. I had known for many weeks that leaving the denomination was the right thing to do. Yet I was crying. Why? The nearest thing I can liken my tears to are the tears one cries when an elderly loved one dies in the faith. The death marks the end of life, as one has known it and the beginning of life in altered relationships. One is aware that the loved one's death is both natural and blessed in the sight of God, yet there is sadness. I had never known "church" apart from the Apostolic Christian Church denomination and the watchful, approving eyes of Grandpa and Grandma Beer. And even though it was my decision to leave, why did the Elders let me go so easily? A part of my tears, undoubtedly, was also the fact that many people whom I loved would now no longer have any use for me.

By the time I arrived home my tears had dried and I was giddy with joy. After changing clothes I lay down on my bed, stared at the ceiling, and began thinking "Now what? Where do we go from here? Was Ned serious when he said we launch (a new church) next week? Where would we meet? How would the service be structured?" As this was going on I heard my daughter Trischa ask Tammy in the next room "Mom, is Dad OK?" We all got a good laugh out of this. We realized when I had come home from church upset in recent months (which had been nearly every Sunday) that I had laid on the bed and stared. Trischa had come to correctly associate these two things, but this day she was wrong! To this point I had thought the children were oblivious to my feelings and that I had hidden them well. Even though his incident was funny, I took note of it and decided to be more careful to guard my feelings in the future.

Like so many other things in my life, being a part of founding a new church "just kind of took place." I did not give it a great deal of study or think about it for long periods of time before the fact. In the fall of 1986 I was certain about three things. I was certain that leaving the AC denomination was the right thing to do. I was

A Lifetime of Church

certain about what I believed. I was certain that I wanted to openly share the Gospel of Jesus Christ. All three of these certainties fit well into the vision some others had about founding a new church. When it was assumed that I would be a part of it, I became a part of it. I am not suggesting that I was not a willing participant. I was willing. It was just not my vision. When the church was founded, I remember being pleasantly surprised how quickly and naturally "future possibilities" became present realities.

In the week following my departure from the AC Church, Tammy and I were one of five couples who met twice to plan our first Sunday. Early in the week, Ned made arrangements with the Wawasee School Corporation Superintendent for us to rent the cafeteria area of the Milford School. We were given a one-month contract that was renewable. One morning that week Ned and I drove to Goshen and met with a lawyer about the legalities of starting a church. As we approached our first Sunday everything was in place. I would preach. This was decided in our first meeting. We thought it would be best to begin with one Pastor. I remember one of the men, who was an avid fisherman, saying it should be me because I was "a proven lure." Another man would be in charge of the music. We had enough teachers and Sunday school classes to include the ages of our children and an adult class. We decided we would have a fellowship time with drink and snacks between the Sunday school service and the church service. We had no bank account, so we decided to set out a nice shoebox for offerings. This initial shoebox would serve us faithfully for nearly a year! Near the end of the first week we agreed to name our church "Wawasee Community Bible Church." We reasoned that "Wawasee" would be recognized throughout the area. "Community" was consistent with our desire to reach the community with the Gospel. "Bible Church" is what we wanted to be known for more than anything else. The name seemed to be a beautiful "fit" for our vision.

I remember two events from this first week. On Wednesday morning Ned and I went to Grandpa and Grandma Beer's for lunch. Apart from the "bloody noses" of the previous two years, this meeting would have been unthinkable for both Ned and me. They took the news of a new church much better than I thought they would. They were very sad, of course, but both understood that Ned and I had no future in the denomination. They also were both deeply disappointed by the way the AC leadership had dealt with us. I remember Grandpa Beer sternly looking me in the eye and asking, "Tom, do you realize what a responsibility you are taking on here? It will be a tremendous responsibility. Tremendous!" The fact that he pronounced tremendous as "tree men'jus" probably helped keep the warning clear in my memory over the years. I told Grandpa that morning that I understood what I was getting into, but I know now that I did not have the foggiest idea what founding and pastoring a church would involve. If I had known, I doubt I would have undertaken it.

This meeting marked the end of an era. My relationship with Grandpa and Grandma Beer remained extremely close to the day they went to be with the Lord, but the dynamic of the relationship was changed. In some ways the relationship was even better. For one thing, since we no longer attended the same church our conversations centered on the Word of God instead of the Apostolic Christian Church denomination. In this we continued to have sweet fellowship. We rarely encountered scriptures that we could not agree upon. While Grandpa and Grandma were life-long devotees to the AC church, they were life-long devotees to the Word of God to a significantly greater degree. There is another reason why I feel our relationship was better after I left the denomination. Until this point in my life I had worked to please Grandpa and Grandma Beer by fulfilling their expectations of me within the context of the social order of the AC church. I had assumed previously to this that just being a member in the AC church placed me on a higher plane of approval in their eyes than I could have achieved under any other circumstances, and in their younger years I am sure that this would have been true, at least in part. After leaving the denomination, however, I discovered that they loved me apart from my fulfilling their expectations of me in the AC church. I found that they were proud of me for taking a stand for what I believed was right. I found that they were proud of my service of Christ regardless of my denominational affiliation. Until they went to be with the Lord they listened to tapes of nearly every sermon I ever preached. For a few months after starting the new church Grandpa Beer would write notes to me critiquing my sermons. Then one day he came to my house to tell me that he had begun to pray for my church. He added,

"You are reaching people we cannot reach." After this the critiques of my sermons stopped. I have dear memories of Grandpa and Grandma Beer for many reasons, but in my mind the greatest measure of their character and their love of Jesus Christ is the fact that they continued to love me and support my ministry after I left the denomination they held so dear.

The second significant event of the first week took place on Saturday, September 6th. An old woman named Edna Graff asked that I visit her at her home in Goshen. She was a single woman who had spent her entire life in the AC Church but had never joined it. After visiting with her for a while I shared the Gospel. God had prepared her heart and she prayed to receive Jesus Christ as her Savior. This greatly encouraged me that I was on the right track.

That same afternoon Ned and I went to the Milford School cafeteria to set up for Sunday morning. After my visit with Edna Graff I was dizzy with excitement. This began to wane as the reality of what we were preparing to do began to sink in. It seemed like a million questions were racing through my brain, including: "Would anyone come to our service? If so, how many? What if no one showed up? How long would we keep trying before giving up? How many chairs should we set up? How should we arrange them?" Ned seemed to be the epitome of calm and confidence. He had it all pictured in his mind and we set up accordingly. As for anyone showing up, he pointed out that we already knew enough people who had told us they planned to come to keep our first service from being a total failure. Hearing this helped quiet my unconfident feelings. Once we had things the way we wanted, we headed home to wait the morrow.

The next morning Tammy and the kids and I arrived early at the school. My heart was pounding. At 9:30am Ned welcomed those who had come. He made some announcements and after we sang a song together the Sunday school classes were dismissed one at a time. Ned then taught the adults who remained. He began by teaching through our Statement of Faith. After Sunday school we had a half hour fellowship time. I remember thinking how nice it was to hear Deb Speicher playing the piano throughout the fellowship time. At 11:00am we began singing. Before I knew it I was on my feet preaching my first sermon as Pastor of Wawasee Community

Bible Church. We had no sound system. I put a cassette tape recorder on the floor in front of me to record everything. I do not remember much about the sermon, other than the thrill of being a part of what was happening. What I remember most about this first Sunday was how excited everyone was to be there. Sixteen years have come and gone, but the memory of the excitement of that first service remains clear in my memory.

As we drove home that day I no longer had the sense of foreboding that I had warred against for most Sundays in recent memory. The day had been a success. Sixty-six people had attended and I was confident they all would be back, plus Dad and Mom and my sister Sue and her family were gone for the day. They would be there next week — at least Dad and Sue and her family would be. Mom was still a question mark. No one wanted to be free of the Apostolic Christian Church more than she did, but her fierce sense of obligation to her parents might compel her to stay. Time would tell.

Someone had asked me a few days before what my dream would be for the new church. After a few questions to be sure what he was asking, I had replied, "If in ten years we had a solid church of one hundred people, I would be satisfied." After church on September 7, 1986 this dream seemed to be very realistic.

Chapter Forty-Nine

In early December 1972, Tammy and I were riding in an Army bus to our new home in Bad Toeltz, West Germany. It was an overcast, foggy day and the light was fading as it neared its end. I was mindlessly looking out the window when I saw the fog momentarily lift. In front of us was a mountain. My heart seemed to skip a beat at the excitement. I had never seen a mountain before. It was love at first sight, and the love affair between mountains and me has continued to the present day. Some of the happiest times in my life have been the vacations Tammy and the children and I have taken to various mountainous areas. Few things can make me feel closer to my Heavenly Father than to hike in His handiwork with my family. When one embarks on a long hike in the mountains, the end is not in sight. At the end of each valley and through each pass one assumes he is about at his destination, but most often each pass just leads into another previously unseen, beautiful valley. Generally all one has to navigate by is the trail which continues to wind upward through the ever growing network of valleys and passes, which all have their own unique beauty and challenges. It is usually when I am exhausted and sure that I am about to where I set out for that I encounter some hikers heading the opposite direction who tell me that I am about halfway to the end. There have been many times when I have had to use my best persuasive skills to get Tammy to continue on, times when I would not have convinced her to continue if the hikers had not encouraged us that the beauty ahead is well worth the toil.

After ten years of at least some annual mountain hiking I have made some general observations. First, it has been my experience that the longer and more difficult the hike, the greater the beauty at the end. Secondly, without being told of the beauty at the end of the hike, most hikes would not be taken. If one is not convinced ahead of time that the end is worth it, then the physical strength and the desire to continue on will both be gone well ahead of the goal. My third observation is that when one reaches the top and looks back neither the trail nor the valleys can be seen beyond the most recent distance. One can see only the peaks. The areas between the peaks are memories that were created by what was seen, heard, and felt by each individual hiker, and while these memories may be similar, they are all unique. While there might be differences of opinion about how the way was negotiated on the way up, nothing can change the decisions that were made. My fourth area of observation is regarding the return trip. It is not as much fun as the way up. It goes faster than the way up. It taxes a different area of the body than the way up. The progress can be more easily measured. One sees things differently on the way back: in a different light, from a different angle, and with the benefit of hindsight. Mistakes made on the way up are easy to see on the way back. My fifth and final observation about mountain hiking is that when the hike is over the memories of the pain begin to fade while the memories of the joy increase — so much so that one cannot wait to undertake another grueling hike!

As I reflect on the past sixteen years it occurs to me that Pastoring Wawasee Community Bible Church was like a long mountain hike in many respects. In 1986 I was "long" on zeal to serve Christ in the ministry and "short" on experiences in life and in dealing with people in an organizational context. The "end" I envisioned was a congregation of people who loved Jesus Christ, who shared the Gospel, who honored God with their daily lives, and who loved each other. I had no doubt that the "end" would be worth striving for, no matter how difficult the way there would be. I was certain that if one was in God's will and held to sound doctrine that the path to be taken would be mostly flat, mostly straight, and mostly beautiful. As the path I was on passed through each phase of our existence and approached another "pass" I was confident that the end would be in sight on the other side. I believed that everyone would want to stay on the same path unto the same end, that sharing the same "sights" and experiences along the way would bring this about, that the "rightness" of our quest and the beauty of the "end" would be more than adequate to preserve our strength and ensure our determination. In 1986 I had a lot to learn!

My tenure Pastoring Wawasee Community Bible Church spanned thirteen years. Although it took place on the flat farmlands of Northern Indiana, the experience was remarkably similar to a long hike in the mountains. Three realities guided the unfolding of the history of Wawasee Community Bible Church, realities which must be borne in mind if one wishes to understand the history. The first reality was that we were an all-volunteer church. Whatever was accomplished happened because people freely chose to offer their time, talents, and resources to meet the needs of the congregation. The second reality was that our numerical growth consistently ran ahead of our expectations. This reality weighed heavily in all our decisions, from facilities, to programs, to leadership. The third reality is one that is common to all congregations within the Church, the Body of Christ. We were all human beings: zealous, well-intentioned, seeking of God's direction, but imperfect nonetheless.

The history of Wawasee Community Bible Church and the thirteen years of my pastorship were comprised of five distinct phases in the congregation's development. The first phase was when we met for our services in the Milford School Cafeteria. This phase began with our founding on September 7, 1986 and continued a little over fourteen months. News of a new church quickly spread through our little community. The fact that this new church's founding families were former members of the Milford Apostolic Christian Church especially aroused the curiosity of the townspeople. In our second week the local newspaper included a brief "bio" of who we were in the "Milford Main Street" section. It was not much later that the local newspaper interviewed me for the first time. I remember being very careful in my comments to not say anything that might be hurtful to Grandpa and Grandma Beer. I had also told my boss at the pharmacy that I would be careful not to allow church business to interfere with my pharmacy work. This proved difficult to do at times over the years, although I knew early on that my boss was as curious as everyone else about what was going on.

In our first several months every Sunday was an adventure. Each week new people came to visit. Some were just curious to see what was going on, but others liked our services and became a part of our group. On several Sundays in these first months we had carry-in dinners after church. Everyone seemed to enjoy the fellowship and the dinners helped build our sense of oneness. A number of families cited these dinners as influential in their decisions to affiliate with Wawasee Community Bible Church (WCBC). In the early days of the church we had a fellowship time between the Sunday school and church services that included cookies and drinks. This was a holdover practice from the AC Church, but it was helpful in getting new people to feel a part of the congregation. We continued this practice all the time we were in the school. Another practice we kept from the AC Church was not passing an offering plate. People gave as they felt moved to give, putting their offerings in our shoebox. Raising the money we needed was never a problem in our first phase, although our expenses were minimal, being an all-volunteer group.

One of the first issues before us in our first days was deciding where we would meet in the long run. The school had given us a one-month, renewable rental contract, but they were under no obligation to renew it indefinitely. The first idea we had was to look into buying a little church building in the country that was unused and owned by the United Methodist denomination. I saw the church one day as I was driving. The kids and I stopped and checked it out. It was in a state of disrepair, but it had possibilities. We checked with a man who owned land adjacent to it and he said he would be willing to sell some to us if we wanted. After discussing the idea we decided to make an offer to the United Methodist Church for the building. Some of us even spent a Saturday cleaning the lot and putting plastic over some broken windows. After several weeks the Methodists came back with an offer that we considered far too high. We counter-offered. While we were waiting to hear back we explored ideas for the building in the event they accepted our offer. We even estimated the cost of putting a balcony in the church. We figured the maximum occupancy with a balcony would be about one hundred twenty-five people. At this point we realized pursuing this little church was a bad idea because we were already having groups nearly this large on Sunday morning. The idea was abandoned and a committee was formed to investigate our long-term church home options. They began meeting in early November.

In November 1986, Edna Graff, who had trusted Christ as her Savior the day before our first service, asked if we could baptize her. This request led to a discussion among the leadership about formalizing our positions before the congregation. The men of the five founding families had been functioning as Elders since the beginning. We now agreed that we should ask the congregation to formally support us in an ordination service. Apart from one woman asking me why there were no women Elders being ordained, the congregation supported our request. The ordination service was held before our church service on December 7, 1986. The five of us came to the front. We thanked them for their support, and then I ordained the other four as Elders with a prayer. They then ordained me as an Elder and as our Pastor with a prayer. Three days later on a Wednesday evening, we drove to Edna Graff's house and held a baptismal service. Because Edna was a semi-invalid, we sprinkled her rather than immersing her. It was a special evening. I remember especially how thrilled Edna's elderly sisters were for her. Edna spent the final years of her life bed-ridden in a nursing home, but she never wavered in her faith and I never once heard her complain. She remains an inspiration to me to this day.

The committee we formed to consider options for a permanent church home worked efficiently and harmoniously. By mid-December they had a plan to present for a modest, functional, new post-frame building. They presented it to the leadership on December 18, 1986. Everyone agreed to the concept and we sent their work to an engineer for pricing and initial blue prints. At that time two other committees were formed, one to look into financing any future project, and one to investigate possible building sites. The "building site" committee began their work with the hope that we could eventually buy some land from a family farm that was located on the main road half way between Milford and the neighboring town of Syracuse. We all agreed that this would be an ideal site.

March of 1987 was a very special month in the history of

WCBC. The work of the land, finance, and building committees came together and their package proposal for a church building was presented to the congregation early in the month. The land committee had made arrangements to purchase five acres along the road between Milford and Syracuse for five thousand dollars per acre. This was the site we all had hoped for. The finance committee had made arrangements with a local bank. The total cost of the project was three hundred and twenty thousand dollars. The bank President had interviewed some of our congregation and agreed to make the loan with no collateral. His decision was based solely on the reputation of the members of our congregation. This greatly touched me at the time.

The building committee had created a plan for a post frame building 128 feet long and 56 feet wide with a porch on the two sides facing the road. The auditorium would be 56 feet by 56 feet with a three-step stage at the south end. The committee estimated that the auditorium would hold up to two hundred and seventy five chairs. They had even made a model of the building that showed the interior rooms. On March 22, 1987 the congregation voted and gave the project a one hundred percent approval. When the results of the vote were announced the congregation broke into a spontaneous applause. This was one of the very rare times I remember a vote being one hundred percent approval in the church.

Very soon after this we paid for the land that we were to build on. The next Saturday morning a number of us met at the building site. We tore out the fence along the road, burned the fencerows, and cleaned up the site. I distinctly remember how thrilled everyone was to be a part of this initial activity. Indeed, it is not difficult to recall the "feel" of the excitement in the spring of 1987. The congregation was growing. I had begun preaching through the Gospel of John. I was thrilled about what I was learning and the congregation seemed thrilled about what they were hearing. On Sundays people came early to "set up" and stayed late to "tear down." They did not need to be asked. At times we had more volunteers than we had jobs to do. Some adults had trusted Christ as their Savior by that spring, as well as at least a dozen teenagers. We had mid-week Bible studies for the adults and for the teenagers that were well attended. Everyone seemed to genuinely love one another. I believe everyone realized they were a part of something special, something that the Holy Spirit was bringing about. It was a period of time when the congregation seemed to be collectively enjoying a spiritual high like one experiences when one is first saved: forgiven, free, joyful, and zealous to live for Christ.

Experience has since taught me that it is times like these Satan always launches a counter-attack. The spring of 1987 was no exception to this. The attack came in the form of an anonymous letter to the Elders. One of the Elders had received the letter and brought it to an Elder meeting. The letter contained a number of complaints against one of the Elders, the one who was not in attendance at the meeting. None of the complaints were serious. All of them could have been expressed easily face to face or in a signed letter. They concerned procedures in our services and personality issues. After a long discussion about what to do about the letter, we decided that one of us would share the letter with the Elder it concerned sometime in the future. By chance, it happened that several of the irritations mentioned in the letter were procedural changes that we intended to alter that evening anyway. Six days later I learned that the wife of the Elder whom the letter concerned was very hurt. Before one of us was able to speak to her husband about the letter she learned about it through another Elder's wife. I spoke to her at length about it twice that day, which was a Saturday when I was at work. It was embarrassing and extremely frustrating. Because several of the things mentioned in the letter had been addressed, she concluded that we were against her husband also.

I was very upset by this for several reasons. First of all, our changes were not in response to the letter, although I saw how she concluded that they were. Secondly, I knew she was deeply hurt and my nature is to hurt when others hurt. Thirdly, I was angry with both the author of the letter and the Elder and his wife who did not do what we agreed as a group to do. This deep hurt and my time spent to work through it did not need to happen. I was left with a question, also. What does one do with an anonymous letter, especially one that mentions legitimate issues? Does one throw the letter in the trash because it is not signed? Or does one consider the issues? To this day I am not certain what is the best thing to do, although in this case I would throw the letter away if I had it all to do over again. Perhaps this is just because of how it turned out, however. This incident produced some significant hurts and worse yet, these hurts contributed to the formation of a basis for interpreting future actions of the church leadership.

We held a groundbreaking ceremony at our building site on May 17, 1987. As soon as our service was over that day the congregation drove to the site. After a short program we prayed together and took a group picture. One hundred forty-one people are in the picture. It is a classic and still hangs in our church fellowship hall.

Although the excavating for our new church was accomplished in early May, the actual construction began on June 23rd when the corners were staked out. This initiated a frenzy of activity that culminated in a new facility. Once the building was framed we often had more volunteer help than could be used. This created a special challenge for our contractor, whom I felt sorry for at times. I remember being astonished how quickly the sheeting and shingles went on once the roof rafters were set. It was during this roofing that we had our only significant construction accident when one of our volunteers fell off the roof and broke his leg. Apart from this our volunteers suffered only one chipped tooth and many smashed thumbs!

It was a period of time when everyone in the congregation was helping. There seemed to be a committee for everything, from the kitchen to the furnishings to the decorating to the landscaping. There were a few "ruffled feathers" along the way, but for the most part everyone got along remarkably well.

Despite the frantic pace of activity in building our new church home we had five special events that summer and fall. On June 28th we had an all-church picnic with Living Gospel Church, a church whose Pastor was Otto Beer, Junior. On July 12th we had our services at Camp Alexander Mack and spent the day enjoying all the camp's activities. During the second week of August our children attended church camp with several other Independent Bible Churches. Most of our children had never attended a church camp before and they thoroughly enjoyed the week. On August 2, 1987 we had a baptism service at a local church. A woman had requested that she be baptized then rather than wait until our church building was finished. This woman had spent her entire life attending the Apostolic Christian Church, but she could never accept their conditions for salvation. She and her husband had come to WCBC from the beginning. It was only several months after attending that she came to me and confessed that she had trusted Jesus Christ as her Savior. She did not want to wait to be baptized, because she was in her mid-sixties and had "waited long enough already!" The evening was a precious one. The woman gave a touching testimony prior to being baptized. Some of our congregation had never witnessed a baptism by immersion and they were especially moved by it. This was my first immersion baptism. It would be the first of many such precious services in the years to come.

Our final special event took place on September 20, 1987. Don and Virginia Hoover had begun attending WCBC very soon after our founding. They had a farm with large yards that were bordered by a wood. It was a beautiful outdoor setting. Don and "Ginny" invited the entire church to their home for a day of fellowship, food, and fun. The day began with a church service. I preached in my bib overalls while the congregation listened from their straw bale seats. We then ate dinner. The Hoover family had roasted two hogs and the rest of the church carried in other foods. Following dinner, the Hoover family had games, hay rides, and "rope and tire" swings for the children. As these activities were in full swing the older kids and young adults played volleyball and football. Everyone else sat, ate, watched, and talked. What a day! The "Hoover Hog Roast" became an annual event that continues to this day.

There was only one year that the "Hoover Hog Roast" was not held — the year that Don Hoover died. Don had trusted Jesus Christ as his Savior several years after the founding of the church. Soon after he unashamedly gave a public testimony and was baptized. From the beginning of WCBC until the day he died Don was an inexhaustible worker in the church — so gifted, so willing, so positive. He and Ginny and their children are precious to WCBC and me beyond what I am able to express. Families like the Hoovers are the life-blood of any local congregation within the Body of Christ. My fondest wish for any Pastor is to have at least one such family in his congregation!

One final significant event took place in the frenzied midst of building our church home. Three young couples in the congregation felt moved to start an AWANA Club. They did their research and planning very well and presented a plan to us on July 26, 1987. We learned that AWANA was a proven, worldwide evangelistic organization for children. The program format was one-third Bible memorization, one-third devotional time, and one-third game time. We also learned that the AWANA organization had their own Statement of Faith and that charters were only awarded to churches of like doctrine. We Elders were all in agreement that this was a program that would fit very well with our vision of community outreach and evangelism. We approved the plan, set to begin concurrently with the school year. The school agreed that we could hold the AWANA meetings there on Wednesday nights. Even though intellectually I was one hundred per cent behind the plan I confess it was a touch unsettling to imagine sponsoring a child evangelism club. It was an idea that would have been absolutely anathema in my former church. I suppose my feelings had not fully caught up with my mind at the time.

AWANA has proven its worth over and over again throughout the history of WCBC. Many people over the years have testified at their baptisms that they trusted Jesus Christ as their Savior while at an AWANA meeting. In addition, AWANA provides many opportunities for ministry in the congregation, from simple jobs suitable for new Christians to leadership and teaching jobs for those more mature in their faith. AWANA is an organization I am thankful to have been associated with since 1986.

The building of our new church home took about exactly five months. The effort was truly Herculean in nature. I had never been a part of any project in my life where there was more single-mindedness and cooperation within a group than on this building project. If I had not kept a journal I would remember it as a time of pure bliss, but my journal entry of November 3, 1987 refreshes my memory.

What a period of time. It seems that in the last week everything is going waco. (I then listed six "people" situations.) *This is all so ironic in light of the fact that all of these people say how excited they are about the Word and the fellowship of the church. I guess this is the closest I have come to burnout. The toughest part for me* *personally is the **guilt** and this is on two fronts: home — that I'm not being a proper husband/father, and these people — I feel so impotent to help them.*

Chapter Fifty

The second distinct phase in the history of Wawasee Community Bible Church began when we moved from the Milford School cafeteria to our new church home. Our first Sunday in our new church was November 15, 1987. My journal entry of January 4, 1988 tells the tale.

The last two months went past in a blur. They were two of the finest in my life. December 16th we dedicated the church. On November 15th we had our first service (in the church) and pushed the building to capacity. On December 13th Tom Kroh (my brother-in-law) came forward (after the service) and committed his life to the Lord. (Six others) came forward to make their commitments public as well. On the morning of December 28th I met with Missy and Nikki (two teenage nieces) and they both received Jesus as their Savior. On New Years morning I met with Don Hoover and he testified that he gave his life to the Lord last summer and that he wanted to make it public.

I am simply overwhelmed with what God had done. I am equally overwhelmed with the responsibility. There are not enough hours in the day and I am suffering a lot of guilt. I have to really wait upon the Lord about this and count on Him to make something happen.

*John (my boss) left for Hawaii tonight. I am not looking forward to the next two weeks **at all**.*

We dedicated our new building on a Sunday evening. I remember that night as one of the finest over the years. We had a community open house all afternoon. It was well attended. The church was full that night as I challenged the people to be obedient to the Biblical commands to faithfully propagate the Gospel of Jesus Christ. The highlight of the evening for me, however, was when our choir finished by singing "Bless This House." I had not sung in a large, accompanied choir since my freshman year in high school and I was very touched by the moment. The following is a transcript of my charge to the congregation the night we dedicated the building.

December 16, 1987.

Today (dedication Sunday) was a day which was almost beyond description. We are to the heights, the zenith, the apex, if you will, of our emotions to think that God has brought us to this point. We are so excited that we have this church and that we are full and that the fellowship is sweet and that we love one another. Today is really something, quite frankly, that I could not have even imagined not too many months ago.

I would like to tell you a parable about a church tonight. And I would like all of you to decide as we go through this where we are now as a church, and, if the Lord tarries, where will we be one year from now, or five or ten or twenty years from now.

There was a dangerous seacoast, along which there were many shipwrecks. Along this seacoast a crude little edifice was built. As a matter of fact, it was just a hut. And they had just one boat. But the several individuals who manned this seacoast outpost, without any fear for themselves, would day after day brave the turbulent waters in search of people who were the victims of ship wrecks. With no thought for themselves, these few devoted people went out and sought out those who were perishing. They threw out the lifeline to those who were lost, and through the efforts of these few people many lives were saved. So many lives, in fact, that before long the little outpost became famous. Many people, those in the surrounding communities and those in the area, as well as those who were saved, wanted to get involved in the work. So they gave their time, they gave their talents, they gave their money. More boats were

A Lifetime of Church

bought, more crews were trained, more souls were pulled out of the clutches of death of those waters. The work grew.

But time passed, as it always does, and it was not long before some of the members of these life-saving crews decided that "Hey, our fame has spread far and wide. What are we doing in this little hut? We need more than this. Our building is too crude. We need a larger, a nicer place for the first refuge of those we save from the sea!" And so the building was enlarged. The emergency cots were put away and hospital beds were put in their place.

Slowly, inexorably, as time passed, this life-saving station began to be a place where the people gathered and discussed the work. And it became more and more a place that took on the characteristics of a social club. The remodeling continued and the building grew and grew and before long more and more people became less and less interested in going out and risking their lives in the waters to pick up potential drowning victims. Fewer and fewer people were involved in the life-saving activities. They said, "We enjoy our club. We enjoy our social life. We really cannot be bothered with this. We need to hire people to do the life-saving work." Professional crews were then hired and they were sent out to search the waters. And as time went by less and less people were involved in the work. Their stationary letterhead still had the motif of the life-saving boat and the room in which they held their initiations still sat under the gaze of one of the original lifeboats. But more and more and more these were merely symbols commemorating a previous era as this group and this edifice took on the look of a social club.

One day there was a particularly large ship which crashed on the rocks off the seashore and the hired crews went out and brought in many people by the boatload. They were cold, they were wet, they were dirty. Some of them were diseased and nearly at the point of death. They brought them into this new building, this club, and the place was a mess.

The next day the building committee met and immediately decided "We need to build a station outside of our building. We need a shower house. We cannot bring these people in until we clean them up and make them acceptable to us!" At the next meeting there was a split in the club. Most of the club members wanted to get rid of life-saving activities altogether, reasoning, "It is too messy. It requires too much of me. Let someone else do it." But others said "No! We can't do that. Isn't that what we are called — a life-saving club? Isn't this what we were founded on?" And they held a vote. Those who wanted to search the waters; those who wanted to save lives were told, "If you want to continue this activity, go start your own place."

And time passed. Soon the same cycle began to repeat itself. And should you go by that seacoast today you will find many, many, many exquisite clubs along the seashore. Ships still wreck. People are still thrown into the sea. Most still drown.

Where are we? Where are we tonight? What are we to be about as a church? We now have the building. We are the Body. Right now we are on fire. Our zeal is unchecked. What lies in the future? What would Jesus tell us if He was speaking tonight? Remember — at the end of His public ministry, when He went to Jerusalem for the last time knowing full well He would be rejected and crucified ultimately — he was to cry from the depths of His soul in Matthew 23:37 "O Jerusalem, Jerusalem, you who kill the prophets and stone those sent to you, how often I have longed to gather your children together, as a hen gathers her chicks under her wings (lovingly, tenderly, securely), but you were not willing." He would say repeatedly that, "The Son of Man came to seek and to save that which was lost." What a lifesaver! For salvation we need to look no farther than our Savior, the God-man Jesus Christ.

You know, any of you who have been in the military that no soldier moves without orders. And what are our orders, from the lips of Jesus Christ? In all four Gospels and in the Book of Acts, the last thing He told us was very similar. Matthew 28, verses 18 through 20, He said, "All authority in heaven and on earth has been given to me. Therefore go and make disciples of all nations, baptizing them in the name of the Father and of the Son and of the Holy Spirit, and teaching them to obey everything I have commanded you. And surely I am with you always, to the very end of the age." Mark 16:15. "Go into all the wold and preach the good news to all creation." What about Luke? Luke 24, 45 through 47. "Then he opened their minds so they could understand the scriptures. He told them, 'This is what is written: The Christ will suffer and rise from the dead on the third day, and repentance and forgiveness of sins will be preached in his name to all nations, beginning at Jerusalem.'" What about John? Chapter 20, verse 21. Again Jesus said, "Peace be with you! As the Father has sent me, I am sending you." And what about Acts? Chapter1, verses 6 through 8. So when they met together, they asked him, "Lord, are you at this time going to restore the kingdom to Israel?" He said to them: "It is not for you to know the times or dates the Father has set by his own authority. But you will receive power when the Holy Spirit comes on you; and you will be my witnesses in Jerusalem, and in all Judea and Samaria, and to the ends of the earth."

So in Matthew, "Go!" In Mark, "Go!" In Luke, "Go!" In John, "Go!" And in Acts, "You will be my witnesses!" "Go!" "Go" is an active term, in our church, in our homes, in our communities. "To the ends of the earth" we are to make, make, make disciples!

Where are we in the little parable? Right now we are the little group — more are saved and love the work — our fame has spread, we want to get out and do the work. And time will only tell if the cycle will repeat itself with us and we will sink more and more into complacency and mediocrity. And if we do, it is not of God because our orders are clear. We are to "Go — and make disciples!" The charge is before us tonight. And none of us will have any excuse to say that we didn't have anything to work with. The same Holy Spirit who empowered the Apostles, the Twelve, is empowering us! If we were the one hundred and twenty that were in the upper room on the day of Pentecost, where would the Church be today?

We are here, some three hundred people tonight, and only God knows what the future holds. But if we continue to exalt the Lord Jesus Christ and preach His Name and if everything else comes secondary to this Great Commission, there is no reason to not believe that God will not continue to bless us beyond our wildest expectations, as He has — praise God — until this very hour. I lift up my eyes and I say "Abba, Father. Thank you! I love you!"

As my journal entry indicates, our move to the new church building ushered in a period of time in which there was intense activity. Many people believed in Christ for salvation. I was dizzy with joy over this, but the joy was tempered with guilt over not having enough time to disciple them. Over the years, though, it seemed like

I was always able to find enough time to bring most of the converts to the point of giving a public testimony and being baptized. Requests for funeral services and wedding services also began to come my way. In addition, there were administrative meetings, counseling sessions, and meetings with disgruntled people. Every week there was sermon preparation. In retrospect, I honestly do not know how I kept my sanity. I have to conclude it was due to two factors: the people who were praying for me, and the fact that I was married to Tammy. I have never stopped being amazed at her ability to quietly and efficiently manage any situation she finds herself in. The most amazing aspect of all this as I look back is the fact that in this early stage in the history of Wawasee Community Bible Church I had no idea of what real pressure was. I still had much to learn.

On January 19, 1988 we held our first WCBC annual business meeting. I recall being surprised that we would conduct such a meeting. I was so focused on preaching and pastoring that it never occurred to me that part of being a leader was to be an organized and responsible steward of the congregation's contributions and business matters. Fortunately, there were others who saw the need and addressed it. I remember being very impressed how thoroughly and efficiently the agenda was covered that evening. My brother Ned wrote the agenda and conducted the meeting, displaying his giftedness as an administrator throughout.

It was during this meeting that the congregation gave their support for our plan to expand the church leadership. The plan had been conceived in the months prior to the move to our church home. We five Elders were all in agreement. The plan was relatively simple. We would bring one man into the leadership the first year and in the second year expand our leadership board to seven members. The new leadership group would be referred to as the Board of Directors. There were two reasons for this. The first reason was that we Elders did not feel it was a proper time to add more Elders. Because we were such a new church and because we were a melting pot of people from differing religious backgrounds, we wanted to move slowly in adding new people to the group responsible for the spiritual oversight of the church. The second reason for calling the group a Board of Directors was because our church by-laws spoke of our leadership as a Board of Directors.

A Lifetime of Church

The attorney who created our incorporation papers used this terminology. This was not a problem to us five original Elders because we all understood that the "Board of Directors" terminology in our by-laws referred to us. The long-term vision was for the church to have two leadership boards: a Board of Elders and a Board of Directors. The Elders would attend to the spiritual matters of the congregation and the Directors would attend to the operational matters. According to the rotation we set up, by 1990 we would have a board of five Elders and a board of seven Directors. It was envisioned that the Pastor would be the liaison between the two boards. As we Elders developed this plan we all understood that the Board of Directors would serve in the capacity of the Biblical office of Deacons. We all understood that scripture clearly gave final authority in the local church to Elders. Looking back, it is my opinion that we Elders made a critical error at this point in not changing our by-laws to reflect our belief in leadership by Elders and Deacons. We failed to take into account that an issue of semantics between the terms "Deacons" and "Directors" might possibly become an issue of authority in the future. We also did not take the time to consider future scenarios that might create an authority issue out of a semantics issue. We should have asked ourselves questions like "Who will decide what is a spiritual issue and what is an operational issue? Who has the authority to make a decision if the two boards cannot agree? Are financial matters spiritual or operational — or both? Who will control the finances of the congregation?" We did not ask ourselves these questions. In January 1988, things were running so efficiently and harmoniously at WCBC that I remember no objections whatsoever being raised about our plan for future leadership.

The winter months of 1988 were full of special activities at WCBC. On January 17th we had our first baptismal service in our new building. My niece Dawn and a friend of hers gave their testimonies and were baptized. On January 24th our first missionary visited us and we agreed to support him. The following week we had an all-church outing Sunday afternoon at Wawasee High School. There was swimming and a gymnasium full of activities. This was topped off with carry-in pizza and pop. It was such a success that we did it again in March. On February 14th we had an all-church trip to a local state park for tobogganing. We filled two school buses and enjoyed a very special afternoon and evening together. Several weeks later our church went to the neighboring town of Nappanee for a praise gathering with Living Gospel Church.

These activities were all influential in improving our fellowship and sense of oneness. They were also excellent opportunities for our people to invite visitors. The visionary and agenda setter for all of these activities was my brother Ned. As the Principal of Wawasee High School he had the connections to make these things happen. More important, though, was his insightfulness regarding what the congregation would take part in and enjoy. I may have been the voice of the congregation, but Ned was clearly the leader. It is my firm conviction that WCBC would never have come to exist, let alone flourish, without his vision and leadership.

We had no sooner moved into our first church home than we realized we had under built. The shortage of space was particularly acute in Sunday school classrooms. When use of our church kitchen and our hallways for classrooms was inadequate we decided to purchase an old mobile home. By April 1988 we had the old mobile home refurbished and in use as two large classrooms. Before long we purchased two more mobile classrooms from a neighboring church. This overcrowding was a nice problem to have, but we knew we needed to find a long-term solution. This realization gave birth to a new committee in the church, the "Planning for the Future" committee. It was open to anyone who wanted to attend. This committee's first meeting was held on June 13, 1989. They began by exploring all issues pertaining to overcrowding. They continued to meet for many years, providing a very valuable service to the leadership of the church. Many of their proposals were approved without change and many others were approved with modifications. I do not remember any instance when they were not generally "on the same page" with the leadership. An example of their work came to be known as "Faith Sunday." Studying issues of overcrowding seemed to always come back to the fact that we were wedded to the debt of our building. The Planning for the Future Committee proposed that the church begin "Faith Sunday," where the entire offering that day would be applied to the principle of our debt. September 4, 1988 was our first "Faith Sunday" at WCBC.

This would continue on the first Sunday of each month for about a year and a half, during which time we significantly lowered the debt on our church home.

The Planning for the Future Committee was the author of another project in 1988, one that was very special to me. The church surprised Tammy and me in the fall of that year by building a finished room in the basement of our home so that I would have an area to study in and to counsel in. We had just arrived home from our first significant family vacation when we learned about the church's gift. We had flown to Florida and spent a week at Disney World. Having such a nice surprise on the heels of this fantastic vacation was more than we could have imagined. The only letdown was that our son Travis needed to be hospitalized for several days with asthmatic bronchitis when we returned. Tammy was with him in the hospital when the room was built. It was built in one day. There were so many workers helping that they got in each other's way. The new room was beautiful. It was a project that we could not have afforded by ourselves. Tammy and I were both humbled by this act of love and were so grateful.

The other "first" in 1988 was our first Vacation Bible School. Like everything else in those early days, the VBS greatly exceeded our expectations, straining our staff and supplies. We were fortunate in that the weather was beautiful and we were able to have many of the kids outside. I was especially thrilled with the success of the VBS. My three children all took part and they loved it. Travis enjoyed himself so much that he broke his collarbone when the boy who was carrying him fell down. He was in a lot of pain for a few days but much of this was offset by the notoriety he received as a result of the injury.

In 1988 we held five baptism services, during which twenty-one people gave their public testimonies and were baptized. We had three baby dedication services, one funeral, and one wedding. By the late fall of 1988, I was already aware of five weddings scheduled for 1989. I knew of more converts who would want to be baptized and I assumed there would be more funerals. (There would be five.) To meet this increasing workload I came up with an idea to name two more Pastors, one for Christian Education and one for the Youth. The leadership embraced this idea and it became one of our approved church goals for 1989. On July 9, 1989 we held a special church meeting where the congregation gave their support to the new church leadership structure and to the two new Pastors. The schematic of our leadership structure presented and approved at the meeting was in the shape of a diamond. At the top of the diamond was Jesus Christ, reflecting the biblical truth that Christ is the Head of the Body, the Church. On the side points of this diamond-shaped schematic were the Board of Directors and the Board of Elders, respectively. The Board of Directors was responsible for the oversight of the operational matters of the congregation, to include the finances and budget. The Board of Elders was responsible for the spiritual oversight of the church. At the bottom point of the diamond-shaped schematic was the Pastorate. The Pastorate was made up of three Pastors. The Senior Pastor was responsible for preaching, weddings, funerals, and other special services. The Christian Education Pastor was responsible for Sunday school and adult education. The Youth Pastor would oversee the youth. Presumably, all Pastors and Elders were responsible for visitation and outreach. Matters brought to the Pastors would be directed to the appropriate leadership board. Matters brought to the leadership boards would be dealt with and the Pastors would be given direction regarding carrying out the decisions of the leadership boards. The Pastors were to attend the meetings of both boards and serve as the liaison between them. When instituted, this new leadership structure seemed balanced and logical. It seemed to have appropriate checks and balances. Lacking in our new leadership structure, however, was one critical element – clear levels of authority. I do not recall anyone raising the issue at the time.

As 1988 became 1989, it was apparent that our overcrowding needed to be addressed. Ideas for expansion of our facilities were being expressed in many corners of the congregation and being seriously explored in the Planning for the Future Committee. I remember being very surprised when I began to realize that so many people were seriously thinking about another building project. The first written allusion to needing a new building appeared in the church bulletin on March 5, 1989.

FAITH SUNDAY

Today is Faith Sunday! (When all donations for that Sunday are put against the building loan.) To keep everyone aware of the EXCITING problem we have of overcrowding, we will be noting the attendance at both Sunday school services and for the church service in the bulletin each week. Watch how our numbers grow! It is GREAT and we want it to stay that way. With all of us working together we have made it grow in numbers, now we need to make the building grow!

*** Attendance for Sunday, February 26, 1989 ***
Sunday School Service - 248
Church Worship Service - 335

An initial study about our facility needs had been completed by the summer and was presented in our July 9th organizational meeting. No one disagreed that our facility needs were legitimate. There was, however, considerable disagreement about where the money would come from if we decided to build. By the fall of 1989 the leadership decided to present a detailed building plan to the church. This was done on Sunday morning, November 5th. The plan called for a new five hundred-seat auditorium. On one side of the auditorium would be a new Sunday school wing the size of our original building. The other wing would be our original building, converted to a fellowship area. The cost was projected to be over five hundred fifty thousand dollars. The next step was to survey the congregation. This was done during church on November 12th. The bulletin announcement read as follows:

Today a Faith Survey will be distributed during the church worship service. This will be filled out at that time and turned back in. These will be done totally anonymously. No name will be written down or noted. This survey will be an evaluation of the congregation's ideas and support on the concept of church building expansion.

This was a two-page survey. Among other things, it asked how many people the survey represented, how much the respondents were currently giving to the church, how much they would be willing to increase their giving if a project were approved, and whether they were in favor of a building project or not. The decision to conduct this survey was made after considerable discussion among the leadership. Two of our leaders felt the project was simply too much, too soon. The others were fully in favor of proceeding. I was on the proceeding side, but I privately expressed some concern about taking on such a large debt. Until we actually surveyed the congregation, however, we were all working largely on assumptions.

The results of the survey were a very pleasant surprise to those who were in favor of building. The results indicated strong sentiment within the congregation to build. They also indicated that the increased giving would be adequate to support the project. The results of the survey were shared with the congregation on Sunday, December 3rd. The bulletin announcement that day explained what would happen.

Church Service
"The Plan"
FAITH SURVEY RESULTS
and recommendation to the congregation.

To all visitors and those coming today to especially receive a message from the Bible during the worship hour, we do apologize. WCBC is growing so much and we are so excited from this growth and the love that is filling this building that necessity dictates that we must take time to talk of the work we must do to keep this excitement, love and God's word flowing from all of us. Please return to us on a more "normal" day to receive the Gospel message, but for today share in the enjoyment and excitement of "The Plan." By the way, be careful.....it can be very contagious.

On the morning the building proposal was presented the congregation was told there would be an approval or disapproval vote in two weeks. How was I feeling about this? Events were flying by at such a furious pace then that it is difficult to answer this. I remember having a strange mix of emotions. On the one hand I was humbled at the realization that so many people were so excited about the future that we were on the verge of another building project only two years after we completed our first building. As I considered the zeal of the congregation and the number of people who were coming to faith in Jesus Christ, I was convinced that God was responsible for it all. In this line of reasoning it seemed foolish to do anything other than to "ride the wave" the Holy Spirit had created. Balancing this, however, were three sobering thoughts. The first was "What happens if conflict comes or if people get offended by the preaching of the Word and leave the church?" The second thought was "What if people do not honor their financial commitments or if the economy turns down?" The thought of being stuck with such a big debt was frightening. The third thought was "I am struggling to keep up now. How will I possibly be able to handle the increased work load that will surely follow an expansion?" Following the loop of these three questions were always three thoughts: Nothing in my life has ever gone as I have planned. If all these people whom I highly respect are in favor of the project, then it must be the right thing to do. I need to be very careful what I say because my feelings would likely be unduly influential. Like so many other things in my life, the second building project at WCBC "just sort of happened."

The congregation voted on the project two weeks later, before my morning message. Before the ballots were handed out we had a prayer. After the prayer I told the people "Please do not vote in favor of this project unless you intend to support it." The results of the vote were announced at the end of the service. There were one hundred and seventy five "yes" votes and twenty-nine "no" votes. The project was thus approved by eighty-six per cent of the congregation. While construction would not begin until the next summer, our course was set. Eleven committees were formed to begin work on various aspects of the project. One other significant decision was made in the fall of 1989. When it became official that we would be entering into another building project, I spoke to the leadership about some concerns I had. I expressed my conviction that we needed to be preparing for the day when we would need professional help to meet the spiritual needs of the congregation. Even at that early date I was certain it would not be possible to remain all volunteer and keep the congregation satisfied in the long run. There were simply not enough off-work hours for all the calls, visits, evangelism, descipling, sermon preparation, meetings, counseling, weddings, funerals, and conflict resolution that was necessary. I was willing to continue as long as I could, but even if I stayed healthy and if others maintained their high level of activity, I was sure professional help would be required in the future. The leadership's response to my concerns was to budget one hundred dollars per week for whoever did the Sunday morning service. This was not what I had in mind when I approached them about the matter. I was not seeking monetary compensation. I simply wanted them to include the likelihood of needing help in their future planning. The leadership's reasoning was that this new line item in the budget would serve as a first step in preparing the congregation for this possible future need. Initially, I accepted this money for about one year. I then told the leadership that I did not feel right taking it when so many others were also working sacrificially and were not being paid. After I stopped taking it, the money was still budgeted, but it was applied to the principle of our church debt.

Chapter Fifty-One

While hiking in the mountains I have on more than one occasion become so enthralled with the scenery around me that I have not paid adequate attention to the trail I am following. On these occasions there has been a cost for not choosing the best path, a cost of extra time and energy. As one looks back on the trail these wrong choices are easy to see, but they are difficult to see amid the distractions on the way up. As the decade of the eighties came to a close and we entered the nineteen nineties, the leadership of Wawasee Community Bible Church set out on a path that was not the best path available to us. In the midst of the beauty of what we were experiencing in the congregation, we started on this path innocently. There was absolutely no malice of forethought. There would be a price to pay for our choice in the future, however.

By January 1990, a subtle, but critical metamorphosis had been completed in the leadership of WCBC. The path we were now on in terms of leadership structure looked very different than the one we began with in 1986. In 1986 a board of five Elders led us. When we decided to expand our leadership, we Elders began rotating off the Board of Directors unto the end of creating two leadership boards, one to manage the spiritual affairs of the congregation and the other to manage the operational affairs. Three Pastors, who were from the original Elders, would serve on both boards and act as the liaison between them. By January 1990, there was an active board of seven Directors, and three man Pastorate and the two remaining original

Elders. The meetings of the Elder Board began to be less and less frequent. There were a number of reasons for this. The first was the frantic pace of activities in the congregation. As a Pastor the last thing I wanted was another meeting. I assume the other two Pastors felt the same way. The second reason was the differing opinions among the Elders as to what our role was to be. I viewed the role of an Elder as one of spiritual oversight, marked by teaching, prayer, visitation, and evangelism. In my vision we Elders would make our own work among the people and that our Elder meetings should be both short and infrequent. To me, administration was of lesser importance than any of these Elder responsibilities. It was my opinion that some of the Elders believed administration was among the most important of their duties. I now know my view was only partially correct. I knew full well that the Bible clearly gave the leadership responsibility to Elders. A third reason our meetings became less frequent was because the two non-Pastor Elders both had serious reservations about the timing and scope of the new building project. They also felt their voices had been somewhat excluded in the building project decision process. I understood some of their misgivings. I had some misgivings of my own, but once the decision had been made, I felt I needed to be fully supportive of it. The fourth reason our meetings became less frequent was because the Board of Directors was doing such an outstanding job managing the affairs of the congregation. Additional meetings simply were not necessary. There was, however, a very clear reason why the Board of Directors was operating so efficiently: my brother Ned was actively involved in their leadership. There clearly was tension among the original Elders in January 1990, tension that would wax and wane in the years to come. In my opinion, none of we five were free from blame for the production and maintenance of the tension. Given the personalities involved, I do not know to this day what could have been done to produce lasting harmony.

1990 was a beautiful year at WCBC. The storm clouds in our leadership seemed so far away that we barely took note of them in the midst of our activities. Our weekly attendance hovered around three hundred people. A five-week average in March and April for example, was two hundred and eighty three. Souls were coming to Christ for salvation and most were being obedient in water baptism.

On July 22, 1991, I had the rare privilege of baptizing my daughter Trischa. She was one of thirty souls baptized that year, but definitely the one I will never forget. As she stood in the water to be baptized I held her hands to ask her some foundational questions of faith. At this point I welled up with emotion. I paused to clear my throat and she whispered "It's OK, Dad. Just take your time." This was typical Trischa — mature beyond her age. What a day!

In May of 1990 I was receiving so many phone calls at home and at work that I felt my sanity was in jeopardy. The other two Pastors and I met to find a solution. A retired Pastor who had become involved in WCBC met with us. We all agreed that we needed to institute an on-call and day off schedule. The retired Pastor agreed to be a part of this schedule and we announced our plan to the congregation. The plan was well received. Everyone understood the need — or so it seemed. The schedule did not last long. It turned out that there were many who felt the day off and no call times were a good idea for other people to honor. It was not very long until there was no distinction from one day to another and we abandoned the idea. I realized later that we made a mistake in the conception of our plan. About a year later I learned that the non-Pastor Elders were upset by the fact they were not included. They were right. We should have included them, but it never occurred to me at the time. In the fall of 1990 I made another attempt to organize my schedule and free up some time. I made my attempt public in the church bulletin on November 18th.

> **From the Pastor:**
> *Beginning this week I want to set regular hours for appointments and counseling. I will set aside alternating Monday mornings and Monday evenings for this purpose. If you want to meet, please call for an appointment during one of these blocks of time. This week I will be available tomorrow evening after 6:00PM. Thanks!*
>
> *Pastor Tom*

This failed also. Over the years nothing ever was effective in organizing my schedule and freeing up blocks of time. The congregational response to my attempts was always positive. The response of individuals within the congregation, however, was different. There were always those who "just wanted to run something by me" or who needed "just a minute of my time" that no time at home or at work was ever off-limits. Part of the problem was my fault. I found it nearly impossible to say "No." After all, how could I be a good Pastor and say "No" to people's needs? I also never quite caught on to the fact that "just a minute of my time" was only a figure of speech. Over the years, though, I only remember several people who I felt took unfair advantage of my inability to say "No." I believe most callers sincerely felt they had legitimate problems that could not wait for scheduled times. I believe most really did expect to take "just a minute." Talking to other Pastors over the years I learned this was not a problem unique to me.

After the congregation gave final approval to our building project a "Project Coordinating Committee" was formed to oversee it. I was invited to one of their meetings on June 13, 1990. The purpose of the meeting was to formally decide to begin our construction in the early fall or to postpone it until the spring of 1991. Following a review of the project I was asked my opinion. I expressed that I had concerns about the long-term level of commitment of the congregation. I also wondered aloud if our volunteer staff could keep up with the work a bigger congregation would require. I finished with the thought that we might be unwise to begin a project heavily dependent on volunteer labor during a season when the weather would likely be bad. I remember stating "I think we should be like NASA with the Space Shuttle and recycle the launch for next spring." The six other people at the meeting immediately began to affirm their zeal for the congregation's readiness to begin and their confidence in the congregation's commitment. After hearing their enthusiasm I agreed to support the decision to proceed. This was the first and last time I publicly expressed any concerns about the second building project.

Several months before this meeting I had prepared a "Think Sheet" for the leadership to privately consider. In this "Think Sheet" I expressed my concerns about not being able to keep up with the spiritual needs of the congregation at its present size and wondered aloud how we might do it with the bigger group the new building would surely bring. I include this document here.

Think Sheet *March 15, 1990*

1. *Facts:*
   A. *My first responsibility is to love God above all.*
   B. *My second responsibility (given by God) is to love, serve, provide for, and nurture Tammy and the children.*
   C. *No responsibilities can supercede #1 and #2. They can be assumed only as they compliment and reinforce #1 and #2.*
   D. *I am presently not being Biblical in observing the above order. Tammy is suffering. The children are suffering. I am being drained spiritually.*
   E. *Maintaining the status quo is not acceptable to me long term.*

2. *Options:* *Full time pharmacist*
   Full time pastor
   Full time pharmacist/limited pastor
   Full time pastor/limited pharmacist
   (Full time pharmacist/full time pastor -my present capacity- is neither an option, nor feasible beyond the near future)

   A. *Full time pharmacist. This best meets responsibilities #1 and #2.*
      1. I could still remain great asset to WCBC: song leader, teacher, youth worker, fill-in preacher, choir, counselor/soul-winner, giver of money, etc.

   B. *Full time pastor.*
      1. Responsibilities #1 and #2 **possibly** *could be met here.*
      2. I believe if we go with a professional staff the workload would dramatically increase. (A trusted

pastor friend) has repeatedly pointed this out to me. People would feel freer to ask for help and for our services and people also would want their "money's worth."
3. *We would probably need at least two pastors and one secretary to do it right.*
4. *I would feel unqualified to undertake this job alone.*
5. *At this time I seriously doubt that I would be willing to do this even if asked.*

C.   *Full time pharmacist/limited pastor.*
1. *With limitations this might become consistent with responsibilities #1 and #2.*
2. *Currently, the "Pastor" is to preach, marry, baptize, do funerals, evangelize, counsel, attend meetings, trouble shoot, and conduct other special services (communion, baby dedications, etc.)*
3. *Preaching, baptizing, and funerals would seem to be inseparable. The rest, theoretically, could be delegated. Practically, though, I doubt it is possible.*
4. *Trouble shooting, soul winning, marrying, and counseling go hand in hand with the above.*
5. *The pastor must also be at least somewhat a part of the church administration, too.*

D.   *Full time pastor/limited pharmacist.*
1. *Theoretically this might be possible, but the same pitfalls as ("C") above apply.*

3. Opinions.

   A.   I believe that it is **imperative** that this matter be dealt with **before** we undertake the building project. I believe it is folly to do otherwise.

   B.   What do I want? I want to fulfill responsibilities #1 and #2.

C.   *I have been telling people that these problems exist for the last year and a half. Everyone has listened sympathetically, but nothing has changed.*

D.   *I am an optimist by nature, but I fear I am nearing the point of physical, emotional, and spiritual bankruptcy. It is unwise to predicate any long-term church planning on my "staying the present course."*

E.   *Finally, I feel that we need to hire a full time trained Pastor who is capable and enthusiastic. Our experience and infrastructure could then support him in setting our church on a course that is solid and stable and marked by continuity.*

If the leadership ever responded to this "Think Sheet," I do not remember it. I also do not remember feeling as frustrated as this document portrays me to be. I remember being in awe of what was happening at Wawasee Community Bible Church and I know I was thrilled to be a part of it all. I also remember speaking out for a professional Pastor very early in our history. The passing of time must have dulled my memory about the frustrations and overload of these years.

Once ground was broken on July 29, 1990 events unfolded at a furious pace. The energy of the congregation was incredible as we undertook our goal. On August 22, 1990 we held an open meeting where the construction bids, the contractors selected, and a time line was presented to the congregation. The Friday of Thanksgiving weekend in November 1990 was our first big volunteer workday. The work was to be done on our new Sunday school wing, whose footers and concrete slab had been completed by our contractor. By day's end all of the wing's exterior walls were erected and braced. By December 12th the rafters had been set. Every Saturday was a volunteer workday until the project was completed. The nearby communities watched in wonder as WCBC volunteers built the entire educational wing, most of the interior of the new auditorium, most of the adjoining structures, and laid all of the shingles. An electrician in the congregation oversaw a team that did all the electrical work as well. It was a beautiful example of what can happen when a group of people works together to achieve a common goal.

If there were any conflicts during the project they were minor enough that I do not remember them.

In early March 1991, we held an Elder meeting. On the agenda was the upcoming Good Friday Communion Service. As we discussed the service it became apparent to me that there were some unresolved offenses within our Elder group. The two Elders who were not Pastors confirmed that there were some things that needed to be resolved among us. When they insisted they were not prepared to talk about the problems at that time, we scheduled another meeting for the following week. We agreed in advance that we would "leave no stone unturned" and that the purpose of the meeting would be to seek total reconciliation within our group.

The reconciliation meeting was held on March 10, 1991. I went to the meeting aware of the fact that the two Elders who were not Pastors would express some hurt and offenses. As the meeting unfolded, however, the number of offenses each man made known stunned me. My notes of the meeting filled up one side of four full pages of paper. One man listed twenty offenses. The other man listed twenty-one. The subject of the offenses fell roughly into three categories. About one third of the offenses were personal in nature. Another third concerned the organization, direction, and functioning of the church. The final third of the offenses came about as the result of decisions that had been arrived at in the past. The men held me responsible for some of the offenses. They held another Pastor responsible for a few of them. Most of the offenses, however, were directed at my brother Ned. As we responded to the list of offenses we discovered that many of the personal ones could be talked through. Some were the result of inadequate communication. They were simple misunderstandings. Third parties "speaking for us" had caused some other personal offenses. These were more difficult to resolve because what we allegedly said, whom we allegedly said it to, and the context of what we allegedly said was virtually impossible to establish. Undoubtedly, others occasionally misunderstood our words. On other occasions it is possible our words were intentionally distorted and used maliciously by others. I recall specific instances when my brother Ned was misrepresented in this way. Resolution of these types of offenses basically boils down to whom one chooses to believe. In this category, I had two apologies I needed to offer. One was for some words I had said to one of the men in the wrong tone at the wrong time and wrong place. The other was to apologize to the two men for not including them in the time management initiative I wrote about earlier.

The other two thirds of the offenses were more difficult to address. The organization, direction, and functioning of the church and decisions made in the past were largely matters of opinion. Assuming there was no violation of the Scripture, one can only hold two general views about these areas. Either what was done was the best that could have been done, given the circumstances, or it was not. If one concludes that the best was not done, then there are also basically two choices regarding what came to be. Either my opinions were not considered or the opinions of others were considered to be better than mine by the group. If one concludes that the opinions of others were considered to be better by the group, then there are basically two more conclusions that one can arrive at. Either the opinions of others were more reasonable and acceptable to the group than my own or someone manipulated others to accept opinions other than my own. Strong leaders are often accused of the second of these two conclusions and my brother Ned was no exception to this. I was occasionally accused of exerting undue influence, too, but to a far lesser extent.

To this day it breaks my heart that this undercurrent was present in the midst of all the good that was going on in the congregation of Wawasee Community Bible Church at that time. I am certain that it grieved the heart of God. At the end of this evening, however, I was hopeful that the gnawing forces of division within the leadership of WCBC had been stilled. Stapled to my notes of the meeting is a note that reads: *"Three plus hours. All concerns expressed. Apologies offered and accepted. A new beginning covenanted."* As we left for home that evening I sincerely believe we all intended to honor our conclusions. After this meeting the relationships among the five of us were considerably better. Time would prove, however, that dividing the leadership of WCBC was a goal that the Adversary of our Souls did not cease to pursue. In retrospect, I cannot imagine anything else that would have been capable of undermining what God was accomplishing in our congregation.

Chapter Fifty-Two

The third distinct phase in the history of Wawasee Community Bible Church began when we moved into our new auditorium on May 12, 1991. In my mind, the congregation's efforts in completing this project so quickly were even more impressive than they were in building our first building. The leadership of the Project Coordinating Committee was amazing. I believe the cooperation, hard work, and single-mindedness during this project was truly WCBC's finest hour.

As is often the case when one finishes a big task, one is left with a feeling of "Now what?" Our move into the new auditorium was no exception to this phenomenon. We immediately found that a series of adjustments were necessary. Our new stage area was so much larger that we needed to reconfigure everything on it. We also needed to change how the music was led and where it was led. The sound people had a special challenge, as nothing was the same as in our first auditorium. The thrill of moving in was also somewhat tempered by the fact that "nothing felt the same" as it did before. Because we were "not on top of each other" anymore, many had the feeling we were "losing our sense of oneness" since our move. People no longer had their "place to sit." The padded pews felt different than the padded interlocking chairs had felt. Gradually we became accustomed to our new building, but the "feel" of the packed old auditorium was gone forever, just as the "feel" of the school cafeteria had gone before it.

In June of 1991, Tammy and I took the children to the Outer Banks of North Carolina for a week of vacation. Tammy's entire family was there, too, and we all stayed in two large beach houses. We had just arrived at our destination when we received a call from back home. "Calls from back home" are seldom good news while one is on vacation, but this call bore news that was worse than bad. It fell into the tragic category. We were told that the older son of one of our Elders had been critically stricken by bleeding in his brain and was not expected to survive. This was an especially nice young man who was full of promise. At age fourteen he was an athlete, a leader, and a friend to everyone he knew. He freely shared his faith in Jesus Christ whenever he could. He was the picture of health. His fatal brain bleed came without any warning whatsoever. He lingered for most of a week before passing away. The entire community was stunned by his death.

It is an understatement to say that our week in North Carolina was tainted by this tragedy. When the young man died we left for home early. I drove all night in order to be home in time for the visitation. After catching a few hours of sleep, Tammy and I drove to the home of the family. I had never dealt with anything like this before. I will never forget the agony that was on their faces that morning. I will never forget how desperately we wanted to ease their pain and how impotent we were to do so. I will never forget trying to grasp the magnitude of their sorrow and loss. I will never forget their courage to stand in the face of their loss and the surety of their faith that God would not forsake them. I know now that nothing could have prepared any of us for what we were experiencing. We were all on uncharted waters.

The viewing was held in our old auditorium at Wawasee Community Bible Church. It had been converted to a fellowship hall and was well suited for this purpose. The viewing began on a Sunday afternoon and did not end until late that evening. The funeral the next morning was the largest I have ever been a part of. Our new auditorium was filled to capacity. In the crowd there must have been several hundred friends and schoolmates. Addressing this crowd and maintaining my composure was the most difficult service I ever undertook. I can testify, however, that once I got started I felt the Holy Spirit's power more than at any other time in my life. To this day I cannot understand why God allowed this young man to die, but I can take comfort in the fact that the occasion of his death brought me the largest, most diverse crowd that I ever had the privilege of preaching the Gospel to. While I will never know for sure in this life, I believe that God had purpose in this aspect of his tragic death.

On the weekend following the young man's funeral a group of sixty people from the church was scheduled to go to Whitewater Rafting in West Virginia. Many of us did not feel like doing this after the funeral, but the trip was paid for and non-refundable, so we went. It turned out to be good that we went. Tammy and I rode in a van with two other couples. The thing I remember most about the weekend was getting very sick from a sandwich we allowed to get too warm on the way there. Although the fellowship and rafting were great, the people who went tend to remember the bad sandwich story more than anything else.

The remainder of 1991 went by in a blink of an eye. According to our church bulletins, a five-week average attendance in September and October of 1991 was three hundred and fourteen at our worship service. The only other significant thing in 1991 was coming to an agreement with my boss that I would buy the business from him. True to the pattern of my life, purchasing Walter Drugs, Inc "just sort of happened." After years of dismissing the idea because of the time required for ministry, I began to think differently when my boss was gone on vacation in July. I placed the following note in our church bulletin on July 21, 1991.

FROM THE PASTOR

A note from Pastor Tom: My boss is gone on a two-week vacation. I will be working double shifts until he returns. During this time I will need to limit my activities to preaching and emergencies. Please feel free to contact one of our Elders or other Pastors if you need help.

It was during this vacation that I changed my mind and decided to approach my boss about purchasing the business. There were basically four reasons why I changed my mind. The first reason was that my boss, John Perry, was getting older and wanting to retire.

He needed knee replacements also. I knew that he would not be able to continue to work full time for too much longer. Secondly, I took note of the fact that my children were beginning to grow up. My daughter Trischa would be a sophomore in High School that year. She had been helping me in the pharmacy since she was a fifth grader. If I bought the store I knew I could provide her with a job that she would like and be safe doing. As I looked into the future a third reason to buy the store became clear to me. Owning the store would provide the family with a much larger income. With college and weddings ahead of us, I knew this would come in handy. I also knew this would allow our family to go more places and do more things while the children were still home. The fourth reason for wanting to buy the business had to do with church. Simply stated, by the end of 1991, it had become clear to me that Wawasee Community Bible Church had no interest in hiring me as a full time Pastor. I had known from the beginning that our philosophy was that we were an all-volunteer congregation. In the previous several years, however, I had hoped this would change as our congregation grew beyond all expectations. But with a new building and a six hundred and seventy thousand dollar debt, I now knew that nothing would change in the foreseeable future. Nevertheless, in the spring of 1992, I formally notified the leadership that I was planning to buy the store and that this was essentially "their last chance" to hire me. No one expressed any interest in changing our present course. In fairness to the leadership, I doubt I would have given up pharmacy to pursue full time ministry even if the church had asked me to, but prior to this I had been unwilling to place myself in any circumstances that would have precluded this possibility. With these reasons in mind, Tammy and I agreed we should approach my boss about the idea. He was very receptive and from that point on we began to work toward a goal of making the transition at the end of the fiscal year in October 1992.

The winter of 1992 was a quiet one at WCBC. A five-week average attendance in March and April was three hundred and twenty one. In 1992 there were two initiatives to meet the rising spiritual needs in the congregation. In the spring we began Shepherding Groups. After a lot of recruiting we secured enough people to serve as leaders. We had some training sessions for these leaders before we began, which included some guest speakers. Soon all active attenders were placed in a Shepherding Group. One Sunday I officially began the ministry before my sermon. After the sermon that day, a man who had been active in the church pulled me aside and said "You guys are only fooling yourselves if you think that Shepherding Groups can take the place of a professional staff." That was the last Sunday I saw him or his wife in church. Our Shepherding Groups produced mixed results. A few of the groups functioned as designed and lasted several years. A few more of the groups met for a while. Most of the groups, however, never got off the ground. After an introductory letter or an initial meeting they simply ceased to exist. After continuing several years and undergoing at least one major reorganization, we abandoned the idea of Shepherding groups. I think it was a good concept and I feel we gave it a good try, but it simply was not a good fit for WCBC. There was a "first" in this, however. It was the first time we tried something that ended in failure. It would not be the last.

Our second initiative to meet the growing spiritual needs of the congregation was to add Elders to our Elder Board. We began to address this 1992 church goal in May when we devoted two Sunday sermons to teaching about the office of Elder. My brother Ned preached these messages while I was in Ohio consulting with my Pharmacist Ritzman cousins about buying Walter Drugs, Inc. After encouraging the congregation to pray about the matter we conducted a nomination vote one month later. The following announcement was in our church bulletin on June 28, 1992.

NOTE FROM THE ELDERS: *The nomination ballots have been counted and reviewed by the Elders. The Brothers with the leading votes will be interviewed according to the criteria in I Timothy 3: 1-7.*

On August 16th, the Elders will announce names to the church for the position of Elder. On August 23rd, the church (after one week of prayer) will be asked to vote on the Elders' recommendation. An ordination service will be held after the church membership approves additional Elders.

Four men received far more nomination votes than anyone else.

In interviews, two of the men removed themselves from consideration. In the end we ordained two additional Elders. Both were good men whom I felt were well suited for the job. One of them was a relatively young man who had come to Christ through the ministry of WCBC. Following a powerful public testimony and baptism he became a tireless worker in many areas of the church, including a three-year term on the Board of Directors. He also had become my best friend by this time. I received some significant criticism for this. One family, in particular, felt I had forced this man on the church. The man was relatively young and although he was my friend and partner in ministry, I exerted no special influence in his becoming an Elder in the church. He simply was the one who received many more nomination votes than others and no one had any Biblical reason to reject him. Even though I knew these were the facts, the criticism still stung. This was one of the first incidents that demonstrated to me that the "honeymoon period" in my ministry had ended. As the years went by I received my share of criticism, some of it just and some of it unjust. While the surprise element of this early criticism went away, the criticism itself never stopped stinging. I came to accept it as a part of the job, but I never became callused to the point that it did not bother me.

The addition of two new men revitalized the Elder Board. Both new men worked hard at their job. The expanded board may have lessened the workload some, but not as much as I had hoped. I found that most people still generally came to "the Pastor." On January 23, 1994, in another attempt to meet the expanding spiritual needs of the congregation, we added four more Elders to the Elder Board. This also helped, but the needs proved to be rising faster than our efforts to meet them. One decision that made a big difference for me, however, was in 1992 when the Elders consented to my suggestion that my brother Ned begin performing weddings. After this decision I still performed some weddings, but only in special circumstances. I found premarital counseling and performing weddings to be frustrating work. For every couple that sincerely sought a church home and sought Christian counseling to prepare them for marriage, there were at least several more who only sought a nice ceremony in a nice building. I found it difficult to determine which type of couple I was working with until after the wedding and we did not see them at church anymore. I understood that it might take longer for the time invested to bear fruit in some than others and that the end to the story was not yet written in the lives of these couples, but I found it to be frustrating, nonetheless.

With the expansion of the Elder Board in 1992 the Elders began to be much more active in the oversight of the church. For years after this the Board of Directors met on the first Tuesday of each month and the Board of Elders met on the first Wednesday. We attempted to hold a joint meeting of the Boards once a quarter. It was the responsibility of the Pastors to attend the meetings of both Boards and to relate what was decided on various issues. I found this to be a very difficult job for several reasons. First of all, I always hated administrative meetings. I understood that they were necessary, but administration was neither an area of giftedness for me nor was it an area of interest. The second reason why I found acting as the liaison between the Boards difficult was because so many of the issues before the church overlapped areas of responsibility of both Boards. Oftentimes the Boards felt differently about the issues, and as time passed both Boards began to be more and more protective of what they saw as "their turf." Being the liaison between the Boards was a far more difficult job for me than preaching sermons. Relating how one Board felt about an issue to the other Board was virtually impossible to do to the satisfaction of everyone. There was the constant peril of being seen as overstating, or understating, or exerting too much influence. To use the illustration of hiking in the mountains, the leadership of WCBC was walking down a path that was leading to conflict over the horizon, but because of the beauty of what God was doing in the congregation we failed to take notice for far too long. The finest, most efficient work of the WCBC leadership Boards took place in the fall of each year when we met jointly for as many weeks as it took to formulate the budget and set church goals for the coming year.

There were some other exciting happenings at WCBC in 1992. In May we began a radio ministry at a local radio station. In the years to come we would receive feedback that our sermons were listened to by many unchurched people in our communities. Our summer Vacation Bible School was a success, too. We averaged one hundred and thirty-five children per day with a staff of thirty adults. The day camp we held for our middle school youth in a wood on a nearby farm was especially popular. In October we held a "Recruiting Sunday" in an effort to get people involved in the church ministries. Between the Sunday school and Worship services, representatives of the various church ministries were set up in the fellowship area to speak to interested people. To our delight, many people signed up to serve. In November we began an all-volunteer church secretary ministry. Tammy was one a group of women who volunteered to work in the church office one morning a week. I remember that we men were astonished at the degree of organization these volunteers brought to the church administration.

My personal highlight of the year was in August when Tammy and I took the children on our first major vacation out west. Tammy and I had fallen in love with mountains when we were in Germany and I had long wanted to see our American Rocky Mountains. I planned the vacation for most of the year. My daughter Trischa and I spent hours pouring over maps at work between customers in the months prior to our departure. All of us were excited as we left, but no one could have possibly been more excited than I was. I was giddy with excitement as I drove through the first night on our way to Colorado. Trischa had just received her student driver permit and by the next morning she was driving on I-80 across Nebraska. Our two weeks took us through Colorado, Utah, Wyoming, and back through South Dakota. Everything went exactly according to plan. What I remember most about those two weeks is how precious it was to be with Tammy and the kids without interruptions. We were blessed to be able to take annual vacations for years to come, but there was something special about the thrill of this one that will remain forever precious to me. I realize as I look back that the long-term planning for our annual vacation was one of the things that helped me remain hopeful and positive during the thirteen years I served as Pastor of Wawasee Community Bible Church. Thinking about the vacation ahead of me seemed to always lift my spirit when frustrations set in. Tammy and I spent many thousands of dollars on these vacations over the years, but I would not trade them for any amount of money.

1993 was a smooth and productive year at WCBC. A five-week average attendance in the summer was three hundred and ten. The highlight of 1993 for me was on October 31st when I had the privilege of baptizing my daughter Traci. She was one of the twelve who gave their testimonies and were baptized that day. I remember how proud and thankful I was when several of the middle school students mentioned in their testimonies that Traci was influential in their decision to give their lives to Jesus Christ.

In July of 1993 my beloved Grandma Naoma Beer died. She had been in slowly declining health for several years, but we were all taken by surprise by her sudden death. It would be difficult to overstate the impact of this godly woman's life upon my own life. I have never known another person who was as selfless or as loving as my Grandma Beer. Her life was one of absolute devotion to God, to Grandpa Theo, to her children, and to her grandchildren. Observing her life taught me about God's grace and what it meant to be "Christ-like." Attending her funeral was the first time I had been in the Apostolic Christian Church in seven years. I attended the funeral knowing that no words could adequately eulogize her life, but I was anxious to hear what someone outside our family would have to say about her. An older Elder from the Detroit, Michigan Apostolic Christian Church conducted the funeral. I was squirming midway through the service when my daughter Trischa leaned over to me and said "Geeze, Dad! Are they going to say anything about Grandma?" She was thinking exactly the same thing that I was. The only statement directly about Grandma that I remember was when the man noted, "She (Grandma) had nice handwriting." The majority of the time he spoke to Grandpa Theo about their years of service as Elders in the denomination. In all my years of conducting funerals, I do not recall speaking about anyone who would have been as easy to eulogize as Grandma Naoma Beer would have been. In all my years of life and ministry I have never seen a more golden opportunity missed more dramatically than this man did when he was asked to preside over her funeral. By the end of the service I was weeping bitterly. Some of my tears were undoubtedly cried because I loved Grandma Naoma, but mostly I cried because she did not receive even a drop of the flood of honor she was due. Even sadder than this, however, was the fact that Grandma Naoma would have been very pleased by the fact that she was barely mentioned at her own funeral.

Chapter Fifty-Three

In the fall of 1993 I was busy planning for our second vacation out west the following summer. In my research I learned that reservations for the historic lodges at the National Parks were made on a first-come, first-served basis. My reservation requests were therefore sent off in the early fall. After the first of the year we learned that our requests were honored at both Yellowstone National Park and Glacier National Park. Our expectations were sky high as we flew to Jackson Hole, Wyoming, to begin the two-week vacation. The vacation exceeded our expectations! One of the most memorable moments of this vacation took place at Glacier National Park. We started on a short hike one afternoon to Saint Mary's Falls. As we left the car Tammy mentioned that she heard thunder in the distance and wondered if we should wait and see if it was going to storm. None of the rest of us heard the thunder, so we all proceeded to the falls. The waterfall was a very loud and powerful one, but as we stood on a bridge overlooking it we all began to hear the thunder of a rapidly approaching storm. Soon the wind began to blow and it began to lightning. As we were thinking "Now what?" I noticed that a nearby trail ran by an overhang on the hill beside it. We had no sooner huddled under this overhang than it began to storm. The water running off the hillside fell just beyond our feet as it thundered, lightninged, blew, and poured down rain. Adding to the roar of the waterfall, we were truly in the presence of nature's majesty. The storm was indeed dramatic, but it did not last long. Huddling together with my family in that little indentation in the hill throughout the storm was one of the most special moments of all our family vacations over the years.

As 1993 turned into 1994 at Wawasee Community Bible Church, any church leaders listening closely could have heard some "thunder" in the distance. The "thunder" of impending trouble was "audible" at this early date, but if anyone noticed it I do not remember him speaking any words of warning. Just as thunderstorms in nature are the product of various atmospheric forces, storms in churches are the product of various human forces. The storm that began to gather on the WCBC horizon in 1994 was no exception to this rule.

The setting of the stage for what was to follow in coming years was comprised of four initiatives, three by the WCBC Board of Directors and one by the WCBC Board of Elders. In my opinion, the "distant thunder" officially began in 1993 when the Board of Directors forwarded a list of nine items they wanted the Board of Elders to act on. I was not in attendance at the Board of Directors meeting during which this list was produced. When I saw the list I knew immediately that it would "raise some eyebrows" on the Elder Board. I include the document here for the record.

March 16, 1993

The Wawasee Community Bible Church Board of Directors at the regular monthly meeting on Tuesday, March 16, 1993, discussed the following items. We recommend that the Board of Elders consider action on these items and report back before our next monthly meeting.

1. *An Elder should be on duty in the church office for two hours each evening Monday through Thursday and Saturday morning. Things that could be done during this time would be walk-in counseling, phone calls to shut-ins and elderly, follow-up phone calls for the secretaries, and prayer time.*

2. *Establish a term limit for Elders. This should be a 3-5 year term (staggered initially). An Elder could re-submit his name*

at the end of his term and this would be voted on by the church.

3. *Recommend that the Pastorate be rotated off the Elder Board and then remain separate from the Board as ex-officio members.*

4. *Elders need to be available for counseling at all times.*

5. *Church paid counseling should be limited to 4 sessions after which further counseling expenditures must be reviewed by the Board of Directors.*

6. *We recommend that the Elder Board appoint a chairman to call meetings and conduct business and a secretary to record minutes.*

7. *We recommend that the Elder Board conduct regularly scheduled monthly meetings.*

8. *There should be regular and ongoing communication between the Elder Board and the Board of Directors.*

9. *We further feel that the Board of Directors reserves the right to make recommendations to the Elder Board either individually or as a group.*

It is fair to say that all the Elders were at least somewhat taken aback by the document and several Elders felt some of the points were clearly unwarranted and inappropriate. The primary reason the Elders were taken aback was because of the overall tone of the document. It seemed to have a tone of admonishment, a tone that seemed to say "We want to remind you that you have a job to do. You are not doing your job. Here is a list that will ensure that you do your job." In addition, the fact that the Elders were presented a nine-point list indicated that they were the focus of an in-depth discussion on points that had previously not been brought to their attention. The obvious follow-up question to this is "What else is being discussed behind our backs?" As a Pastor and fellow Elder, I was mildly offended by the document, even though I did not believe it was directed at my job performance. Some of the Elders saw this document as a clear encroachment by the Board of Directors into their realm of authority. Several Elders viewed the document's second point as a thinly veiled attempt to orchestrate their removal from the Elder Board. In the minds of those most offended there was also a certainty as to the source of the document. They were certain that the document was not created at the Board of Directors meeting, but created previously and approved at the meeting. They were also of the opinion that only a few people in the leadership could have written it. I later heard suggestions as to the author's identity, but to my knowledge those making the insinuations never asked this individual or anyone else on the Board of Directors who authored the document.

After the initial shock the Elders conducted serious discussions on all nine points of the document. Some of the points, like number six and number seven, were moot because the Elders were already operating under them. There was no interest in pursuing point number three. The Elders viewed point number eight as ironic, because the Elders believed they were the ones not being communicated to by the Board of Directors. I never understood the intent of point number nine. It implied that this "right to make recommendations" had been denied to them in the past. I was never aware of an instance where this was the case. Points number one and four were agreed upon as good suggestions to help meet the growing spiritual needs of the church. We may have worked on enacting a plan to address point number one, but I simply do not remember. If we did, it did not last long. Point number two was the one that received most of the Elders' attention. Most agreed that we should be accountable to the congregation for our job performance. After considerable discussion, the Elders agreed to initiate a program for congregational votes of confidence for individual Elders on a rotating basis. It was made one of our church goals for 1994. With the addition of four more Elders in early 1994, the Elder Board began working on the goal in earnest. Implementation of the plan required changes in our church by-laws. We announced the proposed changes to the congregation May 8, 1994. The announcement and proposed changes read as follows:

BY-LAW CHANGE
One of the steps in accomplishing our goals for 1994 is to change our by-laws to: Establish a yearly vote of confidence for 2 - 3 Elders on a rotational basis. The by-laws have been edited and are posted on both bulletin boards in the narthex and the fellowship hallway. If you have any questions concerning this by-law, please see one of the Elders or a member of the Board of Directors. This by-law change will be voted on Sunday, May 22, 1994.

Article V Government
Section 7. Board of Elders.

A. *Qualifications. See Article III, Section V A*

B. *Duties.*
   The Board of Elders shall attend to the spiritual needs of the church. These duties include:
   1. Teaching. 2. Soul winning. 3. Visitation. 4. Counseling. 5. Seeking out the hurting. 6. Interpretation and application of scripture.

C. *Number.*

   The Board of Elders of the church shall consist of at least seven (7) members, or at least (1) Elder per fifty (50) members of the congregation.

D. *Terms of Office.*

   The term of Eldership shall be four (4) years. At the end of a four (4) year term an Elder may choose to continue to serve an additional term or he may choose to sit out a term.

   1. *If an Elder wishes to continue serving, he must submit his name to the congregation for a vote of confidence. A seventy-five (75%) approval will be required. "No" votes*

> *will be counted only if accompanied by a scriptural reason.*
>
> 2. *If an Elder chooses to sit out a term, he will retain the title of Elder but may not function as a part of the Elder Board.*
>
>   a. *Following a four (4) year absence an Elder may: either return to active status or retire. If active status is chosen, the Elder's name must be submitted to the congregation for a vote of confidence (75% approval necessary). See Section 7*

The by-law revisions passed and rotating votes of confidence for Elders became a policy at WCBC. The institution of this policy was bitterly opposed by two of our Elders, and one of them refused to support it even after we agreed to it as a group. Both men felt there was a hidden agenda behind the initiative that sought their removal from office.

As I look back on this document of March 16, 9993, I still feel a tone of admonishment in it. It is possible that neither the Board of Directors nor the document's author intended to admonish the Board of Elders, but this is how the Elders received it, and this was very unfortunate. Whatever results were sought, there were also some unintended results. The first unintended result was that it further polarized the two leadership Boards. At one extreme of this polarization was the idea that "The Elders are a bunch of do-nothings." At the other extreme was the thought that "The Board of Directors is power-usurping and exclusionary." Between these extremes was a solid majority of leaders working to bridge the gap and lead the congregation in an efficient, Biblical manner. The other unintended result of this document was a corollary to the first: The root of bitterness within the extremes of both Boards sank deeper and became more nourishing to those attached to it. It is also possible that even by mid-1993 there was enough suspicion of the Boards toward each other that this document was doomed to be viewed in a negative light no matter how noble its intent may have been. It has always been my opinion that the points in the document were both reasonable and worthy of consideration, but that they should have been presented in a less confrontational format. Perhaps raising a few of the points at a time and in face-to-face meetings would have been a wiser approach.

The second initiative by the Board of Directors that helped set the stage for conflict in years to come concerned the purchase of additional land for the church. There was a five-acre roadside parcel of land along our east property line. This parcel contained the house and farm buildings of the original farm that we bought our first five acres from. Representatives of our Board of Directors had privately approached the family who owned the five acres about selling to the church. Through these negotiations an agreement was reached for the church to purchase the property. The Board of Directors then came up with a plan to present the purchase to the congregation and ask for their approval. Through the church "phone tree" everyone would be invited to a special Tuesday evening meeting at the church to consider "a proposal from the Board of Directors." At this meeting the plan would be presented to purchase the property for the price of fifty four thousand three hundred dollars. The purchase would be paid for with a one-year note from the bank. The goal would be to pay off the note within the year. A committee would then be established to evaluate what should be done with the land and the buildings. The plan was to present the proposal to the congregation and have them vote on the proposal the same night.

I was not in attendance at the meeting when this presentation plan was formulated. I was aware of the private negotiations and the tentative agreement with the owners to buy the property. I thought it was a great idea and fully supported the purchase. The presentation plan, however, scared me. When I learned what the Board of Directors planned to do I warned the messenger that the Elders needed to be made aware of the plan before the meeting. My warning was not heeded and I erred in not making an effort to tell them myself. The Board of Directors had several reasons for proceeding in secrecy. The first reason was that they felt the church could get a better deal working privately with the family. The property was in a prime location between neighboring communities and there may well have been other buyers if it became known that the property was for sale. A second reason the negotiations were conducted in private was because the marriage of the owners was rumored to be in trouble. This would have likely complicated the negotiations. The third reason for the private negotiations was because the Board of Directors believed the purchase of additional property for the church was clearly within their realm of authority. In their minds there was no need to engage in a potentially lengthy process with the Board of Elders.

The special meeting to consider the proposal to purchase more land was held in the church fellowship hall on April 19, 1994. To my knowledge, only four of the eleven church Elders even knew what the meeting was about when they arrived. I remember at least four Elders making comments about the proposal during the meeting. To my knowledge, only one of these four knew what the meeting was about in advance, and he had found out the previous evening. The comments they made at the meeting were reasonable, but it was apparent from their comments that they were not in favor of borrowing more money, no matter how good a deal it was. Overall, the meeting went reasonably well. There was a lot of discussion and many good questions. Things changed quickly when the moderator announced that the plan would be voted on that same night. This announcement was immediately met with many spontaneous "Nos!" from the group. When I saw that the meeting was breaking down I got up and suggested that we give people several weeks to think over their decision and to pray about it. The group agreed to this idea and the meeting adjourned. The following announcement appeared in our church bulletin on April 24, 1994.

The Board of Directors is recommending to the congregation the purchase of additional property. The property is the house, buildings and five acres immediately to the east of the church. The congregation will be asked to vote on the Board of Directors' recommendation on Sunday, May 1st. If you have any questions concerning the purchase, please address your questions to the Board of Directors.

The congregation voted to purchase the property and the bank loan was paid off within one year.

The fallout from this Board of Directors initiative began without

A Lifetime of Church

delay. Nearly all of the Elders felt it was inappropriate that the Board of Directors had conducted the negotiations and approached the congregation with a proposal of this magnitude without informing them of it in advance. Some of the Elders were furious. The Board of Directors had its own members who were angry. These men and some members of the congregation felt it was wrong that some of the Elders had spoken against the plan in public. The essence of their anger was "How could the Elders be so negative and unsupportive?" These Elder's response to this criticism was two-fold: First, the Bible gives us the oversight of the church. We should have been consulted about this before the fact. Secondly, if we do not know any more about the proposal than the general congregation, then we have as much a right as anyone in the general congregation to express our opinions in an open meeting.

The third initiative that helped "set the stage" for what was to follow was put forth by the

Board of Elders. Since the founding of Wawasee Community Bible Church we had only one adult Sunday school class. This class met in the church auditorium and was very well received by a big majority of the congregation. There were some, however, who wanted some options for adults to choose from for Sunday school. While we were in our first church building we had no options regarding this because there was simply no space to do anything other than what we were doing. Things were different, however, now that we were in our new building. There were enough people interested additional options for adult Sunday school that the Elders made a small group class available in April 1994. The class was created on a trial basis. If it went well, the intention was to create more classes in the future. Critics of this initiative portrayed the Elders as being out of step with the congregation and seeking to "fix what was not broken." The Elders heard second hand comments like "Why is it that only the Elders want to change things? Why are the Elders listening to the people who are griping? Can't the Elders see that this will only create cliques in the congregation? Why are the Elders always so negative about what we have here?" Criticism is inevitable in leadership, but the problem with this criticism was that much of it was traced back to members of the Board of Directors and their families. This new class met and went through the book "Growing in Christ." About twenty people attended the class. I never heard anything negative about the class and the people who attended seemed to enjoy it.

The fourth initiative that helped set the stage for what was to follow within the WCBC leadership began in the summer of 1995. The Board of Directors came up with a plan to pave the church parking lot. The cost of the plan was twenty four thousand dollars. The Board of Directors asked for a meeting with the Board of Elders to explain the plan and ask for the Elders' support of it. Upon hearing about the meeting, some of the Elders wanted to hold an Elder meeting in advance of the joint meeting to discuss the concept of the plan. As one Elder explained to me "The Board of Directors comes to these meetings with well-oiled arguments for what they want to do and we never have a coordinated, thought out response." A conflict occurred when one of the Elders called other Elders to come for a meeting about the plan without going through the Elder Board Chairman. The Elder Board Chairman admonished the Elders about this, causing hard feelings that would resurface in the years to come. This admonishment was one of the very rare times that any of the leadership exchanged angry comments. Usually the angry comments were made to others about others. This lack of spiritual maturity and lack of obedience to Scripture was destined to produce a bitter harvest down the road. I do not remember if the Elder meeting to discuss the Board of Directors' plan was ever held, but I do not think it was.

When the Leadership Team (Board of Elders, Board of Directors, and Pastors) met and the Board of Directors presented their plan to pave the church parking lot, the discussion was free and cordial. By the end of the meeting, however, it was clear that the Elder Board did not have a majority willing to give their support to the plan. The Elders who opposed the plan offered three reasons. First, they felt the church was already too far in debt to borrow another twenty four thousand dollars. Secondly, they felt the project was unnecessary at that time. Thirdly, the Elders felt any additional spending would be better directed towards new ministries or missions. The Board of Directors then asked if they could present the plan without the Elders' support. The Elders consented. When the plan was announced to the congregation, it was painfully clear to everyone that the leadership was divided over the proposal. The announcements conspicuously avoided mention of the Elder Board, which was necessary under the circumstances. In the history of Wawasee Community Bible Church this was the only time I remember something being presented to the congregation without the support of the entire Leadership Team. The results were predictable. The vote on the plan resulted in an approval by fifty-nine percent of the congregation, but the Leadership Team had agreed in the past that proposals of this nature required seventy-five percent approval, so the initiative failed. Clearly, this failure did nothing to improve the already strained relations between the two leadership boards.

One of the curious aspects about this fourth initiative was its timing. For the better part of a year the Leadership Team had been working together on a fifth initiative, one that was much more far-reaching than any of the other four. (There will be much more on this "fifth initiative" later.) The Leadership Team was within one month of introducing the fifth initiative to the congregation when the Board of Directors came up with the proposal to pave the church parking lot. Unfortunately, some of the Elders saw this as a deliberate attempt by the Board of Directors to derail this fifth, critical initiative of the Leadership Team. I did not agree with this view, but I felt the timing of the initiative to pave the church parking lot was very unfortunate. At that time I was seeing definite improvement in the trust and cooperation level between the two Boards. I was hopeful that our differences were being bridged. This initiative by the Board of Directors and the timing of this initiative was a definite setback.

The four initiatives just discussed spanned two and a half years in the history of Wawasee Community Bible Church. They all produced their share of conflict, but more importantly they set the stage for the coming storm in the WCBC leadership. The conflict they produced was akin to "distant thunder." Having attended nearly all the Elder Board meetings and most of the Board of Director meetings during this time frame, I can attest that both Boards sincerely loved the Lord, loved Wawasee Community Bible Church, and loved the Word of God. Both groups sincerely felt they were acting in the best interest of the congregation. Within both leadership boards, however, there were individuals who had developed negative attitudes towards the other board. While no open conflict had occurred at this early date, the potential for conflict was real and growing. This was a gnawing concern to me. My nature is to always try to defuse conflict and to "fix" hurt feelings. As often as I had time, I tried to lower the tension. There were times when I felt progress was made, but for the most part people tended to view their feelings as appropriate and justified. As a rule, I tended to believe that harmony among the leaders was more important than the specifics of the operational issues under consideration. Interpretation and application of scripture was different. I would vigorously contend for what I though was right in these questions. Because I worked for harmony rather than specifics on operational issues I was sometimes viewed as being "wishy-washy" by both sides of these debates. They were right. Harmony simply was more important to me than taking a side.

These four initiatives were all basically good and I believe the people behind them had good intentions. There is no question in my mind, however that increased tension between our leadership boards would not have been a result of these initiatives if they had been conceived and presented in a different manner. Two additional results of these initiatives stand out in my mind. One of them was good and the other was not good. The positive result was that our church by-laws were changed to prohibit either leadership board from presenting something to the congregation without first discussion it with the other board. The fact that this by-law addition came about indicated the WCBC leadership understood the potential for conflict and the damage that might result in the congregation if such misjudgements were made in the future.

The second general result of these initiatives was not good. In the aftermath of these initiatives, elements of both leadership boards became even more protective of what they saw as their areas of authority. This, in turn, increased the difficulty we Pastors had in serving impartially as the liaison between them. Two critical leadership questions remained unanswered. The first was "How does one decide what is a spiritual issue and what is an operational issue?" The second was "Who had the final authority to make a decision when there is no agreement?" It was becoming increasingly clear that the WCBC leadership was destined for continued conflict until these questions were answered.

In the two and one-half years when this tension was developing within the WCBC leadership, the big majority of the WCBC congregation was completely unaware of it. As far as the general congregation knew, we were a church on fire for the Lord. There was so much good going on, it was hard to imagine otherwise. A five-week Sunday morning average attendance in February and early March 1994 was three hundred and twelve people. During this time frame we had large groups of men attend Promise Keepers conferences in Indianapolis. A significant number of men's small groups began meeting as a result of these conferences. In July of 1994 a women's ministry began. Many women participated in their various well-planned activities. All committees in the church were staffed. Volunteers, of whom there was no shortage, did all church maintenance and upkeep. During this two and one-half years we had the privilege of hearing forty-two souls give their public testimonies of new life in Jesus Christ and seeing them be baptized. It was also a busy time for some sad work as I performed thirteen funerals. As I look back it seems impossible that I found time to do what I did, but somehow enough time seemed to be available for the " big things."

My time was spent primary at work and in sermon preparation. Buying the drug store was turning out to be an excellent decision. Tammy quit working at the bank after the first year and was outstanding managing the office work of the business. We loved working together. The job provided her with great flexibility to come and to go, as she needed to run the kids around and manage the home. It was also great to have Trischa working at my side whenever she was free. Life was great.

Much remained undone, however, in the areas of visitation, counseling, trouble-shooting, and discipling. This began to become more and more clear to more and more people as time went by. Combining this realization with the reality that our all-volunteer staff was operating at maximum capacity began to convince the church that we needed professional help. There was one more factor that helped form the consensus in our leadership to study seeking outside help. In the fall of 1994 I discovered I had health problems. This discovery came about by accident, as I describe in my journal.

Friday, October 28, 1994

Tammy and I left for KCH (Koscuisko Community Hospital) *this morning at 8:00am, where I had an MRI done on my lower back. This* (problem) *all began about two months ago when* (my sister) *Sue brought a stack of wallpaper sample books to the store. A customer of Doll's Decorating was to pick them up later. I decided to move them and hurt my back as I lifted them from the side. About the time my lower back stopped hurting, my left hip and leg began to hurt. Any time I stand lately my leg and hip have been very painful, especially when I am fatigued. The pain has been centered on my hip joint, down the back of the leg, the upper outer calf region, and topped off with numbness in my big toe.*

The results of the MRI were bad. There was a bad herniation in the L4/L5 disc, bulges in the L5/S1 disc, and spinal stenosis — a congenital problem. (The doctor) *is going to make an appointment with a surgeon next week. Now what? I can't go on with the pain I am having, but I can't imagine finding* (pharmacist) *coverage for the store long enough to recover from back surgery.*

Other medical problems encountered in the last month: high blood pressure (158/110), high cholesterol, and triglycerides in the upper 500's (8.9 out of 10 on the cardiac risk scale). My blood pressure is down to 140/90 after beginning Verelan 240mg daily. I am also working on diet modification for my cholesterol and triglycerides. **BUT** *— what I must do is reduce stress. Last week I informed the church that from now on I will only be preaching and doing funerals. This announcement was made with the support of both leadership boards. So far the 40's are great!*

The congregation was very understanding when I explained the situation to them. It was interesting as I spoke to people after the service that day. For every person who expressed encouragement, there were several who recited a list of their own health problems. From my years of experience in the pharmacy listening to customers talk to one another, this should not have at all surprised me, but I was a bit surprised, nonetheless. The people tried to give me more privacy for a period of time after they learned about my health problems. Before too long, however, things were back to normal.

On January 15, 1995 the following was one of our annual church goals.

Appoint a committee to study the feasibility of hiring a part-time assistant Pastor to minister to WCBC. (Feasibility study due by June, 1995).
    1. Develop Job Description. 2. Develop Funding. 3. Recommend Time Line. 4. Present Complete plan for Consideration to:
       A. Elders
       B. Board
       C. Church
    5. Committee Structure:

Elders	*(2)*
Board	*(2)*
Pastorate	*(1)*
Other	*(2)*
Total	*(7)*

This "fifth initiative" was a combined effort of the Leadership Team. A feasibility committee was formed to begin work on this goal. I was a member of this committee. We did our work within a few months and presented our findings to the leadership boards. We concluded that it was feasible for WCBC to hire an Associate Pastor and still meet our financial obligations. By the fall the Leadership Team was ready to approach the congregation with a plan. Our church bulletin included the following announcement on September 24, 1995.

PRAYERFULLY CONSIDER—

PROPOSAL
    WCBC will hire an assistant pastor to assist the existing

pastorate in meeting the ever-growing spiritual needs of the church. It would be the goal to have this assistant pastor on staff as early as 1996 or late as 1997. The new assistant pastor's duties would include, but not be limited to, helping our current staff with visitation, discipling, teaching, preaching, weddings, funerals, counseling and attending church meetings.

There will be two church meetings to discuss this proposal (please attend one of the meetings) on Sunday, October 1 at 7:00 p.m. and on Thursday, October 5 at 7:00 p.m. The church will vote on this proposal on Sunday, October 8, 1995.

Following these two meetings we conducted a vote asking the congregation if they would support changing our all-volunteer philosophy of ministry. The church agreed to this change. Work continued and in March 1996, a committee was formed to begin the search for an Associate Pastor candidate. I was one of six people who served on this committee. The search progressed quickly. The main reason for this was because we knew whom the most likely candidate would be when the search began.

The likely candidate had attended WCBC for a while several years before. He had grown up in the Apostolic Christian Church in a neighboring community and had left the denomination to attend Bible College in Alaska several years before. Upon returning from Alaska he and his family of nine lived in Milford and attended our church. I found him to be a very personable man. He was witty and a great conversationalist. His testimony of new life in Christ was clear. In addition, he expressed a zeal for the Scripture and a determination to devote his life to Christian service. According to his testimony he had been well on his way to wealth in farming and side businesses when he received the Lord's calling to walk away from it all and enter Bible College. While living in Milford and attending WCBC he attended a Promise Keepers rally with a big group of our men and had fitted in beautifully.

When I learned that he eventually planned to enter vocational ministry I approached him about whether he would be interested in serving at WCBC as an assistant. My brother Ned and I even went to breakfast with him one morning to gauge his interest. He affirmed that he would have an interest in working at WCBC, but only after attending Dallas Theological Seminary. I wondered aloud how it would be possible for him to move his wife and seven children to Texas while he went to seminary. I was especially interested if his wife was agreeable to this. He invited me to their home one evening to discuss the plan with her. She flatly declared to me that if this was what he wanted it was fine with her and they soon moved to Dallas. While he was in Texas we had kept in touch with him, and his completing school was now coinciding with our Associate Pastor search. At the time I saw all of this as the work of the Sovereign Hand of God. How else could the right congregational mood, the right candidate, and the precise timing be coming together as they were? I was not alone in this conviction, either. At no time throughout the eighteen-month process do I recall a serious objection being raised about the goal we were pursuing.

There was another possible explanation, however, for what was happening. This explanation began to surface about one year after the fact. The explanation? "If something appears too good to be true, it probably is."

Chapter Fifty-Four

*"The best laid schemes o mice an men
Often go awry
And lea'e us nought but grief an pain,
For promis'd joy!"* Robert Burns.

The fourth distinct phase in the history of Wawasee Community Bible Church began in the fall of 1996 when we hired an Associate Pastor. Change is difficult. All change. The decision to depart from our all-volunteer philosophy of ministry had come about very slowly and deliberately within the WCBC leadership. Having made our decision we proceeded with the understanding that our congregation would also need time to become comfortable with the change. The period of time from the leadership's decision to the hiring of our first professional staff member was two full years.

The "picture" of the congregation of WCBC in 1996 was comprised of multiple "parts." These parts of the picture were different groups of people at different stages in life in different relationships with different levels of spiritual maturity with different needs. The general age of the congregation was young relative to the congregations of churches in our area. A five-week average attendance at our Sunday morning worship service in June and July of 1996 was three hundred and eight. For a rural church, this was a large congregation in our area.

For people who were believers and whose lives were going

smoothly, things were great at WCBC in 1996. The church services were excellent and the fellowship was sweet. This group was the largest part of the WCBC congregational picture and for them the change from an all-volunteer church was the most difficult. To this group the change was akin to "fixing what was not broken." In other parts of the picture, however, things had a different look. In the lives of these people there were needs beyond what family and friends could help with. Many of these people were in need of special teaching, of counseling, of intervention, and of encouragement beyond what were being provided through the church services and group ministries. These people saw the need for professional help, but they were the ones who generally could not afford to help make it happen. All parts of the picture needed weddings and funerals performed, but we were getting this work done with things as they were.

By 1996, there was a growing phenomenon that all parts of the congregational picture were contributing to, a phenomenon that was simply overloading our all-volunteer staff. This phenomenon was that requests were coming for us to meet with or to visit or to perform weddings or funerals for "my friend, my co-worker, my neighbor, or my relative." Because these requests were for people outside the congregation it was difficult for the general congregation to see the additional strain on our staff.

Early in the history of the church I was on record as believing we needed to plan for professional help in the Pastorate. I had strongly spoken on the issue before our second building project and had even presented the leadership with a document expressing my unwillingness to continue on long-term in my present capacity. I must not have meant what I said however, because I was still in the same capacity six years later. My reason for feeling as I did had never changed. There were simply not enough hours in a day to do what needed to be done in the congregation. Twice we had added additional Elders in an attempt to meet the needs. All of them were good, godly men, but only a few of them helped significantly in the critical areas of visitation and counseling. My brother Ned was an inexhaustible worker who probably put in even more hours than I did at the church. Our youth pastor also put in sacrificial numbers of hours. The volunteer staff was simply "maxed out." One of the final straws was in 1994 when I was found to have health problems. The leadership was then in agreement that we needed full time help and we began our presentations to the congregation.

The presentation of the need to change our all-volunteer system to the congregation was one of our leadership's finest hours. The boards were deliberate in their actions and sensitive to the congregation's feelings and input. Most importantly, though, they were of one mind. The result of the two-year process was a congregation that was prepared to accept a significant change and willing to support it.

Our Associate Pastor search committee (APC) interviewed three candidates. In our opinion, only one of them warranted serious consideration. We flew him from Texas to meet with the committee in June of 1996. The next day we introduced him to the congregation for their consideration. Tammy and I drove to Midway Airport in Chicago to pick up the Associate Pastor candidate. In that he and I had already become friends I volunteered for the job. It was soon apparent that he and his family were as excited at the prospect of working for WCBC as we were at the prospect of hiring him.

At this point I was certain that I would be working with him in the ministry. The prospect of having a full-time person to help visit, counsel, disciple, and evangelize had me excited to the point of giddiness, but I still wanted to be fair with him about the job he was about to take. I felt he needed to know ahead of time that while things were great within the ministries of WCBC, things within the leadership presented a potential for real problems in the future. I began with a history of WCBC. As we made the three-hour drive from Chicago to my home in Milford I described the congregation in fine detail. I explained our leadership structure and how it had evolved to its present form. I recounted the instances of conflict we had experienced, including the personalities involved on both sides, and how our structure had contributed to the conflict. I told him that as an Associate Pastor he would be required to serve as liaison between the leadership boards and sit as an ex-officio member of both of them. I wanted him to know in advance how difficult I had found this role to be. I felt it was critical that he understand how important it would be for him to be positive, even-handed, and of a peacemaker mind set in his dealings with both boards. Above all else, I wanted him to clearly understand how real the potential for division in the leadership was and how critical our role would be in keeping the peace. As we arrived home Tammy and I were both encouraged by the Associate Pastor candidates's willingness to work within the leadership structure he was soon to become a part of. He had not seemed to be alarmed by anything we had discussed and he assured us that he could be a positive force within WCBC.

The weekend at the church went very well. Several weeks later the candidate visited the church with his wife and children. The vote to hire him passed with overwhelming support. With this vote Wawasee Community Bible Church officially entered a new era. The move from Texas back to Indiana was soon accomplished. Many people from the congregation helped prepare the rental house they were going to live in for their arrival. The church gave them a "pounding" upon their arrival, where all participants contributed one pound of something for their household. By the end of August the family was moved in and with the coming of September the Associate Pastor began his work at WCBC.

On September 8, 1996 WCBC marked its ten-year anniversary. We called it "Founders Day Celebration." It was a big day. The auditorium was full for the morning program. I was asked to speak near the end. My assignment from the committee was to express to the church how I had felt when we began and how I felt about my future and the future of WCBC. It was easy to recall and express how I had felt in the beginning, how modest my expectations were and how I had learned over the years not to underestimate God or His plans. I found it much more difficult to describe how I was feeling about my future in ministry. Then one day I heard a song by Twila Paris that exactly described the feelings of my heart about my future. I can still remember exactly where I was when I first heard the song. It had touched me so much that day that I cried. Having finished my comments that morning I projected the words and played the song. I include the lyrics here for the record.

"I Will Listen" by Twila Paris

Hard as it seems
Standing in dreams
Where is the dreamer now
Wonder if I
Wanted to try
Would I remember how
I don't know the way to go from here
But I know that I have made my choice
And this is where I stand
Until He moves me on
And I will listen to His voice

This is the faith
Patience to wait
When there is nothing clear
Nothing to see
Still we believe
Jesus is very near
I cannot imagine what will come
But I've already made my choice
And this is where I stand
Until He moves me on
And I will listen to His voice

Could be that He is
Only waiting there to see
If I will learn to love the dreams
That He has dreamed for me
Can't imagine what the future holds
But I've already made my choice
And this is where I stand
Until He moves me on
And I will listen to His voice.

The hiring of our Associate Pastor ushered in a year of intense activity by the church leadership. I desperately wanted the new

Associate Pastor to be widely accepted and set out to make it happen. I took him with me wherever I went. I helped him wherever I could. We got along famously and I soon considered him one of my best friends. He was an easy man to talk to. In addition, he was interested in what was going on in my heart. I had already lived long enough by then to know what a rare quality this was for one to possess. It became a real comfort to have someone outside my family to whom I could express my frustrations and fears. I remembered thinking early on how beautifully God had provided for both the congregation and me in bringing the Associate Pastor into my life.

Soon after his arrival there was a meeting with the chairmen of both boards with the Associate Pastor to map out an early plan for his teaching activities. I was also present. He had a desire to teach a unit on the history of the Old Testament. This was scheduled. We wanted to conduct classes to teach the recently adopted Core Values of WCBC. These classes were scheduled at multiple times so that many people could attend. At this meeting the Associate Pastor was also scheduled to fill in for me several times on Sunday morning and to teach our large group adult Sunday school class. I left this meeting pleased that he would be getting opportunities to prove himself to the congregation in various capacities from the beginning.

When he was hired the Associate Pastor made it clear that he saw two immediate needs at WCBC. We hired him with the understanding that he would have our support in pursuing these needs. The first need he saw was that the congregation needed more small group opportunities during the Sunday school hour. We had already made some small steps in this direction. They had met with some opposition and murmuring, but the classes that were held had gone well. We knew there would still be opposition to expanding for more small groups but we were willing to pursue the concept. The second need the Associate Pastor saw was that we needed a second Sunday morning church service. He advocated strongly for this, pointing out the fact that many Sunday mornings our attendance was eighty percent of our auditorium capacity or more. He sited studies that demonstrated growth slows or stops when a building is this full. The argument for a second service was an uphill battle, but by the end of 1996 it was one of our church goals for 1997. I remember only one member at our combined leadership meetings being against it in the end.

In the last quarter of 1996 there were three leadership initiatives, all three of which enjoyed the support of both the Elders and Board of Directors. The first initiative concerned the five-acre parcel of land we had purchased in 1994. In the two years since all the buildings on the property were deemed worthless and torn down. Only the house remained. At first we thought we could use the house as a work project to raise money. We envisioned moving the house to the corner farthest from the church, remodeling it with volunteer labor, and selling it. The proceeds would then be used to reduce our church mortgage. With the arrival of the Associate Pastor another idea was conceived for the property. When he expressed an interest in the house for his home the leadership came up with the following property development plan. It was included in our church bulletin on October 27, 1996.

> *Proposal:*
>
> The Joint Board of Elder and Directors, to fulfill the goal for 1996 which is to move the house on the east property and use it as a work service project for WCBC, and because of an interest of the Associate Pastor and family in a permanent home base close to the church, we submit the following proposal.
>
> We propose that the church transfer 1 1/2 acres and the house to the Associate Pastor at the cost of $14,000 to be paid in annual installments of $2,000 over 7 year period. This $2,000 would be rolled into the Pastor compensation package for the 7 year period. If for any reason the Associate Pastor leaves WCBC before the 7 year period is over the balance would be due on the property. The Associate Pastor will pay for the house move and all additional cost incurred. Also the Associate Pastor will give WCBC first right of refusal to buy back the property should they decide to sell at some point in the future.
>
> The Joint Board feels this would be a good use of a portion of the property, and provide a good work service project for the church. This could be accomplished at no additional cost to the church.

The second leadership initiative dealt with the Future Planning Committee. The passing of time had brought about many changes in what the church needed from this committee. In the past it had served as a "think tank" for the leadership about facility needs and church logistics. By late 1996 there was a greatly reduced need for this activity. There were, however, growing needs to assist people in the congregation and community with life's day-to-day problems. The leadership encouraged the committee to reexamine its activities along these lines. The result was a new name and a new direction for what had been the Future Planning Committee. The new name was HELP CORE (Helping Eliminate Life's Problems. Christians Offering Reliable Service.) The new name described the new direction. Following their good leadership the committee began working immediately in a manner consistent with their new name.

The third leadership initiative in the fourth quarter of 1996 dealt with the church's need for improved communications. When we built our new auditorium we had under-budgeted for the sound system. The result was a system and wiring for the system that was inadequate from the beginning. This inadequacy was becoming more troublesome in direct proportion to the tasks we were adding to it. When the sound room operators told the leadership that the system was maxed out a study was done to establish what was needed to fix the problem. We also recognized we needed to upgrade our church computer. It was far too slow and its capacity far too small for the job we wanted it to do. As we researched the problem we also began talking about getting a projector for the auditorium. We had borrowed one from a neighboring high school about as much as we were welcome to. These searches resulted in the following proposals, as they appeared in the bulletin on December 8, 1996.

> *In order to better fulfill our Core Value of Excellence in all that we do, the leadership team (Elders & Board of Directors) of WCBC are recommending two proposals to the church as recommended by the Pastors. These proposals are designed to improve our corporate worship and communication in our sanctuary. Today, at the beginning of the worship service, the leadership will be asking the church to vote on the proposals. We are excited about this opportunity*

to move forward to improve our worship.

> *Proposal #1 -*
> *Improve the existing sound system in the sanctuary.*
>
> *Proposal #2 –*
> *Purchase new computers for the church and install video projection in the sanctuary.*
>
> *If you have any questions about these proposals, please speak with one of the Elders or one of the Board of Directors.*

Several weeks later the congregation, with 92% and 78% in favor, approved both proposals respectively. These proposals were approved with the understanding that we would undertake them only when we had the money. To help raise this money a committee was formed. They were very creative and in the next year held three all-church dinners. The first evening was an "Italian" theme, the second was a "Western" theme, and the third was an "Island" theme. These were all well attended and raised a good amount of money in addition to providing three great evenings of fellowship. It took nearly two years but eventually the money was raised and the projects were completed. The delay in the sound system, however, was to play a role in one of our congregation's saddest chapters.

1996 ended with a precious moment for me. On November 10th I had the privilege of baptizing my son Travis. He was one of eight who chose to be obedient in the matter of baptism that day. The auditorium was nearly full that morning. Travis strode to the microphone and gave his testimony with a calm like he was at home in our living room. I was so proud and so thankful. Of all the privileges a father can have, I cannot imagine any much more precious than to be able to baptize his children. I need to remind myself of this great blessing when I am tempted to hang my head and feel sorry for myself. It is one of many, many blessings I have enjoyed and continue to enjoy in my life.

Chapter Fifty-Five

To commemorate my parents' fiftieth wedding anniversary my bother Ted and his wife Sandy took Dad and Mom on a trip out west. My nephew David Speicher went along also. In addition to providing great company he was invaluable as a servant boy to the traveling party. Tammy and I flew to Montana in early September and joined them for a week in Glacier National Park. It was one of the most fun weeks I have enjoyed in my life. It provided us with a wealth of stories that we have not tired of retelling in the years since. On one of the first days in the park we stopped at the Logan Pass Visitor Center after driving up the breath-taking "Going to the Sun Road" to the continental divide. We were all amused by Dad's fear of heights, which had manifested itself in his insistence on sitting on the "mountain side" of the car during the drive up to the Visitor Center. Across the road from the Visitor Center was a short, but spectacular hike to the "Garden Wall." I had done the hike with Tammy and our children several years before and I was sure my exuberance for the hike would overcome Dad's fear of heights. I was sure that once he saw the majesty of the mountains and valley around the bend that he would continue on the hike. We all assured him that he would be safe and that he would be free to turn back at any time. So off we all went, excited as a bunch of children on Christmas morning. On our way we passed very close to some beautiful White Mountain Goats. Ted, David, and I were leading the way. As we rounded a corner, before us was a narrow trail that had a sheer mountain on the right side and a sheer cliff on the left. The sight before us was stunningly beautiful. When we stopped to enjoy the moment, we suddenly heard an emphatic "Nope!" from Dad, who had just caught up with us. With this exclamation, he turned around instantly and headed back to the Visitor Center. The hike was over for Dad. Case closed.

In many ways this little story is how I remember 1997 at Wawasee Community Bible Church: begun with widespread exuberance about what the Holy Spirit was accomplishing in the congregation, aware of the potential for some of the leadership to head in a different direction than the group, but not giving the possibility much attention, and ending with an abrupt dividing of the leadership that should have been foreseen but was not. The profound difference is that I continue to laugh at the Glacier National Park story years later and I continue to mourn the Wawasee Community Bible Church story years later.

As 1997 rolled around we were a church that was, as the saying goes, "On a roll." Our Sunday morning worship attendance had grown throughout the last quarter of 1996. A five-week average attendance in January and February of 1997 was three hundred and eighty one. We were clearly in the honeymoon stage with our new Associate Pastor, a honeymoon period that was destined to end very soon. The leadership was united as we made plans to institute a second Sunday morning worship service. We were so optimistic about our future that a group was formed from our leadership boards to formulate a plan for future expansion. Even with conservative projections we were facing a space shortage in the near future. While we were in no position financially to undertake an expansion of our facilities, our leadership agreed that it was important we place a plan before the congregation. The thinking in this was two-fold. It was a real need for the near future and, secondly, the sooner the congregation had a plan in front of them the sooner they would be likely to "buy into" the plan. The committee did their research, the leadership approved their plan, and it was presented to the congregation in the spring. It was also included in our church bulletin. I include it here because it gives good insight into the mindset and expectations of the leadership.

WAWASEE COMMUNITY BIBLE CHURCH
VISION STATEMENT
SPRING 1997

VISION: *The church will provide adequate Sunday School classroom space and multi-purpose activity space to provide for a growing ministry.*

In order to achieve this vision the following concerns need to be addressed:
1. *The Sunday School facility is currently overcrowded.*
2. *Our Sunday School is understaffed.*
3. *Additional activity areas are needed for youth and young adults.*

Over the past several years WCBC has continued to experience growth. The growth rate has been approximately 15% per year. If for the next 7 years WCBC would sustain a 5% per year growth (minimal) the following will be needed:

1. *12 - 15 additional Sunday School classrooms.*
2. *Activity / multi-purpose area for youth and young adults: Youth activities, AWANA, basketball/volleyball, aerobics, banquets, receptions.*
3. *Additional trained teachers that are called to teach Christianity to our youth.*

TIME LINE: The vision TIME LINE is to have trained and willing staff in place, the additional educational facility and the multi-purpose areas by 1999.

In order to implement this new step to provide for our growth the following conditions need to be met:
1. *Additional teachers are called to teach and are trained.*
2. *$80,000 are donated over and above our regular budget to prepare to implement the vision.*
3. *The total church debt is reduced.*

The Leadership Team of WCBC (Elders, Board of Directors,

Pastors) is recommending this vision to the church to be proactive in planning for the future.

In March of 1997 we began our second Sunday morning service. In planning for it we had overcome objection from two critical support ministries, the sound people and the music people. They ultimately agreed to give it a try and the second service began on a three to six month trial basis. We held one of the worship services before the Sunday school hour and one of them after it. The services were identical in their structure and content. I went along with the second service because I trusted the men in our leadership who had administrative expertise. I preferred preaching to one full house over preaching twice to two half full houses, but I was convinced the change was necessary to avoid stifling growth. Four things became apparent to me very soon after we began the second service. First, the total increase in attendance did not come as we had anticipated. Secondly, church now had a very different "feel." This was very unsettling. The Associate Pastor encouraged me, saying this change would take some time to get used to. Thirdly, I began to hear grumbling from our core congregation from the onset: Church did not "feel" the same. It did not "sound" the same. People did not "see each other" anymore. Why did the leadership "fix what was not broken?" The Associate Pastor also encouraged me to be patient about this, contending the core group would become accepting when they saw the benefits of the change. The fourth thing that became apparent with the beginning of the second service was that the honeymoon period between some of the leadership and the Associate Pastor was over. In October of 1997, the combined leadership boards evaluated the second service and extended it indefinitely. In July and August our five-week average attendance was three hundred and twenty seven.

Under the leadership of the Associate Pastor, the Elders launched two initiatives in the summer of 1997. The first was to require teacher training for Sunday school teachers in the coming year. All people wanting to teach were required to complete a class on the "MILK" Bible study book. It was a very simple study on the foundational truths of the Christian faith. Classes were offered many different times to accommodate as many schedules as possible. I thought this teacher training was a great idea. The long-term plan was for annual teacher training in more advanced topics. To my shock and dismay we received considerable opposition to this requirement. Many teachers elected to quit teaching rather than take the class. More disturbing than this, though, was the fact that considerable criticism of the plan was traced back to some members of the Board of Directors and their wives. The Elders stood their ground and by the fall there were enough teachers to staff all classes.

The second Elder initiative was to expand the number of adult small group Sunday school classes. On July 13th there was even a bulletin announcement encouraging people to become involved in one of these classes. I was not involved in this particular decision, but I was aware that there were those in the congregation who wanted additional small group Sunday School choices and was therefore not opposed to the idea. I knew, however, that the decision would be met with criticism. I was not to be disappointed in this. The criticism came as expected and, tragically, some of it was again traced back to some present and former members of the Board of Directors and their families. People speaking for "some people" or "they" usually conveyed this criticism to the Elders. It usually was accompanied with the insinuations that the Elders were out of touch with the congregation and that the Elders had no leadership skills or administrative expertise. As time passed, more and more criticism was fired directly at the Associate Pastor, that he was undisciplined, that he was trying to radically change the church, that he was lazy, and that he was only interested in serving certain segments of the congregation. The Associate Pastor simply framed the problem as being a lack of submission to church leadership and labeled it sin. Most of the Elders agreed. By the summer of 1997 the pressure was clearly building within the leadership of Wawasee Community Bible Church. The Elders were becoming more pro-active in the leadership of the church, a role that was clearly theirs according to Scripture. I saw this uneasiness in the leadership as a part of the change we were going through. I was confident that the congregation and the rest of the Leadership Team would become accustomed to it, although I was greatly troubled by the tone and the degree and the on-going nature of the criticism.

There is one more critical piece of the WCBC picture in the

summer of 1997. My brother Ned took a new job as a Superintendent of Schools and moved to Lapel, Indiana, about one hundred miles away. This created an enormous power vacuum in the day-to-day operation of the church, one that the Associate Pastor and the Elders began to assume. Ned had planned to continue his activities in the church when he moved, but it soon became apparent that the distance was going to be too great for him to remain involved at his previous level of activity. He made trip after trip for meeting after meeting, though, trying as only he could to keep up. Sad for Ned, though, was the fact that many people in the church would only be "led" by him and they let it be known. In addition, his supporters who felt they could speak for him in his absence often did him a disservice. Within one year of moving Ned became convinced that the distance was too great for him to continue and he resigned his offices in the church. To this day I have not known a harder worker than Ned. I have never worked with anyone who was a more gifted administrator. People were drawn to his leadership and blessed by his ministry and he led us to our apex in 1997. To this day there are still many in the congregation who long for the days when he was their leader.

I became close friends with the Associate Pastor soon after his arrival. The more the criticism of him increased the more I worked to defend him to his critics. The more his critics said he did not fit in, the more I tried to take him places with me so that they could get to know him. When his wife asked me to speak to him about being home more, I interceded. I tried to help in any way I could. I knew he had significant support within the Elder Board and in some segments of the congregation and I knew if he left that there would be trouble in the church. I also genuinely liked the man and enjoyed being with him. By the end of his first year, I felt there were four areas of his job that he could work on. The first area was visitation. I had hoped he would help me more with this than he had. Part of the problem was mine, though, because I hated to ask him to cover for me. I kept hoping he would notice and offer to help more. The second area was his hours spent at the church. We were receiving complaints that he was not in his office enough and that when he was there he was not available to be seen at times. I had difficulty locating him often enough that I agreed this was an area for improvement. Another area of concern for me was that I had hoped

A Lifetime of Church

he would try harder to work with the Board of Directors and with my brother Ned than he did. I had admonished him in detail about how important I considered this to be before he took the job. As far as I was able to determine, he had ignored my advice on this issue. I felt the building tension within the leadership could still be lowered if he would heed my advice, but he did not seem inclined to do so. The final area of concern for me was doctrinal. I had hoped the Associate Pastor would be a partner with me in evangelism. I had also hoped he would be more active in outreach and in following up with people who left the church. When I first expressed these two concerns to him, I distinctly remember his response and my surprise upon hearing it. He simple told me "God will bring who He wants and He will take who he wants." This response was reflective of his strong Calvinistic view of God's working in the lives of men. While I also believed strongly in the sovereignty of God, I believed the scriptural commands instructing me to actively seek those who are lost and those who are straying. Despite these concerns, I was determined to make it work. He was the only person outside of my immediate family who consistently sought to know my inner thoughts and feelings. In time I came to confide things to him that I would have otherwise only spoken to Tammy about. With Ned moved away and able to do less and less, I had nowhere else to turn. In my mind, the ministry of the Associate Pastor simply had to succeed.

Three more significant things took place in the summer of 1997. One of them was somewhat sad and the other two were good. In August of 1997 my Grandpa Theo Beer died. He died four months before his one-hundredth birthday. I was one of many who expected him to live to one hundred and beyond. He had been in slowly declining health for several years, but went down rapidly after falling down once. My mother had committed herself to his care many years before and she was faithful in this to the end. Grandpa Theo was my primary authority figure from my earliest memories until my mid-thirties. It would be difficult to overstate how important it was to me to have his approval throughout these years. His influence in my life was profound. Of his many attributes, three shine brighter as the years go by. One was his ability to converse with people. He had an amazing ability to remember people's names and some facts about them. He seemed to be able to get anyone to open up and speak with him. He would ask them questions about themselves and was genuinely interested in what they had to say. A second attribute of his that I admired was his ability to not hold grudges. These two attributes were undoubtedly connected to the third attribute that I greatly admired — His love for God. In my life I have known only two other people who matched Grandpa Theo Beer's preoccupation with seeing everything as God would see it. My Grandma Naoma Beer was one of these two. I am sure it hurt Grandpa Theo when I left the Apostolic Christian Church denomination, but he never made me feel it. On the contrary, he was remarkably encouraging of my ministry at Wawasee Community Bible Church. He listened to tapes of nearly every sermon I preached. When we held services that did not conflict with AC services, he sometimes attended. The people loved him and it was obvious he was proud to be my Grandpa. I did not cry when he died. It just seemed to be a beautiful thing that he went to be with the Lord. The Milford AC Elder did a pretty good job at his funeral and I remember how proud I felt to be a part of his family. If I am able to positively influence my children and grandchildren a fraction as much as he and Grandma Naoma positively influenced me, I will feel my life was a success.

The first of the two other good things that took place in the summer of 1997 was our high school youth group taking a mission trip to Mexico. My daughter Traci was one of a group of about thirty youth and sponsors who went. The week was a profound spiritual experience for them. Their leaders had prepared them weekly for months in advance and the net result of the experience was a significant jump forward in their spiritual maturity.

The final significant event of the summer was the instituting of a program for the college and high school young people. Some parents asked the Associate Pastor to create something and he responded. Once a week that summer we had a large group of young people who met for music, devotions, and fellowship. Both of my daughters attended and enjoyed the sessions. To help with the music the Associate Pastor rented two large tower speakers each week. After some weeks of this the owner of the speakers offered to sell them to the church. The Board of Directors consented and purchased them. There was some conflict about the summer youth program that the Associate Pastor could have prevented, but did not. The chairman of the sound committee meticulously maintained the sound room of the church. After the church was burglarized twice, the sound room was made secure with an alarm and a lock. There were only a few people who had access to the area. When the summer youth program began the Associate Pastor allowed the youth into the sound room for whatever equipment was needed. The problem arose when he did not supervise them and the room was left a mess week after week. One evening the sound chairman came in when the kids were in the room and he expressed his displeasure over what was happening. He told them how frustrating it was to come on Sunday morning and not have the equipment he needed. This man was already frustrated by being short of help and by the extra Sunday service. He had continued to serve sacrificially despite frustration, despite an inadequate system, and despite multiple personal health problems. The sad result of this confrontation was that some of the Elders were upset with the sound chairman rather than the Associate Pastor for not supervising the young people. This unfortunate incident left some simmering resentment that would resurface later in a far more dramatic manner. It was only the intervention of more level heads that kept us from losing our sound chairman in the summer of 1997.

The tension among the leaders of Wawasee Community Bible Church rose dramatically over an incident that took place in the mid-fall of 1997. I distinctly remember where I was and what I was doing when I learned about it. I also remember the "chill" in my stomach. At issue were some minutes of meeting of the HELP CORE Committee that were highly critical of the Associate Pastor's job performance. I knew the instant I saw the notes that there would be trouble. The Elders were furious. They were even more furious when they interviewed the people present at the committee meeting and learned that no such discussion about the Associate Pastor even took place. I had to argue vigorously to get the interviews with those present and a revision of the notes of the meeting instead of the Elders' original idea to disband the HELP CORE Committee.

On the heels of this, the Associate Pastor asked the Elders for their support in demanding that the computer disc containing the church bulletin be left at the church each week in case revisions needed to be made just prior to printing. I agreed that this was what needed to happen, but I knew there would be a fight if it were demanded of the woman doing the bulletin. This woman had sacrificially done the bulletin each week for the previous ten years and I wanted to make the change gently. I persuaded the Elders to allow my brother Ned to speak to her about it. They agreed in the end, but they felt I was allowing her to not be submissive to church leadership. The disc was turned in, but it came with the woman's resignation.

As 1997 came to a close the Associate Pastor and most of the Elders were convinced that the most serious issue before them was that the leadership structure of WCBC — a Board of Directors and a Board of Elders of equal authority — was not Biblical. They were convinced, furthermore, that there was sin within some of the leadership and within some of the congregation that needed to be dealt with. The sin in view was the refusal to be submissive to church leadership. All of the leadership conflicts of the previous eleven years were now called into remembrance to support their determination to make a stand. I now began to find myself out of favor with some the Elders for arguing for restraint in the recent conflicts. I even began to hear through back door channels that I was unwilling to "confront sin." At this point in the history of the church I was also convinced we needed to change our leadership structure. I was not opposed to two leadership boards, but I wanted them to be a Board of Elders and a Board of Deacons, to reflect Biblical authority and Biblical roles. I was convinced such a change, while correct, could not be made quickly. I believed it would require patience and a lot of education of the congregation. I was also aware that some members of the Board of Directors would fiercely resist change. At the top of my list of priorities was protecting the "sheep" in the congregation who needed our leadership and who would be most harmed by unnecessary conflict among us. The extremes of both boards, however, were determined to stand their ground. In a sense, the argument before us began to be between the "Power of Tradition" and the Word of Scripture. The Board of Directors maintained they were acting according to the church by-laws and according to how we had set up our church government. The Elders maintained that it did not matter that we had always done it the way we were doing it, because the way we were doing it was not Biblical. In this dispute the Elders were right and I had no choice but to side with the Scripture. What bothered me about the whole argument was that I saw it as not being about right and wrong as much as it was about power. I felt if it was about anything other than power that there would be some love and forbearance being shown by both sides. I saw little of either and it broke my heart.

As 1997 came to an end, Wawasee Community Bible Church was sitting on a powder keg. All we needed was a spark and we would have real trouble. The spark came from a most unexpected source. Several months after the church bought the tower speakers for the summer youth program, the Associate Pastor had an idea about how they could be used in the church auditorium on Sunday mornings. With no fix for the sound system coming soon, the Associate Pastor suggested we use the tower speakers to augment the system. On one evening when the leadership boards were meeting he arranged a demonstration of the speakers. As I read scripture from the pulpit microphone he showed the Board of Directors how much the speakers helped the sound in the auditorium and then demonstrated them for the Elders. Both leadership boards were impressed by how they increased the sound and it was decided that they should be used until the sound system upgrade could be done. For a while the speakers were used during the services, then they were not. I never heard much input from the congregation about them, good or bad. By late December, however, their non-use was an issue for the Associate Pastor, and because it was an issue for him it became an issue to the Elders also. They saw this as another instance where people were refusing to submit to church leadership. When I saw that a confrontation was brewing I called the sound chairman to ask why the speakers were not being used. He bluntly informed me they the tower speakers were the Associate Pastor's project and that he was not going to use them anymore. I was taken aback by the finality of his words and simply asked "So that's the end of the story?" He said, "Yes." This man and his extended family were a founding family in the church and as hard working and dedicated to the church as any family we had. As I mentioned earlier, this man was stretched to the limit by physical, emotional, and professional problems. Despite this, he had continued to serve. He and his family felt the Associate Pastor had behaved irresponsibly in allowing the youth unsupervised access to the sound room in the past. They were also hurt that the Elders had taken the Associate Pastor's side in the dispute. This family was clearly of the opinion that the sound room fell under the authority of the Board of Directors and was therefore none of the Elders' business.

It is my opinion that by this time the Elders had taken all they were going to take and they were looking for a place to take a stand. At the next Elder meeting I saw they were determined to stand up to this refusal to use the speakers. As the discussion progressed I knew two things were going to happen. First, the Elders were going to demand that the speakers be used. Secondly, I knew when this demand was made there would be trouble. The soundman would surely resign and his family would be furious. I believed the only hope for a peaceful resolution of this was to have both boards request the speakers be used. So while the discussion was going on I walked into the next room and typed the following on a piece of paper. The actual letter has been lost, but I am confident this is nearly identical to the original.

> *Dear (*Sound Chairman*):*
> *We are in agreement that the sound is better in the auditorium using the auxiliary speakers. We therefore ask that you continue to use them until the sound room upgrade can be done. Thank you for your sacrificial service to WCBC.*

With this in hand I went back to the Elder meeting and presented it to them with the suggestion that all members of the two leadership boards sign it. I offered to deliver the letter and to speak to the man about it. Some of the Elders still preferred to send a delegation to speak to him instead, but ultimately they agreed to my suggestion. One of the Elders volunteered to take the letter around the next day and obtain signatures from all members of both leadership boards. I made an appointment to go the man's home the next evening. As we spoke on the phone he and I each expressed regret for the terse tone of our previous conversation. There was a complicating factor in the logistics of this meeting, however. I was set to leave with my family to spend the Christmas week in Colorado skiing. In order to fit the meeting in with the sound chairman I needed to delay our departure. Tammy agreed to this, but did so reluctantly. Further complicating this meeting was the fact that I was late getting out of work that night. As I rushed from work to the man's home I remembered that I needed to pick up the signed letter at one of our Elder's homes. I knew this stop would only delay me more so I made the decision to go directly to the sound chairman's home for the meeting. I decided I would tell him about the letter and someone else could get it to him later. This impulsive decision would prove to be a very costly one for me and one that would come back and haunt me later. Years later I still wish I could turn back the clock and make this additional stop that frantic evening. I cannot do this, of course, so I am left to take comfort in the knowledge that the decision was made with no malice of forethought or improper motives.

The sound chairman and I had a very cordial and informative meeting. He began by telling me that his life would be so much easier if he gave up the sound room chairmanship, but that he was continuing because he wanted to serve and he felt the church needed him. I assured him that he was greatly appreciated, but that we needed to break the impasse about the auxiliary speakers. I told him that the leadership was unanimously on record asking him to use them until the entire system could be upgraded. He repeated his refusal to use them, but this time he gave me a detailed explanation about why he would not use them. I learned it was not that he simply was refusing to use the speakers, but that he could not use them and use all the other sound equipment at the same time. There was simply not enough power in the system for everything. His explanation made sense to me. When I asked him why he had not told anyone this before he said he had told some people about it, but that the leaders who were upset with him had never asked. When I asked if he would meet with the leaders and explain to them what he had explained to me, he agreed. As I left I thanked him and told him someone would contact him after Christmas to set up the meeting.

I left the meeting greatly relieved. I was overjoyed that the meeting had gone so well. I was sure that the other leaders would be satisfied when they heard his reasoning. I was beyond relieved that the crisis had been averted. As I drove home I saw that the Associate Pastor was at the church, so I stopped and reported to him about the meeting. I asked him if he would take responsibility to set up the meeting the sound chairman and I had agreed to and he said he would. He then specifically asked me if I gave the man the letter. I said I had not done so and explained why. I added that the sound chairman knew that the leadership had unanimously gone on the record with their desire he use the speakers. He seemed satisfied and I left for home. When I got there we all hopped in the Suburban and left for Colorado.

The week in Colorado was a preview of coming attractions for me. We had no sooner arrived in Breckenridge to ski when I got sick. For two days I had vomiting, high fever, and diarrhea. I was just beginning to feel normal about the time we left to return to Indiana. I was greatly discouraged by this. I had planned for this week for six months. During those months I would force myself to think about the vacation whenever I became discouraged. Last minute complications at work had nearly ruined the plans. When we finally left I had felt free as a bird, like I had been released from prison. Now this! As we approached home I was feeling very sorry for myself and I was dreading returning to work and church. The reality of what I encountered upon my return was far worse than what my heart was innocently feeling.

As I was sitting at my desk opening the mail at work the first day after our return, a man from the church walked in and told me some startling news. The sound chairman had resigned. There had been an ugly confrontation between an Elder and the sound chairman's father. The sound chairman and his extended family were finished at Wawasee Community Bible Church. This news shocked me as much as anything has ever shocked me. I called the family to see if we could talk and was informed that they felt I had become like "the Elder" of the Milford Apostolic Christian Church in my leadership at WCBC. I do not know how I filled prescriptions that day, but somehow I did. As the day wore on I began to learn what had happened after I left for Colorado. One of our Elders, whom I considered one of my two closest friends outside my family, was told by the Associate Pastor that I had not delivered the letter signed by both leadership boards to the sound chairman. I do not know if the Associate Pastor explained my reasons for not doing so to the Elder, or if he explained that I had conveyed the contents of the

A Lifetime of Church

letter to the sound chairman, but I seriously doubt he did. Upon learning this from the Associate Pastor, the Elder called the sound chairman that same night and informed him that the letter existed and that it should have been delivered by me, but was not. The result of this conversation was that the sound chairman resigned from the sound team, effective immediately. Both men later said that the other had been unreasonable during their phone conversation. The Elder next called the sound chairman's father, hoping to reason with him and enlist his help. By all accounts this call was a disaster. Both men maintained the other was accusatory and rude. This was the last straw for the sound chairman and his extended family. They were finished with WCBC.

Later in the awful first day back from Colorado I spoke to the Associate Pastor. He confirmed to me the essence of what I had been told about the crisis by others. A full week had passed since the blow-up and I asked him what he had done about it. It made me angry when he simply replied, "Nothing." When I expressed my displeasure he calmly replied "I believe it is best to let people have some time to calm down in situations like this." I strongly disagreed with this approach and told him so. I viewed this approach as nothing more than laziness on his part, or worse yet, as "good riddance" to the sound chairman and his extended family. I immediately began to seek a resolution of the crisis. After getting home from work I called my Elder friend at the center of it all to get his side of the story. He confirmed the essence of what I was hearing, but differed on who had been rude and unreasonable during the two phone calls. I asked him why he had made the follow-up phone call the night I met with the sound chairman. He said he had made the call when he learned I had not delivered the letter. He explained that he viewed this omission on my part as one of a number of times recently that the Elders' wishes had not been followed by others and me. He added that he felt it was important the man knew there was a letter and that all the leaders had signed it. I asked if the Associate Pastor had told him what I had learned from the sound chairman and what arrangements I had made as a result of our meeting. I do not remember any reply to this. He wanted me to understand that he saw this whole situation as a simple case of people not being submissive to church leadership. He added, "You said you do not compromise the

Scripture, Tom. This time you are compromising." These words really stung and I have never forgotten them. If all my Elder friend knew was that I did not deliver the letter — and I strongly suspect this is all the Associate Pastor told him — then his words were true. I knew my heart, though. I also knew what I had done and why I had done it. I had gone to the sound chairman's house that night hating what I was about to do, but fully intending to carry out the Elders' wishes. When I learned there was good reason for the sound chairman's behavior, I was elated to change roles to become what I saw as being a peacemaker. Being at peace with myself, though, did not change the fact that I was devastated emotionally. This was one of the very worst days in my entire life.

The next day was Sunday. I preached, but my heart was far from settled. The tower speakers were prominently placed and in use, but I thought the sound was as strained as my nerves. That afternoon three of the leadership met with the sound chairman and some of his family. It was painful to hear what they had to say. They felt the speakers were clearly a symptom of a much bigger problem. They were adamant that the Elders were intruding into an area where they had no authority, that the Associate Pastor was doing a pathetic job, and that I was being led astray by him. I was determined to listen to everything both sides wished to say, but this meeting strained my resolve. By the end of the meeting, however, the words were less harsh and the anger seemed to be considerably less. I left the meeting with a ray of hope, although I had no rational basis for it.

At that time in the history of Wawasee Community Bible Church we had an Administrative Advisory Team (AAT) made up of representatives from the Board of Directors, the Board of Elders, and the Pastors. Among other things, their job was to prepare the agendas for the monthly meetings. After the conflict earlier in the year between the sound chairman and some of the youth and the Associate Pastor, the AAT had met with the sound chairman to hear his ideas for avoiding this sort of conflict in the future. The members of the AAT then took the information from this meeting back to the two Boards. This had worked well at that time. After some meetings with the injured parties in our present conflict had not made much progress, I suggested that the AAT meet and formulate some ideas for resolving the conflict and preventing such conflict in the future to present at the February Board meetings. Which AAT, though? We were exactly in the middle of the annual changeover in our leadership. The out-going AAT was still officially the AAT, but by the February meetings the new AAT would be in charge. I decided to have the meeting with the new AAT because they were the ones who would have to present the ideas and deal with Leadership Team. All the men on the new AAT were currently on the leadership boards. They would just be assuming new roles in a week or two. This seemed like the simpler and more reasonable course to take. The Associate Pastor was not a member of the AAT, but because he was at the center of the present conflict I invited him to attend the meeting. He agreed, but later the same day he called and asked if I thought the meeting would really do any good. This struck me as strange, but I explained my view that the meeting would help the leadership boards intelligently address the issue at their February meetings. He agreed to come. On our way to the meeting that night the Associate Pastor said two things that absolutely floored me. At one point in our conversation I asked rhetorically "What is the answer going to be to all this conflict?" He replied, simply, "Maybe the answer is a new church." I could not believe what I had just heard. He must have sensed that this shocked me because he added, "We have two distinct groups that are not meshing, Tom." Later he said a second shocking thing. "I think we will lose some Elders over this." I remember thinking "Who is he talking to? How is it that I have never heard this before?" This was all like a horrible nightmare to me, a nightmare that I was awake for. In mid-January, 1998, though, my nightmare had just begun. Looking back, I honestly do not know how I maintained my sanity during the first eight months of the year. I know that sleep became a precious and elusive thing. It was only with great restraint that I did not resort to sleep aids every night.

Several days after the AAT meeting, the Associate Pastor called me and wanted me to come to an Elder meeting. It was an unscheduled meeting, so I assumed it would be about the on-going conflict. I told him I would be there after my son Travis' eighth grade basketball game. When I arrived at the meeting I saw that everyone was looking unusually grim. As I took a seat it was clear that all eyes were on me. The Associate Pastor took the lead and asked me

"We need to know, Tom. Will you be in submission to the Elders?" I realized at this point that the meeting was about me. I was taken aback by the question, but I replied, "Yes. Why do you ask?" They went on to explain that they felt I had gone against their wishes a number of times, most recently in the matters of the letter to the sound chairman and the "secret" meeting of the AAT. I maintained my composure and patiently explained what I had done in the matter of the letter and why I had done it. Most of the men seemed to accept my explanation. I added that in my mind there was nothing "secret" about the AAT meeting and that we had held many such meetings in the past without notifying the members of the leadership boards. More of the Elders were upset about the "secret" AAT meeting than about the letter to the sound chairman. It was clear to me at this point that the Associate Pastor had misrepresented me to them. As the conversation continued, it became painfully clear to me that the Associate Pastor had taken other private concerns I had shared with him from my heart as friend to friend and had used them against me. I was numb. Even years later, it is not possible for me to describe how it felt to first realize that I had been betrayed by a trusted friend. The strange combination of the emotions of fury and shock and sorrow and embarrassment felt like a suffocating weight on my chest. I could not deny the concerns I had expressed to him. I could only tell the Elders that they were all things I had wondered aloud about to a trusted friend in confidence, things I would never have said in open meetings.

The conversation eventually turned from me to another leader, one who was not present at the meeting. For a while I listened as accusation after accusation was made about him and offense after offense was recounted. My mind soon cleared and I confronted the situation. I demanded of them, "How many of you have confronted this man according to the Scripture?" After a moment of uneasy silence, one man said he had confronted him about some offenses in the past. I was present at this particular confrontation. It had taken place many years before and I remembered that the issues were agreed to be resolved and forgiveness was granted at that time. I told the man that I did not think it was right for him to bring the matter up again when they had agreed to put it behind them. He disagreed, but some of the Elders agreed with me. The other Elders reluctantly admitted that they had not confronted the man according to Scripture and I reminded them, "Then you have no right to be saying the things you are saying." At this point the Associate Pastor and I had to leave the meeting to meet with the Board of Directors. As we were leaving I heard some of the Elders making plans to confront the leader who was not present according to Scripture. To my knowledge, they never did.

I had nothing to say to the Associate Pastor as we walked across the building to join the other meeting. I was in a state of shock. Once at the Board of Directors meeting, I was again asked to explain what had happened with the sound chairman and to explain about the "secret" AAT meeting. I did this, patiently and calmly. Like in the previous group, though, more people were upset about the "secret" AAT meeting than the other issue. This greatly puzzled me. We had never announced AAT meetings in the past. We simply held them when they were needed. There had never been a word of criticism that had come to my attention before. In my mind there was only one reasonable explanation about why there was now an outcry about a "secret" AAT meeting. The Associate Pastor had to have misrepresented the AAT meeting and its conception to the other leaders. As this realization was sinking in, my mind came back to the meeting that was in progress. People around the table were angry and arguing about things that seemed so silly to me. It felt like my brain was about to explode, when suddenly I lost control. I slammed my fist on the table and shouted "I can't take this anymore! We have a half million dollar debt and people are dying and going to hell every minute and here we are, threatening to blow this church apart arguing about things that don't matter a bit for eternity!" By the end of this outburst I was in tears and left the room. A few minutes later I went back and said "I have to go home and prepare a sermon for Sunday."

As I walked out of the church I was sobbing. It was as if my world had come crashing down around me in a matter of hours. The thought of the congregation splitting up over a power struggle in the leadership was inconceivable to me. My mind was like a stew as I tried to comprehend how we had come from a relative calm to this crisis so quickly. One of the men from the Board of Directors followed me out and called to me. "You can't leave like this, Tom.

Let's talk," he said. On this night this man's kindness was a Godsend to me. As we talked, his gentle manner calmed me down. His words encouraged me. By the time I left I was back in a normal state of mind. Before going home, I stopped at the pharmacy and delivered some medicine. I took it to a man who was in very poor health, a man whom I had recently had the privilege of leading to Jesus Christ. It was good I made this delivery on this night. It helped me refocus my mind on the purpose we had for founding Wawasee Community Bible Church in the first place. When I got home Tammy did not even notice that I had been crying. She did not ask me about the meeting and I did not offer anything about it. I sat clicking through the TV stations long after everyone else was in bed, but it was mindless clicking. My mind was consumed with concern for the future of WCBC. The sun came up the next morning, but it did not follow much sleep.

Chapter Fifty-Six

There is an old saying in the medical community that "The light burns brightest before it goes out." It refers to the fact that many elderly people seem to have a burst of life prior to dying. In the congregation of Wawasee Community Bible Church the light was burning very brightly in January 1998. A five-week average attendance in January and February was three hundred and ninety five in the Sunday morning worship service. On January 18th seventeen people gave their testimonies and were baptized. It was the largest one-day group we ever had. There were five hundred and ninety five people in attendance that day. On the weekend of January 23rd we conducted a seminar on spiritual gifts that was well attended, as the one the previous fall had been. The light at WCBC was not going to go out, but it was about to dim. In January we adopted church goals for 1998 that demonstrated we were a congregation set to tackle the future. I include them here.

WAWASEE COMMUNITY BIBLE CHURCH
RECOMMENDED GOALS FOR 1998
VISION: Reaching the community for Jesus Christ

1. Provide opportunities for all WCBC attendees to complete Network training, to identify and understand their spiritual gifts.
2. Begin an additional non-Sunday Morning Service to serve the

following purposes:
> Provide an opportunity for inexperienced people to use their gifts.
> Provide a casual worship time.
> Provide more opportunities for testimonies and corporate prayer.
> Provide a "family night" atmosphere to include a basic, inexpensive meal.

3. Have all members of the WCBC Leadership Team and spouses attend a leadership training conference at Willow Creek Church.
4. Provide times of coordinated topical teaching in our sermons and Sunday School Classes, with materials provided to facilitate corresponding family devotions.
5. Create a WCBC mentoring program and begin to establish mentoring relationships within the church body.
6. Define a WCBC Youth Pastor position and research issues pertinent to the future hiring of a Youth Pastor.
7. Provide the leadership of the MOPS and AWANA groups with the needed support to become leading outreach tools of WCBC.
8. In order to maintain our physical plant and be good stewards of our provided financial resources, we will:
> Develop a long-range capital improvements plan.
> Computerize our church accounting.
> Continue to accelerate our mortgage reduction when all budgets are fully funded.
> Complete the ready rooms in the church auditorium.
> Repair and resurface asphalt parking lot.

As these goals were adopted, very few people in the congregation had any idea that there was a crisis in the leadership of the church. Most of the people would not have believed it if we had told them. There were, however, those who were hearing the thunder of the approaching storm, a storm that would soon be upon us. In I Corinthians 3 the Apostle Paul admonished the congregation at Corinth for some sin that many of them were taking part in. In verses 1 through 4 he wrote *Brothers, I could not address you as spiritual but as worldly — mere infants in Christ. I gave you milk, not solid food, for you were not yet ready for it. Indeed, you are still not ready. You are still worldly. For since there is jealousy and quarreling among you, are you not worldly? Are you not acting like mere men? For when one says, "I follow Paul," and another, "I follow Apollos," are you not mere men?* In January 1998, this is exactly what was beginning to be seen at WCBC. It was already being actively seen within the leadership. Here the people were lining up behind one of two leaders, one of whom was the Associate Pastor and the other was the one who was the object of the accusations I had challenged the Elders to confront according to Matthew 18 or to be silent about. As the conflict began to boil over into the congregation in the early months of 1998, the congregation began to divide along the same lines. Basically, there were three groups. Two of them were small and vocal and one was large and confused. One of the small groups supported the Associate Pastor. They felt he was being treated improperly. This group soon began to parrot the line that "There is sin in the leadership." The problem with this line was the fact that the "sin" was left undefined to the congregation. A second aspect of this persuasion was that there was also sin in the congregation. This sin **was** defined, though. It was defined as a refusal on the part of some to be submissive to church leadership. People who believed there were clear and distinct areas of authority for both the Board of Directors and the Elders and that there was no overarching authority of either board and who believed some areas were off limits to the Elders were the ones deemed to be guilty of this sin. The source of this line was clearly the Associate Pastor and his supporters in the Elder Board.

The second small group was not at all supportive of the Associate Pastor. They believed he lacked work ethic, that he was unorganized, that he spent too much time at play while his family and the church were ignored, that he was determined to change the church into what he thought it should be, that he ministered only to those who supported him, and that he was divisive. The people in this group tended to also believe that the Elders were out of touch with the congregation and that they wanted all of the power but none of the work. This catch phrase of this group was "Stop trying to fix something that is not broken!"

The third group was by far the largest. For the most part they were not resistant to change and they had no objection to the church's leadership structure. These people wondered what all the fuss was about. They did not see the "sin" that the one group was talking about and they did not see the faults of the Associate Pastor and the Elders that the other group was talking about. These people attended, served, and contributed. They were respectful of authority and willing to be led.

My greatest concern was for this group. I viewed them as the "sheep" and that it was our duty as leaders to nurture and protect them. On multiple occasions I pleaded with people from the first two groups to keep this group in mind when they were inclined to engage in "wolf-like" behavior. In my opinion neither of the first two groups were blameless. Both groups expressed willingness to see numbers of people leave the congregation if they did not agree with their point of view. With regard to the one group, I had also seen some of the shortcomings of the Associate Pastor and had worked with him so that he could improve. I understood the frustrations of those who had worked so hard in the past to bring the church to its present state and who were not seeing the same zeal in him. In early 1998, though, I was so hurt by what I saw as the Associate Pastor's personal betrayal of me that I found it very difficult to advocate for him. I continued to do so in the first months of the year, however, because I could see no viable alternative to his continuance. I was also hurt by this small group's militance and lack of love. If they had any room for compromise or any willingness to change their minds, I did not see it.

Intellectually I felt I had no choice other than to side with the Elders on the subject of authority. It was clear that the Bible gave Elders the role of leading the church. Our leadership structure and our tradition could not change this fact. I also knew that the Bible commanded Christians to submit to the Elders' leadership. There was no changing this fact. I was bound to uphold the scripture. This did not mean, however, that I supported all the Elders in their attitudes and actions. My disagreement with some of them was in three areas.

The first area of disagreement was about their desire to discipline a fellow leader and how they were going about it. The man and his alleged wrongdoings were discussed among themselves without requiring those making the accusations to first confront him according to scripture. The conclusion of a few within the group was that the fellow leader was a liar. Having reached this conclusion, they searched for evidence to support it. Several even went so far as to ask former co-workers and acquaintances of the man if they knew of any instances where he had been untruthful and if they would be willing to testify about them. In the end they never found the necessary "two or three witnesses" to make their case. One of the Elders offered to be one of the witnesses, but he wanted to bring up instances that he and the man has agreed to put behind them many years before, things they had agreed to disagree about and had forgiven each other for. Of the several witnesses who spoke against him, only one would agree to do it on the record. In addition, this witness and the man in question met face to face about the charge and could not agree. The witness said he lied. He said he did not. There was no proof either way. In the end the Elders were deeply divided about this discipline. Some insisted that they could not bring the man before the church without agreed upon charges and witnesses. I agreed with this group. Others stood by their conclusion that he had lied on at least several occasions and wanted him disciplined. Because there was no agreement there was no action taken against the man. By the time this point was reached, however, the point was moot, because the man had resigned his offices and discontinued his duties in the church.

A second area of disagreement I had with the Elders was the fact that often they protested among themselves that the church leadership structure was not Biblical, that the Board of Directors was exclusionary, and that the Board of Directors often ventured into areas that were in the Elders' realm of authority. Some of them made their feelings known to people in the congregation also. By early 1998 this was a major issue in the present conflict. Yet in all the meetings that were conducted in joint session with the Board of Directors I never witnessed or heard about a single instance when an Elder or Elders directly addressed the issue. This would have been the forum to make any changes necessary. This issue did not come to the forefront until the arrival of the Associate Pastor, but I do not remember him ever addressing it directly in a forum where change could be brought about, either.

My third area of disagreement with the Elders was about what the real issue was in the present conflict. The Associate Pastor and his supporters among the Elders said the issues were confrontation of sin, correct authority structure, and submission to church authority. I believed that the underlying issue was **power** — who has the power and who has the right to exercise it. I believed this to be true of the extremes of both leadership boards. I realize that it can be argued that these are two sides of the same coin, but I differentiate between them on the basis of the driving emotion behind them. A church leader can say, "I have power — the Bible gives it to me — and I have the right to exercise it in confronting sin, in insisting on correct authority structure, and in insisting that those under my authority submit to it." This can be a true statement and still not be one that honors God. This happens when the motivation of the leader is compromised by anger and bitterness. In this case it amounts to doing the right thing in the wrong way. A church leader can say the exact same thing, but approach the responsibility lovingly, with determination to deal with people in the same way he has been dealt with by God. It has been my experience that the people subject to church leadership are able to discern the emotions that drive their leaders' actions, whether they are predominantly motivated by love or by anger and bitterness. God knows the difference, too. It is my belief that anger and bitterness were root motivations for much of the activity that led to our leadership crisis at WCBC in 1998. I saw the anger build over the years and I saw the repeated frustration give root to bitterness. I also hasten to add that I saw this only in some of the Elders, not all of them. In most of them I saw none of it.

In February 1998, the issue of our second Sunday morning worship service surfaced again. A congregational survey had been conducted in January and we found that the church was split. Half wanted to retain it and half did not. The Board of Directors discussed the matter and decided to return to one service. I was present at this meeting and argued for keeping it. I personally did not want to keep doing it but I felt we had not given it an adequate try yet. The Board of Directors made their decision on the facts that attendance had not increased as anticipated and that the support staff was burned out. The next night the Elders discussed the issue and decided to keep the second service. Their answer to the staff burnout was to use recorded music and have the Associate Pastor operate a single pulpit microphone. A joint meeting was then scheduled to discuss the service and the Boards' opposite conclusions about it. This meeting proved to be the quintessential illustration of why it is not good to have two Boards of equal power with no clear areas of authority. After several hours of discussion we were no closer to agreement than when we had begun. As the discussion wore on I began asking myself what I really felt was best for the church. The competing arguments in the congregation were going something like this: "Those early service people just want to continue so they can have the day to play. They don't support the church anyway." Or, "Why do those second service people criticize me? They go to the second service so they can sleep in." I had to acknowledge also that the attendance had not increased as we had hoped. I knew the toll the service was taking on me so I understood how the support staff felt. The sound room was especially short-handed with the resignation of their chairman the month before. I finally decided that continuing the second service was not worth the fight and I expressed my change of mind to the group. Several more of the Elders then agreed and the second service at WCBC was history. When the decision was made, one of the Elders got up shaking his head and walked out. He resigned from the Elder Board the next week. If I had this decision to make again I would still do the same thing. Someone needed to break the impasse and I could do so without violating what I thought was right. I simply did not think the church needed another on-going controversy. We lost a few attendees when we returned to a single service, but the change back went very smoothly for the most part. I include our February 15, 1998 bulletin announcement for the record.

Wawasee Community Bible Church
Facing The Future

One year ago one of our church goals was to institute a second Sunday morning worship service on a three to six month trial basis. We began this additional service last March. The Leadership Team evaluated the two service format last fall. At that time the decision was made to continue it for an additional period of time.

In January we asked for your input in a survey. You submitted 146 surveys for our consideration. 45.9% of the surveys favored the two service format. 49.3% favored returning to one worship service 4.75% did not state a preference.

After repeated meetings and hours of discussions, in which all aspects of all views were considered, we have decided to return to a single Sunday morning worship service format, as in the past.

Our decision primarily rests on the fact that we have not had enough volunteers to staff two services. We also heard your consistent concerns that the two service format was diminishing our sense of community.

This had been as agonizing of a decision as we have ever had to make, and we feel that we made the best one in light of the information we have. We are convinced that we must have your support to proceed. On Sunday, February 15th we will ask for your support by ballot. If your support is forthcoming, we will return to our one worship service format on Sunday, March 1st.

> *Thank You*
> *The WCBC*
> *Leadership Team*

As March rolled around in 1998 it became apparent that the congregation was becoming caught up in the leadership struggle. By this time four Elders had resigned from the Elder Board. Offended people were talking. Curious people were speculating. There was growing unrest as people were seeking to get the story and place blame. I knew I needed to address the matter from the pulpit. I hated to do this, but I knew the problem was here to stay and was likely to get worse if I did not address it before the church. An idea how to approach the subject came to me early one morning and I began working on the message. I never was big on entitling my sermons, but I entitled this one "The State of the Church Address." The following is a transcription of the sermon recording of March 15, 1998.

A Lifetime of Church

March 15, 1998

I want to extend a very heartfelt and warm welcome to everyone who has come today. It is an exciting thing to come and see the church nearly filled up. I trust that you all have come today to center yourselves around God's Word and to be taught by it. These are really the only good reasons that we have for coming to church. Our fellowship and our interaction with one another are important, but they should be a fruit of the teaching and the understanding and the application of God's Holy Word. So at this time I would like to invite everyone here today to please get a Bible in your hand. If you did not bring one with you, please use one from the pew in front of you.

(Note: After these introductory remarks I reminded the congregation about the upcoming Good Friday Communion service. I read from I Corinthians, chapter 11 and challenged them to examine themselves before coming to take part in the communion. I then challenged them to ask themselves why they come to church and what one is to look for when looking for a church. I told them that a church's view of the scripture was the most important factor to look for and I offered a list of consequences that follow when a church views the scripture as anything less than infallible and authoritative. Having finished this I began the main part of the sermon.)

Now with this in mind, let's examine ourselves. I'm going to examine myself. I have been doing it for two weeks already. It has been on my heart a lot longer than that. I'm going to ask that you examine yourselves, too — not who is sitting across the aisle from you — you examine yourself this morning. So lets begin.

WCBC takes a physical. Let's imagine ourselves this morning in an examining room to be examined by the Great Physician and the Spirit of God, in the light of the Word of God, will take a look at us. First, let's look at our patient history. In September 1986, WCBC came into being. At that time we had a common purpose, a common message, a common view of Scripture. The common purpose was to institute a community outreach that was active. We all wanted to win souls through the Gospel of Jesus Christ. We all wanted to see these converts and ourselves framed and molded in ways that would honor God. We all wanted to be a shining light in the community. Our message was crystal clear: that we all are hopelessly lost, that at best we can never be any better than sinners saved by grace and servants who serve out of love and gratitude for what God has done for us. That Jesus died to save us and that He is the Way and the Truth and the Life and that no one is going to come unto the Father except through Him. And we were all excited to invite people to church to hear the Word of God taught. We were all excited to bring people to church so that they could share our fellowship and so that they could feel our love. We all were. Our view of Scripture was right on target and our statement of faith states, regarding the Holy Scripture, "We teach that the Bible is the written revelation of God, verbally inspired in every word, absolutely without error in the original documents. We teach the Bible alone constitutes infallible and final authority in faith and life." Friends, our patient history says that in the beginning we were a bouncing, healthy, happy, baby church and our potential was without limits.

This brings us to **The Patient Complaints.** After all, we usually don't go and have an examination until we have something start to go wrong. Most of us don't, anyway. In recent years, I am hearing a wide variety of concerns, complaints — call them what you will — concerns which are not only increasing in frequency but which are increasing in intensity. It is like four or five years ago a little snowball started rolling down the hill and we have a big one rolling down now. Like what, you ask? Some fall under the category of what I'll call **Growing Pains.** Things like — and we could take these in any order — "I don't like our Sunday school set up; we have too many classes." Others say, "No, we have too few." Others say, "No, they are too big," or "No, they are too small." Some say, "There is too much interaction," others say "Not enough." Or, "I'm not satisfied with our music; it is too traditional. No, it's too contemporary, No, it is too slow, No, it is too loud, Too fast, Too soft, Not creative, No, it is too creative." Or, "I don't like that we are getting so big. I don't like that. As a matter of fact, I talked to someone who I thought was a visitor and found out that they had been here six months. We are too big. No, for community outreach, you can never be too big." Or, "I don't know what is going on, no one communicates." Or, "Why do they go through those bulletins in detail every week?" Or, "I never hear from the leaders. They don't seem to care about me or my needs. I don't feel

I have a voice in anything anymore." Or, "The leaders are too distant. No, they are too smothering, too authoritative, too strict. No, they are too lenient, too innovative. No they are too stuck in the mud, etc, etc." Or, "Church is too early," or "Too late." Or, "Church is too long. No, it is too short. Church has too many services. No, not enough." Or, "I am being worked to death. I'm getting burned out." Or, "There is nothing for me to do, nowhere to fit in. I'm just not able to find a connection, etc, etc."

Other concerns fall under the category of what I will call **Aging Pains.** I look at myself and I can see that my needs now are not the same needs that I had when I was in high school. My needs are not the same now as when I had three little children at home. And my needs now are not what they will be when I retire. I think we can all relate to the fact that our needs change as we go through different stages in life. So we are hearing things like, "Man, things are not like they used to be," or "Hey, this thing isn't broken. Why are you trying to fix it?" Or, "You are only concerned about the young people." Or, "You are only concerned about the older people." Or, "You are not paying attention to the people who do all the work and give all the money." That's right. I have heard that one a lot. Etc, etc, etc.

Other concerns fall under the category of **Anxiety or Endogenous Depression.** Anxiety like "Man, I'm worried about what I'm hearing. I don't know what people are so upset about. I don't know what is going on. I'm nervous." Endogenous depression is a feeling of blues without any apparent cause. Things like "I don't know why, but I feel hopeless. I feel helpless. Something is going on and I feel it but I don't know why. It is like there is a cloud over this church." Friends, I have heard all this and much more. Many of you could add things to the list, but you notice that the complaints are multi-faceted. They are not coming from any one particular area. And I have found it nearly impossible to gauge for one very simple reason. Listen carefully — Very few will come forward to speak about their own concerns. Very few. But many are speaking of concerns of un-named others. Things like, "Some people say." Or "Someone said." Or "Well, **they** say..." WHO IS "THEY??" The answer? "Well I can't say, but they are out there." How do you gauge that? How do you work with that? How do you remedy that? I have found this to be an almost debilitating frustration!

So — in our WCBC physical we have examined the patient history and the patient complaints. This brings me to **The Findings.** As your pastor for eleven years, I'm going to tell you what I see as the problem and what I see as the solution. Now — everyone look up here! I am talking to everyone, but I am talking to no one in particular. If what I say here today hits you between the eyes, it is because it needs to. It is not because I aimed it at you. OK? Friends, if you are here as visitors today, I apologize to you. But every local assembly of believers is a family and we have all come from families and we all know that in families sometimes we have troubles that need to be addressed. So be aware of the fact that I am not always a crank and usually I am very upbeat and happy and we go through the scriptures verse by verse and apply it to our lives. And if you are here today and have been a part of the church and are happy-go-lucky, God Bless You! Apply these principals to other areas of your lives. But since I don't know who you are and I can't gauge it because of the reasons I have given, I'm going to throw it out and hope that it lands on receptive hearts. I'll tell you, I have never agonized over my words more than what I have over what I have been telling you and what I am about to tell you. Someone asked me how I felt before I came up here and I said I feel like I have never stood before a group in my whole life. These words are going to cut deep, but they are going to have to cut deep to have their effect.

My **First Finding** is this: We have **A Cancer Spot** and I am calling it a melanoma. Melanoma is a skin cancer that is fatal if it is left untreated. If it is caught early, it can be cut out and the patient is cured. If it invades the system, neither radiation nor chemotherapy will kill it. Ultimately the patient dies. Our melanoma is this: I believe our melanoma is a refusal to be obedient to the clear demands of Scripture regarding the resolution of conflict. Again — I believe that our melanoma is a refusal to be obedient to the clear commands of Scripture regarding the resolution of conflict. And this is primarily being manifested in two areas. First, in the undermining of our leadership and, secondly, in the undermining in our brothers and sisters in Christ.

Now — What do I mean by undermining of leadership? Throughout the New Testament leadership is demonstrated and there is only one model for church leadership. It is Elders and

Deacons. You will search your Bible in vain to find another NT model for church leadership other than Elders and Deacons. I would say that Elders and Deacons leading the church in the New Testament is as foundational as representative democracy is to the United States of America. It is that clear. And Biblically, the focal point of all church leadership is the Elder. If you don't believe me, check your Bibles. Throughout the New Testament, it is the Elders who are charged with feeding, teaching, and protecting the church. Peter writes this in I Peter 5: 1-3. *To the Elders among you, I appeal as a fellow Elder, a witness of Christ's sufferings and one who will also share to the glory to be revealed. Be shepherds of God's flock that is under your care, serving as overseers — not because you must, but because you are willing, as God wants you to be; not greedy for money, but eager to serve; not lording it over those entrusted to you, but being examples to the flock.* And according to Hebrews 13:17 it is the Elders who will one day be accountable to God for their shepherding of the church.

Now I know that some of us had never heard the term "Elder" before we came to WCBC. Others of us have come from backgrounds where we have seen Elders rule wrong and misapply scripture and abuse their power. Some of us are at various phases in between. The clear command of Scripture regarding Elder leadership must stand. You do not throw out the baby with the bath water, friends. And our Board of Directors serves in a Deacon capacity and really correctly should be called a Board of Deacons. We have split our leadership responsibilities into two realms: Spiritual direction, teaching, interpretation and application of Scripture for the Elders and the Board of Directors serve in a Deacon capacity over our operations. And Friends, these realms overlap all the time. It takes great wisdom to know which problem belongs to which group — and sometimes they belong to both. That's the fact of the matter. Now listen carefully, please. The individual Spiritual leader, whether an Elder or Deacon, will earn the respect for his person based on the performance of their job. But — Scripture demands respect for the office itself. And that is why the Word of God is very clear that you don't flippantly bring accusations against Spiritual leaders. If there is to be an accusation, it must be made in a godly, Biblical manner. The only analogy I can think of that is this: I don't respect our current President of the United States as a person, but as an American, I greatly respect his office.

I am now going to drop the one and only bombshell of the day on you right now. In the last three months, three of our Elders resigned their office: (The men are named). All three resigned with the same primary reason: they not only believe that there is no respect for them as a person in their office, but there is no respect for the office itself, and therefore there is nothing for them to do. As a fellow Elder, I know that this is true, at least in part. I disagree with them resigning their positions and we have been holding their resignations hoping for a change of heart. All I can say to you at this time is that if you do respect their person and if you do respect their office, tell them.

Leadership is lonely, and I'll tell you, it is really lonely when people refuse to see the needs of the whole as opposed to their own personal needs. I want to say that again. Leadership is always lonely, but it is especially lonely when people insist on their own personal needs and refuse to look at the needs of the whole. I have been a part of every leadership team that has ever existed here at WCBC. Listen — every one of them — every one of them — has made mistakes. Every one of them has made decisions that they would do differently if they had it to do over again. And you know what else? Not one leadership team in the future is ever going to get it one hundred percent right, either. It won't happen. Why? Because we are at best, sinners saved by Grace. Count on it. But there are two points I want to make regarding this and I want you to burn these into your brain. I have never at any time, in eleven years at WCBC, with the hundreds of decisions that have been made, ever believed that any of them were made with anything other than what the collective wisdom of the church leadership thought was in the best interest of the church. Never. Secondly, if you must disagree with the leadership, there is a biblical way to do it. Again, there is a biblical way to disagree, if you must. We are going to get to that in a minute.

This brings us to the second facet of our melanoma, the undermining of our brothers and sisters in Christ. James wrote in James 3: 8 and 9: *"..no man can tame the tongue. It is a restless evil, full of deadly poison. With the tongue we praise our Lord and Father, and with it we curse men, who have been made in God's likeness."* This, friends, has been going on ad nauseam in the last few months. I don't want you to do it now, but sometime when you get home I want you to get your Bibles and I want you to go to the concordance and I want you to look up words like gossip, slander, jealously, discord, dissensions, selfish ambitions, factions, envy. When you do this you are going to be shocked because you are going to find in Matthew 14, Mark 7, Romans 1, I Corinthians 6, Galatians 5, and other passages that words like gossip, slander, jealously, discord, dissensions, selfish ambitions, factions, and envy are going to be included in lists of sins right alongside words like murder, idolatry, adultery, theft, etc. When we enter into these practices, friends, we are not just ignoring the clear commands of scripture, we are ignoring God who wrote that scripture. It is not just our brothers and sisters we are sinning against, it is God. It is not just the Bible's word that we are under-estimating; it is God's word. This is sin and it must stop. Now!

Let me try and illustrate just how communications and words are distorted — even when intentions are good. I'm going to use an illustration called "Communication Deterioration." I tried to get the first paragraph up on a slide there. It might be a little small. You might have to get your opera glasses out to read it. I want to read this together and I want you to realize that this communication goes from the school's Superintendent to the school's Principals, to the teachers, to the students, to the parents. I want you to see how things can break down when we don't properly communicate.

A school Superintendent told his Assistant Superintendent the following: "Next Thursday morning at 10:30 Halley's Comet will appear over this area. This is an event that occurs only once every 75 years. Call the school Principals and have them assemble their teachers and classes on the athletic field and explain this phenomenon to them. If it rains, then cancel the day's observation and have the classes meet in the auditorium to see a film about the comet."

Now with this in mind, the following went from the Assistant Superintendent to the school Principal: "By order of the Superintendent of schools, next Thursday at 10:30 Halley's Comet will appear over your athletic field. If it rains, then cancel the day's classes and report to the auditorium with the teachers and students and you will be shown films of a phenomenal event that occurs only once in 75 years."

From the Principals to the teachers: "By order of the phenomenal Superintendent of Schools, at 10:30 next Thursday, Halley's comet will appear at the auditorium. In case of rain over the athletic field, the Superintendent will give another order, something which occurs only once every 75 years."

Teachers to students: "Next Thursday, at 10:30, the Superintendent of Schools will appear in the school auditorium with Halley's Comet, something which occurs only once every 75 years. If it rains, the Superintendent will cancel the Comet and order us out to our phenomenal athletic field."

Students to parents: "When it rains next Thursday at 10:30 over the school athletic field, the phenomenal 75 year old Superintendent of Schools will cancel all classes and appear before the students in the auditorium accompanied by Bill Halley and the Comets".

Now friends, we laugh at this — and it is funny — but I'll guarantee you that this is about how ridiculous it has become in the church recently when we, as leaders, try to trace back what "THEY" or "SOMEONE" or "HE" or "SHE" — that is UNNAMED — has supposedly said or has supposedly had a concern about. The "facts" become as elusive and contradictory as the story we all just laughed at! People get hurt, the name of Christ is sullied in the community and in the church and we become a party to sin and we — all of us — are going to STOP IT! You want to disagree with each other and with the leadership? Fine. But there is a biblical way to do it. I want you all to turn in your Bibles to Matthew, chapter 18, and we are going to see how to biblically disagree with each other. Matthew chapter 18, verse 15. *"If your brother sins against you, go and show him his fault, just between the two of you. If he listens, you have won your brother over."* These are the words of Jesus. They are so clear, so clear, so absolutely clear that we cannot misunderstand them — but yet we REFUSE to obey them so frequently. I have thought about all of this a lot lately. In the Bible we are told to love one another. We are told to share our faith. We are told to do something simple like we just read. And many other simple things. I often wonder — for the most part, Christian people don't steal, don't commit idolatry, don't commit adultery, don't commit murder, don't cheat, don't lie — Why is it that biblical "don't do's" are so much easier to accept and obey than biblical "do dos?" I have never figured this out, but there IS a big difference in how we view biblical "dos" and "don'ts."

In conflict, there is a clear command of scripture that we are supposed to live by. If you have a disagreement, if someone sins against you, if you want to register a complaint, then you are to follow Matthew 18:15 and *"go and show HIM his fault, just between the TWO of you."* Now Jesus does not say "If your brother sins against you — after you have told twenty other people about it, go..." — does He? No. He says, *"If your brother sins against you, go and show him his fault, just between the two of you."* If this does not work, Jesus gives us a second step to take. Look at Verse 16. *But if he will not listen, take one or two others along, so that 'every matter may be established by the testimony of two or three witnesses.'* This is step two. Step three in the process follows in Verse 17. *"And if he refuses to listen to them, tell it to the church; and if he refuses to listen even to the church, treat him as you would a pagan or a tax collector."* In other words, all fellowship with such an individual is to be broken at this point.

It is very simple, friends. If you have a problem with someone, if someone offends you, if there is a leadership decision that you do not understand or you do not agree with, come and talk to US or to the individual you have a problem with — Not to everyone else — Go and talk to directly to the individual in question. If you try it yourself and have no luck, we will go with you the next time. You say, "I can't do that!" Well, you HAVE to do it. It is biblical. When we don't do things according to scripture, things break down. Mark this very carefully friends — I am serving notice on behalf of the leadership that from this point on, we are going to be very, very proactive in putting "offenders" and "offendees" in touch with each other. Our efforts are going to be to make Matthew 18 the norm rather than the exception and we are going to call refusal to do this what it is — "SIN" — where this is refused.

This brings me to **My Final Finding**. The first finding was a cancer spot, a melanoma. We are cutting it out before it kills us. The second finding is **Anemia,** or "iron poor blood." I believe this accounts for our weakness. It accounts for our sluggishness. It accounts for our melancholy. The treatment plan is very simple. First we are going to cut out the cancer before it metastasises and kills us. And secondly, we will treat the anemia.

There are **Three Steps To Cure Our Anemia. First,** we are going to get a massive vitamin B-12 shot. By this I mean we are going to get a "jump start." I am going to do it and you are going to do it. We are going to take our grievances before the Lord and examine them in the light of God's Word. Where we need to repent for the sin of not following biblical commands for conflict resolution, we are going to do it. We are going to repent and we are going to get together with those whom we are at odds with and we are going to fix it. This is our "jump start." We must begin here. If we do, we will have renewed fellowship. If we do not, we are doomed to have more of the discord we have been having.

Secondly, we need a nutrient rich diet. By this I mean that we have to feed on God's Word, not on the words of other people. We have to regularly take in a rich diet of God's Word. We need to do it until we are stuffed. Because when we do this, we will understand who God is, what He has done, what He is doing, what He has promised to do, and we will measure all things against the inestimable gift of the Lord Jesus Christ to us. We will grow in our love for Him and guess what's going to happen? Things will change.

Thirdly, we need exercise. We need exercise and I am giving everyone here a three-fold exercise plan. First of all, I want you to pick one area of service that you have let go and re-involve yourself. Secondly, I want you to take one word of slander or one word of gossip or one word of offense that you have committed against someone else and you make the wrong right. Thirdly, I want every one of us to pick one instance when a word of encouragement was in order and we did not give it — and give it now. One area of service, one area of slander or gossip or offense, and one word of encouragement is our three-fold exercise plan. You will feel better. The Body of Christ, the local assembly, will be built up. But most importantly, God will be glorified. Do this friends, and we will gather on Good Friday to celebrate Communion in a joyful worship such as we have never experienced before.

Finally, Paul writes the following in Galatians 5: 14,15 *The entire law is summed up in a single command: "Love your neighbor as yourself." If you keep on biting and devouring each other, watch out or you will be destroyed by each other.* On the third of January, I had Tammy type this out on a large piece of paper and I hung it up in my office. It has been there ever since. What I have seen since then is Verse 15 coming to fruition. Every single day. The command here is very clear and so are the consequences for disobedience. Friends — today, right now, we choose. Every one of us. We choose. Not someone else chooses — we choose. It starts with us. And from this day on — in this local assembly of believers — we are either going to be a part of Verse 14 and be a part of the solution or we are going to be a part of Verse 15, in sin against God, sullying the Name of Jesus in our communities, and a part of the problem. The choice is YOURS! I have made mine. And by the Grace of God, I intend to try to live it out. Friends, I am confident that beginning today, we will choose to honor God's word, and in so doing, honor God our Father and our Lord Jesus Christ. May God bless these words. Let's arise for prayer and remain standing for our closing hymn.

Chapter Fifty-Seven

I had preached enough sermons over the years to know when the message made an impact. "The State of the Church Address" made an impact. The response of most people was very positive. I received many hugs and words of encouragement. Several people made a point of telling me that they "wanted to be a part of the solution" to our on-going crisis. I would estimate that half of the congregation's response was shock. They had heard rumblings but did not know how serious the problem was. One man summed up the sentiment of the big group in the middle of the extremes when he told me "I did not know we had so much trouble in our church." I encouraged him by saying, "It really is not that big a problem in the congregation yet, but it has the potential to be if people do not begin following biblical commands for conflict resolution." I went on to explain that one of the most frustrating aspects of what was going on was that the people who were talking always seemed to be talking for other people. We kept hearing things like "some people" are upset or "they" are saying. We were finding it impossible to find out who these upset people were so that we could talk to them. The man said he would do what he could to help. For the big group in the middle of the conflict the message served two purposes. It made them aware that we were in the middle of a leadership crisis and it challenged them to be Christ-like in their response to it.

The message produced mixed results in the two smaller groups at the heart of the conflict. In the majority of each group it is fair to say that the passion for their views moderated. There were even some efforts made by some individuals for reconciliation. It soon came back to me, however, that the Elders who had resigned were telling people in the congregation that I had not told the church the "real" reasons they had resigned. What hurt me even more was the fact that some were assuming I was not being completely truthful with the church. Upon hearing this I re-read the three resignation letters I had in my possession. They were all very general in what they said and after re-reading them I concluded that I had been honest with the church. The church would not have known any more specifics about the conflict than what they did if I had read the letters in their entirety. Perhaps I should have read the letters, but none of the former Elders had asked me to read them before the church and in the absence of such a request I did not think it was appropriate to do so.

When we continued to get feed-back that the remaining Elders and I were not being honest about the "real" reasons the four Elders had resigned (one more Elder had resigned since The State of the Church address) and that we were "sweeping the truth under the carpet," we addressed the issue again. The Associate Pastor encouraged me to say more, so we all reviewed the resignation letters again and went over the events of the previous months another time. Together we came up with five reasons to report to the congregation. I remember everyone at the meeting being satisfied, including the Associate Pastor. On April 5, 1998, I read the following letter to the church. I told them that anyone was welcome to a copy of it.

To: The WCBC Congregation   *April 5, 1998*
From: The Board of Elders

On March 15th it was announced that three Elders had resigned their office. Since then there has been one more resignation. The four are (I read their names). Their reasons for resigning, as we understand them, are as follows:

1. *They feel that the "real decisions" are often being made outside of the Elder and Director Boards.*
2. *They feel that the "core group" of WCBC has no respect for the*

office of Elder or desire for Elder leadership.
3. *They feel that they as Elders were often constrained from confronting what they saw as sin.*
4. *There were instances of conflict between the Elders and (Pastors) over what they saw as a misuse of the power of their office. This was in the area of Pastors' roles as communicators between the leadership boards and between the boards and the congregation. Nothing could be established regarding these conflicts to the satisfaction of the entire Elder Board. (The Pastors) apologized to both leadership boards for any offenses which they have caused.*
5. *They feel that our church leadership structure — an Elder Board and a Board of Directors of equal authority — is not Biblical and therefore destined to cause ongoing conflict.*

These are their reasons for resigning, as we understand them. There are no other reasons that we are aware of. We view these Brothers as godly men of impeccable integrity who have faithfully served our congregation. It is our hope that they will reconsider their resignations and one day be restored to their leadership positions.

I willingly read this letter before the congregation in the hope that doing so would quiet the ongoing murmuring. I was troubled, however, by the fact that we stated some "reasons for their resignations" that were not included in their resignation letters. The Associate Pastor was confident that the list of reasons was accurate and that reading it publicly "would help." I hoped the congregation would understand that just because these former Elders "felt" things were a certain way did not necessarily make it so.

After the service the Associate Pastor walked up to me in the parking lot and said, "You are my hero. That took a lot of courage. Thank you." The "You are my hero" expression was one that I often said to people. I took it to mean that he appreciated my willingness to do what I had done, not that I actually was his hero. The reason I mention this is to illustrate how clearly I remember the conversation. The reason I recall the conversation is because not too much time would pass before it began to come back to me that the

Associate Pastor agreed with the former Elders that the remaining Elders and I were not being honest with the congregation. By this point in my dealings with the Associate Pastor I was not surprised to be hearing this, but it was still exasperating. As I look back, the only other thing we could have told the congregation was about the disagreement among the Elders about disciplining a fellow leader. In my mind it would have been very wrong for us to mention this to the church. It would have created more questions than it would have answered and would have been grossly unfair to the individual under consideration. Leaders simply cannot rightfully bring a believer before the congregation without an agreement concerning the charge or charges. To this day one can find people who were once a part of WCBC who will say things like "There is sin in the leadership," or "The leadership won't confront sin." There will probably never be enough time elapse that statements like these will not frustrate and hurt me.

By April 1998 I was emotionally and physically drained. On the wall at Walter Drugs I had placed Galatians 5: 13-15 *"You, my brothers, were called to be free. But do not use your freedom to indulge the flesh; rather, serve one another in love. The entire law is summed up in a single command: 'Love your neighbor as yourself.' If you keep on biting and devouring each other, watch out or you will be destroyed by each other."* It seemed like this was exactly what was happening at WCBC. In the preceding months God had given me the peace of mind to prepare a sermon each week and to preach it, but the conflict had taken a toll on me. I decided I needed to rest so I took the month of May off. It was the first time in twelve years that I had done anything like this. I spent three of the weekends away from Milford hunting morel mushrooms. This helped clear my mind and I returned refreshed.

In the spring of 1998 the Associate Pastor began to pursue an idea he had been talking about for some time. His idea was that the church would buy a stock car and race it. He felt this would be a good way to reach out to people who were racing enthusiasts. The first time he told me about his idea I laughed. When I saw that he was serious I told him that the idea was fine with me but I was not interested in being a part of the project. The church leadership ultimately gave their blessing to the idea, but it was to proceed on its own merits. The Associate Pastor was free to work within the congregation to enact his plan but it would be without any financial backing from the church. The Associate Pastor's critics felt this was a foolish waste of time and resources and were open in their opposition. Their view was "If you want to reach out to racing enthusiasts, why not just go the races and reach out to them?" The criticism must have made its way back to the Associate Pastor, as the following bulletin announcement of July 21, 1998 indicates.

> *FYI a handful of men from WCBC have purchased a stock car to race at New Paris. The purpose is for local outreach. The car will not bear the name of WCBC, and will not be funded in any way by WCBC. Direct any questions to* (the Associate Pastor).

The racecar never made it to the track. The men who contributed money to the project could not agree on whether they were "Ford" men or "Chevy" men. They also could not agree on who would drive the car. One of the men involved in the project later complained to me that he felt his money was used up for nothing. He added, "I don't think this was ever about outreach. I think he (the Associate Pastor) just wanted to be a race car driver." This may or may not have been true, but it illustrates the frustration those involved were left with. I do not know what ultimately became of the car. I have never spoken to anyone who knows what became of it.

Around this same time there was an Elder meeting. I remember it as being a very frustrating one, as we hashed and re-hashed what had transpired earlier in the year. I found it incredibly frustrating that we could not seem to get beyond this past conflict. On this evening the Associate Pastor was being very negative and pessimistic. After listening quietly for quite awhile, one of our Elders spoke up. "I have not heard one positive word come out of your mouth tonight," he said, "And I am sick of it!" For a moment we all sat in stunned silence. The Associate Pastor finally said "OK. I will bring some plans for the future next week." In this rebuke our quiet, contemplative Elder had summed up both the nature of the content and the tone of the previous year's Elder meetings. We needed to move on.

In early August of 1998, Tammy and I and the kids went on vacation for two weeks. It was to be the last vacation that just the five of us would go on together. Like many vacations before it, I had planned and planned and dreamed about it for the previous year. It met all of our expectations. We flew to Las Vegas and rented a van. After spending a day at our drug wholesaler's trade show, we headed out. During the two weeks we spent time at the Hoover Dam, Zion, Bryce Canyon, and Yosemite National Parks, San Francisco, and back to Las Vegas. It would be hard to pick a highlight but for me it was probably fulfilling a life-long dream of seeing the Giant Sequoia Trees in Yosemite. We also had some very special times hiking in Zion National Park, particularly our early morning hike to the top of Angels' Landing. I would not take any amount of money in the place of the precious memories we have shared on our family vacations over the years. I feel so blessed to have had the wherewithal to go on them.

Over the years I had learned to brace myself for bad news when I returned from vacation and the return from this one was to be no exception to this rule. On the first night back the Associate Pastor called and informed me that he was resigning, effective the end of the month. He asked me to meet him for breakfast the next morning and I agreed. At breakfast he explained that he felt there were just too many hard feelings and too many differences with the core group at WCBC for him to continue. He felt there was even a cultural difference between his family and the core group. He assured me that he would leave peacefully. I asked him what he was planning to do. He said he did not know for sure but that he might move back to Alaska. He added that one of the former Elders was encouraging him to start a new church in the area. I asked him if he really wanted to be the cause of the upheaval in WCBC that would follow such a move. To this he replied that he would not be a part of starting another church in the area. I learned later that he had given the WCBC leaders the same assurance the previous night. I asked him what he planned on doing with the house and the land the church had given him as part of his compensation. With all the conflict in the congregation the work on the house had proceeded at a snail's pace and the house was not ready to be lived in yet. He said he would pay WCBC for the land, according to the agreement he had made. He planned on finishing the house and then selling it. Before we left I asked him "Could I have told you anything more than what I did to prepare you for this job?" He said, simply, "No, I knew what I was getting into." The next Sunday, August 6th, he put the following announcement in the church bulletin.

> *To WCBC: On August 31, 1998, I will have completed my two-year contract as the Associate Pastor. I have decided that I will not pursue a future contract with WCBC. The reasons for this decision are personal and are not connected with the situations that transpired in the fall of 1997 and spring of 1998. I pray for the success of the ministry of WCBC and for each person who walks through her doors.*
>   *Your Servant,*
>   (The Associate Pastor)

This announcement was met with mixed responses. Some were sad. Some were elated. Very few were surprised. And no one believed the statement that the resignation was "not connected with the situations that transpired in the fall of 1997 and spring of 1998."

I did not know how to feel. The Associate Pastor's tenure began with so much hope for me and ended with so much despair that I was numb. While I knew he had become a focal point of controversy and that it was probably best he leave, I knew his departure would stir up yet more controversy in the church. He had formed close relationships with a number of families who remained in the congregation. I knew his departure would leave a void that I would not have the time to fill. I did not know how I would be able to find the time necessary to preach and minister to the congregation, especially in the light of the reality that I would face the task with two less Pastors and four less Elders than I had to help one year before. In addition to despair, I was filled with anger bitterness at the former leaders who had found it so easy to walk away — away from our financial obligations, away from the "sheep" who were counting on us for leadership, away from the Biblical imperative that spiritual leaders were to set the example in love, in forbearance, in forgiveness, and in reconciliation. In my mind, our financial obligations **alone** should have been reason enough for all the Elders to remain at WCBC and continue working at resolving our differences.

After a few weeks I knew I needed to ask God to change my heart. Even though my bitterness felt good and right to me, I knew it would only hurt me and dishonor God in the end. I needed to let it go. God was faithful and answered my prayer. I came to the conclusion that it was my responsibility to faithfully preach His word and minister to His people no matter how I felt. When I considered the scriptural accounts of God's servants, there was no other conclusion that could have been right. Looking back I see that God encouraged me in a way that I could not have imagined. In the summer and fall of 1998 a number of adults believed in Christ for salvation. I had prayed for three of them off and on for over twenty years. This was the perfect encouragement for me. In October I began teaching a Sunday school class for the new believers. We went through "Growing In Christ" together. Teaching during the Sunday school hour and preaching during the worship service kept my mind on the Word of God and off of my own heartache.

In the fall of 1998 the Elders came to me and asked me what I wanted to do in the future. They wanted to know if they should seek another Associate Pastor or a Senior Pastor. I knew the answer right away and told them to search for a Senior Pastor. Years before I had concluded that I could not be a full-time Pharmacist and a full-time Pastor and still adequately meet the needs of the congregation. In addition to this I was convinced that after twelve years of preaching to them that I had taken them as far as I could. It was time for a change. I announced my decision to the congregation right away. I wanted them to hear it from me that this was what I wanted and what I felt was best for them. I coupled this with my assurance that I intended to remain in the congregation and to serve in whatever capacity was most beneficial. With this direction the search committee began their work.

Chapter Fifty-Eight

The Canadian air was crisp and cool as we left our hotel for a day-hike one morning in Banff National Park. The hike was a loop from our parking lot, through a moderately difficult mountain pass, and back again. The hike was to be a "man-trip" as the women elected to stay in the town of Banff and shop. Several of us had thoroughly researched the trail the night before and the Park Ranger had told us the best way to go. My son-in-law Charlie grilled the Ranger with questions because the mileage was different going one way than it was the other, a fact that cannot be when considering a loop. We were assured that the map was correct. Our concern was based on the fact that we were on a tight schedule. The hike could not take much longer than the estimated six hours without messing up the day's plan. We were to begin on Edyth Pass and make our return on Corey Pass — hence the name of the hike, the Corey Pass Loop. The first information sign we saw after the trailhead confirmed the Ranger's instructions, with Edyth Pass and Corey Pass side by side and arrows pointing in opposite directions.

The walk up to Edyth pass was beautiful, through boulders and mature trees. There were enough breaks in the trees for us to see the sharp mountain peaks we were heading towards. We were amused when we came to a second trail information sign. Beside "Edyth Pass" people had scratched graffiti like "Don't go!" and "Totally boring!" We laughed and moved on, convinced we would soon encounter Corey Pass. Two hours later there was no indication of where Corey Pass might be. We continued to walk an hour or so more before we accepted the fact that we were lost. Reluctantly, we turned back. Hours later, after ascending back through the thick underbrush we had descended through earlier and back downhill again, we came back to the sign with the graffiti about Edyth Pass. It was then that we saw the arrow pointing to Corey Pass. It was at the very bottom of the sign, as far away from the arrow pointing to Edyth Pass as it could be. We all had simply failed to see it the first time! It was too late in the day to complete the Corey Pass Loop by this time, so we continued to retrace our steps on the Edyth Pass trail back to the parking lot.

Our plans for the day had obviously fallen through. We were very tired and with each step downhill our knees, ankles, and skin on the bottom of our feet seemed to cry out in pain. Despite all of this, our final leg of the journey was fun. It was all downhill. We were in familiar territory. We knew with each step we were closer to our loved ones, to rest, and to supper. Our discomfort and fatigue would soon give way to comfort and refreshment. We also knew we would have quite a story to tell. By the time we got back to our starting point we estimated we had walked nearly twenty miles and much of it had been, as the sign had warned, "totally boring!"

In many ways this hike was similar to my last months as Senior Pastor of Wawasee Community Bible Church. It seemed "all downhill" as I worked in "familiar territory." With the passing of each day I was getting closer to a time when I would enjoy more time with my family. The joy of this prospect dulled the disappointment over the past. While I did not know it at the time, I would also have "quite a story to tell."

The fall and early winter of my final year passed quickly. Most of my energy was spent in sermon preparation and teaching our new converts. The congregation was in a "wait and see" mode. Our five-week average attendance in October and November of 1998 was two hundred and seventy one. In February and March it was three hundred and twenty eight. We had lost some people through our leadership crisis, but it could have been much worse. The leadership's primary challenge in these months was to remain proactive and positive in the face of an uncertain future. I think everyone understood my decision to step back from my role as

Senior Pastor. I do not recall anyone trying to change my mind. This could have been because the congregation wanted me to resign, but I do not think so. I believe I would have been aware of that kind of opposition. I had felt the love and support of the congregation from the beginning. I think there was just no reasonable argument to make against my decision. It did contribute to painting a picture of an uncertain future, however.

I received a big dose of encouragement near the end of 1998. One of the members of the Board of Directors lost his job. When it was apparent that he would not be finding another job soon I suggested that he could help out at the church. The man was excited at the prospect and both leadership boards, which were now meeting jointly, wholeheartedly supported the idea. The congregation agreed and the man began working in the capacity of our former Associate Pastor. He was excellent at the job. The church offices were soon organized, as they never had been before. He **looked** for people to visit and encourage. He efficiently did the "leg work" for our Pastor Search Committee. He was so hard working and enthusiastic that I might have reconsidered retiring if he had not made it clear that his financial needs were such that he could not continue in the job long-term. His months as our Associate Pastor were truly a Godsend to both the congregation and me. By the end of February he found another job, but he had gotten the congregation and me "over the hump."

In mid-January of 1999 we had a Pastor candidate visit the church. I liked the man and his wife immediately. The church seemed to like them also. On February 7, 1999 the leadership unanimously recommended him to the congregation. Several weeks later the congregation overwhelmingly approved them and they accepted the job. The plan was for them to move to our area from Washington, DC and begin work in July 1999. I was **so** excited. He and his wife were both from homes where Evangelical Christianity was not known. Both had forsaken professional careers to pursue full-time ministry. Both were evangelical in their thinking. When they came to look for a home in the springtime they stayed with Tammy and me for seven days. They were so easy to be around that I was sad to see them leave. This was a man I would be able to "hand the reigns over to" with confidence that he would work hard and be a man of integrity. I had lived long enough to know that God could do great things through such people.

There were two clear highlights in my final year. The first highlight was my final baptisms. On the last Sunday evening in February 1999, we had a baptism service. Six people gave their testimonies and were baptized that night. I remember we were so short-handed that night that I led the singing. It did not matter, though. Nothing could have dampened my enthusiasm that night. Four of the converts were adults that I had prayed for all of my Christian life. Another of the converts was a man who had attended WCBC since the beginning and finally had given in to God's calling. The final convert was the younger son of one of the adult converts. This was the only entire family (husband, wife, and two sons) who found their salvation through the ministries of WCBC in my tenure. These people all gave powerful testimonies about how they had come to faith in Jesus Christ. I doubt I will ever live long enough to forget the thrill of this evening. The final baptism service of my tenure was held on Sunday morning, March 14, 1999. Nine were baptized and the church was nearly full. What a privilege it was to be a part of these services over the years!

A second highlight of my final year was the Mission trip to Mexico by our youth. My daughter Traci and son Travis were among a group of nineteen youth and four adults who went for the week. Their leaders prepared them for months in advance. It was exciting to see the group's zeal and spiritual growth during this training. The congregation seemed to catch their zeal and gave accordingly. The week was a dream come true for the group. Traci and Travis felt it was the most touching experience of their lives to that point.

As June rolled around in 1999 I knew my journey as Pastor of WCBC was nearing an end. Our new Pastor was scheduled to begin in July. I remember the end of that May and the month of June as being every special. My daughter Trischa had become engaged to a young man named Charlie Zercher that Spring. He was the oldest child of a Christian family very similar to our own from a neighboring town. In the previous year he had shown himself to be very adept in the discipline of "Speicheresque" humor and was a joy to have around. He led a work team of young men in those weeks that included my son Travis and my nephew Joey. As Trischa worked with me in the pharmacy, they painted the exterior of Walter Drugs, re-coated the roof, and painted our home. These three jobs desperately needed done. This crew behaved like "The Three Stooges" but got the work done and had a lot of fun in the process.

During these final weeks of June I was working on my final message to the congregation as their Senior Pastor. I wanted it to be a challenge to the church as well as a message of remembrance. I worked unto this end. Things were heading toward a big crescendo on that final Sunday in June. The plan was that I would preach the sermon and we would then leave on a family vacation to Colorado. There was a hectic pace as we held Traci's high school graduation reception, ironed out all the details for our vacation and work coverage at the store, finished up the house painting, and prepared my farewell sermon. We were also in the middle of planning Charlie and Trischa's wedding, which was to take place in August. It was an especially happy time in our lives.

On Sunday, June 20, 1999, I delivered my final sermon as Senior Pastor of Wawasee Community Bible Church. I entitled it "WCBC: Thirteen Years and Counting." What follows is a transcript of this sermon.

June 20, 1999 "Wawasee Community Bible Church: Thirteen Years — And Counting."

I want to welcome you today in the name of our Lord Jesus Christ. I thank you for coming. I trust you are going to be blessed for having come here today to sit under the sound of God's word.

Today is a day that I personally have anticipated for a long time. Any of you who know me well knows this to be the case. It is with some degree of emotion that I approach this final sermon as your Senior Pastor, but I am at peace that what I am doing is both good and right. Before I enter into anything this morning, I want you to know two things: First, I am not going anywhere. I am still going to be here at WCBC working as hard and as long as God gives me strength — so you can dispel that concern. And secondly — now what was the second thing? Oh, yes. Just in case you hear anything to the contrary, I want all of you to know that my stepping back from the position of Senior Pastor was my idea — mine alone. When we started a search committee for a new Pastor, the leadership team came to me and said "Tom, what do you want?" Without hesitation I told them that I wanted to become an assistant to a well-trained, hard working, energetic new Pastor. That is exactly what I wanted and that is exactly what I feel we are getting.

At this time I would like for everyone to get a Bible in your hands. Please. Everyone. If you did not bring one, reach under the pew in front of you and grab one. I know I say this every week, but I feel it is important that everyone sees the words for themselves and I will continue to say this whenever I teach from God's Word. Let's open up to the book of I Corinthians and turn to chapter 12.

The story begins, friends, when I was thirty-three years old. That was thirteen years ago. It was an August afternoon and I found myself in the parking lot of the church of my youth — the church of my heritage, the church of my family, the church of my baptism, the church of my marriage. I was standing out there in tears. Hard to imagine a tough guy like me doing that, isn't it? But at the time, I was really crushed. I don't remember all the people that came and talked to me that day, but I do remember that Steve Kaiser was one of the first. I remember that he came up and put his hand on my shoulder and said, "It's ok. It's going to be fine." I remember my frustration wasn't so much that I knew I was finished in the church of my youth. Actually, that realization brought a sense of relief because I believed it to be the right thing to do. Only two years before I had been put in as a Pastor there and it was just sinking in how easily they had let me go. I guess I had over estimated my own value — whatever. But I remember that moment was kind of hard. I knew it was the end of an era. As I was feeling the hurt, my brother Ned came up to me confidently and said, "Well, we launch next week!" I remember thinking, "Whoa!"

Doctrinally, I was fine. I knew that leaving was the right thing to do. As a matter of fact, with the beliefs I held I knew I could not stay there even if I had wanted to. But, if you know anything about me, you know I am not an aggressive type of person in the things I do. Thinking about starting a new church placed me in uncharted waters and I was uncomfortable. I was uncertain where to go and what to do so I guess I became a follower at that time — not that I was taken in kicking and screaming, though. I believed starting WCBC was the right thing to do. I just didn't exude the confidence about it that many around me did. I remember that first week. Wow. It was a week of meetings — something that I have come to progressively hate more and more over the past thirteen years — but meetings, meetings, making plans with interesting people, meeting with a lawyer to set up articles of incorporation for the new church. I remember the hardest thing I did that week was going to see my beloved — and now deceased — Grandma and Grandpa Beer, the people to whom I owe most of my spiritual fervor. Ned and I went out and we told them we would not be coming back to the AC church and that we would be starting a new church. Grandpa Beer asked us if we realized the TREMENJOUS responsibility we were taking on — he couldn't say "tremendous," I guess. I said, "Yes, Grandpa, I do." But I did not have a clue, in retrospect, what we were entering into. During that week I also prepared a sermon for the first time. This was the first time I had done this because in the church of my youth you just opened the Bible and you trusted God to give you a message. I did this all with a lump in my throat that first week, wondering "Should we be doing this?" and "Would anyone bother to come if we did?"

There were three things that took place that week that gave me a great amount of courage. One of them was a note that I received from Mary Ann Rassi. In it she quoted from Habakkuk 1:5 which says *"Look at the nations and watch — and be utterly amazed. For I am going to do something in your days that you would not believe, even if you were told."* The note turned out to be prophetic. If anyone had told me thirteen years ago that I would be standing here talking to all of you today, I would not have believed it.

The second thing that happened that first week concerned Edna Graff, one of the three lovely Graff sisters, who has since gone to be with the Lord. She sent word to me that she was troubled about her soul and wanted to talk. I was new at the evangelism game, but I went. We talked and I shared the gospel with her. She prayed to receive Christ as her Savior. I vividly remember seeing the joy in the room that day. I believe it was Mary — maybe Tillie — who was there with us. They hugged and cried together and I remember thinking "Man! This really works! This is so cool." This shows how immature I still was at the time.

On the night before our first service, Otto Beer Jr. called me on the telephone and prayed with me. This was the first time anyone had ever done that with me. I remember him saying "Never forget, Tom, it is the greatest of privileges to handle the Word of God." I have never forgotten this.

That first Sunday, in that school cafeteria, there were sixty-six people in attendance. It blew away my fondest anticipation. Some of you were there, weren't you? Fifteen months later we moved into our first building, which is now our fellowship hall. I think back to our first baptism — in a borrowed church -and to this past winter and spring when I had the great spiritual privilege of hearing the testimonies and doing the baptisms of some souls who were close friends of mine growing up and whom I had prayed for over twenty-five years. It is almost like God brought this to fruition to show me "Yes, Tom. It is time that the guard changes." Through the years we saw church government develop, we saw church ministries develop. I have seen children grow up as my hair got gray. What a thrill this had been. But more than anything it has been a thrill to see lives of people changed and to see it over and over again. From some deep personal hurts to some indescribable spiritual highs, it had been quite an experience. And one, in retrospect, that has gone by in a blur.

Now, this morning I want to share my heart with you. I want to share my own observations, my own thoughts — just some conclusions I have come to over the last thirteen years. I will be sharing in three areas. I'm going to start with my greatest frustrations in ministry. Then I will share my greatest blessings and I will close with my greatest aspirations for WCBC in the years to come. And by the way, I will not be sharing about any event in particular or anyone in particular. If anything hits you between the eyes this morning, it is just because it hits you, not because I am aiming at you.

Let's begin with my three greatest frustrations. First, a **Consumer Mentality in the Church.** And when I say this, I am talking about a consumer mentality in church among professing Christians. I'm not talking about unbelievers. Unbelievers are only acting naturally when they do the things they do, but Christians should never have a consumer mentality towards church. What do I mean by "a consumer mentality in the church?" I mean people approaching church or viewing church or treating church as they would a store of general merchandise where all the merchandise is unlimited in supply and free to anyone who wants to take it. This is what I am talking about! Those with consumer mentality go to church primarily to be entertained and to be served. Many people, professing to be Christians, take and take and receive and receive until their needs are met or their needs change and then they are gone — either gone to another church or to no church at all. We have all known and worked with many, many such people over the years.

Friends, a consumer mentality among Christians is not Biblical. It is not Biblical. No one is ever saved by God to just sit — to just sit and grow old. "Doing nothing" is never God's will in the life of a Christian. Why is this consumer mentality so destructive to the church? I can give you three reasons. First of all, consumer mentality in the church drains the energy of the ministries of the church. It drains them. Secondly, consumer mentality takes ministry efforts away from those in the church who are both ministering to others and in need of ministry themselves. It takes it away from them. Thirdly, it also takes ministry efforts away from the un-churched and the unsaved who need it most desperately. Consumer mentality creates bitterness. It creates bitterness and burnout among those who are ministering — and you know this is true.

How should it be in the church? Every blood-bought, born again child of God is called to both minister and to be ministered unto. This is the economy of the church. Just like you don't go into a store without money and expect to take what you want, in the church believers are called to both produce ministry and receive ministry. Now, granted, time frames and circumstances in our lives will from time to time alter this balance, but the principle none-the-less holds true. Paul describes this balance and this interdependence upon one another in I Corinthians, chapter 12. I would like for you to look, if you will, at verse 12. This is how it is supposed to be in the Church, the Body of Christ. Here he uses the illustration of the human body. *The body is a unit, though it is made up of many parts; and though all its parts are many, they form one body. So it is with Christ.* He continues in Verse 17. *If the whole body were an eye, where would the sense of hearing be? If the whole body were an ear, where would the sense of smell be? But in fact God has arranged the parts in the body, every one of them, just as he wanted them to be. If they were all one part, where would the body be? As it is, there are many parts, but one body.* See how dumb it is when a Christian says something like "I don't need church. I just worship God on my own?" Such statements are baloney. God wants us to be in a specific role in a specific group within the Body of Christ. All of us! Look at verse 26. *If one part suffers, every part suffers with it; if one part is honored, every part rejoices with it.* Just as if you get a hangnail and it drives you nuts. Your whole body is affected by it. Or if you have a tiny canker sore — it can drive you nuts. Or if you stub your toe, can you think of anything else until the pain lets up? So it is in the church. When one part of the church does not function at all or functions improperly, the whole church ministry suffers. We are all in this together, friends. No one is ever saved just to sit and consume ministry. No one! OK?

Let's move on to "greatest frustration number two" of my thirteen years of being the Senior Pastor at WCBC: **Non-Spiritual Fathers**. Sorry, dads, to do this on Father's Day. I didn't plan it this way. It just worked out like this. This frustration is by no means less frustrating than the first one. Dads, we are given a HUGE responsibility before God and frankly, our performance record, based on my observations during thirteen years of ministry, is dismal. Dismal! Let's look at the Book of Ephesians, chapter 5. In your pew Bible it is on page 829 or 1136. Now friends, in our day this is a culturally offensive passage of scripture, but it is absolutely clear. There is not a one of us who cannot understand what this passage is saying. Now let's look, if you will, at Verses 22 and 23. Hold on, women. Remember, this frustration is directed at the men. *Wives, submit yourselves to your husbands as to the Lord. For the husband is the head of the wife as Christ is the head of the church, his body, of which he is the Savior. Now as the church submits to Christ, so also wives should submit to their husbands in everything.*

Now lets just speak real frankly here. Why is it that women hate those verses? Now I know we are all spiritual and we all love all of the Word of God, but practically speaking, why is it that the women, in general, don't like those verses and try everything in their power to explain them away? Why? Well, men — it is OUR fault! Because we like to point to these verses and say "Look at this — Submit, submit!" We don't read on in the passage. This morning, we are going to read on..... Verse 25: *Husbands, LOVE YOUR WIVES.* How much, Tom? *Just as Christ loved the church.* And how much is that, Tom? *And gave himself up for her to make her holy, cleansing her by the washing with water through the word, and to present her to himself as a radiant church, without stain or wrinkle or any other blemish, but holy and blameless. In this same way, husbands ought to love their wives as their own bodies. He who loves his wife loves himself. After all, no one ever hated his own body, but he feeds and cares for it, just as Christ does the church — for we are members of his body. "For this reason a man will leave his father and mother and be united to his wife, and the two will become one flesh." This is a profound mystery — but I am talking about Christ and the church. However, each one of you also must love his wife as he loves himself, and the wife must respect her husband.* Dads, there is more. Look at chapter 6, verse 4. *Fathers do not exasperate your children; instead, bring them up in the training and instruction of the Lord.*

Now — What is it that we do not understand in these verses? If you don't understand what these verses are saying, please see me afterwards. But my thought is that it is pretty clear who it is that has the first and the greater responsibility in this passage. DADS, HUSBANDS — It is us! It is us, dads and husbands, who have the responsibility to *"love our wives, even as Christ loved the church."* I'll guarantee you, if we actually treated our wives this way that we would never hear our wives say "No way! I'm not going to submit to his leadership over me!" It would be the most natural, blessed thing any woman could ever hope for — to be loved and treasured and nurtured in the way that Christ loved the church. We have dropped the ball, men. Brutally!

I would love to have a dollar for every time over the past thirteen years that a husband came to me and complained about a non-submissive wife, when it was absolutely clear to both her and to me — and should have been clear to him — that he was showing her no love, no treasuring. I have lost track of the number of times I have had wives come to me crushed, broken, pleading, in despair that their husbands, who profess to be Christians, WILL NOT take any responsibility at home. WILL NOT pray at home. WILL NOT speak of spiritual matters at home. WILL NOT, without exacting a great price, come to church with them. WILL NOT nurture and teach and help discipline the children. Where the husband takes the approach "You go ahead. I will criticize if I don't like what you go ahead and do." I would love to have a dollar for every time this has happened!

Here's the pattern, friends. In relationships there is a basic difference between men and women that even secular psychologists will acknowledge. Women tend to take and take, and they do and they do, and they are long-suffering and more long-suffering, and they try and try and try, while men assume and assume and assume, and promise and promise, and put off and put off and put off. And you know what? When a woman is done, she is DONE. I have seen this play out so many times — to the breaking of my heart and to the shame of the Body of Christ. It is usually at this point that the husband goes "What? What did I do? I'll do anything to make it right! Tom, help me! Will you talk to her?" I've seen this until I am sick, sick, sick! And you know what? Unfortunately, when it gets to this point, the relationship is seldom retrievable. Usually the marriage fails, the home breaks up, the kids — who knows what happens to them — and the husband spends the rest of his life going around and feeling sorry for himself and saying, "Boy, I can't believe she did that to me." Dads — the Bible gives us a GREAT responsibility. A GREAT responsibility. Ours' is the first responsibility. Don't ask your wife to submit to your leadership until you love her as Christ loved the church. And to not assume this responsibility, men, is SIN, pure and simple.

Frustration #3: Oh, it's going to get better, by the way! **Abusing God's Grace.** And you know what? My first two frustrations find their roots in this frustration. We are in the book of Ephesians. We are going to go back to chapter 2, but I want to read a few verses from Galatians. You don't need to turn to them. You can just listen. By chapter 5, Paul had used this entire epistle to the Galatian churches to remind them that they had been saved by grace alone, through faith alone, in Jesus Christ — alone. He reminded them that they don't need ceremonies or religious works or circumcision to be right with God, like the Jews were telling them. When he gets to the end of this discussion, he says in chapter 5, verses 1 and 2 *"It* *is for freedom that Christ has set us free. Stand firm, then, and do not let yourselves be burdened again by a yoke of slavery."* Paul warns them not to even think of going back into that religiosity, that legalistic bondage that Christ had set them free from. In verse 13 he continued, *"You, my brothers, were called to be free. But do not use your freedom to indulge the flesh;"* In other words, Paul says, don't take this freedom and say, "Hey, I'm free. I can go do whatever I want to do." Rather, he says in the end of verse 13 and in verse 14, *...Serve one another in love. The entire law is summed up in a single command, "Love your neighbor as yourself."* And then in verse 16 he says *So I say, live by the Spirit, and you will not gratify the desire of the flesh.* In other words, do the things of Christ and you won't have to worry about doing things of Satan. He is saying don't just be on defense, go on offense for Christ.

Now, Ephesians chapter 2. The question is this: So — we are free. OK, free from what? And, secondly, free unto what? Ephesians chapter 2, verses 8 and 9. I hope after thirteen years that most of you can quote this: *"For it is by grace you have BEEN saved, through faith — and this not from yourselves, it is the gift of God — not by works, so that no one can boast."* Now let's go through this again. *For it is by grace* — that undeserved gift of God, where we stand in His favor based on the merits of His son, Jesus Christ, and His finished work on the cross of Calvary and His resurrection from the dead. And what activates the grace of God? *Faith.* We believe in Jesus Christ as the way and the truth and the life. We trust Jesus Christ, God's blessed Son, as our Savior from sin and as our only merit before God. So it is by this gift of grace you have BEEN saved, through the gift of faith. This is what the Bible says, friends. And just so no one gets it wrong, Paul adds *"NOT BY WORKS, so that no can boast."* We don't earn it with works. We don't maintain it with works. Salvation is a gift. Period.

Now listen — with this knowledge some people decide, "I don't have to grow. I don't have to serve. I don't have to live a Christian life. After all, I'm saved by grace, not by works. Christ paid for all my sin. God will forgive me. I can sin all I want." There are tons of Scripture that undermine such thinking, and this is usually what it remains — thinking. Very few are actually bold enough to say such stupid things, but I have seen enough people LIVE this way over the last thirteen years to make me want to vomit my guts inside out, to be honest! Only God knows for sure the condition of the soul of man, but when I see a life-pattern like this I can only conclude that either God is going to bring that soul under such condemnation that he will come back into fellowship or he has never come to truly know the Savior and will go to hell if he or she dies. GOD WILL NOT BE MOCKED!

Consider the change that takes place when one is born again. We have been through this many times. Before Christ we are "in sin." It is a state into which every man is born and we commit acts of sin that demonstrate this throughout our lives. After we receive Christ as our Savior, we are "in Christ." Before Christ, we are "dead" spiritually. After receiving Christ as our Savior, we are "alive" spiritually. Before Christ, we are "citizens of this world" and we are subjects of the ruler of this world, Satan. After trusting Christ, we are "citizens of heaven," children of God. Before Christ, we have a "sin nature." After Christ we are given a new "divine nature." Now — think with me, friends. If, in fact, we are freed from "sin," if we are "in Christ," if we are "citizens of Heaven," if we are "alive" spiritually, and if we are declared to be "children of God," and, if on top of all of that, we are indwelt by God the Holy Spirit, does it not stand to reason that there is, of necessity, a change that will take place in one's life?! That is why Jesus said, *"Every good tree bears good fruit."* EVERY.

Abusing God's grace, friends, has to be one of the greatest affronts to God. Look at verses 8 and 9 again. *For it is by Grace you have been saved, through faith — and this* (that is the faith) *not from yourselves, it is the gift of God — not by works, so that no one can boast.* Now listen, friends. God has a distinct purpose in all of this. What is His purpose? Verse 10. *For we are God's workmanship, created in Christ Jesus to do good works, which God prepared in advance for us to do.* All of us who name Jesus Christ as our Savior have been made new by God — we are His workmanship — and He has good works for us do. All of us! And friends, if you are a Christian and are sitting here today and you are doing nothing for the kingdom of God, then the works that God foreordained for you are not getting done. This is sin, pure and simple!

So, my three greatest frustrations over the years — and I think I have run them into the ground — are consumer mentality in the church, non-spiritual fathers, and Christians abusing God's Grace. Maybe you have felt these frustrations, too, but one thing for sure, these frustrations suck the energy out of the local church, out of the Body of Christ, in general, and out of Pastors, in particular.

But, far out weighing my greatest frustrations have been my greatest blessings. This was tough, but I boiled my blessings down to three areas. I would like for you to turn to the Book of Romans, chapter 1. Greatest blessing number one, for me, is **Seeing the Power of God in His Gospel.** If your life needs changing, read through the book of Romans. Read it over and over and over again and — I guarantee you — you will not err theologically. Your life will be changed. By the way — the word "Gospel" literally means "good news." Now — Romans 1, verses 1 through 4. *"Paul, a servant of Christ Jesus, called to be an apostle and set apart for the gospel of God — the gospel he promised beforehand through his prophets in the Holy Scriptures regarding his Son, who as to his human nature was a descendant of David, and who through the Spirit of holiness was declared with power to be the Son of God by his resurrection from the dead: Jesus Christ our Lord."* Paul, the Apostle, had been set apart by God to proclaim the best news the world had ever heard, ever imagined — good news that the Old Testament prophets had promised. Paul saw himself under obligation to do this. Verses 14 and 15. *"I am obligated both to Greeks and non-Greeks, both to the wise and the foolish. That is why I am so eager to preach the gospel also to you who are at Rome."* What is the Gospel? He goes on to tell us in verse 16. *"I am not ashamed of the gospel, because it is the power of God for the salvation of everyone who believes."* Now why, Paul is the gospel "the power of God for the salvation of everyone who believes?" How can this save someone? Verse 17. *"For in the gospel a righteousness from God is revealed, a righteousness that is by faith from first to last, just as it is written: 'The righteous will live by faith.'"* If you mark your Bibles, underline the phrase *"a righteousness from God."* Then underline the next phrase *"a righteousness that is by faith."* These are critical phrases, my friends — as critical as any in the entire Bible. Faith in the gospel brings the righteousness of God into the eternal account of whoever believes. And this is the only righteousness that God will ever accept! In the end we will all either try to commend ourselves to God with our own righteousness — which is human righteousness or "self" righteousness — and go to hell because of it — or we will be commended to God based on the righteousness from God which comes through faith in the gospel. It will be one or the other, friends — not a combination of the two!

Now — specifically — what is the gospel, or the "good news?" Turn to I Corinthians, chapter 15. We are asking the question, "What is this God News?" Verses 1 and 2. *"Now, brothers, I want to remind you of the gospel I preached to you, which you received and on which you have taken your stand. By this gospel you are saved, if you hold firmly to the word I preached to you. Otherwise, you have believed in vain."* Paul is telling us that if we are taking our stand on anything other than the gospel, we are in trouble. We are believing in vain. What is the Gospel? Verses 3 and 4. *"For what I received I passed on to you as of first importance: that Christ died for our sins according to the Scriptures, that he was buried, that he was raised on the third day according to the Scriptures."* Did you get that? The best news in the history of the world is that Jesus Christ died for our sin — yours and mine — and that He was raised from the dead. Why is this such good news for man? Because — instead of standing before God to account for our own sin and to be condemned eternally for it, we now have a choice. Our alternative choice is to believe that Jesus Christ died for our sin in our place and trust His perfect work to make us acceptable to God. And because Jesus rose from the dead, death no longer has a hold on anyone who trusts in Him. To put it simply, a sinful human can now be saved! Without this good news this would not be possible.

The Apostle Paul knew there would be those who doubted that Jesus rose from the dead so he added verses 4 through 7. Look at them! *"That he was buried, that he was raised on the third day according to the Scriptures, and that he appeared to Peter, and then to the Twelve. After that, he appeared to more than five hundred of the brothers at the same time, most of whom are still living, though some have fallen asleep. Then he appeared to James, then to all the apostles, and last of all he appeared to me also, as to one abnormally born."* When Paul wrote this there were still probably hundreds of live eyewitnesses to the fact that Jesus was alive. If the literal, physical resurrection of Jesus was not true there were certainly a lot of people who were willing to lie about it. The fact of the matter is that it was the resurrection of Jesus that energized and emboldened the Apostles and first Christians.

Friends, I never cease to marvel — never cease to marvel — at the power of this "Good News" which, when received by faith, takes the sin of a man and replaces it with the righteousness of Jesus Christ in that individual's eternal account. I never cease to marvel at the change the Gospel brings in the life of an individual when he believes it and receives it. It changes lives. It always has and it always will. And one of the greatest blessings I have had over the last thirteen years has been the privilege of sharing this Gospel, sharing it apart from any religiosity or man-made rules tacked on to it to get in the way of it. I would go so far as to say that whatever good we have seen happen in this church over the last thirteen years has been the result of the power of the Gospel of Jesus Christ! And we must continue to take our stand on it!

OK. Greatest blessing #2. **Testimonies and Baptisms.** This really is a critical "first fruit" of the Gospel in the life of a believer. In Acts 1:7,8 Jesus said *"It is not for you to know the times or dates the Father has set by his own authority. But you will receive power when the Holy Spirit comes on you; and you will be my witnesses in Jerusalem, and in all Judea and Samaria, and to the ends of the earth."* We are called to be witnesses, to testify for Christ, to be ambassadors for Christ. All of us. In Matthew chapter 28 Jesus gave us our "Great Commission" when He said in verses 18 thru 20 *"All authority in heaven and on earth has been given to me. Therefore go and make disciples of all nations, baptizing them in the name of the Father and of the Son and of the Holy Spirit, and teaching them to obey everything I have commanded you. And surely I am with you always, to the very end of the age."* Christ did not leave us to do this alone. He promised He would be with us. He sent the Holy Spirit to live in us.

Over the years Tammy has kept a record of baptisms, weddings, funerals, and other important happenings in the church. I have never done this before but this past week, I counted our baptisms. In thirteen years there have been two hundred and five souls that have been obedient in the matter of water baptism. I was shocked by this.

I really was. And we have heard the public testimonies of even more souls than that.

I know whenever I tried to get people around for testimonies and baptisms, it was hard work. Sometimes it was like pulling teeth. But it was always worth the effort. And you know that else? I cannot think of a single case where I saw any significant spiritual growth apart from obedience in the matters of water baptism and public testimony. I cannot remember a single exception. If a person won't be obedient in this first area they likely will not be obedient in other areas either.

It seems like over the years whenever I got discouraged, I mean really discouraged — it didn't happen often and very few of you ever saw it — but there were times when I got down to the point I didn't care if I went on or not. It seemed like these were the times that God would invariably bring someone along who would believe in the Gospel and be saved and be willing to be obedient to the command of Jesus to be baptized. When this happened everything else faded into relative obscurity. Nothing thrilled me more, or sustained me longer than those of you — and God bless you — who trusted Jesus Christ as your Savior and were willing to be baptized to identify with Him publicly and to tell assembled people about your conversion experience!

Greatest blessing #3, for me, was **The Youth**. The writer of Ecclesiastes said in Chapter 12, verse 1 to *"Remember your Creator in the days of your youth."* Friends, this was a missing element in my own youth. It really was. Oh — I knew the stories of the Bible. I knew them better than most people I came into contact with. And I never missed church without a good reason. Never. And I was very proud of that.

In my youth, though, I didn't think a young person could be a Christian. Why!? Is there anything in the Scriptures that tells you that? Absolutely not! You can't find one hint of teaching like that in the Scriptures, but this is what I was taught. Did I check it out? No! That is why I have told you for thirteen years not to believe any of my teaching unless I can back it up with the Word of God. If you don't know the Word of God you are a "sitting duck" for anyone who wants to come along and lead you astray!

Salvation was a missing element in my youth. As early as I can remember — I am embarrassed to say this — as early as I can remember, from childhood through age eighteen I would pray every night "God, please let me live long enough that I can give my life to you." What an affront to God that must have been! But, thank heaven, He did.

What a great privilege — of all the great privileges I have had — it was to see my own children come to know Jesus Christ as their Savior from sin at a young age! And seeing them growing up loving Him. Seeing them spared many of the heartaches young people have who don't know Christ. Truly, this was one of the great blessings of my life. I can't count the number of times, young people, that I have marveled at your spiritual maturity and commitment — most recently in your trip to Mexico. God bless you! Or how proud I have been of you over the years — as proud as if I watched you hit a home run! The influence you have had among your peers has been so impressive. I have been so proud of our youth programs over the years, from AWANA. What a great organization! From AWANA, to Sunday school, to Junior-Senior High youth groups, to the College and Career group! How thankful I am for all of you who have served so sacrificially and faithfully in these ministries over the years. I don't know, maybe it is just a case of especially treasuring something you didn't have — a personal relationship with Jesus Christ at a young age — but the youth of the church are among my greatest blessings!

Now that you have heard my greatest frustrations and blessings, I would like to conclude with my greatest aspirations for WCBC in the future. Based on thirteen years of experience, I offer a list of what I believe are imperatives for future success.

First: **Spiritually Mature Leaders**. Leading the church is tough. If you have any aspirations of being in a church leadership position because of prestige or whatever else it can bring you, forget it! It is tough and largely thankless work. That is why it takes spiritual maturity to do it well. Serving effectively in the church requires a sound understanding of scripture AND a committed life. The scriptures are very clear on the qualifications. Church leadership, friends, is not a place for spiritual development. It is not. You don't put someone into the position of leadership hoping they will grow into it. That is why I encourage you, I ask you, I charge you to pray that God will raise up spiritually mature men to lead you in the future. And always, when you are asked for nominations, pray about it and nominate only those who are already showing themselves to be spiritually mature and who are already serving faithfully in the ministries they have undertaken.

Second aspiration: **Open and Honest Communication**. You know what? Nothing creates more problems than poor communication. And the converse of this is also true. Nothing prevents more problems than good communication. It is really that simple. Over the years it seems like it is always the littlest, dumbest things that have caused the biggest problems. It usually starts this way: with a misunderstanding — an honest, simple misunderstanding. Then a little disobedience is added. Instead of going to the person you have a misunderstanding with, you go to someone else. Then you throw a little gossip into the mix — just like you would throw spices on a plate — then the presumptions start, and then the imaginations take off. "They aren't really with me. They are just ignoring me. They are out to get me." And when this happens you get more gossip, etc, etc, etc, until a molehill has become a mountain. Please, please — I implore you — speak to your leaders. They cannot lead you if they don't know your aspirations, the needs of your heart, your frustrations, and your hurts. They cannot do it. When you have a problem, speak to the person you have a problem with or to people who are in a position to do something about the problem — not to others who will just feel sorry for you and trash the people you have a problem with. Open and honest communication.

Third: **A Church-Wide Working Knowledge of the Scriptures**. Paul exhorted Timothy in II Timothy 2:15 — and this is the AWANA verse — *"Do your best to present yourself to God as one approved, a workman who does not need to be ashamed and who correctly handles the word of truth."* Friends — learning the Scripture energizes us. Knowledge of the Scripture protects us from error and keeps our minds focused on God. No one grows spiritually apart from this. If you want to grow spiritually you must spend time in the Word of God. If I could have WCBC known for one thing during my thirteen years as Pastor it would be that we are a church comprised of students of God's Word. That would be the greatest compliment that could be paid to us, in my opinion. Friends, learning requires hard work and I pray that many more of you will take advantage of opportunities to study God's Word in the future.

My fourth aspiration for you is **An Awareness of Our Spiritual Gifts and Involvement in our Areas of Giftedness.** Write a note. I Corinthians, chapter 12, verses 12-27. Read this. Read it until you understand it. We are all responsible to know our areas of giftedness. We are all responsible to be an active part of the total effort of the church, the Body of Christ, and to be an active part of a local assembly of believers. It is simple. Learn where you are gifted, then get busy and work in those areas.

Fifth: **A Strong Commitment to Family and Youth.** Need I say more? The churches are only as strong as the families that make them up and the youth, friends, are always and forever the future. We must always make an investment in them and in our families. To neglect these areas is to write off tomorrow! Now, parents — look up here! Parents, LOVE EACH OTHER! Let your children see it. Let your children see that the things of Christ are important to you. Support the youth programs. Support the youth leaders. Pray for them. Communicate with them.

Sixth: **Working Within Our Purpose Statement.** Now, friends, we put this into our bulletin every week and we all need to learn it. "Our purpose is to transform people into fully devoted followers of Jesus Christ through the power of the Holy Spirit and the Word of God." Learn it! Measure your activities in the church against it. Everything you want to see in the church, every direction you want to go — is it consistent with our purpose statement? What this does, friends, is to keep us all basically going in the same direction with a generally unified effort.

My seventh aspiration for WCBC is that **We Measure All Things By Christ.** Want to know if something you are about to do is right or wrong? Just simply ask yourself "What do the scriptures show me that Christ would have thought about it?" This makes such decisions "no-brainers." Friends, measure all things by Christ.

One final aspiration: **Worship.** We need to work on corporate and individual worship, because as we focus on God, we see Him more and more for whom He is. And as we see Him more and more for whom He is, we are progressively willing to submit to His Word. We are more and more willing to obey what it teaches. This is the exercise from which all other Christian discipline will flow.

Friends, this will not be my last sermon to you, but it will be my last as your head Pastor. It has been a great thirteen years. If I get a bit rhapsodic here, please bear with me. To everyone who has worked so hard — whatever discipline you have worked in — God Bless you! Thank you. To my parents-in-law, George and Pat Sheets, God Bless you. They stuck with me in my early years of hardheaded, dogmatic legalism. They were patient and never ceased to pray for me. And it turned out OK, didn't it? No one could have asked for better parents-in-law than what God has given me.

Dad and Mom, thank you. You started out your married life with all the cards stacked against you. I want to thank you for giving me a value system which included hard work and — especially — commitment, without which you guys would have gone the way of the world and divorced years ago. And through all those years of hard work and commitment, you really raised some pretty good kids. Thank you. I love you.

To those of you who have been my encouragers, God bless you. I don't know how you knew it, but every time I got down and wondered if it was all worth it, you were there, time and time again. It is your gift. Keep using it. Prayer Warriors, there were many times when I wondered, why am I not losing my sanity here? Why am I able to put one foot in front of the other? People would ask me that from time to time and the only thing that I could attribute my stability to were the prayers of those who were praying for me. I don't know who you are. God does. God bless you. Keep it up.

To my children, Trischa, Traci, and Travis: Thank you for never making me feel guilty about doing the church's work, because it was often at your expense. Anyone who knows me well knows that they could have easily done this, but they never did. Never. Thank you, secondly, for never (that I can ever remember) resisting going to church or youth. Never. Thank you for never behaving in a way that I would have had to explain to others. Maybe there were such times, but if there were, I didn't know about it and I'm glad. You see, I grew up a pretty good kid, seriously, but I was pretty sneaky. As I was growing up there was kind of an unwritten rule in my social setting that all kids went through a time when they made their parents' lives hell. I don't know why that rule was written or where it came from but I honestly expected it to happen in my own life. Thank God, it never did. Thanks guys.

This is the toughest of all — Tammy. Whatever giftedness you have seen in me over the years, whatever organization, whatever timeliness, whatever preaching ability — behind it all was Tammy. Typing, filing, managing the calendar, organizing, encouraging me, loving me unconditionally. All the while managing our home, the drugstore office, and being a five-star mother. Tama, thank you. Often I say of her "What a woman!" And today I say of her all-the-more, "What a woman." You always have been, and after twenty-seven years, you are still, more than ever, the love of my life, my rock. You are the wind beneath my wings. May God bless His Word. Let's arise for prayer.

When I finished the sermon I told the church that I was going to go to the bottom of the steps in front of the pulpit and face the front. I invited everyone to come forward and stand with me if they were willing to face the future together as one. I had not planned on doing this, but it seemed right at the time. As the song was being sung I remember Tammy and my mom being at my side and that others were there, too. When the song was finished our song leader said, "Well, Tom, everyone has come forward to stand with you. We should have a bright future."

The crowd stayed up front and one by one they expressed their gratitude to Tammy and me for our years of service. I only remember what two people said in the hour or so that followed. My beloved mother-in-law hugged me, said she loved me, and added, "Now that's enough! I never want to hear you apologize again for you and Tammy's beginning!" The other person I remember was the same man who had come up to me the day we walked out of the AC Church for the last time. On that day he had reassured me with the words "It's going to be OK." On this day he shook my hand, smiled, and said, "It's **still** going to be OK. Two hundred and five. That is the only number that matters." As the last person expressed their thoughts and departed, Tammy and I walked out of the church for the last time as the Senior Pastor. Driving home my mind wandered back to that first nervous Sunday in the Milford School cafeteria thirteen years before. It had been quite a journey!

Chapter Fifty-Nine

Years ago I was browsing through a craft shop and saw a plaque that amused me. It pictured an old couple sitting in their rocking chairs. The caption simply said, "Too soon old, too late smart!" Even years ago I knew that this observation was true of most people. At age forty-seven in 1999 I already knew it was true of me and was becoming profoundly truer of me with each passing year. Even with this observation, though, there was an irony. In 1978 I graduated from college at the apex of my academic knowledge. By 1999 only a fraction of this academic knowledge remained, but I considered myself to be much smarter. In 1978 I thought I had all the answers to life's questions. In 1999 I felt I had only a few of the answers to life's questions and still felt smarter. Why? Because in 1999 I was sure of the answers to a few of life's critical questions, and these were the only answers that I felt mattered. Why? Because the questions and answers concerned my relationship to God and were therefore eternal in nature. If how "smart" one is relates to the number of facts one knows, then "smart" is not the best word for what I gained over the years. The better word for what I gained is **wisdom**, something I am convinced one cannot possess in great measure apart from living a life of seeking to serve God. Nevertheless, I have learned some things on my journey: about people, about organizations, about God, and about myself.

The first thing I have learned about people is that human beings fail where Jesus succeeded. When tempted by Satan at the onset of

His public ministry, Jesus passed tests in the three foundational realms of human experience: "The lust of the flesh" (Matthew 4: 2,3), "The lust of the eyes" (Matthew 4: 8,9), and "The pride of life" (Matthew 4: 5,6). Even the most devout, godly individuals fail to pass tests in these foundational realms from time to time. No one **ever** gets it right **all** the time. I believe scripture teaches that all human beings are born "in sin" and it has been my observation that all human beings spend the remainder of their lives demonstrating this fact. Obviously, some demonstrate the fact with greater frequency and more clarity than others, but we all demonstrate it to some degree. Jesus Christ **alone** was sinless. We can call our imperfect actions, inactions, thoughts, and intentions things like mistakes, shortcomings, and oversights, but the Bible calls them **sin**. I have learned when people accept the fact that they are sinful that they are more apt to rejoice in God's grace and to serve Him out of love and gratitude. They are also generally more patient and loving in their interactions with other believers.

Three more things that I have learned about people have their origin in the fact that people fail where Jesus succeeded. The first of these is that people justify their behavior by comparing themselves to other people rather than examining themselves in the light of scripture. We can always find a fellow believer who is living less righteously than we are, whether it is in doing less good or in doing more wrong. This is comforting to our consciences, but it is a false comfort. God is omniscient and always knows what is going on. Manufacturing this balm for our consciences dishonors God in that we take our eyes off the standard, Jesus Christ. The second thing I have learned in this trio is that most people are good at "weeping with those who weep," but very few are good at "rejoicing with those who rejoice" (Romans 12:15). I am not sure why this is the case, but I have observed it over and over again. Undoubtedly, part of this phenomenon is rooted in the sins of envy and jealousy (Galatians 5: 19-21).

The third part of this trio of observations about people over the years is that most Christians consistently disobey Christ's clearest and simplest commandments. In Matthew 22: 34-40 we read the following. *Hearing that Jesus had silenced the Sadducees, the Pharisees got together. One of them, an expert in the law, tested him with this question: "Teacher, which is the greatest commandment in the law?" Jesus replied: " 'Love the lord your God with all your heart and with all your soul and with all your mind.' This is the first and greatest commandment. And the second is like it: 'Love your neighbor as yourself.' All the Law and the Prophets hang on these two commandments."* John records more of Jesus' words on the subject of love. In John 13: 34,35 He said *"A new command I give you: Love one another. As I have loved you, so you must love one another. By this all men will know that your are my disciples, if you love one another."* In John 14: 15 He flatly declared, *"If you love me, you will obey what I command."* The New Testament puts forth these love commandments as the bedrock instructions for Christians to live by. From these bedrock commandments spring many other corollary commandments. I have observed that two of these corollary commandments of Christ are willfully ignored or directly disobeyed by professing Christians more than any others. The first is His command that we share the Gospel. In Matthew, Mark, Luke, John, and Acts we are clearly instructed to share our faith throughout the world. Very few Christians do this at all and far fewer do it consistently. Innumerable excuses and rationalizations are made to explain this disobedience, but a Christian simply cannot get around this universal commandment of Jesus Christ to His followers.

Why are believers not obedient in sharing their faith? I believe there are several reasons.

The first is that sharing our faith makes us vulnerable. We might suffer rejection. Our lives might be subject to scrutiny. We might have to be responsible for people who respond to our message. A second reason we do not share our faith is because it is hard work. We have to know what we believe and why we believe it. This requires time and effort. We have to pray for opportunities, and take advantage of opportunities. This requires time and effort. It requires that we be flexible with our time and plans. This also requires us to be conducting a running inventory of our behavior, as no one will listen to what we say if our lives are openly sinful. A third reason we do not share our faith is because it is so much easier to fill up our free times with other Christians or other "church activities." There is safety and comfort in this. It also helps soothe our consciences for not sharing our faith. More common than this, though, is the mind-game we so often play of justifying ourselves for not doing what we are commanded to do by reciting a list of "worldly things" that we do not do. Granted, it is good to not be involved in worldly activities, but it is far better to be actively involved in evangelism. Christians are to play both "offense" and "defense" as we live out our lives in Christ. When we are involved in the "offense" of evangelism we will also play our best "defense" against the world. They go hand in hand. My times of greatest spiritual growth and joy in the Lord have come in direct relationship to my time spent sharing my faith. I am sure this is true of other believers, too.

The second most frequently disobeyed direct commandment of Christ, in my opinion, is found in Matthew 18: 15-17. *"If your brother sins against you, go and show him his fault, just between the two of you. If he listens to you, you have won your brother over. But if he will not listen, take two or three others along, so that 'every matter may be established by the testimony of two or three witnesses.' If he refuses to listen to them, tell it to the church; and if he refuses to listen even to the church, treat him as you would a pagan or a tax collector."* Simply stated, if one has a problem with someone he is to go directly to that individual and discuss the problem — **just the two of them**. Ideally, this is to take place after the offended individual has done some self-examination (Matthew 7: 3-5). In my lifetime of church I have seen disobedience to this clear command cause more trouble than anything else in the local church. I cannot think of anything that ranks a close second. Consider the case where individual "B" offends individual "A". Oftentimes individual B is not even aware a problem exists. Other times individual A has misunderstood an action or inaction of individual B. Still other times individual A has misunderstood words from individual B or has misunderstood what was meant by those words. In all these instances a simple conversation between the two individuals may be all that is required to settle the matter. In my experience there have been very few exceptions to this. The problem is that it usually does not play out this way. Most of the time individual A speaks to others about what individual B did or said. Then other individuals are offended at individual B, too. Invariably, word gets back to individual B that individual A has been offended. One of two things generally happens at this point. Either individual B will speak to individual A and try to work things out or individual B will speak to others about individual A's accusations and how individual A did not follow scripture and come directly to him or her about the offense. This, of course, happens more often than individual B going back to individual A. Now the situation is that both individuals A and B are offended and each individual has offended supporters. At this point, even if individuals A and B settle their dispute, what about their respective supporters? Disobedience to this commandment of Christ is so destructive to the church. Church leaders often unwittingly contribute to this problem by listening to the offended people complain about those who have offended them, without insisting they speak to each other first. Having been in this situation more times than I can recall, I know all too well how much easier it is to listen to the offended person than it is to lovingly, but firmly insist that he go directly to the person who has offended him. Not doing so amounts to enabling the offended individual to sin and makes the leader a party to the sin. I believe the leader only has two morally upright choices when presented with this problem. The leader can insist the offended individual go directly to the person who has offended him or the leader can offer to go along with the offended person to talk to the person who caused the offense. In either case, though, I believe the offended person has the obligation to state the offense.

There are many other things I have learned about people, but I will mention only two more. The first is negative and the second is positive. When people are troubled they are reluctant to express the real reason or reasons for their pain. This is particularly true if they are troubled by personal or spiritual failure. I observed this most often with regard to two changes: changes of spouses and changes of churches. In supporting these changes people become very creative in their justifying reasons. The reasons offered generally have three characteristics. They portray the individual as a victim. They are for the individual's pursuit of spiritual growth. They preclude other courses of action. I have never ceased being amazed by various actions of people that they attribute to the leading of the Lord.

The final thing I have learned is that all people deeply want and need what God has to freely offer them in Christ. All people want freedom. Jesus promised believers in John 8: 31,32 *"If you hold to my teaching, you are really my disciples. Then you will know the truth, and the truth will set you free."* Freedom can take no higher form than the freedom from sin and condemnation that believers in Jesus Christ receive. All people want to belong. As Christians we belong to God. He is our Father. Nothing can separate us from His love. (Romans 8:28-39). All people want to have a sense of worth. What greater worth can one have than the fact that Jesus Christ died for them? (Romans 5:6-8; John 3:16,17; II Corinthians 5:17-21). All people want to be competent. All believers are infinitely competent through the ministry of the indwelling Holy Spirit. (Romans 8:9; I Corinthians 6:19,20; Galatians 5:22,23; Ephesians 1:11-14). All people want to be happy, or joyful. The only true, lasting joy in this life is found in Jesus Christ. (John 15:9-11; I Peter 1:3-9).

I have never counseled with anyone who did not have these deep needs. Everyone I have met in my life consciously or subconsciously seeks after the fulfillment of these needs. I cannot imagine anyone denying they desire the things God freely offers them in Christ. Why, then, do so many people refuse to believe in Jesus for salvation? I have heard a legion of excuses throughout my journey, but they all boil down to three basic ones. The first reason is that people simply do not believe the Bible is true. The sad irony here is that most people who say they do not believe the Bible have never even **read** the Bible. It is hard for me to imagine making such an important judgment in ignorance. Others, however, are aware of what the Bible teaches about God's provision for our needs in Christ and still refuse to believe it. This alludes to the second reason why people refuse to believe in Jesus for salvation. People refuse to believe that something so great could be free. In their minds there has to be a "catch." There has to be some work to be done. The third reason people refuse salvation is because they refuse to see that they need it — that they are lost and unreconciled to God and that sin is the cause. This is not to say that most people do not accept the fact that they have sin in their lives. Very few people would say this. The problem is either that they do not believe they have **enough** sin to need salvation or that God does not require a remedy for sin unless it is "really bad."

I have learned some things about organizations during my journey. I believe the Church is the body of Christ and that it is made up of all true believers in Jesus (Ephesians 5:25-30; Colossians 1:15-24). What people normally refer to as "churches" are actually local assemblies of believers within the body of Christ. These local assemblies, as we know them, are organizations. Organizations are made up of people. Because of this, none of them are perfect. The old saying "If you ever find a perfect church, don't join it because it won't be perfect anymore," is true. All local assemblies will have their strengths and weaknesses. All will have room for improvement. No exceptions.

Another thing I have learned about organizations is that they are made up of basically two groups of people. One group is made up of producers of ministries and the other group is made up of consumers of ministries. The producers of ministries are invariably the happier, more contented group of people. Another way of expressing this same observation is that the two general groups of people are "those who do" and "those who benefit from what others do." A sub-group within the second general group of people in organizations is "those who critique what others do." Not all consumers of ministries are "those who critique," but "those who critique" are nearly always consumers of ministries. The "battle cry" for this subgroup is something like "You go ahead. I'll criticize." I realize this sounds sarcastic, but this had been my honest observation. This dynamic in churches creates a three-fold ongoing challenge for Pastors: to encourage the producers of ministries, to transform the consumers of ministries into producers of ministries, and to diminish the effect of those who critique on those who produce.

On my journey, I have noted that organizations are founded in simplicity and progress to ever-increasing complexity with the passing of time. With this increasing complexity also comes ever-increasing inefficiency. As complexity and inefficiency increase, something else begins to happen. Those within the organization increasingly consume the energy produced by the organization. The unfortunate net result of all this is less and less outreach and community ministry relative to the size of the organization.

The final thing I have learned about organizations has to do with leadership. Simply stated, organizations mirror their leadership. Good organizations have good leaders. In the Church, Christ is the ultimate leader. No church leader is a good leader unless he is Christ-like. Libraries have been filled with books about what it means to be Christ-like, but I will mention a few critical attributes of one who is Christ-like. The first is that one is born again. Nothing in the life of a human being matters for eternity until one comes to know Jesus Christ as his Savior. Christ-like leaders love their Savior and seek to serve Him with the lives they live and the words they speak. Christ-like leaders acknowledge Christ as the head of their homes. They love and honor their spouses and children. Christ-like leaders know and understand God's word. Christ-like leaders are patient. They know when to speak and when to listen. They also know when to be stern and when to be gentle. Christ-like leaders love people. They relate well to people and enjoy working with others. Finally, Christ-like leaders speak the truth in love. I have learned that there is absolutely no relationship whatsoever between the possession of these attributes and one's social or economic status. There does seem to be a relationship, however, between the possession of these attributes and one's age and life experiences. Congregations with leaders like this will become progressively more Christ-like themselves. This, in turn, produces congregations who impact their neighbors for the good. They also tend to spiritually reproduce themselves.

My earliest beliefs about God are not all that different than those I hold today. What I have learned about God on my journey is that His attributes are absolute. For example, I always believed God was sovereign. On my journey I learned He is absolutely sovereign over nations, peoples, events, rulers and the universe. Nothing catches God by surprise. My appreciation of this fact has grown in direct proportion to my familiarity with His Word. The area of God's sovereignty that I have come to appreciate most, however, is His sovereignty over our salvation. (Romans 8:28-30). The more I see the universal imperfections of man, the more amazing God's work of transforming people into the image of His Son becomes. I find it embarrassing when I recall the years I was of the opinion that my good works somehow played a role in securing and maintaining my salvation. Even if I were capable of an absolutely pure action with an absolutely pure motive with an absolutely pure attitude, it would be isolated and would not be good enough to earn God's favor. An honest inventory of myself tells me this rarely, if ever, happens. Do I have a low self-esteem because of this? No. I just am reminded I am human. I am also reminded of God's absolute love for me in Christ. I am reminded of how absolute are God's attributes of holiness, justice, grace, and mercy. I am reminded how these attributes worked in absolute harmony when Jesus died on the cross for the sin of the world. The penalty for sin was death and justice was served when Christ died for sin. Holiness was preserved, as sin was not tolerated. Mercy upon sinful man was now possible because holiness was preserved and justice was served. After the death of Christ at Calvary, God could justly accept sinful humans who came to Him through faith in the finished work of His Son. Throughout my journey I have come to increasingly treasure and marvel at this absolutely gracious provision for the salvation of man. This motivates me to live for God far more than any amount of fear and obligation ever could.

Finally, there are a number of things I have leaned about myself on my journey. Life has taught me that I am too idealistic. My nature is to be very optimistic. I am very trusting of other people. I expect happy endings and am still surprised when endings are sad. I am nearly always happy and upbeat in dealing with people. I tend to believe that I can make everyone else happy, too. I deeply value relationships and loyalty. I am fulfilled by meaningful conversations with people of all backgrounds.

After a lifetime of dealing with people one would think I would have changed, but I have not. I do not know why, but I am **still** stunned and hurt when I deal with people who are not kind or honest or loyal. I should know better by now. I suppose my mindset is a product of my upbringing. I grew up around honest people, people who were "doers." All of my extended family and the adults in my childhood were fiercely loyal. They were people who could be counted on in good times and in bad. This is probably why I never remember being afraid as a child. I was blessed to marry into a family that also was marked by these qualities. I entered adulthood expecting the whole world to be this way. Despite overwhelming evidence and experience to the contrary I still have these expectations of people. This tells me there must also be a genetic component that makes me be the way I am.

When we founded Wawasee Community Bible Church I entered into it convinced that correct doctrine would ensure smooth sailing. This was a "given" in my mind. I was certain when people understood the riches of God's grace in Jesus Christ that they would be committed to the work, loving towards one another, and loyal to the congregation. Even though my intellect tells me otherwise, my heart remains idealistic to this present day. I have learned to try and lower my expectations of others and, with my dear wife's reminders and encouragement, I have begun to have some modest success at this in recent years.

On my journey I also learned quite a bit about my spiritual gifts. This learning curve began when I was in the Apostolic Christian Church, before I knew anything about what the Bible taught on the subject. When I taught my first Sunday school lesson I was nervous as a cat. By the end of the lesson, however, I saw that the third graders were listening and responding to what I was saying. I knew I could sing well, but when it was time to try directing a choir I was sure I could not do it. It turned out to be a very natural thing for me to do. Still later, I leaned that I could keep people's attention preaching. By this time I had learned about spiritual gifts. Understanding that these abilities were God-given helped remove my reluctance to use them. When Wawasee Community Bible Church was founded I began preaching with greater passion. Feedback from the congregation and the radio audiences over the years confirmed this gift to me. I soon knew I was gifted in evangelism also. With pastoring came funerals and counseling. Working in these areas showed me that I could feel and show compassion. I learned that it was far easier for me to encourage others than to confront them. Confrontation has always been difficult for me unless I am confronting cruel or insensitive behavior, or erroneous doctrine. In these early days of WCBC I thought I was very discerning, too. Time showed me, however, that I was not gifted in discernment. I have been wrong about far too many people to be accurately described as discerning. I also learned over the years that I am not gifted in administration. I lack vision, I am not effective in organizing people, and I detest administrative meetings. On my journey I learned that my strengths are much better utilized in supporting another gifted leader. I have learned much about myself on my journey. I have some areas of giftedness and some areas of weakness. I believe this is exactly how God planned it. Others will benefit from my strengths and will offset my weaknesses. This knowledge of my strengths and weaknesses should serve me well in the future as I decide how to effectively involve myself in the work of the church.

Has my journey been a success? Ultimately, only God knows the answer to this. Only He knows how everything works out in the end. I am left with a few facts and many feelings. Sometimes I feel like a success and other times like a failure, depending upon what I am remembering or presently observing. I could write much on this subject but I will limit the discussion to two things that make me feel like my journey has been a failure and two things that make my journey feel like a success. The first thing that makes me feel like a failure is the fact that the leaders of the congregation I pastored parted ways rather than resolve their differences. All the while the pressure was building within the leadership of WCBC I was confident that the common doctrinal base of our leaders would transcend their personal differences. All the while I was confident that their concern for the "sheep" in the congregation would override their personal hurts and unmet expectations. Until the moment we reached a crisis point I was confident that our leaders would follow the biblical framework for conflict resolution, that they would seek forgiveness and reconciliation among themselves. Until the moment of our crisis, I could not have imagined any of our leaders leaving the church over anything less than a clear violation of sound doctrine. I feel like a failure for not accurately judging the depth of the division and for not being able to be an effective peacemaker once the division began to play itself out.

The second area in which I sometimes feel I failed was in teaching the congregation the importance of sound doctrine. Since my spiritual renaissance in the early 1980's I have believed that nothing is of greater importance than sound doctrine. What one believes directs how one lives. Throughout my thirteen years as Senior Pastor of WBCB it was my passion to teach the people the preeminence of knowing and living according to sound doctrine. It was my passion that the congregation of WCBC was made up of people who would insist on sound doctrine and be loyal only to congregations who also taught sound doctrine. This was my unwavering passion.

Over the years many families came and went from WCBC. Many of them became affiliated with congregations of like doctrine. While I missed these people, their leaving did not make me feel like a failure. Many others, however, became involved in denominations with notably different views of scripture and doctrinal bases. The two most common reasons people offered were "better music" or a "better youth group." Whenever this happened over the years I felt as if I had failed. Many of these people would defend their actions by saying something such as "I know what I believe. Their different teaching does not change my mind. I still hold correct doctrinal views." Such reasoning was never a comfort to me. Their attendance at these churches amounted to them supporting the propagation of that congregation's doctrine, whether they personally believed it or not. What about those who did not know better? What about their children? What about the churches teaching sound doctrine that needed their support?

Two stories illustrate this problem more than any others over my years of pastoring. Over the years our AWANA Clubs were a critical part of our community outreach. Many souls trusted Christ as their Savior through AWANA. The AWANA organization has their own Statement of Faith and they will only go into the churches that hold to like doctrine. Early in the history of WCBC three families began our AWANA Club. For years these families championed AWANA and their sound doctrinal base. Today two of these families attend churches that would never agree to sign an AWANA doctrinal statement; churches AWANA likely would not affiliate with even if they were willing to sign the doctrinal statement. The reason these families changed churches was "for their children." Both families still profess to intellectually support the AWANA doctrine. Try as I might, I simply cannot understand such reasoning.

Another time a Youth Pastor search committee was formed. The committee did its work, made its recommendation, and the candidate they recommended was ultimately hired. Within months after the candidate they recommended was hired, two members of the committee and their families began attending other churches, churches with different doctrinal views on some foundational issues. One of the families later said they had been praying about changing churches "for months" and just felt it was "time for a change." The other family made the change so their child could attend another youth group. These families clearly had the right to change churches if they wanted to, but why did they continue working on the search committee if this was their intention? These are two stories from my years of pastoring that continue to elude my understanding even years after the fact. Perhaps I did not fail in my efforts to teach people the importance of sound doctrine over the years — God knows — but stories like this certainly make me feel as if I did.

Was I successful on my journey? I suppose that affirmative arguments could be made in a number of areas, but one fact convinces me to answer "yes" far more than any other. The fact? In the thirteen years I pastored WCBC two hundred and five people were obedient in regard to water baptism, publicly identifying with their new Savior. Many others made professions of faith in Christ, perhaps many more than I ever knew about. It is still my prayer that they will all become obedient in regard to water baptism and openly live their lives for Christ. If their professions of faith were sincere, I believe they will. Relative to these new believers in Christ, anything else I might point to as a reason for feeling my journey was a success is woefully inconsequential.

What would I change if I had it to do all over again? I often think about this. Sometimes people ask the question. If I had it all to do over again I would actually change very little. At Wawasee Community Bible Church I would do three things differently. The first thing would be regarding the leadership structure. Either we would have had two leadership boards with clear levels of authority, or we would have had one leadership board. I cannot imagine anything that might have altered the course of events at WCBC more than this. Secondly, I believe it would have been better to delay our second building project a year or two. More time would have allowed us to more accurately evaluate the level of commitment of our crowds to the church. We would not have needed to borrow as much money as we did. We would have had a freer hand to make decisions and deal with people without such a large debt. The third thing I would do differently at WCBC is to not devote as much time and effort attempting to transform dissatisfied people into satisfied people. Trying to change the minds of dissatisfied people required an inordinate amount of time, it was emotionally draining, and I cannot remember a single situation where it was successful in the long run.

The only significant change I would make in my personal life if I had it to do over would be to purchase the pharmacy business at least five years before I did. My former boss would have been willing to sell it to me earlier. I loved working side by side with Tammy and the kids and would have had more years to do so. The profitability of the store was considerably better before the large-scale institution of managed health care that began about the same time I bought it. My life would have been no more chaotic if I had. Why did I not buy the business sooner? One reason. I did not want to rule out full time ministry in the event that WCBC wanted to hire me.

At the ripe old age of fifty, if I had to choose one word to characterize my life it would be "blessed." I have never met anyone whom I thought had a better marriage than I do. We have had the privilege of rearing three children to adulthood. They are a continuing source of pride and joy to me, as is our first "in-law." We have had the resources over the years to go places and do things. I have a beautiful house that is a far more beautiful home. We are all relatively healthy. We all are believers in Christ. I am just a happy guy! The only time I think much about my minor disappointments is when others remind me of them. If life ever brings sorrow my way I hope I will have the presence of mind to continue to praise God for all my blessings.

I rarely, if ever, think about death, probably because I am so content with life. At times, however, I find myself thinking about the Judgment Seat of Christ (I Corinthians 3:5-15; II Corinthians 5:1-10) and how it will be. This divine judgment of the works of every believer's life, to include the motives behind those works, is a process too great for me to imagine, let alone comprehend. I wonder what will remain when the works of my life are tried in the perfect fire of this judgment. With my motives and attitudes included, probably not too much. How thankful I am that my merit before God is in Jesus Christ!

One question springs up in my mind from time-to-time in recent years. It is a question I imagine being asked at the Judgment Seat of Christ. I do not particularly fear the question; I just do not yet know how I would answer it. The question goes something like this: "Tom, I gave you a gift to preach my word. Why did you quit in your prime?"

Chapter Sixty

The spring of the year is an inspiring time for me. Observing the vegetation emerging from the dormancy of winter always reminds me of the complexity of creation. It demonstrates anew the majesty of God. As far back as I can remember I have associated two things with the arrival of spring: turtles and morel mushrooms. I still love turtles but my involvement with them has waned since my son stopped collecting them. My passion for morel mushrooms, however, continues to develop with each spring season.

In the last decade the Speicher family quest for mushrooms has become legendary. On the second or third weekend in May of each year the Speicher men wend their way north to spend three or four days hunting mushrooms. Without the women of the family to keep us organized and acting civilized we often laugh to the point of exhaustion. Between my dad, brothers, nephews, in-laws, my son Travis, and me there are enough stories to keep us going the whole year until we can go again and generate some new ones. We usually find a lot of mushrooms, too.

Why mushrooms? What is the attraction? Why would grown men pursue mushrooms to the point of obsession? I do not have an absolute answer to this, but I do have a number of partial ones. Why mushrooms? First, one must go outside to find them. This is about the only inviolable rule. The outdoors is alluring to a bunch of men who spend the year working inside. Still, it is difficult to explain to one who has never hunted them why it is so challenging and so much fun to walk around outside in search of them. Another attraction of morel mushrooms is their diversity. No two are alike. There are blacks, whites, longnecks, grays, and yellows. Some are found in early season, some mid-season, and some in late season — and sometimes they are all mixed together. They literally seem to "pop up" when conditions are right and they only last a few days. To find them one must be in the right place at the right time. They differ dramatically in size, color, and shape, but they all taste remarkably alike. Remarkably good!

Perhaps the greatest attraction of morel mushroom hunting, however, is the fact that their appearing is at the same time both very predictable and very unpredictable. One can make an experienced prediction when they may be found. One can make an experienced prediction where they may be found. They will be found, however, at times and in places that defy both logic and experience. Experienced mushroom hunters know how to examine an area for moisture, slope, heat, sun exposure, tree species, and ground vegetation to predict the likelihood of finding them. Yet every experienced morel mushroom hunter also knows novices who are not even looking for them often stumble upon mushrooms. Morel mushrooms are mysterious, elusive, and a culinary delight. Throw in an element of "friendly" competition among mushroom hunters and it is no wonder they are so much fun to search for!

Jesus Christ instituted His Body, the Church two thousand years ago on the Day of Pentecost. As people believed in Christ as their Savior from sin the Church has grown over the millennia. These believers have come together in local assemblies since the beginning. According to the sovereign plan and activity of God, people come to faith in Christ and the Church is built. I recognize that the sovereign plan and activity of God is beyond the realm of human understanding, but I have thought about it oftentimes throughout my lifetime of church.

What is the building of the Church, the Body of Christ, like? How has it been in the past? How does it continue until the present? The best analogy of the building of the Church in the realm of nature, in my opinion, is morel mushrooms. I have a number of reasons for making this observation. First, both are conceived and grow according to God's sovereignty. At all times conditions are right somewhere on the earth and mushrooms are growing. Local assemblies of believers will never cease to exist on the earth until Christ returns. At all times conditions are right somewhere on the earth that local assemblies of believers are growing. Throughout history, when conditions create hostility toward Christians, the church goes underground. When conditions are favorable again, the church re-emerges. The same is true of mushrooms. When conditions are right, they pop up and flourish. When conditions are hostile, they literally go underground. Like the persecuted church, they do not cease to exist; they simply exist in a different form. Like saving faith, morel mushrooms cannot be produced by the efforts of human beings. Both are gifts of God to man — saving faith being a direct gift and morel mushrooms a gift via nature.

Like mushrooms, the appearance of saving faith is at the same time both predictable and unpredictable. The same is true of the appearance and growth of local assemblies of believers. Christians can predict in whom saving faith will appear. An individual's background, life experiences, and degree of open-mindedness can point to a likelihood of that individual receiving the Gospel or rejecting it. Christians can also make educated predications about where congregations of believers will spring up and where they will not. Any experienced Christian or student of church history knows, however, that saving faith and congregations of believers often appear in places and at times where they are least expected. In addition, while faith in the Gospel is the only saving faith, such faith is manifested in many ways. True worship can look and sound dramatically different, depending on cultures, localities, individuals, and congregations of believers. While mushrooms make no sound, they certainly are manifested in many, many different shapes, sizes, colors, and groupings. Finally, church history demonstrates that while local assemblies of believers tend to spring up, level off, and decline in relatively short periods of time — just like mushrooms — the Body of Christ continues to grow throughout the world without interruption.

In my lifetime of church I have learned that morel mushrooms are mysterious, elusive, and a culinary delight to those who will pursue them. To this point in my lifetime of church, the Church, the Body of Christ, that I became a part of through faith and in which I have endeavored to serve remains somewhat mysterious. A clear understanding of how God works everything out for the accomplishment of His plan for man remains elusive. Just as the finest of foods bring delight to our sense of taste, however, the Body of Christ remains my passion and delight.

CPSIA information can be obtained
at www.ICGtesting.com
Printed in the USA
LVOW12s1307020117
519400LV00001B/287/P